Sean M. McDonough

YHWH at Patmos

Rev. 1:4 in its Hellenistic and Early Jewish Setting

WIPF & STOCK · Eugene, Oregon

SEAN M. MCDONOUGH, Born 1964; B.A. in History, Harvard College, 1986; Master of Divinity, Gordon Conwell Theological Seminary, 1993; Master of Theology, Gordon Conwell Theological Seminary, 1994; PhD, University of St. Andrews, 1997; since 1997, Lecturer in Biblical Studies, Pacific Theological College, Suva, Fiji.

Wipf and Stock Publishers
199 W 8th Ave, Suite 3
Eugene, OR 97401

YHWH at Patmos
Rev. 1:4 in its Hellenistic and Early Jewish Setting
By McDonough, Sean
Copyright©1999 Mohr Siebeck
ISBN 13: 978-1-61097-155-3
Publication date 5/1/2011
Previously published by Mohr Siebeck, 1999

"This edition reprinted 2011 by Wipf and Stock through special arrangement with J.C.B. Mohr (Paul Siebeck). Copyright J.C.B. Mohr (Paul Siebeck) 1999".

Preface

> ...Pascal used to say of those authors who always refer to their works as: 'My book, my commentary, my history, etc.,' that they sound like solid citizens with a place of their own, always talking about 'My house.' They would do better, this excellent man added, to say: 'Our book, or commentary, our history, etc.,' considering that there is usually more of other people's property in it than their own.
> – Sayings Attributed to Pascal, no. I; in Pascal, *Pensées* (Translated by A.J. Krailsheimer; Harmondsworth: Penguin Books, 1966), p. 355.

The present work is a revised version of my doctoral thesis, which was accepted at the University of St. Andrews in July 1997. It is my pleasure to thank those who have helped me in the task of completing the thesis and this revision.

Thanks first to my supervisor at St. Andrews, Professor Richard Bauckham. He has provided a model of careful, insightful scholarship, and his contribution to the thesis far exceeds the acknowledgments made at various points in the footnotes. I am also grateful to Professor Dr Martin Hengel, Professor Dr Otfried Hofius, and Herrn Georg Siebeck for accepting the work for publication. Dr William Horbury of Cambridge and Dr. James Davila of St. Andrews provided several helpful insights during their examination of the thesis at St. Andrews.

I am greatly indebted to the faculty and students of Gordon Conwell Theological Seminary, who first taught me the exegesis of Scripture; and to the faculty and students of St. Mary's College, University of St. Andrews, who have helped me grow further in this area. The Principal, Vice-Principal, faculty, staff, and students at the Pacific Theological College have provided a wonderful setting for the process of revision; *vinaka vakalevu* (thank you very much). Special mention may be made of Dr Gregory Beale of Gordon Conwell, who laid the foundation for my study of Revelation and kindly allowed me to look at the relevant portions of the draft of his forthcoming commentary on Revelation. Thanks also to the Department of Classics at St. Andrews for their assistance in completing this project, and in particular to Professor Stephen Halliwell, who read much of the Greek material, and Professor Harry Hine, who provided valuable insights along the way. I am also grateful to Professor Richard Sorabji of King's College, London, who took time from his schedule to offer helpful comments on Aristotle and the hellenistic philosophers; and to Dr

James Aiton of the School of Biological and Medical Sciences, St. Andrews, for technical support. Special thanks to Jeanette Little of the Pacific Theological Library for her assistance in producing the manuscript, and to Herrn Matthias Spitzner of the Mohr Siebeck production department for his help.

Much appreciated material support has come from many quarters. The Committee of Vice-Chancellors and Principals of the Universities of the United Kingdom provided an Overseas Research Student Award for my studies, while St. Mary's College added a Cobb Scholarship. The congregations of St. Andrews Baptist Church and Waltham Evangelical Free Church, and friends too numerous to mention, have provided various forms of help before and during our time in Scotland and Fiji. The Colin Hemer fund of Tyndale House allowed me a very profitable week of study in Cambridge.

On the personal side, I would like to thank my parents, Robert and Dorothy McDonough, and my siblings, Lisa, Alex, and Hugh, for all their help through the years. My daughter Siobhan and my sons Patrick and Keanu have brought me much joy and have contributed in their own ways to the book. My greatest debt is to my beloved wife Ariana, who has given me incalculable support and encouragement in the completion of this work. (This is in addition to her computer skills, without which this manuscript would no doubt be languishing in the waste places of cyber-space.) Finally, it is especially appropriate given the nature of the topic at hand to give due thanks and acknowledgment to ὁ ὢν καὶ ὁ ἦν καὶ ὁ ἐρχόμενος.

March 1999 Sean M. McDonough
Suva, Fiji

Table of Contents

Preface V

Introduction 1
   History of Research 2
   Plan and Goal of the Present Study 5
   Methodology 6

Chapter 1: Greco-Roman Material 7
   Etymology 7
   Τὸ Ὄν in Greek Thought 11
      Presocratic Philosophy 15
      Plato 20
      Aristotle on Being 27
      Aristotle on Eternity 31
      Later Thinkers 32
   The Dreizeitenformel in Greek Literature 41
      Homer 41
      Hesiod 42
      Presocratic Thinkers 45
      Plato and Beyond 47
      Summary of the Dreizeitenformel 56

Chapter 2: The Use of the Name YHWH 58
   Septuagint 58
      Writing the Name 58
      Saying the Name 62

Qumran	65
Writing the Name	65
Greek and Aramaic Texts	70
Saying the Name	71
Apocrypha and Pseudepigrapha	74
Writing the Name	74
Saying the Name	77
Philo	79
Josephus	84
Greek and Roman Writers	87
Magical material	93
New Testament	97
Rabbinical Literature	98
Writing the Name	98
Saying the Name	99
Targums	109
Why was the use of YHWH restricted in Early Judaism?	111
Discursus: The Pronunciation of the Tetragrammaton	116

Chapter 3: The Significance and Meaning of the Name ... 123

The Significance of the Name	123
The name in or on people, angels, and things	124
Jesus and the Name	126
The Power of the Name	128
The Meaning of the Name	131
The LXX Translation of Ex. 3:14	131
Ὁ ὤν in the LXX of Jeremiah	137
אני הוא and ἐγώ εἰμι in Is. 40–55	138
Qumran	141
Apocrypha and Pseudepigrapha	153
Magical material	159
Philo	162
Josephus	169

New Testament 170
Rabbinical Literature 176

The Dreizeitenformel in Jewish Literature 187
Jewish Literature 187
Later Materials 191

Summary: The Name's Encounter with Hellenism 192

Chapter 4: Revelation 195

Sources 195

Use of the Dreizeitenformel 202
Context 203
What is in a Name? 203
ὁ ὤν 205
ὁ ἦν 211
ὁ ἐρχόμενος 214

Variations on the Formula of 1:4 217
Rev. 1:8 217
Rev. 1:17–8 220
Rev. 1:19 222
Rev. 4:8 223
Rev. 11:17, 16:5 226
Rev. 17:8, 11 227

Comparison with Other Formulae in Revelation 229

Conclusion 232

Bibliography 235

Indexes 251

Index of Sources 251
Old Testament 251
Apocrypha 254
Pseudepigrapha 254
New Testament 256
Dead Sea Scrolls 258
Rabbinical Literature 259

Ancient Authors 262

Index of Modern Authors 269

Index of Subjects 274

Introduction

"Grace and peace to you from the One who is and who was and who is to come, and from the seven spirits before his throne, and from Jesus Christ, the faithful witness, the first born of the dead and the ruler of the kings of the earth (Rev.1:4–5)." With this most unusual greeting John begins his most unusual letter.[1] The subject of our investigation is the phrase, "the One who is and who was and who is to come" – ὁ ὢν καὶ ὁ ἦν καὶ ὁ ἐρχόμενος. It has long been recognized that this description of God is indebted to Jewish reflection on the name YHWH,[2] and in particular to reflection on the enigmatic words of Ex. 3:14, "I am who I am." Parallels in the hellenistic world have also been duly noted. But the story of how the name YHWH arrived at Patmos in the form it did is little known. We intend to tell a part of that story here.

Our emphasis will be on the understanding of the name YHWH in early Judaism,[3] and how this shaped John's formula in Rev. 1:4. We do not thereby intend to minimize the importance of the earlier Old Testament material. The burning bush of Moses will always be flickering in the background of our discussion. We may be thankful that this part of the story is fairly well known, and has been the object of intense scholarly study (see below). The later history of the name YHWH is far more obscure – but no less interesting. While it is sometimes suggested that the name fell into more or less total oblivion in the second temple era, in fact it continued to have a rich underground existence, and it occasionally made a dramatic public appearance. More than this, the question of what the name meant was a constant stimulus to creative reflection on the biblical tradition.

---

[1] For Revelation *as a letter*, see e.g. Richard Bauckham, *The Theology of the Book of Revelation* (Cambridge: Cambridge University Press, 1993), chapter 1. John is of course transforming the traditional formula, "Grace and peace to you from God our Father and the Lord Jesus Christ." See e.g. Rom. 1:7; 1 Cor. 1:3; 2 Cor. 1:2, etc.; cf. 1 Pet. 1:2–3; 2 Jn. 3; Jude 1–2.

[2] We will generally employ "YHWH" for the tetragrammaton. As we will see in chapter 2, the pronunciation "Yahweh" is not absolutely certain, and we would not want to privilege this vocalization.

[3] By "early Judaism" we mean Judaism in the period from the mid-second century BCE to the mid-second century CE. We will also use the designations "second temple Judaism" and "the New Testament era" to designate this same period.

None of this, of course, took place in a vacuum. During the period of our concern, Judaism and Christianity were challenged to understand and articulate their beliefs in the midst of the dominant hellenistic society. Central to this endeavor was the identity of God, and central to the identity of God was God's name. The very fact that most Jews were reluctant to state the name YHWH to outsiders was a powerful way of declaring their separation from the broader society. At the same time, they were willing to use other epithets for their God which would have made at least tolerable sense to those around them: "the God of Heaven," "the Most High," "the Lord," and so on. The engagement with Greco-Roman culture is even more evident in the interpretations offered about the meaning of the name. This becomes clearest in the LXX description of God in Ex. 3:14, "I am the one who is," and in the theological implications which were drawn from this translation. The idea that God "was, is, and will be/is to come" was likewise a response to three-times formulae or *Dreizeitenformeln* (to use Otto Weinreich's term) already present in the hellenistic world. The story of the name YHWH thus affords us a unique opportunity to explore the complex interaction of Greek, Jewish, and Christian thought in the ancient world.

History of Research

As we have indicated, most modern commentators on Revelation recognize the importance of the name YHWH for understanding the phrase "the One who is and who was and who is to come" in Rev. 1:4. In the early part of the century, Charles, Swete, and Beckwith all included hellenistic and Jewish background material in their commentaries, and later commentators have followed suit. The most detailed treatments may now be found in the recently published commentaries by G. K. Beale and D. E. Aune.

Research on the name YHWH itself has focused on Old Testament texts and their ancient near eastern background. Not surprisingly, the MT of Ex. 3:14 has been the *crux interpretum*. D. N. Freedman and M. O'Connor provide a thorough treatment of the relevant ancient near eastern materials in their article "Yhwh" in the *Theological Dictionary of the Old Testament*.[4] Also noteworthy is the scholarly but very readable discussion in T. D. Mettinger's book *In Search of God: The Message and Meaning of the Divine Names*.[5] One might also mention Martin Rose's *Jahwe: zum Streit um den alttestamentlichen Gottesnamen*, which devotes particular attention

---

[4] Freedman and O'Connor, "YHWH," in *TDNT* 5: 500–21.

[5] Tryggve Mettinger, *In Search of God: The Meaning and Message of the Divine Names*, trans. Frederick H. Cryer (Philadelphia: Fortress, 1988).

to the relationship of YHWH to the related names Iao and Ia.⁶ Ex. 3:14 itself has been well-served by scholars. Among the many commentaries, the discussion of Brevard Childs is particularly enlightening, and there are a number of important articles on the verse, including those of de Vaux, Schild, and Albrektson.⁷ This is not to say that there is a firm consensus as to the original meaning of Ex. 3:14. But researchers may at least be content that the major interpretative options have received thorough discussion and critique.

The discussion of the divine name in early Judaism has been more diffuse. The most thorough treatment of the material remains vol. 2 of W. W. G. Baudissin's *Kyrios als Gottesname*.⁸ The central thesis of the work – that the use of *kyrios* in the Septuagint did not derive from the *qere* of Adonai – has not been well received by scholars. It was also published long before the discovery of the Dead Sea Scrolls. But neither of these points diminishes the amazing breadth of material contained in the volume, or the sharpness of his observations. A. Marmorstein assembles an impressive array of Jewish texts concerning the use of the tetragrammaton in his opening essay in the volume *The Old Rabbinic Doctrine of God*.⁹ The problem for modern scholars is that Marmorstein is extremely generous in what he considers to be valid evidence for second temple practice. A somewhat more critical discussion may be found in E. E. Urbach's *The Sages*.¹⁰ G. H. Parke-Taylor's *Yahweh: The Divine Name in the Bible* contains an extensive survey of the divine name in early Judaism and Christianity, in addition to a helpful overview of the Old Testament and ancient near eastern materials.¹¹

Two of the most useful recent discussions are J. E. Fossum's *The Name of God and the Angel of the Lord*, and C. T. R. Hayward's *Divine Name*

---

⁶ Martin Rose, *Jahwe* (Theologische Studien 122, Zürich: Theologischer Verlag, 1978).

⁷ Brevard Childs, *Exodus* (London: SCM Press, 1974); R. de Vaux, "The Revelation of the Divine Name YHWH" in *Proclamation and Presence* (London: SCM Press, 1970): pp.51ff,; E. Schild, "On Exodus 3:14 – I am that I am," *VT* 4 (1954): 296–302; Bertil Albrektson, "On the Syntax of אהיה אשר אהיה in Exodus 3:14," in *Words and Meanings*, eds. Peter R. Ackroyd and Barnabas Lindars (Cambridge: Cambridge University Press, 1968): 15–28.

⁸ Wolf W. G. Baudissin, *Kyrios als Gottesname* 4 vols. (Giessen: Alfred Topelmann, 1929).

⁹ A. Marmorstein, *The Old Rabbinic Doctrine of God* (London: Oxford, 1927).

¹⁰ E.E. Urbach, *The Sages*, trans. Israel Abrahams 2 vols. (Jerusalem: Magnes Press, 1975).

¹¹ G.H. Parke-Taylor, *Yahweh: The Divine Name in the Bible* (Waterloo, Ont.: Wilfrid Laurier University Press, 1975).

and Presence: The Memra.¹² Fossum's work is quite wide ranging, as one can see from the subtitle – *Samaritan and Jewish Concepts of Intermediation and the Origins of Gnosticism*. Strictly speaking, the implications for early Christianity lie more with christology than theology *per se*, which is our chief concern. We must also point out that Fossum includes in his analysis some material whose relevance to the New Testament era might well be questioned (e.g. the Samaritan texts). Despite these caveats, *The Name of God and the Angel of the Lord* is indispensable for the study of the divine name. Fossum's research is extremely thorough, and he provides crucial insights on several important points. As we will see below, his recognition that the tetragrammaton should be connected with the "let it be!" of the creation narrative is foundational for understanding the interpretation of the divine name in early Judaism. Hayward presents a more balanced, if less detailed, survey of the same material in his work. Its distinctive contribution is the close attention paid to the use of *Memra* in the Targums, and its relationship to the tetragrammaton. Hayward makes a strong case that the *Memra* represents God's אהיה, his name for himself, and that this name signifies not merely God's existence, but his merciful presence with his people. God says, אהיה, "I am there!," and his people respond, יהיה, "He is there!"¹³

Another important study of the Targums is M. McNamara's *The New Testament and the Palestinian Targum*, which includes an extensive investigation of the Jewish background to our text in Rev. 1:4.¹⁴ Scholars had long recognized a connection between the Targums and Rev. 1:4, but McNamara was the first to devote considerable attention to their relationship. He pays less attention, however, to the use of *Dreizeitenformeln* in Greco-Roman literature. For this we may turn to O. Weinreich's article "Aion in Eleusis," and W. C. van Unnik's "A Formula Describing Prophecy."¹⁵ Between them they cover most of the *Dreizeitenformeln* in the ancient world.

Finally, a word may be said concerning the literature on the Septuagint translation of Ex. 3:14, "I am the one who is," which is a major theme of the present work. Despite the immense significance of this translation, it

---

¹² Jarl E. Fossum, *The Name of God and the Angel of the Lord* (Tübingen: J.C.B. Mohr (Paul Siebeck), 1985); Robert (C.T.R.) Hayward, *Divine Name and Presence: The Memra* (Totowa, NJ: Allanhead, Osmun, and Co., 1981).

¹³ Hayward's basic argument is ably complemented by P. Vermes' article, "Buber's Understanding of the Divine Name Related to Bible, Targum, and Midrash," *JJS* 24 (1973): 147–66.

¹⁴ M. J. McNamara, *The New Testament and the Palestinian Targum* Analecta Biblica 27 (Rome: Pontifical Biblical Institute, 1966).

¹⁵ Otto Weinreich, "Aion in Eleusis," *ARW* 19 (1919): 174–90; W.C. van Unnik, "A Formula Describing Prophecy," *NTS* 9 (1962): 86–94.

has received little attention in comparison with the Hebrew text of Ex. 3:14 and later rabbinic traditions. The LXX version is ignored by most commentators on Exodus.[16] Exceptions do exist. W. Wevers makes some very helpful comments in his *LXX: Notes on the Greek Text of Exodus*, as do A. Le Boulluec and P. Sandevoir in *La Bible d'Alexandrie: L'Exode*.[17] But the nature of these works makes it impossible for them to pursue the issues at length. We may be thankful that the concept of "Being" in Greco-Roman thought has received more extensive coverage. Most noteworthy is the work of J. Whittaker, who has pursued this theme in a number of articles and monographs.[18]

Plan and Goal of the Present Study

We begin by examining material from the Greco-Roman world (chapter 1). We do not wish to imply by this that hellenistic philosophy or religion was the *fons et origo* of Jewish and Christian reflection on the name. The consideration is practical. It is assumed that most readers of this study will have at least a basic acquaintance with Old Testament history and theology, but that the Greek and Latin texts will be less familiar. For this reason we will also include in our survey material which considerably pre-dates the New Testament period. We begin with a brief discussion of divine etymologies in the Greco-Roman world, and follow this with two extended sections on Being and the *Dreizeitenformeln*.

With this background information in hand, we proceed in chapter 2 to look at the use of the name YHWH in early Judaism. In addition to technical questions concerning how the name was written and pronounced, we attempt to establish when the name was used by Jews, and why its use was so restricted in the second temple period.

---

[16] Although Childs does not defend the LXX translation *per se*, he recognizes the legitimacy of drawing implications about the Being of God from the verse (pp.84–7). Writers of Old Testament theologies seem particularly offended by the translation; see, e.g., the comments by Preuß and von Rad, cited below (chapter 3) in our discussion of the Septuagint rendering of Ex. 3:14.

[17] Wevers, *LXX: Notes on the Greek Text of Exodus* Septuagint and Cognate Studies 30 (Atlanta: Scholars Press, 1990); Alain Le Boulluec and Pierre Sandevoir, *La Bible d'Alexandrie: L'Exode* (Paris: Cerf, 1989).

[18] See his works: "Ammonius on the Delphic E," *CQ* n.s. 19 (1969): 185–92; "The 'Eternity' of the Platonic Forms," *Phronesis* 13 (1968): 131–44; *God, Time, Being. Symbolae Osloenses* Fasc. Supp. 23 (Oslo: Universitetsforlaget, 1971); "Moses Atticizing," *Phoenix* 21 (1967): 196–201; "Seneca, Ep. 58.17," *Symbolae Osloenses* 50 (1975): 143–48; "Plutarch, Platonism, and Christianity," in *Neoplatonism and Early Christian Thought*, eds. H.J. Blumenthal and R.A. Markus (London: Variorum, 1981): 50–63.

In chapter 3, we move on to the interpretation of the name. Here we make a distinction between the general "significance" of the name and its specific "meaning" in the sense of etymology (real or imagined). Such a distinction, if a bit artificial, is nonetheless necessary. "The Name" could stand for all the attributes and activities of the God of Israel, and so a full estimate of its significance is impossible. There is more than enough material to examine concerning the supposed meaning of the name. While most explanations of YHWH are variations on the etymology, "He is" (and perhaps, "He causes to be"), this etymology was unpacked by Jewish and Christian writers in a variety of ways.

We conclude in chapter 4 by examining the formula "the one who is and who was and who is to come" in the book of Revelation. We first attempt to assess to what extent John is indebted to his Jewish and Greek predecessors, and to what extent he is making his own theological contribution. We then note how John employs the formula (and variations upon it) throughout his work.

It is hoped that this investigation will give us a deeper appreciation of the theological message of the book of Revelation. The importance of Rev. 1:4, however, extends beyond the small circle of specialists in the Apocalypse. For it is a particularly striking case study in influence in early Judaism and Christianity. Scholars often speak of Greek "influence" on Judaism, or Jewish "influence" on Christianity. But influence can imply many different things. It may sometimes, for instance, convey the idea of an unwilling, or unwitting, acceptance of alien ideas in order to make up for some deficiency in one's own faith. We will see that such a model is singularly inappropriate for the subtle interplay of Greek, Jewish, and Christian ideas which eventually led to John's formula "the One who is and who was and who is to come."

Methodology

Our investigation is primarily historical in nature. We will attempt to trace the development of the Jewish and Greek traditions which impinge on the study of Rev. 1:4, and then see how John adapted these traditions for his own purposes. In terms of contemporary scholarship, we would hope to make a contribution to the growing body of literature concerning the relationship of Jews and Christians to their hellenistic milieu. Naturally, the question of the name and identity of God has important theological, philosophical, and sociological implications. This study may provide a stimulus for further research in these areas.

Chapter 1

Greco-Roman Material

The impact of Hellenism upon Judaism has been well documented, particularly in recent years. While crucial questions remain as to the extent of Greek influence upon the Jews, no one would dispute the importance of this cultural and religious encounter. The matter of the divine name is no exception. The name was indeed shrouded in secrecy, but this very secrecy may have been engendered by the pressures put upon Jewish identity by the dominant hellenistic culture. As for the meaning of the name, it was almost inevitable that a God who declared, "I am who I am," would at some point run up against Greek definitions of ultimate reality.

This survey of Greek and Roman literature is not intended to nullify Jewish contributions to theology. On the contrary, only by fully exploring the Greek background can we fully appreciate the creativity and intellectual power of the Jewish response to the hellenistic world. At the same time, we cannot simply portray the Greeks as the villains, threatening to taint the ancestral Jewish faith with their abstract philosophizing. The relationship was far more complex.

We begin by examining Greek etymologies of divine names. After this, we turn our attention to the question of Being in Greek philosophy. This is of prime importance for understanding the LXX translation of Ex. 3:14 and the subsequent use of ὁ ὤν in Jewish and Christian literature. We conclude with a survey of the *Dreizeitenformel* in Greek literature. The "was, is, will be" motif was prevalent in all kinds of Greek literature, and its importance for our text in Revelation is self-evident.

Etymology

The Jews were not alone in the ancient world in seeking to elucidate the meaning of the name of their deity. In the Babylonian epic of creation, for instance, the god Marduk is praised with fifty names. Of these, writes William Hallo, "...nos. 2–4 represent transparently 'unscientific' etymologies based on the syllabic or logographic orthography of the name..."[1] The Greeks were equally adept at such word-play. This was not always done with complete seriousness, nor was it believed that a particular etymology was the only true or valid one. Many thinkers probably viewed them as pedagogical tools rather than as historically verifiable pieces of data.

Nonetheless, divine etymologies were a common feature of the religious landscape from (at least) Hesiod onwards. They play a crucial role in the *Theogony*, particularly for the older deities like Night, Heaven, Earth, etc.[2] As time went on, such interpretations were pressed into the service of philosophy. We may take Plutarch as an example. In the *De Iside et Osiride* he informs us that the name of Isis' temple, the Iseion, "clearly offers recognition and knowledge of that which is (εἴδησιν τοῦ ὄντος); for it is called the Iseion to indicate that we shall know that which is (εἰσομένων τὸ ὄν) if we approach the sanctuaries of the goddess with reason and reverence" (352a). In the *De E ap. Delphos*, Plutarch's mentor Ammonius draws lessons about the unity of God from the name of the Delphic god, Apollo. He takes it to mean "not many" – ἀ-πολλοί.[3] This etymology has many parallels in the ancient world and may be Pythagorean in origin.[4]

One of the most commonly adduced etymologies was that which explained Zeus/Dios as "he through whom all things have life." Pherecydes, a sixth century figure "on the borderline between myth and philosophy,"[5] began his *Theogony* with, "Zas (=Zeus) and Chronos always existed (ἦσαν

---

[1] Hallo, "Scurrilous Etymologies," in *Pomegranates and Golden Bells*, eds. David P. Wright, David Noel Freedman, and Avi Hurvitz (Winona Lake, IN: Eisenbrauns, 1995), p.768.

[2] Cf. Werner Jaeger, *The Theology of the Early Greek Philosophers*, (London: Oxford University Press, 1947), pp.68–9. One may also note the etymological significance of the names of the Muses, ll. 77ff.; Aphrodite/Cytherea, ll.195ff.; and the Titans, ll. 207ff.

[3] *De E* 393b; cf. 388f. See *Plutarque: Sur l'E de Delphes*, ed. and trans. by Robert Flacelière, Annales de l'Université de Lyon (Paris: Société d'Édition Les Belles Lettres, 1941), p.84 n. It is worth noting that even a relatively minor god such as Proteus could take on a new importance based on etymology. In an admittedly late Orphic hymn, Proteus is described as πρωτογενῆ, πάσης φύσεως ἀρχὰς ὃς ἔδηνεν. This seems to derive from the interpretation of his name as "the First." (For text see Apostolos N. Athanassakis, *The Orphic Hymns* (Missoula, MT: Scholars Press, 1977, p.120); cf. van Unnik, "Formula," p.92. Athanassakis (vii–viii) believes the hymns date from the first four centuries of the Christian era, perhaps from the second half of the third century. He concurs with Nilsson (cited in van Unnik,p.92 n) that they are likely from Asia Minor.)

[4] See John Whittaker, "Ammonius on the Delphic E," *CQ* n.s. 19 (1969): 187.

[5] W.K.C. Guthrie *A History of Greek Philosophy*, 6 vols. (Cambridge: Cambridge University Press, 1962–78), 1: 29 n; cf. G.S. Kirk, J.E. Raven, and M. Schofield, *The Pre-Socratic Philosophers*, Second Ed. (Cambridge: Cambridge University Press, 1983; henceforth, *KRS*.), pp.50ff.

ἀεὶ) and Chthonie..."⁶ W. Jaeger suggests quite plausibly that Pherecydes is employing an etymology in which Zas = "he who liveth."⁷ We may also compare a portion of the Orphic "Rhapsodic" Theogony,⁸ which reads:

Ζεὺς πρῶτος γένετο, Ζεὺς ὕστατος ἀργικέραυνος
Ζεὺς κεφαλή, Ζεὺς μέσσα, Διὸς δ'ἐκ πάντα τέτυκται (φρ.168, Κερν)
Zeus became first, Zeus of the bright lightning last.
Zeus is head, Zeus middle, and from Zeus all things have their being.⁹

While this ancient text is not an etymology *per se*, the sentiment is close to the view of Zeus presented by later writers, particularly the Stoic Cleanthes.¹⁰ (The second line also bears comparison with Plato's *Laws* 715e ff., see below.)

The first literary evidence outside of Pherecydes we possess for an etymology connecting Zeus and Life comes in Plato's *Cratylus* 396a. In the course of a discussion concerning the names of the gods, Socrates explains the meaning of Zeus in the following way: Ἀτεχνῶς γάρ ἐστιν οἷον

---

⁶ *KRS*, p.56. Compare the similar account (also in *KRS*, p.56) of Damascius Ζάντα μὲν εἶναι ἀεὶ καὶ Χρόνον καὶ Χθονίαν τὰς τρεῖς ἀρχάς. That Pherecydes should have already worked out an abstract notion of Time (Chronos) at this point in history is surprising, but it is possible. See *KRS*, p.57.

⁷ Rather than simply employing Zas to emphasize the ζα-, an intensive prefix, as suggested by *KRS*, p.57.

⁸ The fragment (in Otto Kern, ed. *Orphicorum Fragmenta* (Berlin: Weidmann, 1922)) is from Porphyry, ap. Eusebius, but it also appears in the "Derveni Theogony," an ancient papyrus containing an Orphic theogony (close enough to the Rhapsodic for our purposes) with philosophizing commentary. The papyrus itself may be as early as the fourth century BCE, and the commentary appears to be pre-Socratic. See M.L. West *The Orphic Poems* (Oxford: Oxford University Press, 1983), pp.75-82; 108-110. A provisional transcript may be found in "Der Orphische Papyrus von Derveni," *Zeitschrift für Papyrologie und Epigraphik* 47 (1982), following p.300.

⁹ Translation in W.K.C. Guthrie, *Orpheus and Greek Religion* 2nd ed. (London: Methuen, 1952), p.140. He provides a translation of the metrical fragments of the "Rhapsodic Theogony" on pp. 137 ff.

¹⁰ The original meaning of this portion of the poem may be traced to particular points of Orphic belief. In the Rhapsodic theogony, the first god to be born is Phanes (also called Protogonos, among other names), who becomes creator of the world. Zeus – having already escaped being eaten by Kronos – eventually swallows Phanes, and with him, the created order as well. Zeus then brings this forth in a new creation. The mention of "first and last," thus appears to refer to the fact that Zeus is the *last*-born of Kronos, yet he is also *first*-born in that he alone did not require "re-birth" after Kronos' swallowing of his children. The second line we have cited seems an obvious allusion to Zeus' role as "second creator." For detailed summaries, see West, pp.70-75,91; Guthrie, pp.78-83. With reference to Zeus' swallowing of the creation, note also fr. 167: "...all that was then in being and all that was to come to pass, all was there, and mingled like streams in the belly of Zeus." Trans. in Guthrie, p.81.

λόγος τὸ τοῦ Διὸς ὄνομα.[11] This λόγος may be divided into two parts: Ζῆνα and Δία.[12] The two elements taken together give an accurate picture of the nature of God: he is the one "through whom (δι' ὄν) all beings have life (ζῆν)."[13] Plato no doubt draws upon commonly known etymologies throughout the *Cratylus*, and this may be one such traditional reading. In any case, this reading of Zeus' name appealed to the "philosophically tinged piety" of hellenistic times.[14] Variations of it appear in Chryssipus,[15] (cf. the account of the Stoics in Diogenes Laertes),[16] the Pseudo-Aristotelian *De Mundo*,[17] and, most notably for us, in the Letter of Aristeas 16[18] and (in abbreviated form) Josephus, *Ant.* 12:22.[19] There are evident similarities between this etymology for Zeus; the LXX understanding of YHWH as "the one who is"; and Jewish traditions which take YHWH as "the one who causes to be." We will examine the relationship between these later.

---

[11] Text in *Platon: Oeuvres Complètes* Vol. 5, part 2, ed. Louis Méridier (Paris: Société d'Édition "Les belles lettres," 1931). Méridier gives "En effet le nom de Zeus est à proprement parler comme une définition;" H.N. Fowler takes οἷον λόγος as "like a sentence" (Plato, *Cratylus*, LCL; Cambridge: Harvard University Press/London: Wm. Heinemann, 1926).

[12] These correspond to the declension of Zeus as nom. Ζεύς, gen. Διός, thought to be derived from *Ζήν and *Δίς respectively. I have followed Plato in giving the accusative forms, since they best suit his purported etymology.

[13] 396b: Συμβαίνει οὖν ὀρθῶς ὀνομάζεσθαι οὗτος ὁ θεὸς εἶναι, δι' ὃν ζῆν ἀεὶ πᾶσι τοῖς ζῶσιν ὑπάρχει...

[14] For the phrase in quotation marks see D.C. Feeney, *The Gods in Epic* (Oxford: Oxford University Press, 1991), p.138.

[15] Ap. Philodemus περὶ εὐσεβείας 12: Δία μὲν γάρ φασι δι' ὃν τὰ πάντα, Ζῆνα δὲ καλοῦσι παρ ὅσον τοῦ ζῆν αἴτιός ἐστιν ἢ διὰ τοῦ ζῆν κεχώρηκεν; cf. a similar remark in Stobaeus *ecl.* 1.1.26. Texts in A.B. Cook, *Zeus* 3 vols. (Cambridge: Cambridge University Press, 1914–40) 1: 29 n.

[16] Diogenes Laertes 7.147, on Zeno. The text is identical to that found in Philodemus περὶ εὐσεβείας 12, quoted above.

[17] Ps-Arist. *De Mundo* 401a: καλοῦμεν δὲ αὐτὸν καὶ Ζῆνα καὶ Δία, παραλλήλως χρώμενοι τοῖς ὀνόμασιν, ὡς κἂν εἰ λέγοιμεν δι' ὃν ζῶμεν. Text in Aristotle, *On the Cosmos*, trans. D.J. Furley, LCL (London: Wm. Heinemann/Cambridge: Harvard University Press, 1955).

[18] "They (sc. the Jews) worship the same God...though we call him by different names, such as Zeus or Dis. This name was very appropriately bestowed upon him by our first ancestors, in order to signify that *He through whom all things are endowed with life and come into being* (δι' ὃν ζωοποιοῦνται τὰ πάντα καὶ γίνεται), is necessarily the ruler and lord of the Universe." (italics mine; Ep. Arist. 15/16.) Text and translation in Martin Hengel, *Judaism and Hellenism*, trans. John Bowden; 2 vols (London: SCM, 1974), 1: 264. Cf. Hengel's comments on p.265.

[19] In his account of the LXX translation, Josephus too has Aristeas say that God is called Zeus (Ζῆνα) because he breathes life (ζῆν) into all things.

We conclude with two etymologies which, while not nearly as widespread as the previous one, are still of interest for our study. Shortly after ps-Aristotle makes us of the Ζῆνα/Δία motif, he offers a long list of equivalencies for Zeus. Many of them are different words for "destiny," which the author, in typically hellenistic fashion, sees as the equivalent of the supreme deity. One of these names is Aisa (Αἶσαν), which ps-Aristotle takes to mean "always existing" – ἀεὶ οὖσαν (401b). Furley takes this in conjunction with the previous name (Adrasteia) and translates "Aisa – a cause that exists forever."[20] The second etymology concerns the word αἰών. Aristotle says the following in the *De Caelo*: "...By the same analogy also the sum of existence of the whole heaven, the sum which includes all time even to infinity, is *aeon*, taking its name from ἀεὶ εἶναι ("to be everlasting"), for it is immortal and divine" (*De Caelo* 279a17-28).[21] While Aristotle did not treat "Aion" as a divinity, later generations did. We will see later in our study of Aion that the Aristotelian concept of eternity influenced the author of the inscription to Aion found at Eleusis. We would suspect, then, that the author of the inscription was likewise aware of the purported etymology αἰών=ἀεὶ ὤν, which he then extrapolated into ὁποῖος ἔστι καὶ ἦν καὶ ἔσται.

Τὸ ˝Ον in Greek Thought

Introduction

When John used the phrase ὁ ὤν to describe God in Rev. 1:4, he landed himself (wittingly or unwittingly) in the middle of a long and complex philosophical conversation concerning God and Being. Since this particular reading of the name YHWH first appeared in the LXX translation of Ex. 3:14, however, it will be most helpful to focus our attention there. Did the LXX translation in fact "depend on" Greek philosophy? And if so, what would such dependence actually mean? Was the ancestral Jewish faith necessarily polluted by such contact with Greek thought?

The first, and most precise, way to explore these questions is to look for *verbal parallels* between Greek texts and the LXX's ἐγώ εἰμι ὁ ὤν. If we were to find this precise formulation in Greek literature before the translation of the Septuagint, we could rightly speak of "dependence" in an absolute sense. It is true that we are hampered by a certain lack of data. Much of our knowledge of hellenistic philosophy comes from fragments col-

---

[20] In LCL. We may compare 401a, "He himself is the cause of all" (ἅτε πάντων αὐτὸς αἴτιος ὤν).

[21] Translation in Aristotle: *On the Heavens*, trans. by W.K.C. Guthrie LCL (Cambridge: Harvard University Press/London: Wm. Heinemann, 1939).

lected by later authors, and there is always a possibility that a crucial teaching has dropped out of the tradition. This should not completely discourage us, however. The questions of God and Being were much discussed in the ancient world, and if someone had been bold enough to equate the two it would likely have been preserved. It is significant that one of our most important sources for Greek philosophy, Eusebius, had a particular interest in this question, and would have been more than happy to note such an equation as a *praeparatio evangelica*.[22]

As it happens, no such formulation exists. The phrase ὁ ὤν is not used of God (or Being) in Greek philosophy until Numenius in the second century CE (and even here the evidence is disputed).[23] The similar expression τὸ ὄν, however, is used quite frequently. We might settle, then, for an equation of God, or a god, with Being, τὸ ὄν. Even if such a parallel were to emerge, of course, the use of a personal ὁ ὤν would still constitute a significant innovation on the part of the LXX. We will demonstrate, however, that such an equation is *not* attested in Greek thought until the time of Seneca and Plutarch – in other words, long after the translation of the LXX.

Although verbal parallels provide the surest foundation for establishing conclusions about dependence and independence, we must also deal with broader *conceptual parallels* which might give evidence of a more subtle or indirect influence of Greek thought on the LXX of Ex. 3:14. These are far more difficult to examine and must be treated with great care. The Presocratic philosopher Anaxagoras, for example, taught that Mind (νοῦς) is everlasting: ὁ δὲ νοῦς, ὃς ἀεί ἐστι (fr. 14; see discussion below). The material is of obvious relevance to our topic, but one cannot say the LXX "depends" on Anaxagoras' description. Even if we stay close to the word "god" (θεός/deus) our problems are not minimized. The Greek and Latin terms could cover a wide range of meanings, from "ultimate reality" to "the world" to "the divine." The singular and plural forms could be used interchangeably in many instances.

We may venture one general observation which may be of help. It is true that the word "god" as used by the philosophers often connotes something very different from the speaking, acting God depicted in the Hebrew bible. (This applies even more, of course, to terms like "Mind," "Logos," and so on.) We will note examples of this below, particularly with regards to the Stoics. At the same time, the word "god" was still inextricably linked with the *persons* of Zeus, Apollo, and the rest of the Olympians, whose exploits remained standard fare in Greek education. The

---

[22] We discuss below Eusebius' warm embracing of Plutarch's equation of Apollo and τὸ ὄν in *Praeparatio Evangelica* 527b ff.

[23] John Whittaker, "Moses Atticizing," *Phoenix* 21 (1967): 196–201.

tension between personal gods and philosophical abstractions, then, does not simply arise on the fault line between Jewish and Greek thinking. It is present within the Greek tradition itself. On occasion an author may assist us by making a clear distinction between, say, the gods and the Forms (as Plato does in the *Phaedrus*). But this will not apply to someone like Cleanthes, who names the Stoic designing fire "Zeus," and sings him (it?) a hymn which could easily find its way into Jewish or Christian worship, after a simple exchange of names.

All of this should highlight the importance of verbal parallels for our investigation. In the (notable) absence of ὁ ὤν in Greek philosophical texts, we will concentrate our attention on actual occurrences of τὸ ὄν in the literature. We are especially interested in those texts where τὸ ὄν is brought into close conjunction with θεός. The best we can do in terms of conceptual parallels is to try and understand the various thinkers on their own terms and to keep the categories of God and Being as clear as possible. We will also need to devote attention to the closely related issues of time and eternity, and how these relate to God and Being. This should put us in a better position to see how these ideas may have contributed to the translation of Ex. 3:14 LXX, and the interpretation of that verse by later writers.

With this framework in place we may begin our investigation of τὸ ὄν in Greek literature. We make no claim to exhaustiveness. "Being is said in many ways," wrote Aristotle – τὸ ὄν λέγεται πολλαχῶς,[24] and we cannot hope to explore all of them.[25]

A few general remarks about τὸ ὄν are in order before we investigate specific texts. Following Charles Kahn, we may speak of four basic uses of the verb to be: predicative ("He *is* white"); static or durative ("Justice *is* a virtue"); veridical ("*It is true that* he *is* a man."); or existential ("He *exists*").[26] The last three categories will be of particular interest as our study proceeds. As for τὸ ὄν (= τὸ ἐόν) itself, we may render it "that which is," but this can have various shades of meaning. Τὸ ὄν (and related forms like τὰ ὄντα) can mean simply "something that is"[27] or more generally "the

---

[24] See, e.g. *Met.* Z 1; he repeats the phrase throughout the *Metaphysics*.

[25] Those who do wish to explore the verb to be in depth may turn to Charles H. Kahn, *The Verb "Be" in Ancient Greek* (Dordrecht: Reidel, 1973). Of particular interest is "Appendix C: The Nominalized Forms of the Verb," pp.453–62.

[26] The terms used in the analysis of "to be" vary from author to author. I have employed those given by Kahn, "Some Philosophical Uses of 'to be' in Plato," *Phronesis* 26 (1981): 113–4. For a good overview of the general philosophical problems connected with Being, see C. J. F Williams,. "Being," in *A Companion to Philosophy of Religion*; Blackwell Companions to Philosophy; eds. Philip L. Quinn and Charles Taliaferro (Oxford: Blackwell, 1997): 223–28.

[27] Kahn, *The Verb "Be,"* pp.455–6; Guthrie, 6: 204.

things that are."[28] One could further distinguish "that which is *the case*" from "some*thing* that is (i.e. that exists)." Herodotus, meanwhile, uses τὸ ὄν to refer to "the facts" of a situation. Thus at Hdt. 5:50.2 we read:

χρεὸν γάρ μιν μὴ λέγειν τὸ ἐόν, βουλόμενόν γε Σπαρτιήτας ἐξαγαγεῖν ἐς τὴν Ἀσίην.

He should not have told the truth, if he wanted to lead the Spartans on an expedition into Asia.[29]

Since our primary concern will be with the use of τὸ ὄν in philosophical literature, it is worth quoting Kahn here:

> This veridical construction for the nominalized participle [such as we see in the text from Herodotus] is certainly the oldest and probably also the most common use of the articular form in non-philosophic literature; and I believe that it exerts a powerful influence on the meaning of the participle in philosophical contexts from Parmenides on.[30]

As we will see, Parmenides and Plato exploit this veridical nuance of the verb when they speak of τὸ ὄν as "that which *really* is," as opposed to that which only seems to be.

The participle could also be taken more abstractly as the "Being" or "Is-ness" of a thing. Just as something could partake of "Heat" or "Cold," so it could be said to partake of "Being." Most apposite for our discussion, of course, is the use of τὸ ὄν for "*the* Being," the Being *par excellence*, namely God. Most Greeks would have agreed that the gods *are*,[31] although certain men like Protagoras might confess uncertainty even on that score.[32] Moreover, the gods could be described as early as Hesiod as μακάρων γένος αἰὲν ἐόντων.[33] We will argue that the explicit equation of τὸ ὄν and deity, however, was not made until the first century BCE.

---

[28] Note that Jonathan Barnes is happy to render τὸ ὄν in the *Metaphysics*: "things that exist." See Barnes, ed., *The Cambridge Companion to Aristotle* (Cambridge: Cambridge University Press, 1995), p.70.

[29] Text and translation in Kahn, *The Verb "Be,"* p.352. He gives several other examples from Herodotus on pp.352–55.

[30] Kahn, *The Verb "Be,"* p.455.

[31] See especially Plutarch, *De E* 393a, where Plutarch believes the sentiment that ἔστιν ὁ θεός is so obvious that he adds εἰ χρὴ φάναι. For a discussion of the existence of the gods from a linguistic point of view see Kahn, *The Verb "Be,"* pp.300ff.

[32] See below.

[33] Hesiod, *Theog.* 34; cf. Plato, *Tim.* 34a, which speaks of the reasoning of the "ever living God" – ὄντος ἀεὶ θεοῦ (presumably a reference to the Demiurge). This is in some ways even more relevant to our discussion, since unlike the gods of Hesiod, the Demiurge does not appear to have a beginning or an end. Note that at *Tim.* 41b Plato says explicitly that the traditional gods (if one believes in them at all) are not even ἀθάνατοι. This is of course in contradiction to the classical description of the gods.

Presocratic Philosophy[34]

The first philosopher to use τὸ ὄν (or more precisely the older form τὸ ἐόν) in a technical sense appears to have been Parmenides of Elea (6th/5th c. BCE; see fr. 8, ll.19–20). Parmenides portrays his search for "what is" in vivid religious terms which echo Hesiod, and which also bear similarities to later heavenly journey narratives.[35] This does not necessarily make him a theologian, as becomes evident when we take a closer look at what he actually says.[36] He aims to show through reason not only that "what is" is one, but also that it is eternal, ungenerated, and immovable. If this runs counter to what we observe, so much the worse for our observations. The senses must go, and reason alone must be judge. The premise from which Parmenides argues is laid out in fr. 2. "The goddess" who gives him the revelation of "what is" tells him of:

> ὁδοὶ μοῦναι διζήσιός εἰσι νοῆσαι/ἡ μὲν ὅπως ἔστιν τε καὶ ὡς οὐκ ἔστι μὴ εἶναι/πειθοῦς ἐστι κέλευθος (Ἀληθείῃ γὰρ ὀπηδεῖ)/ἡ δ' ὡς οὐκ ἔστιν τε καὶ ὡς χρεών ἐστι μὴ εἶναι/τὴν δή τοι φράζω παναπευθέα ἔμμεν ἀταρπόν/οὔτε γὰρ ἂν γνοίης τό γε μὴ ἐόν (οὐ γὰρ ἀνυστόν)/οὔτε φράσαις....
>
> the only ways of enquiry that are to be thought of. The one, that [it] is and that it is impossible for [it] not to be, is the path of Persuasion (for she attends upon truth); the other, that [it] is not and that it is needful that [it] not be, that I declare to you is an altogether indiscernible track: for you cannot know what is not – that cannot be done – nor indicate it.[37]

The words "it is" in this text should likely be read as "anything that can be talked or thought about," since this makes the best sense of the statement "you cannot know what is not" towards the end of the fragment.[38] Par-

---

[34] Unless otherwise noted, texts and translations for the Presocratics are drawn from *KRS*, which provides text, translation, and commentary for most of the major passages in the Presocratics. For a more lengthy collection of texts, see Hermann Diels and Walther Kranz, *Die Fragmente der Vorsokratiker*, Eleventh Ed., 3 vols (Zürich/Berlin: Weidmannsche, 1964; henceforth *DK*).

[35] For a brief overview, see *KRS*, p.244; Guthrie, 2: 6–13; Hermann Fränkel, *Early Greek Poetry and Philosophy*, trans. Moses Hadas and James Willis (Oxford: Basil Blackwell, 1975), pp.350ff.

[36] Jaeger, who is quick to point out "theology" wherever it might exist among the Presocratics, does ascribe a genuine religious sentiment to Parmenides; nonetheless, he emphasizes that Parmenides "definitely fails to identify Being with God." Jaeger, p.107. On Presocratic theology in general, see also Olof Gigon, "Die Theologie der Vorsokratiker," in *Studien zur antiken Philosophie* (Berlin/New York: Walter de Gruyter, 1972): 41–68.; and Gregory Vlastos, "Theology and Philosophy in Early Greek Thought" in *Studies in PreSocratic Philosophy*, 2 vols, eds. David J. Furley and R. E. Allen (London: Routledge and Kegan Paul; New York: Humanities Press, 1970), 1: 92–129.

[37] *KRS*, p.245.

[38] Thus G.E.L. Owen, "Eleatic Questions," *CQ* n.s. 10 (1960): 90ff.; and Richard Sorabji, *Time, Creation, and the Continuum* (London: Duckworth, 1983), p.99. *Contra*,

menides begins his discourse with the question of the guidelines which in his mind ought to inform any discussion. It is not, at least at this stage, a disquisition on Being in the abstract.[39] As it turns out, he will go on to reach conclusions about Being or Reality as such, so different interpretations at this point are not necessarily crucial for understanding his thought as a whole.[40]

The goddess goes on to tell him (fr. 8, 1–4):

μόνος δ' ἔτι μῦθος ὁδοῖο/λείπεται ὡς ἔστιν ταύτῃ δ' ἔπι σήματ' ἔασι/πολλὰ μάλ', ὡς ἀγένητον ἐὸν καὶ ἀνώλεθρόν ἐστιν/οὖλον μουνογενές τε καὶ ἀτρεμὲς ἠδὲ τέλειον.

There still remains just one account of a way, that it is. On this way there are very many signs, that being uncreated and imperishable it is, whole and of a single kind and unshaken and perfect.[41]

The implications of what appeared to be a simple problem of logic – you can only talk about what is, not what is not – turn out to be far-reaching. Apparently this affirmation "it is" holds the secret to the nature of reality. In this regard, Parmenides' affinity for singular forms of the verb to be ("it is," "that which is") is not accidental. The singular contrasts with the plural forms used by his predecessors and successors.[42] While they speak of the things in the world as τὰ ὄντα, Parmenides explains that this apparent multiplicity is an illusion. There is really only τὸ ὄν.

The next line of the fragment also grabs our attention: "It never was nor will be, since it is now, all together, one, continuous"; οὐδέ ποτ' ἦν οὐδ' ἔσται, ἐπεὶ νῦν ἐστιν ὁμοῦ πᾶν/ἕν, συνεχές. If we assume that Simplicius has accurately reported Parmenides here,[43] we have a statement that stands in a puzzling relationship with Rev. 1:4. On the one hand, the notion of a "timeless eternity" – if indeed this is what is being taught here (see below) – might have affinities with the idea of God as ὁ ὤν. But the denial of past and future stands in direct antithesis to the formula in Revelation. The passage merits further investigation.

---

e.g. Fränkel (p.353n), who believes ἔστιν is an impersonal verb like "it rains"; and Guthrie, 1: 15–17 (cf. 2: 14–15), who takes "it is" etc. as tautology.

[39] Cf. Montgomery Furth, "Elements of Eleatic Ontology," in *The Presocratics*, ed. Alexander Mourelatos (Garden City, NY: Doubleday, 1974), p.248.

[40] Guthrie, 2: 15.

[41] KRS, p.248.

[42] Kahn (*The Verb "Be,"* pp.455–67) believes the use of τὰ ὄντα for "the things in the world" pre-dates Parmenides. Cf. his words on p.456 n: "This use of the plurals is a perfectly natural expression for the Ionian (and originally Milesian) endeavor to construct a single explanatory scheme for the whole cosmos and for 'everything there is'."

[43] A point which has been questioned by John Whittaker in *God, Time, Being*; *Symbolae Osloenses* Fasc. Supp. 23 (Oslo: Universitetsforlaget, 1971), pp.17ff.

There are essentially two ways of understanding οὐδέ ποτ' ἦν οὐδ' ἔσται, ἐπεὶ νῦν ἐστιν.⁴⁴ In the first, Parmenides is thought to be teaching that "what is" is timeless. It is a state of affairs in which temporal distinctions are obliterated.⁴⁵ This view has been challenged, and it has been asserted (e.g. by Fränkel) that the phrase ought to be rendered: "Nor is it the case that X existed at some time (*but not now*), or will exist at some time (*but not now*)." In other words, there are no gaps in Being with respect to time.⁴⁶ It is a question of infinite duration rather than timelessness. Owen has effectively dismantled the linguistic basis for Fränkel's interpretation, but this has not been the end of the discussion. Whittaker has questioned whether Parmenides would have expounded such a novel and abstruse doctrine as "timeless eternity" in a few simple words with no further explanation, and wonders why later philosophers like Plato and Aristotle did not respond to such a provocative thesis.⁴⁷ Schofield gives a detailed argument from the context of fr.8 that defends the substance of Fränkel's idea while admitting many of Owen's critiques.⁴⁸

There are formidable names on both sides of the issue. I am inclined to side with the first group. Certainly Parmenides did not articulate the timelessness of "what is" in great detail, but something like timelessness seems to be implied in his words, at least as we have them from Simplicius.⁴⁹ If this is abstruse and novel, one can only say that those two words characterize Parmenides' thinking in general. It is true that ll.6ff. of fr.8 go on to

---

⁴⁴ This is of course a simplification. Sorabji, *Time*, pp.99 ff., provides a thorough and lucid survey of *eight* possible interpretations.

⁴⁵ Adherents to this view include Guthrie (2:29), who credits Parmenides with being the first to articulate the difference between eternal and everlasting; *KRS*, p.250; Owen, who gives a detailed discussion of the whole matter in "Plato and Parmenides on the Timeless Present," in Mourelatos, *The Presocratics*, pp.271ff; Sorabji, *Time*, pp.99–108;128–30; and Leo Groarke, "Parmenides' Timeless Universe," *Dialogue* 24 (1985): 535–41. Groarke stresses that the fact that ἐστι is in the present tense is of immense importance to Parmenides, since this means that past and future "lack an existing referent" (pp.536–7).

⁴⁶ See Owen, "Plato and Parmenides," p.274. The other name often associated with this view is that of Tarán in his book *Parmenides* (cf. the summary of this approach in Malcolm Schofield, "Did Parmenides Discover Eternity?" *Archiv für Geschichte der Philosophie* 52 (1970): 113–4.)

⁴⁷ Whittaker, *God, Time, Being*, pp.11,16ff. The second half of Whittaker's thesis depends, of course, on his particular understanding of Plato's discussion of time and eternity in the *Timaeus*. Most scholars see Plato using Parmenides there to bolster his own doctrine of an eternal present, but Whittaker dissents. See the counter arguments in Sorabji, *Time*, pp.105ff.

⁴⁸ Schofield, pp. 113–135.

⁴⁹ This is one of Whittaker's prime objections, since he believes the rendering of Simplicius may have been the result of Neoplatonic interpretations of Parmenides creeping into the sources used by Simplicius.

speak of "coming to be," which might lead one to adopt the interpretation of Fränkel. But consider ll.19–20:

> πῶς δ' ἂν ἔπειτα πέλοι τὸ ἐόν; πῶς δ'ἂν κε γένοιτο;
> εἰ γὰρ ἔγεντ', οὐκ ἔστ', οὐδ' εἴ ποτε μέλλει ἔσεσθαι.
> And how could what is be in the future? How could it come to be?
> For if it came into being, it is not: nor is it if it is ever going to be in the future.

It seems as if Parmenides is *not* simply asserting that there can be no future "coming to be" from non-being (since it has already been asserted that one can only say "it is" and not "it is not"). Rather, he is indicating that "what is" can have no "movement" into the future. According to Parmenides, it exists actually and completely only *in the present*. Past and future, as it were, collapse into the present.[50]

Before we leave fr. 8, it is important to point out one of the crucial assumptions of his argument: nothing comes out of what is not – *ex nihilo nihil fit*. After the goddess asks how and whence "what is" could have grown, she says, "I will not allow you to say nor to think from not being."[51] This formulation became standard dogma for philosophers after Parmenides, such that Aristotle could write, "Generation from the nonexistent is impossible: in this opinion all the natural philosophers concur" (*Phys.* 187a34).[52] Its widespread acceptance makes all the more striking the contrasting Jewish idea that οὐκ ἐξ ὄντων ἐποίησεν αὐτὰ (that is, the heavens, earth, etc.) ὁ θεός (2 Macc. 7:28; cf. Rom. 4:17).

Parmenides' teaching naturally aroused much discussion among the philosophers of the fifth century. His follower *Melissus* is reported as saying:

---

[50] The fact that "what is" is later described as ἀκίνητόν, "motionless" or "changeless" (fr. 8, l. 38) might be adduced as further support for this view. Just as there is no "physical" movement by or within that which is, so there is no progression or movement through time. Whittaker (*God, Time, Being*, p.11) asserts that neither the Presocratics nor Plato nor Aristotle thought of duration as a process. Owen by contrast argues that Parmenides is working with the idea of "the identity of indiscernibles." In order to distinguish past from present or present from future, one would need something to change; otherwise they "look" exactly alike. Since he has already affirmed that nothing changes, tense distinctions must therefore be abandoned. (See Owen, "Plato and Parmenides," pp.272-3; and the discussion in Schofield, pp.127ff.) The fact that Parmenides later says that what is "remains" the same (fr. 8, l. 30: μενεῖ or μένει, according to one's taste; see Schofield, p.129 n) does not destroy Owen's argument. Parmenides is making concessions to human understanding, just as he does by including "is not" statements and alpha-privatives in his earlier discussion of what is, despite his principle that such things are inherently meaningless. See Owen, p.275; Sorabji, *Time*, pp.104–5. Owen also suggests (pp.278ff.) that Parmenides may be of two minds on the whole issue.

[51] fr. 8, l. 12; *KRS*, p.249.

[52] Quoted in Guthrie, 2: 29.

ὅτε τοίνυν οὐκ ἐγένετο, ἔστι δέ, ἀεὶ ἦν καὶ ἀεὶ ἔσται καὶ ἀρχὴν οὐκ ἔχει οὐδὲ τελευτήν, ἀλλ' ἄπειρον ἐστιν.

Since, then, it did not come to be, but is, it always was and always will be, and it has no beginning nor end but is unlimited. (fr. 2)[53]

Depending on how one interprets Parmenides fr. 8, Melissus is here either correcting him or explaining him more clearly. In any case, he affirms that what is is everlasting, without raising the question of a timeless eternity or some such concept.[54] Whether this makes Melissus a sub-standard philosopher is a matter of opinion.[55] What matters to us is that he describes τὸ ἐόν (the word is not used, but it is implied by the analogy with Parmenides and the presence of ἐστι in the text[56]) as that which "always was and always will be."[57]

Empedocles, meanwhile, is in open revolt against the monism of Parmenides. In his two poems, *On Nature* and *Purifications*, he reintroduces four elements (water, earth, air, and sun/fire) into his scheme,[58] and sets over them the forces of Love (φιλότης) and Strife (νεῖκος).[59] He is willing to say, however, that τὸ ἐόν cannot be "utterly destroyed," and he affirms that "it is impossible for anything to come to be from what is not" – ἔκ τε γὰρ οὐδάμ' ἐόντος ἀμήχανόν ἐστι γενέσθαι (fr.12).[60] In a similar way, *Anaxagoras* sought to maintain Parmenides' dictum that nothing comes into being from what is not, while allowing for multiplicity and change in the world.[61] Thus in one place he can affirm Parmenides, writing οὐδὲν...χρῆμα γίνεται οὐδὲ ἀπόλλυται[62], and in another he can directly oppose him, saying, ὁμοῦ χρήματα πάντα ἦν – "all things were together."[63] As Owen notes, this statement is in "flat contradiction" to Parmenides, both in its affirmation of multiplicity and in its employment of the past tense ἦν.[64]

---

[53] *KRS*, p.393; cf. fr.1: "It always was whatever it was and it always will be..."; ἀεὶ ἦν ὅ τι ἦν καὶ ἀεὶ ἔσται.

[54] Cf. *KRS*, p.393: Melissus "allows the tenses 'was' and 'will be', and ascribes a more readily intelligible everlasting existence to what is."

[55] For a word in favor of Melissus see Jonathan Barnes, *The Pre-Socratic Philosophers*, 2 vols. (London: Routledge and Kegan Paul, 1979), 1:180; cf. Guthrie, 2: 102; *KRS*, p.392 n.

[56] Cf. Simplicius' remark (*KRS* p.400) that Melissus believed τὸ ὄν to be ἀσώματον.

[57] See, e.g., his discussion in fr. 7, *KRS*, pp.397–8.

[58] See fr. 71, Guthrie 2: 147.

[59] See, e.g., fr. 17, *KRS*, p.287.

[60] *KRS*, pp.291–2; cf. Jaeger, p.137.

[61] See, e.g., Guthrie 2: 271.

[62] Fr. 17, *KRS*, p.358.

[63] Fr. 1, *KRS*, pp.357–8.

[64] Owen, p.276; *KRS* make the same point, p.358.

Anaxagoras is also of interest to us for his concept of Mind (νοῦς). In fr.14, we learn that Mind is everlasting: ὁ δὲ νοῦς, ὃς ἀεί ἐστι...[65] More than that, it set the entire universe in order (and in motion):

καὶ ὁποῖα ἔμελλεν ἔσεσθαι καὶ ὁποῖα ἦν καὶ ὅσα νῦν ἔστι καὶ ὁποῖα ἔσται, πάντα διεκόσμησε...

And all things that were to be – those that were and those that are now and those that shall be – Mind arranged them all...(fr. 12)[66]

There has been some debate over whether Anaxagoras understood Mind to be an incorporeal or corporeal entity (albeit the "thinnest" [λεπτότατόν] and "purest" [καθαρώτατον] one),[67] and whether or not he thought of it as "divine."[68] What is important is that the ordering principle of the universe, which can make at least some claims to a divine and incorporeal existence, is described as that which "always is." Furthermore, this Mind organizes all others things that have been, are now, or will be.

Parmenides' teaching met with other criticisms as well. The *Atomists* asserted that non-being exists just as much as being.[69] They were arguing for the existence of void, which enabled them to get the universe in motion again after Parmenides had (in theory) ground it to a halt. *Gorgias* (fr. 1) argued, perhaps simply in mockery of Parmenides, that nothing existed. *Metrodorus* toned this down slightly, saying first that we do not know if anything exists (fr. 1), and then asserting that whatever anyone perceives exists (fr. 2). *Protagoras* writes in a similar vein, saying that "man is the measure of the things that are, that they are, and the things that are not, that they are not (fr. 1)."[70] He was agnostic concerning the gods: περὶ μὲν θεῶν οὐκ ἔχω εἰδέναι, οὔθ' ὡς εἰσὶν οὔθ' ὡς οὐκ εἰσὶν οὔθ' ὁποῖοί τινες ἰδέαν (fr. 4).

Plato

Plato's understanding of τὸ ὄν is foundational for all subsequent discus-

---

[65] *KRS*, pp.363–4.
[66] *KRS*, pp.362–3.
[67] Guthrie (2: 279) takes it to be incorporeal; *KRS* (p.364) corporeal.
[68] Guthrie, 2: 279. Jaeger (p.161) is in full agreement on this point, saying "this must...have been his doctrine." Gigon, p.55, believes Anaxagoras goes out of his way to *avoid* using the word θεός of Mind. See the replies of Verdenius and Chapouthier, both of whom think Anaxagoras' Mind is divine (p.67 of the same article).
[69] See e.g Arist. *Phys.* A3, 187a1:...ἔστι τὸ μὴ ὄν (*KRS*, pp.407–8); Arist. *Met.* A4, 985b4: ...διὸ καὶ οὐθὲν μᾶλλον τὸ ὄν τοῦ μὴ ὄντος εἶναι φασιν, ὅτι οὐδὲ τὸ κενὸν <ἔλαττον> τοῦ σώματος (*KRS*, pp.413–4).
[70] Translation in Kathleen Freeman, *Ancilla to the Pre-Socratic Philosophers* (Oxford: Basil Blackwell, 1956).

sion.[71] While he appropriates some key concepts from Parmenides, he is sensitive to the criticisms levelled against his Eleatic forebear. As a consequence, he develops his philosophy in ways that would have been anathema to Parmenides. He is willing, for example, to countenance the idea of something sharing in Being and Not-Being;[72] and, at least by the time of the *Sophist*, he is willing to grant genuine Being to things in the sensible world.[73] At the same time, he is so close to Parmenides that one can justifiably speak of a "Platonic-Eleatic conception of Being." As Kahn says:

> The Platonic-Eleatic conception of Being is defined by the convergence of two antitheses: 1) the opposition of Being and Seeming (εἶναι and φαίνεσθαι) which exploits the veridical value of εἶναι, and 2) the opposition of Being and Becoming which exploits the static value of the verb (in contrast to γίγνεσθαι as "mutative" copula), the value which serves to express the idea of eternal constancy and uniformity.[74]

This concept of Being, we will see, was to have its effect on Jewish as well as Greek thought.

---

[71] Plato employs various words and phrases in his discussions of Being: οὐσία, τὸ εἶναι, and ὃ ἔστι are all used, as well as τὸ ὄν. It is often difficult to see a real difference between the meaning of these terms. It appears, for instance, that οὐσία and τὸ ὄν are functionally equivalent in *Rep.* 521d, 523 a; *Theaetetus* 185c; and *Sophist* 262c (cf. *Phaedo* 78d). Thus while we will pay particular attention to τὸ ὄν because of its similarity to ὁ ὤν, we need not restrict ourselves to that form of the word in exploring Plato's view of Being. For discussion, see Édouard des Places, "La langue philosophique de Platon: Le vocabulaire de l'être," *CRAI* 1961: 88–94; F.M. Cornford, *Plato and Parmenides* (London: Kegan Paul, Trench, Tubner, 1939), p.111; Richard Ketchum, "Plato on Real Being," *American Philosophical Quarterly* 17 (1980): 213–220; Charles H. Kahn "Some Philosophical Uses of 'to be' in Plato," *Phronesis* 26 (1981): 110. More generally see Kahn, *The Verb "Be,"* pp.453ff.

[72] *Rep.* 477b ff.; *Sophist*, passim. For general comments on the *Sophist*, with an emphasis on the issue of Being, see: A.E. Taylor, *The Sophist and The Statesman* (London: Thomas Nelson, 1961), pp.3ff.; Paul Seligman, *Being and Not-Being: An Introduction to Plato's Sophist* (The Hague: Martinus Nijhoff, 1974), pp.2ff.; John Malcolm, "Plato's Analysis of τὸ ὄν and τὸ μὴ ὄν in the *Sophist*," *Phronesis* 12 (1967): 130–46; Cornford, *Plato's Cosmology*, pp.61–2. Seligman speaks of Being as a "form of forms," since "being, though non-descriptive, does refer, namely to all the things that are, including motion and rest. They are encompassed by being and in this sense share being (p.43)."

[73] Seligman, pp.19, 37. Cf. R. Waterfield, *Theaetetus* (Harmondsworth: Penguin, 1987; p.162), where he says that in his later work Plato no longer holds that the world is in complete flux; "[it] must have enough stability to allow for meaningful conversation." S. Halliwell speaks in a similar vein of the *Theaetetus* in his commentary on *Republic 5*, (*Plato: Republic 5*; Warminster: Aris and Phillips, 1993), p.214. See also Cornford, *Plato and Parmenides*, p.193: "There is nothing irrational in attributing some sort of existence to the objects of belief and perception, and taking them as the subjects of discourse."

[74] Kahn, "Some Philosophical Uses of 'to be' in Plato," p.111.

We will concentrate our efforts on three dialogues, the *Republic*, the *Phaedrus*, and the *Timaeus*, since they are most illustrative of the concepts which were to affect later views of τὸ ὄν.[75] In the first two works, generally taken to be from his middle period, Plato's thoughts about Being are driven by his developing theory of Forms, and attendant questions of epistemology.[76] One can point out instances of justice in the world – but what is "the just"? What is the *unchanging reality* or Form behind the particular appearances of justice or goodness or beauty? It is here that Plato betrays his debt to Parmenides. The essence, or reality, of things is to be sought not in the visible realm of the sensible, the world of Becoming, but rather in the unseen realm of the intelligible, the world of Being. In the *Republic*, this quest for being is seen as the mark of the philosopher, whose nature is described as follows:

> Τοῦτο μὲν δὴ τῶν φιλοσόφων φύσεων πέρι ὡμολογήσθω ἡμῖν, ὅτι μαθήματός γε ἀεὶ ἐρῶσιν ὃ ἂν αὐτοῖς δηλοῖ ἐκείνης τῆς οὐσίας τῆς ἀεὶ οὔσης καὶ μὴ πλανωμένης ὑπὸ γενέσεως καὶ φθορᾶς (Rep. 485a–b).[77]

Education accordingly should turn the mind from τοῦ γιγνομένου and towards τὸ ὄν (*Rep.* 518c). In case one misses the significance of τὸ ὄν and its equivalents, Plato explains himself more clearly with phrases like: "that which purely (εἰλικρινῶς) is" (*Rep.* 478d); "that which by nature (πεφυκώς) is" (*Rep.* 490a)[78]; and "that which completely (παντελῶς) is" (*Rep.* 477a).[79] The philosopher is not primarily interested in that which is sometimes beautiful (and sometimes ugly), or that which is partly just (and partly unjust). He is searching for the thing itself, that paradigm or standard by which beautiful things are accounted beautiful, or just things just.[80]

---

[75] In the *Sophist*, Being is conceived of as a Form, which participates in other Forms such as Sameness, Difference, etc. Not-Being ends up being something like Difference. See Seligman for a thorough discussion of the dialogue.

[76] For the chronology of Plato's works, I rely on Richard Kraut, "Introduction to the Study of Plato," in *The Cambridge Companion to Plato*, ed. Richard Kraut (Cambridge: Cambridge University Press, 1992), pp.1–50. For details on the process of dating the dialogues, see in the same volume Leonard Brandwood, "Stylometry and Chronology," pp.90–120. The *Republic* and *Phaedrus* are thought by Kraut (p.9) to be from late in the middle period.

[77] Texts for the *Republic* are from *The Republic of Plato*, ed. James Adam, 2nd ed. by D.A. Rees (Cambridge: Cambridge University Press, 1963).

[78] The Loeb appears to take πεφυκώς with the "lover of truth," who *naturally* seeks after that which truly is. It is admittedly difficult to choose between the two options.

[79] The examples are taken from Ketchum, p.216. A. J. Festugière understands τὸ παντελῶς ὄν in *Soph.* 248e to mean "la somme totale de l'Être." See Festugière, *La révélation d'Hermès Trismégiste*, 4 vols.; vol. 2: *Le dieu cosmique* (Paris: Libairie Le-Coffre, 1949), p.104.

[80] See the discussion in Ketchum, pp.216ff.

Of course, one of the things that makes a standard a standard is its constancy. That which *really* is must therefore be that which *always* is. Mathematics provides a good model for this idea. One plus one *is* two: This proposition always holds true. It does not change with the passage of time.[81] Plato says as much in *Rep.* 522c ff., where he asserts that counting can lead one towards οὐσία. Why? Because the knowledge of geometry is τοῦ ἀεὶ ὄντος γνώσεως, ἀλλ' οὐ τοῦ ποτέ τι γιγνομένου καὶ ἀπολλυμένου (527b).

But Plato is not wholly under Parmenides' spell in the *Republic*. He will not dismiss the entire sensible world as some kind of fantasy. In *Rep.* 478e ff., he essentially posits three levels of Being: that which truly is (the realm of the Forms, or of Being); that which simply *is not*; and that which in some ways is, and in some ways is not (the world of the senses, or of Becoming).[82] This last admission makes him a heretic by Parmenidean standards, but he affirms it nonetheless. In his later dialogues, it appears Plato is willing to ascribe an increasing degree of reality to this world of Becoming.

We conclude our discussion of the *Republic* with a brief mention of *Rep.* 509b, which states that goodness confers upon known things not only their "known-ness," but also their "Being" (τὸ εἶναι) and "Essence" (τὴν οὐσίαν). Plato goes on to say: οὐκ οὐσίας ὄντος τοῦ ἀγαθοῦ, ἀλλ' ἔτι ἐπέκεινα τῆς οὐσίας πρεσβείᾳ καὶ δυνάμει ὑπερέχοντος. This statement led the Neoplatonists to argue that the Good is beyond Being in the sense that it does not exist. The First Principle is essentially unknown and unknowable. This interpretation of Plato is, I believe, effectively refuted by R.E. Allen, who concludes: "The Good is beyond Being because it surpasses Being in dignity and power. It surpasses Being because both good things and evil things participate in Being, whereas only good things participate in Goodness insofar as they are good."[83] (This is consonant with the view of Being put forward in the *Sophist*. Here Being is pictured as a Form alongside other forms such as Motion, Rest, Sameness, and Difference. Just as things may partake of Sameness or Difference, so by virtue of their very existence they may be said to partake of Being or "Is-ness.")

We now turn to the *Phaedrus*. *Phaedrus* 246ff. gives us a vivid picture of the concepts which we have already encountered in the *Republic*. When the gods in their chariots pierce through to the region above the vault of heaven (τὸν ὑπερουράνιον), they enter the region which is occupied by

---

[81] Cf. Owen, "Plato and Parmenides," p.271.

[82] See Cornford, *Plato and Parmenides*, pp.80–1; Ketchum, p.215.

[83] Allen, *Plato's 'Parmenides'* (Oxford: Basil Blackwell, 1983), p.194. See further Allen, pp.189–95; see also Waterfield, *Plato: Republic* (Oxford: Oxford University Press, 1993), note on 509b); Cornford, *Plato and Parmenides*, p.132.

"Being which really is" (οὐσία ὄντως οὖσα; 247c; cf. 247e).[84] Here in the ὑπερουράνιον they gaze upon justice, temperance, and knowledge, which may equally be called τὸ ὄν, τἀληθῆ (247d), or τὸ ὄν ὄντως (249c). (The unfettered contemplation of these Forms is in fact what *makes* a god divine (249c).[85]) Human souls (or more precisely, souls which will later occupy human bodies) catch at best only a glimpse of these Forms. It is incumbent upon them to follow up on these recollections and pursue true wisdom during their time on earth (248a ff.). The world of Forms, then, is equivalent to τὸ ὄν, that which really or truly exists.

This equivalence between τὸ ὄν and the world of Forms takes on its most influential shape in the *Timaeus*, Plato's account of the origins of the world. Timaeus begins his discourse with this question (27d–28a):

τί τὸ ὂν ἀεί, γένεσιν δὲ οὐκ ἔχον, καὶ τί τὸ γιγνόμενον μὲν ἀεί, ὂν δὲ οὐδέποτε;

What is that which ever is, but never comes to be, and what is that which is ever coming to be, but never is?"[86]

The answer is not long in coming: "that which always is" is the intelligible realm inhabited by the Forms (described in the dialogue as "the Eternal Living Creature"), and "that which is ever coming to be" is the sensible world.[87] The former provides a kind of blueprint for the latter: the Demiurge "looks at" the intelligible world and "creates" the sensible world in its image. The world of Forms possesses, or experiences, a plenitude of life or Being to which the world of Becoming continually aspires but by its very nature can never attain.

Later in the dialogue (37e ff.), Plato speaks in more detail of the mode of being enjoyed by this world of Forms. Again his debts to Parmenides become obvious[88]:

All these [days and nights, months and years] are parts of Time, and "was" and "shall be" are forms of time that have come to be; we are wrong to transfer them unthinkingly to eternal being. We say that it was and is and shall be; but "is" alone really

---

[84] Texts and translations in this section are from C.J. Rowe, *Plato: Phaedrus* (Warminster: Aris And Phillips, 1986). The ascent of the soul in the chariot may be a conscious mark of Plato's indebtedness to Parmenides.

[85] Gk. πρὸς οἷσπερ θεὸς ὢν θεῖος ἐστιν. Cf. G.J. De Vries, *A Commentary on the Phaedrus of Plato* (Amsterdam: Hakkert, 1969), pp.146–7. One could of course translate θεός simply as "God" – Plato does tend to use "God" and "gods" somewhat interchangeably – but I have followed the translation of Rowe, which seems to better fit the context.

[86] Translation in A.E. Taylor, *Plato: Timaeus and Critias* (London: Methuen, 1929); text in Plato, *Timaeus...*, trans. R.G. Bury LCL (Cambridge: Harvard University Press/London: Wm. Heinemann, 1929).

[87] See Cornford, *Plato's Cosmology* (London: Kegan Paul, Trench, Tubner; New York: Harcourt, Brace, 1937), p.24.

[88] As Cornford notes, *Plato's Cosmology*, p. 102.

belongs to it and describes it truly; "was" and "shall be" are properly used of becoming which proceeds in time, for they are motions. But that which is for ever in the same state immovably cannot be becoming older or younger by lapse of time, nor can it ever become so;[89] neither can it now have been, nor will it be in the future; and in general nothing belongs to it of all that Becoming attaches to the moving things of sense; but these have come into being as forms of time, which images eternity and revolves according to number.[90]

While Time has parts (μέρη), the world of Forms is "always abiding in unity" – ...μένοντος αἰῶνος ἐν ἑνί...(37d). The regular, repeated, cyclical movements of the heavenly bodies offer an image or likeness of eternity, but because they can be broken down into discrete units (days, months, years) they cannot be eternity itself. Closely related to this is the notion of change. In December the sun will (appear to) trace one path through the sky. In June this path will be noticeably different. The change is regular, it can be predicted, but it is nonetheless change. Such alteration has no place in the world of Forms.[91] Not only do they not *happen to* change – they are constitutionally incapable of it.[92]

Not surprisingly, Plato's statements here, like those of Parmenides, have led to a debate as to whether he is discussing non-durational eternity, the *totum simul* of later thought,[93] or whether he only intends to contrast eternal *duration* with existence in time.[94] The arguments on both sides are es-

---

[89] It has been generally noted that this line is dependent upon Plato's *Parmenides* 140e ff. See, e.g. Richard D. Mohr, "Plato on Time and Eternity," *Ancient Philosophy* 6 (1986): 44. The *Parmenides* as a whole is difficult to interpret and deliberately contains apparently contradictory statements. (See Allen, *Parmenides*, pp.vii-x, 181-199, for a convincing argument that the dialogue consists of a series of *aporiai*, or puzzles, which are *designed* to issue in contradictions, so that the reader might sharpen his dialectical skills by seeking out the false assumptions or logical mistakes which lead to such absurdities.) It is perhaps for this reason that Mohr explicitly states, "The reasoning of the *Parmenides* passage is sound..." We might even say that the conclusion of this section of the *Parmenides* – "the one, if it is such as we have described, cannot even be in time at all" – is valid.

[90] Cornford's translation.

[91] See Cornford, *Plato's Cosmology*, pp.103-5 for a discussion of the circular nature of time. Cf. J. Whittaker, "The 'Eternity' of the Platonic Forms," *Phronesis* 13 (1968): 140: "Thus change is an necessary concomitant of the former [i.e. χρόνος] but essentially absent from the latter [αἰών]"; and Mohr, pp.44-5.

[92] Mohr, p.44; cf. Richard Patterson, "On the Eternality of Platonic Forms," *Archiv für Geschichte der Philosophie* 67 (1985): 35, who cites Aristotle's and Aquinas' principle that time is a measure "not only of change but also of rest in things liable to change."

[93] The "traditional interpretation," according to J. Whittaker, "Forms," p. 131; cf. p.143. Held by, e.g. Cherniss (Whittaker, p.131); Owen, "Plato and Parmenides," pp.283ff.; Patterson, p.35.

[94] The view of Cornford (p.98 n), argued for most thoroughly by Whittaker, "Forms," pp.131ff. Sorabji (*Time*, p.112) concludes that "Plato did not decide between making eternity timeless and giving it everlasting duration..." He bases the latter conclusion on

sentially the same for the *Timaeus* as they are for the Parmenides fragment, and need not be repeated here. As in the case of Parmenides, I believe Plato is referring to something like "timeless eternity" in this passage.[95] Since we have much more information about Plato's thought as a whole, however, we are justified in following Mohr and suggesting further that the Forms are eternal in that they "are not within the category of things which are subject to temporal judgments."[96] As he says:

> We may casually ask "Did the Ideas exist prior to the making of this statement?" that is, "Are the Ideas in the past?" or even ask "Did the Forms exist at 6:30?" But to do so, in the first example, is to treat the Forms as mere relata in a merely relative comparison, rather than to treat them as that from which we take measurements, and in the second, as instances of standards rather than as standards themselves.[97]

Several important points emerge from this survey of τὸ ὄν in Plato. First, Plato does not unambiguously identify God and τὸ ὄν in his writings. In the texts we studied, τὸ ὄν refers to the invisible realm as a whole, the world of Forms where Justice, Truth, Beauty, etc. "dwell." In other dialogues, notably the *Sophist*, Being itself is viewed as one of the Forms. For this reason, one cannot say that the translators of the LXX were simply "Platonizing" the bible in their equation of God and ὁ ὤν in Ex. 3:14. Even if one disregards the very important shift from neuter to masculine, the fact remains that God and τό ὄν are not identical in Plato.[98]

On the positive side, Plato says that τὸ ὄν is eternal, unchanging, and genuine, in contrast to the visible world around us. While this distinction between ἡ γένεσις and τὸ ὄν may be traced back to Parmenides, Plato put

---

Plato's frequent use of ἀεί for the Forms in the *Timaeus*. This is in sharp contrast to Parmenides, who avoids ἀεί in *The Way of Truth* and employs it only in *The Way of Opinion* (his avowedly imperfect account of the cosmos). See Sorabji, *Time*, pp.108–12.

[95] Whittaker, for instance, stresses that one cannot establish that the Forms do not experience duration. But he still can make statements like these ("Forms," p.141): "To take an example, Justice is, was and will be exactly what it *is*, for otherwise it would be something changeable and not an immutable Form. Justice *is* what it was and what it will be...at whatever moment we may choose to speak of the Forms the only applicable tense is the present simply because the Forms are τὰ κατὰ ταὐτὰ ἔχοντα ἀεί." This is not to say that Whittaker is contradicting himself. It is merely to point out that the distinction between "timeless eternity" and perfect immutability is a fine one, and may not have been recognizable to later readers. I have some difficulty, for example, seeing a clear distinction between "duration...that is exempt from change" (Whittaker, p.141) and "timelessness."

[96] Mohr, p.44.

[97] Mohr, p.44. In a footnote (p.46), Mohr compares trying to measure the idea of eternity by the celestial clock like trying to measure the Standard Meter in Paris with a balsa wood meter stick.

[98] Even if one is inclined to equate God and "the Good" in Plato (which I am not), "the Good" and Being are clearly distinguished in *Rep.* 509b.

this idea in a more developed philosophical framework. His conception of "that which is" was to have a profound effect on later generations. It was a formulation which had obvious attractions for philosophically minded Jews and Christians eager to demonstrate the rationality of their faith. Did the Greeks' greatest philosopher speak of a realm distinct from the material world which was everlasting, stable, and real? The Jews and Christians could match that, or even do one better – their God encompassed all of these things, with the added dimension of personality.

Aristotle on Being

At the beginning of this section we cited Aristotle's dictum τὸ ὄν λέγεται πολλαχῶς. This serves as a warning that there is no easy way to handle the question of Being in Aristotle. As one commentator has remarked, "...to follow out Aristotle's uses of this word [οὐσία, the verbal noun counterpart of τὸ ὄν] would be to expound his whole philosophy."[99] We will confine ourselves to a few brief comments and an extended discussion of one particularly relevant issue.

The fact that Aristotle can say τὸ ὄν λέγεται πολλαχῶς indicates that no single "definition" of τὸ ὄν may be forthcoming. One thing we can be certain of, however, is that Aristotle will not restrict true Being to the Platonic Forms, since his rejection of independently existing Forms constitutes his major break with Plato. If anything, true Being belongs to concrete individuals, "this horse" or "Socrates." These have Being in the "full and proper sense."[100] He is willing to posit universals, but they are "secondary substances," in contrast to the Platonic Forms.[101] Space precludes further discussion of this central feature of Aristotle's doctrine.

There is one question, however, which we must address: What does Aristotle mean when he writes in *Metaphysics* Γ 1 (1003a21): "There is a discipline which studies *Being* qua *Being*..."?[102] The italicized phrase is the usual rendering of τὸ ὄν ᾗ ὄν. At least two radically different interpretations of the phrase have been offered.[103] According to the first view, championed by G. Patzig and Philip Merlan, the statement in *Met.* Γ about "Being *qua* Being" must be read in the light of a later statement in *Met.* E 1 which appears to equate ontology with theology: τὸ ὄν ᾗ ὄν is taken to mean a *specific type of Being*, namely "Being in itself" or "essential Be-

---

[99] Guthrie, 6: 204, citing Bonitz.
[100] See *Cat.* 2a 11ff.; discussion in Guthrie, 6: 141ff.
[101] Guthrie, 6: 143–4.
[102] Translation modified from *Aristotle Metaphysics*, trans. by Christopher Kirwan, 2nd ed. (Oxford: Oxford University Press, 1993).
[103] See, e.g., D. M. MacKinnon, "Aristotle's Conception of Substance," in *New Essays in Plato and Aristotle*, ed. Renford Bambrough (London: Routledge and Kegan Paul, 1965): 112.

ing."[104] This "essential Being" is to be equated with Aristotle's God, the famous "Prime Mover" of *Metaphysics* Book Λ.[105]

Patzig believes Aristotle subsumes "substance," οὐσία, under the primary substance (πρώτη οὐσία; see E 1) which is changeless and separable, that is, God. The study of metaphysics culminates in the study of God, the unmoved mover, and thus theology in a certain sense *is* ontology.[106] Aristotle completes this "journey to the highest principles and causes...in a few giant strides" in Book Λ, culminating with the words, "On such a principle [i.e. the Prime Mover], then, depend the heavens, and nature" (ἐκ τοιαύτης ἄρα ἀρχῆς ἤρτηται ὁ οὐρανος καὶ ἡ φύσις; 1072b 13–15). The brevity of the climax in 1071b3 ff., says Patzig, arises from "aesthetic motives": ordinary discursive language cannot bear the weight of such grand ideas.[107] Patzig concludes: "God is the *ousia ousiôn*, on which all other substances rely for their being and which preserves their being..."[108] Merlan takes a very similar view of things, equating τὸ ὄν ᾗ ὄν in Γ 1 with the πρώτη οὐσία and the ἀκίνητος οὐσία of E 1. This is "die göttliche, prozeßfreie οὐσία."[109]

If Patzig and Merlan are correct, we would have something of obvious interest for our study of the Jewish understanding of ὁ ὤν. But their view has not gone unchallenged. A second group of scholars believes that Aristotle is speaking of a general metaphysics which will investigate everything that is. The "...*qua* Being" refers to the *way* in which this investigation will take place. It is an adverbial phrase meaning something like "Being *insofar as it is*" or "existing things *insofar as they exist*."[110] In the phrase τὸ ὄν ᾗ ὄν, the ᾗ ὄν serves to explain the scope of the study – it will study Being insofar as it is Being. According to J.P. Stevenson, this makes the best sense of the grammar of the phrase, particularly when it is

---

[104] Philip Merlan, "ὄν ᾗ ὄν und πρώτη οὐσία: Postskript einer Besprechung," *Philosophische Rundschau* 7 (1959): 152; G. Patzig, "Theology and Ontology in Aristotle's *Metaphysics*," in *Articles in Aristotle: 3: Metaphysics*, eds. Jonathan Barnes, Malcolm Schofield, Richard Sorabji (London: Duckworth, 1979), pp.41–2.

[105] MacKinnon (p.111) describes the relation of Aristotle's ontology to his theology as "the most besettingly obscure problem in the interpretation of the Metaphysics."

[106] Patzig, p.37.

[107] Patzig, pp.44–5.

[108] Patzig, p.41. Cf. Merlan's description of God as "die Quelle des Seins für alles andere, das ist"; Merlan, p.152; and MacKinnon's comment (p.103), "Is he [Aristotle] not rather stressing [in Book Λ] the fact that God in a way unique among substances exists of himself?"

[109] Merlan, pp.148–9. The connection between the two is clearer in *Met.* K, which has led many scholars to question its authenticity (Merlan, 150).

[110] Barnes, *Aristotle*, pp.69–72, Kirwan, pp.202–3; J. G. Stevenson, "Being qua Being," *Apeiron* 9 (1975): 42 ff.

viewed in light of similar phrases used by Aristotle.[111] Through the idea of "focal meaning," he is able to compress this wide-ranging topic into an investigation of substances, which have "Being in the primary sense," since they are those things of which others things are predicated. The claim in E 1 that theology, the study of "changeless and separable" substance, is "primary philosophy," must be dismissed as an earlier view which Aristotle later abandoned (thus Jaeger), or as a later interpolation (thus Natorp), or as a simple contradiction.[112]

An equally serious objection is that we cannot be sure when and how the *Metaphysics* were arranged.[113] Hence we cannot be certain whether Aristotle intended to make the logical connections which Patzig and Merlan employ in their argument. Patzig himself acknowledges that Books Z, H, and Θ "cannot be fitted" into the account he gives of Aristotle's ontology.[114] Is this due to some change within Aristotle himself? Or is it the work of a later editor – and if so, how much later? Even if we were to grant that the *Metaphysics* was in something like its present shape before the translation of the Septuagint, problems would remain. We have already noted the grammatical objections to Merlan's reading of τὸ ὂν ᾗ ὄν as "Being *an sich*." There is also the question of whether "changeless and separable substance" refers to God alone or to the whole group of unmoved movers which guide the heavenly bodies. We may concede that Aristotle intends to track down the one Prime Mover of everything. But he makes plain statements about a plurality of unmoved movers (Book Λ 1073a23 ff.) which also appear to be changeless and separable.[115]

Before we abandon Merlan and Patzig altogether, however, we must examine some other texts from Aristotle. The first is from *De Caelo* I 9. Aristotle is discussing the notion of eternity:

> In dependence on it [antecedent uncertain; see below] all other things have their existence and their life, some more directly, others more obscurely. In the more popular philosophical works, where divinity is in question, it is often made abundantly clear by the discussion that the foremost and highest divinity must be entirely immutable, a fact which affords testimony to what we have been saying. For there is nothing supe-

---

[111] Stevenson, pp.42–50.
[112] See Patzig, pp.3 ff.
[113] See Barnes, *Aristotle*, pp.66–9.
[114] Patzig, p.46.
[115] In *Met.* Λ 1071b5 ff., for example, he says "...it is necessary for there to be some substance that is eternal and immutable..." ἀνάγκη εἶναι ἀΐδιόν τινα οὐσίαν ἀκίνητος (text in Aristotle, *The Metaphysics* trans. Hugh Tredennick 2 vols. LCL; Cambridge: Harvard University Press/London: Wm. Heinemann, 1933–5). In 1072b21–2, however, he begins to speak of τὰς οὐσίας as "movers of the celestial spheres." 1073a23 ff. speaks of a plurality of unmoved movers, while 1074a35ff. states that the Prime Mover is "one." While the Prime Mover appears to be supreme among them, the problem of having many "unmoved, eternal, incorporeal" substances remains. See Guthrie, 6:267–76.

rior that can move it – if there were it would be more divine – and it has no badness in it nor is lacking in any of the fairness proper to it (*De Caelo* 279a22–279b1).[116]

There is much that is obscure here. Simplicius, for instance, reports that Alexander of Aphrodisias was uncertain whether the references here were to the Prime Mover or to the heaven itself, and one can scarcely blame him.[117] What catches the eye is the phrase: "In dependence on it all other things have their existence and their life..." – ὅθεν καὶ τοῖς ἄλλοις ἐξήρτηται...τὸ εἶναί τε καὶ ζῆν. The use of ἐξήρτηται is particularly striking because of its similarities with *Met.* 1072b 13–15.[118] As Alexander said, the precise antecedent for "it" is uncertain – is it personified Aion? the eternal movement of heaven? the Prime Mover? One cannot say for certain, but it is plausible to argue that the Prime Mover is in view here, and that this passage should be taken in conjunction with the similar statement in *Met.* 1072b.[119] In his inquiry into motion in *Physics* VIII, Aristotle reaches a similar conclusion. There is something (namely the Prime Mover) which "is the cause of the fact that some things are and others are not and of the continuous process of change" – ὅ ἐστιν αἴτιον τοῦ τὰ μὲν εἶναι τὰ δὲ μὴ καὶ τῆς συνεχοῦς μεταβολῆς (259a4–5).[120]

What underlies all three of these passages is the idea that the things in the world in some sense depend for their Being on a "fundamental" or "ultimate" Being (usually understood as the Prime Mover, although one could argue for heaven in the case of the *De Caelo* text).[121] We hasten to add that Aristotle is not referring to *creatio ex nihilo* in the Jewish or Christian sense. But the motion imparted by this Prime Mover does undergird all other things.

Patzig and Merlan, then, may be amiss in positing a clear connection between τὸ ὂν ᾗ ὄν and divinity. This is an important point, since if Aristotle *had* clearly equated the two we would have a striking parallel to the

---

[116] Translation Guthrie, *On the Heavens*, LCL.

[117] W. von Leyden, "Time, Number, and Eternity in Plato and Aristotle," *Philosophical Quarterly* 14 (1964): 45.

[118] We might add that the presence of ζῆν recalls the etymology of Zeus discussed above. It is of course difficult to establish whether Aristotle had this traditional formulation in mind here.

[119] Patzig includes *De Caelo* 279a28–30 in a footnote, p.45.

[120] Translation in Aristotle, *Physica*, trans. R.P. Hardie and R.K. Gaye (Oxford: Oxford University Press, 1930). Text in Aristotle, *The Physics*, trans. Philip H. Wicksteed and F. M. Cornford, vol. 2, LCL (London: Wm. Heinemann/Cambridge: Harvard University Press, 1934).

[121] The precise way in which things "depend" on the Prime Mover for Being is not altogether clear. Von Leyden (p.47) suggests the following: "The point, I think, that Aristotle wishes to stress is that all periods and processes in nature depend on the eternity of the revolution of the first heaven and imitate its circular motion by being themselves cyclical..."

description of God as ὁ ὤν in Ex. 3:14 LXX. On the other hand, they do bring out an important concept that appears throughout Aristotle's works: the idea of an unmoved mover or primary Being upon which all other things depend for their Being. Questions might well remain. How does one reconcile Aristotle's statements about many divine beings with the apparent unity of the Prime Mover? How does an everlasting universe "depend" on one source for its Being? Is there any sense in which this Prime Mover could be called "personal"? These are difficult questions. But as the later example of Thomas Aquinas demonstrates, Aristotle's system can be pressed into the service of Jewish or Christian monotheism. It is thus possible, though hardly demonstrable, that the translators of our text in Exodus may have been influenced in some way by Aristotle's idea that the Being of all things is dependent upon the Prime Mover.

Aristotle on Eternity

In light of the significance of eternity for Plato's discussion of τὸ ὄν, we may be permitted a a few words on Aristotle's views on the matter, even though he does not explicitly bring τὸ ὄν into the discussion.. Our primary text immediately precedes the section of the *De Caelo* cited above:

> It is obvious then that there is neither place nor void nor time outside the heaven, since it has been demonstrated that there neither is nor can be body there. Wherefore neither are the things there born in place, nor does time cause them to age, nor does change work in any way upon any of the beings whose allotted place is beyond the outermost motion: changeless and impassive, they have uninterrupted enjoyment of the best and most independent life for the whole aeon of their existence. Indeed, our forefathers were inspired when they made this word, *aeon*. The total time which circumscribes the length of life of every creature, and which cannot in nature be exceeded, they named the *aeon* of each. By the same analogy also the sum of existence of the whole heaven, the sum which includes all time even to infinity, is *aeon*, taking its name from ἀεὶ εἶναι ("to be everlasting"), for it is immortal and divine (*De Caelo* 279a17–28).[122]

Aristotle does not, like Plato, say that "was" and "will be" should not be used of this region above the heavens.[123] He does say, however, that the beings there are not subject to time. Is this the same as Platonic "timelessness" (assuming, contra Whittaker *et al.*, that such exists)? Richard Sorabji provides us with an interesting case study of the complexities of this problem. Initially, Sorabji denied that timelessness was in view. In the *Physics*, Sorabji pointed out, Aristotle includes the heavenly bodies among

---

[122] Trans. Guthrie, *On the Heavens*, LCL.

[123] I recognize that the use of "region" seems to violate Aristotle's statement that there is no "place" outside heaven. But since he himself populates it with things (τἀκεῖ) one has to resort to some sort of spatial language. This serves to illustrate the difficulty of the whole discussion.

those things which are not "in time" – τὰ ἀεὶ ὄντα are not ἐν χρόνῳ (*Phys.* 221a26 ff.),[124] since for Aristotle "in order to be *in time*, a things must be *included within*...time and cannot last for the whole of time."[125] This is everlastingness rather than "eternity" in the strict sense.[126] The emphasis lies on the fact that heaven (or the Prime Mover) lies outside the ravages of time. The fact that eternity embraces "all time and infinity" does not preclude it from undergoing duration.[127]

A few years later, however, Sorabji conceded that "in view of the argument in the passage translated [*Cael.* 279a 11–18] the intelligences appear to be timeless in a stronger sense than that which applies to the moving heavens."[128] Perhaps the best statement about the matter is that of W. von Leyden, who says that eternity is the "mode of existence to what lies outside the first heaven," and as such "it must practically come to mean the same as timelessness."[129] While Aristotle avoids the use of a "timeless present," his discussion of eternity leaves us with similar ambiguities to those we faced with Parmenides and Plato.

Also worth noting is Aristotle's description of eternity as "immortal and divine" – ἀθάνατος καὶ θεῖος. The flow of thought is not altogether clear here. As the passage goes on Aristotle appears to be talking about the Prime Mover rather than αἰών, which would seem to be a measure of the divine life, or the "mode of existence" of the divine, rather than a term for the divine itself. One could compare *Met.* 1072b29ff., where God is described as "a living being, eternal, most good; and therefore life and a continuous eternal existence (ζωὴ καὶ αἰὼν συνεχὴς καὶ ἀΐδιος) belong to God; for that is what God is."[130] Whatever Aristotle might have meant in the *De Caelo*, what matters to us is that his language could easily lead to a belief that "Aion" was itself a divine figure worthy of worship. Since such a veneration of Aion in fact appeared in the later hellenistic period, we may be justified in taking this passage in the *De Caelo* as a formative influence on this development.[131]

Later Thinkers

Plato's successors at the Academy do not appear to have generated any ideas of God and τὸ ὄν which can plausibly be viewed as background to

---

[124] See Whittaker, *God, Time, Being*, p.42; and W. Kneale, "Time and Eternity in Theology," *Proceedings of the Aristotelian Society* 61 (1960–1): 103.
[125] Sorabji, *Time*, p.126.
[126] Sorabji, *Time*, p.126.
[127] Sorabji, *Time*, p.127. Whittaker agrees. See his "Forms," pp.141–2.
[128] Sorabji, *Matter, Space, Motion* (London: Duckworth, 1988), pp.132–3.
[129] Von Leyden, p.47.
[130] Translation Tredennick, LCL.
[131] See the discussion later in this chapter.

LXX Ex. 3:14. Speucippus, Plato's immediate successor as head of the Academy, appears to have believed that the "One" was "superior to Being and the source from which Being flowed."[132] He presumably derived this from Plato's *Rep.* 509b, which we have discussed above. This type of theorizing goes well beyond anything present in the LXX's rendering of the Exodus text.[133] The evidence for the subsequent leaders of the Academy, Xenocrates and Polemon, (as well as for the successors to Aristotle) is too sparse to form any judgments about their views on Being. After them, the Academy was dominated by sceptical philosophers, whom we would not expect to produce new, positive theological doctrines (such as the explicit equation of God and τὸ ὄν).[134]

We turn then to the Stoics. The simplest way to begin our discussion is to look at a few of the explicit references to τὸ ὄν in Stoic fragments. The first comes from the Aristotelian commentator Alexander of Aphrodisias, who tells us that the Stoics only speak of τὸ ὄν with respect to bodies: ...ἀλλ' ἐκεῖνοι (sc. the Stoics) νομοθετήσαντες αὐτοῖς τὸ ὄν κατὰ σωμάτων μόνων λέγεσθαι...[135] Real Being is corporeal.[136] This includes God, who could be described as σῶμα ὄντα τὸ καθαρώτατον, διὰ πάντων δὲ διήκειν τὴν πρόνοιαν αὐτοῦ.[137] One could argue that God, or at least the Stoic *logos* with which God is linked, is not *really* body, but

---

[132] See John Dillon, *The Middle Platonists* (London: Duckworth, 1977), p.12. The fragment is embedded in Proclus' *Commentary on the Parmenides*.

[133] This is further supported by another fragment of Speucippus, preserved in Iamblichus' *On the General Principles of Mathematics*, ch. 4. It reads in part, "...the One (*which one should not even call Being* (on) by reason of its simplicity and its position as principle of everything else...)." Italics mine; translation in Dillon, p.14.

[134] Dillon, pp.22–43.

[135] Alex. Aphr. Comm. in *Arist. Topica* IV, p.15. Text in *Stoicorum Veterum Fragmenta*, henceforth *SVF*, ed. by J. von Arnim (Leipzig: Teubner, 1903), 2: 117, fr. #329; cf. SVF 2: 115, #320. (Where possible I will quote from A.A. Long and D. N. Sedley, *The Hellenistic Philosphers* (2 vols.; Cambridge: Cambridge University Press, 1987), since they provide translation and commentary.)

[136] See, e.g., Max Pohlenz, *Stoa und Stoiker* (Zürich: Artemis, 1959); on pp.45,362 he gives references to support this view); A. A. Long, *Hellenistic Philosophy* (London: Duckworth, 1974), pp.152ff.; Jacques Brunschwig, "The Stoic theory of the supreme genus and Platonic ontology," in Brunschwig, *Papers in Hellenistic Philosophy*, trans. Janet Lloyd (Cambridge: Cambridge University Press, 1994), p.92.

[137] Hippolytus *Philosoph*. 21,1=*SVF* 1: 41. Cf. Origen, *Contra Celsum* 4.14, in Long and Sedley 1:276; text 2: 274; "The god of the Stoics, in as much as he is a body...," "...ὁ τῶν Στωικῶν θεός, ἅτε σῶμα τυγχάνων... Diogenes Laertius (VII: 135-6) also says that for the Stoics "God, intelligence, fate, and Zeus are all one..." (in Long and Sedley, 1: 275); and that "the essence (οὐσία) of God is the entire world and heaven (VII: 148=*SVF* 1: 43, #163)." See the similar comments by Lactantius, *De vera sap.* c.9, Tertullian, *Apol.* 21=*SVF* 1: 42, #160.

constitutes body insofar as it is inextricably linked with matter.[138] But such a nuanced view tends to get obscured in the fragments we possess. In any case, τὸ ὄν does not appear as a designation for God. The closest we get is a definition of Being attributed to Chrysippus (fl. latter half of third century BCE) by John Stobaeus:

εἶναι τὸ ὄν πνεῦμα κινοῦν ἑαυτὸ πρὸς ἑαυτὸ καὶ ἐξ αὐτοῦ, ἢ πνεῦμα ἑαυτὸ κινοῦν πρόσω καὶ ὀπίσω.

(Chrysippus held) "that which is" to be a spirit moving itself towards itself and from itself, or a spirit moving itself forwards and backwards.[139]

This "spirit" appears to be related to the primal "designing fire" which gives growth and order to the universe. Long suggests that it is a compound of fire and air which permeates the world somewhat like a gas.[140] As such, one could see how a Greek philosopher might describe it as the essential stuff of the universe, that which (really) is. One could go on to argue that if τὸ ὄν = πνεῦμα, and πνεῦμα = God (in some sense), then τὸ ὄν = God. But we have no evidence that such an equation was ever made.

The first direct evidence we have for the identification of God and τὸ ὄν comes from Seneca in the first century CE. Seneca was a Stoic philosopher, but not a fully orthodox one.[141] In his 58th and 65th Epistles, for instance, he makes use of Platonic sources with apparent approval. It is his 58th Epistle which concerns us here. The letter begins with a discussion about the difficulty of finding Latin equivalents for Greek terms, and ends with a defense of suicide (under certain conditions). In the midst of this Seneca gives us a thorough treatment of τὸ ὄν (Ep. 58.16–22). He begins by declaring that he is unable to find an adequate Latin rendering of τὸ ὄν. He will use *quod est*, although he is not entirely happy with this (ll.7–8). He goes on to say that "a friend of ours, a very learned man" was telling him today that Plato spoke of τὸ ὄν in six ways (l.8).[142] There follows a long digression on the topic of genus and species (ll.8–15),[143] after which we at last get to the topic at hand.

---

[138] See F. H. Sandbach, *The Stoics* (London: Chatto and Windus, 1975), p.74.

[139] *SVF* 2: 152, #471; translation mine.

[140] Long, pp.154–8. Cf. Pohlenz, p.83: "Er [Gott] ist das Pneuma, das alles durchdringt und selbst im niedrigsten Stoffe, im Kot der Straße gegenwärtig ist."

[141] See J. M. Rist, "Seneca and Stoic Orthodoxy," *ANRW* II, 36.3: 1993–2012.

[142] The "friend" may be an actual learned companion; a fiction; or an oblique reference to Seneca's source material. See Willy Theiler, *Die Vorbereitung des Neuplatonismus* (Berlin/Zürich: Weidmannsche, 1964; repr. of 1934 ed.), p.36; Ernst Bickel, "Senecas Briefe 58 und 65," *Rheinisches Museum für Philologie* n.f. 103 (1960): 7–8.

[143] Seneca shows his unorthodoxy here as well. The usual Stoic doctrine is that the τὶ constitutes the Supreme Genus. Seneca argues instead that τὸ ὄν is the Supreme Genus. For a full discussion see Brunschwig, "The Supreme Genus and Platonic Ontology," pp.110–15.

The "six modes of being" have attracted a good deal of attention.[144] John Dillon summarizes them as follows:

1. The Intelligible; "that which is perceived neither by sight nor touch nor any sense" (Seneca's words)
2. Being '*par excellence*' (usually taken to be God; see below)
3. The Truly Existent (=the Platonic Ideas)
4. The *eidos*, or immanent Ideas
5. Ordinary existents (men, cattle, property)
6. Quasi-existents (such as space and time).[145]

The apparent equation of God and τὸ ὄν in point 2 is obviously of primary importance for our study. We should not lose sight of the fact, however, that Seneca provides us with several possibilities for the identification of τὸ ὄν, any of which might have been known to some of John's readers. The structure of the scheme is also relevant. The items appear to occupy a rough hierarchy. Only the first item, as Dillon points out, is hard to fit into the scheme.[146] Whether the scheme is Stoicized Platonism, Platonic Stoicism,[147] Neopythagorean Platonism or something else again, is perhaps impossible to say. But we are clearly working with some kind of hybrid, which may explain the difficulties one encounters in getting a clear understanding of the text. It is a kind of compendium of all the grammatical and philosophical implications which might be (and had been) drawn out of this deceptively simple neuter participle.

Of all the explanations offered for the shape of the list, the soundest seem to be those which trace it back, at least in part, to a commentary on the *Timaeus*, perhaps the one written by the Neopythagorean/Platonist philosopher Eudorus, who flourished in first century BCE Alexandria.[148] As Ernst Bickel pointed out, Seneca's first category of τὸ ὄν, that which "cannot be grasped by the sight or by the touch, or by any of the senses;

---

[144] See Rist, pp.2010; Theiler, pp.1ff.; Will Richter, "Kritisches und Exegetisches zu Senecas Prosaschriften," *Hermes* 84 (1956): 182-98; Bickel, pp.1-13; John Whittaker, "Seneca, Ep. 58.17," *Symbolae Osloenses* 50 (1975): 143-48; Dillon, pp.136-7; Stephen Gersh, *Middle Platonism and Neoplatonism: The Latin Tradition*, 2 vols. (Notre Dame: U. of Notre Dame Press, 1986), 1:181-86.

[145] Dillon, pp.136-7.

[146] Dillon, p.137.

[147] As argued by P. Hadot; see the summary in Gersh, 1:185-87.

[148] Whittaker, who leans towards this view, points out that Plutarch used such a commentary by Eudorus (see *De procr. an. in Tim.* 1013b, 1019e, 1020c). He adds, *contra* Bickel, that there is no proof that Posidonius wrote a commentary exclusively on the *Timaeus* (Whittaker, "Seneca," p.148 n). Rist (p.2010) and Dillon (p.136) concur, although Dillon does not wish to completely exclude Theiler's suggestion of Antiochus (Dillon, pp.138-9; cf. Theiler, pp.37 ff.). Gersh (1:188) favors Theiler's explanation. The commentators agree that the proximate source is probably Arius Didymus' handbook of philosophy.

but...by thought"[149] is an echo of *Tim.* 27d, where Plato describes τὸ ὂν ἀεί as τὸ...νοήσει μετὰ λόγου περιληπτόν, ἀεὶ κατὰ ταὐτὰ ὄν.[150] Bickel's attempt to trace each of the six items in detail back to the *Timaeus* has been criticized,[151] and it is perhaps safer to follow Whittaker, who argues more generally that Seneca's source is commenting on the distinction in *Tim.* 27d–28a between Being and Becoming. (The transitory nature of the world will occupy Seneca in ll.22 ff.[152])

Whatever the source or sources might have been, two problems remain for us. First, is God in fact the "Being *par excellence*"? And if so, why is God put *second* on the list, behind the Intelligible in general? The first question may be answered confidently in the affirmative. Seneca begins l.17 with the words, *Secundum ex his quae sunt ponit Plato quod eminet et exsuperat omnia.* After speaking about Homer as the poet *par excellence*, he says *Quid ergo hoc est? Deus scilicet, maior ac potentior cunctis.* The majority of commentators and translators affirm that God is here viewed as the supreme instance of Being. Whittaker has given strong arguments against W. Richter's suggestion that the supreme God is here only an example of a pre-eminent entity.[153] The most telling of these arguments comes from Proclus' *Commentary on the Timaeus.* At 27d6ff., Proclus notes that people are divided as to what constitutes Plato's τὸ ὂν ἀεί. He then gives three options, which correspond closely to Seneca's first three categories – in the same order:

Αὐτὸ δὲ τὸ ὂν ἀεὶ πότερον τὸν νοητὸν πάντα σημαίνει κόσμον ἢ τὸν δημιουργὸν ἢ τὸ παράδειγμα τοῦ παντός; ἄλλοι γὰρ ἄλλως ὑπέλαβον.

It seems that Proclus is following a source similar to the one used by Seneca. It would not be surprising if they both go back ultimately to the same commentary on the *Timaeus*. The fact that Proclus presents these as *options*, rather than as a hierarchy, only adds to the our confusion. But his mention of the Demiurge as option number two solidifies the case for seeing God as the Being *par excellence* in Seneca's list.[154] From a grammatical standpoint, we might say that the article in τὸ ὂν has taken on renewed

---

[149] *Ep.* 58.16; in Seneca, *Ad Lucilium Epistulae Morales I*, trans. Richard M. Gummere LCL (NY: Geo. Putnam's Sons/London: Wm. Heinemann, 1917).

[150] Bickel, p.1; Whittaker, "Seneca," p.146.

[151] By, e.g., Gersh, 1:184–5.

[152] The last three of the six items are not of course τὸ ὂν ἀεί, and Whittaker ("Seneca," p.148 n) thus argues that the source, for "scholastic or pedagogical reasons...seems to have seized the opportunity to attempt a comprehensive analysis of Being."

[153] See Richter, pp.187–90; Whittaker, "Seneca," *passim*.

[154] It also vindicates Bickel's assertion that the Demiurge is the "God" of Seneca's item two, a conclusion he appears to have drawn without reference to Proclus' commentary.

vigor and dominates the expression: we are not talking about *any* existent thing, but *the* Existent Thing.

As to why God should be second on the list rather than first, there is no definitive answer, but some reasonable theories have been propounded. S. Gersh believes that "the distinction between classifying things and classifying concepts has become blurred – as in Platonic and Stoic syncretism..."[155] Whittaker argues that the first category includes the second two.[156] Proclus, we saw, treats the three as competing views. Whether Proclus is accurately following his source in this matter is impossible to say. What we may say is that Seneca himself does not view things this way, since later in the Epistle (1.27) he describes God and the Ideas as happily co-existing. I would again concur with Whittaker. Seneca does believe God is at the top of the ontological ladder, as it were, and God appears second on the list only because of the nature of Seneca's source. We have said that he is likely working with a commentary on the *Timaeus*. We would expect such a commentary to begin with Plato's own words. Plato's first words on the subject in *Tim.* 27d are, as we have seen, τὸ ὂν ἀεί is τὸ...νοήσει μετὰ λόγου περιληπτόν. The commentator might then have stated that the supreme example of "that which always is" is God, followed by the Forms. Both are eternal and intelligible, but God takes ontological priority.

Here, for the first time, we have concrete evidence that God could be described as τὸ ὄν by some Greek (and Latin) thinkers. The fact that this doctrine almost certainly arose no earlier than the first century BCE means that it could not have influenced the translation of Ex. 3:14 LXX. On the other hand, it may well have contributed to Philo's conjoining of ὁ ὤν and τὸ ὄν in his writings. As we will see, this same doctrine appears in Plutarch's writings, and thus constitutes important background for understanding the first century context of ὁ ὤν.

Plutarch (c.45–125 CE) presents us with several relevant pieces of information. Plutarch's philosophical and religious views are quite complex, but for our purposes we may fairly view him as a representative of Middle Platonic thought.[157] It is in this guise that we meet him in the two works which will occupy our attention now, the *De Iside et Osiride* and the *De E ap. Delphos*.

Plutarch's basic concern in the *De Is.* is to interpret the myth of Isis and Osiris through the lens of Platonic (or Middle Platonic) philosophy. Plutarch is sympathetic to the Egyptian religions, but he believes their true

---

[155] Gersh, 1:186.

[156] Whittaker, p.147 n; cf. Dillon (p.137), who notes that the first item is something of an anomaly, and says that it is "a term common to the second and third categories."

[157] Cf. the discussion in Dillon, pp.184–230; and D. A. Russell, *Plutarch* (London: Duckworth, 1973), pp.63ff.

meaning "is hidden for the most part in myths and stories which show dim reflections and insights of the truth..." (*De Is.* 354b).[158] We have already noted his interpretation of the Iseion: it "clearly offers recognition and knowledge of that which is (εἴδησιν τοῦ ὄντος),[159] for it is called the Iseion to indicate that we shall know that which is (εἰσομένων τὸ ὄν) if we approach the sanctuaries of the goddess with reason and reverence" (352a). This τὸ ὄν is represented in the myth by Osiris, so that Isis is the revealer of truth rather than Being itself.[160] In 373a we read that the soul of Osiris stands for "what is and what is spiritually intelligible and is good [which] prevails over destruction and change." (The latter is embodied in Typhon.[161]) The Platonic overtones of Plutarch's interpretation of this aspect of the myth are obvious.

The *De E*, unlike the *De Is.*, is set up along the lines of a traditional Platonic dialogue. Ammonius and some of his students (including the young Plutarch) are discussing the curious phenomenon of the letter Epsilon which was suspended over the *pronaos* of the temple at Delphi.[162] Various proposals for its significance are offered.

At the end of the dialogue, Ammonius gives his considered opinion. According to him, the E represents the only proper greeting one can give to Apollo, who is here equivalent to the supreme god. Apollo comes to us and says, "Know yourself." We in turn reply εἶ – "you are." This is the only true designation one can use for the god, the declaration that he exists (392a). We humans, by contrast, do not *truly* exist: Ἡμῖν μὲν γὰρ ὄντως τοῦ εἶναι μέτεστιν οὐδέν (392a). The latter theme is then developed in a passage (392b–c) with striking similarities to portions of Seneca's epistles, indicating that this was common Middle Platonic teaching.[163] At 392e, the

---

[158] Trans. in J. Gwyn Griffiths, *Plutarch's De Iside et Osiride* (Swansea: U. of Wales Press, 1970). All quotations from the *De Is.* (including Greek texts) unless otherwise noted are from this work. For Plutarch and allegory see e.g. Russell, pp.81–3.

[159] Griffiths gives "what truly exists," which is probably what Plutarch has in mind. I have modified his translation to a more literal one, since ὄντως is not in the text.

[160] Cf. the mention of Osiris as "the First and Lord, whom only the mind can understand" (352a). See Frederick Brenk, "An Imperial Heritage: The Religious Spirit of Plutarch of Chaironeia" *ANRW* 2:36.1: 299.

[161] Cf. 375c, where Isis is said to "incline towards being" πρὸς τὸ εἶναι.

[162] Coins from the time of Hadrian and Faustinius show the E in this position. See Flacelière, pp.1,12–3.

[163] Cf. Whittaker, "Seneca's Ep. 58.17," 145,8; and Whittaker, "Ammonius on the Delphic E," *CQ* n.s. 19 (1969): 185–92. The similarities include: the citation of Heraclitus' famous "river statement" (*De E* 392b and Ep. 58.23); the preservation by God of the material world, which is prone to disintegration (*De E* 393f and Ep. 58.27–8); the denial of "real being" to the visible world (*De E* 392e and Ep.58.26–7); the ages of man, with the related idea that death happens to us everyday (*De E* 392c–d and Ep. 58.22–4; cf.

attention shifts back to Apollo. Τί οὖν ὄντως ὄν ἐστι; asks Ammonius, in a question that could almost have come straight from the *Timaeus* (cf. *Tim.* 27d). The answer is equally Platonic: Τὸ ἀίδιον καὶ ἀγένητον καὶ ἄφθαρτον, ᾧ χρόνος μεταβολὴν οὐδὲ εἷς ἐπάγει. Since "that which is" has no share in time, it is inappropriate to use words like "then" or "before" or "will be" in connection with it. Only "is" rightly applies. This is of course nothing more than a rephrasing of *Tim.* 37e ff.

The parallels with Plato are so obvious, in fact, that one can easily be unaware that a decisive change has taken place. Whittaker puts it succinctly: "...Plutarch, in describing Apollo as τὸ ὄν, is equating the Delphic deity with Platonic reality."[164] This equation is brought out most cleverly in 393a, where Plutarch adds a new dimension to the well-worn phrase ἔστιν ὁ θεός (which he takes to be so obvious that he adds εἰ χρὴ φάναι). While this would usually indicate only that God or the gods exist, as opposed to not existing, he goes on to say καὶ ἔστι κατ' οὐδένα χρόνον, ἀλλὰ κατὰ τὸν αἰῶνα τὸν ἀκίνητον καὶ ἄχρονον κτλ. Everyone knows God *is*, Plutarch seems to be saying, but we need to see the deeper (=Platonic) implications of that "is."

This has obvious implications for Plutarch's view of God and time. Ammonius continues his interpretation of "God is" with the remarkable words ἀλλ' εἷς ὢν ἑνὶ τῷ νῦν τὸ ἀεὶ πεπλήρωκε, καὶ μόνον ἐστὶ τὸ κατὰ τοῦτον ὄντως ὄν... The first clause is particularly difficult to translate. Flacelière gives "L'être divin, qui est unique, embrasse toute la durée dans un unique instant...," while Edwin Gifford reads it, "but being One, He has filled the 'Ever' with the one 'Now'..."[165] Whatever one thinks of Parmenides' and Plato's understanding of time and eternity, Plutarch's formulation certainly seems like the *totum simul* of later thought. Whittaker, who disputes that Parmenides and Plato taught a non-durational eternity, offers the following explanation for Plutarch's innovation:

> As Plutarch indicates, the Now, which was irrelevant to the being of the impersonal Forms, assumes importance when conscious deity is equated with Platonic reality...Thus the doctrine of non-durational eternity in Greek thought is in origin essen-

---

Ep.24.19–20). The high concentration of similarities between these two reasonably brief passages makes one suspect a common source.

[164] Whittaker, "Ammonius," p.189. He notes that the description of the god Osiris as τὸ ὄν in *De Is.* 373a represents a similar phenomenon.

[165] Gifford is translating Eusebius' *Preparation for the Gospel* 527b ff. (Oxford: Oxford University Press, 1903), which contains most of Ammonius' speech. Cf. Babbitt in the LCL, "But He, being One, has with only one 'Now' completely filled 'for ever'..." (Plutarch, *Moralia* vol. 5 trans. Frank Cole Babbitt; London: Wm. Heinemann, 1936). Sorabji (*Time*, pp.105–6), thinks this "means something like: the whole of God's life is telescoped together rather than spread out."

tially linked with the problems of God's consciousness in relation to his immutability.[166]

Ammonius concludes his discourse with the idea of God's unity, which he sees as a necessary concomitant of God's Being: ἀλλ' ἓν εἶναι δεῖ τὸ ὄν, ὥσπερ ὂν τὸ ἕν (393b).

Thus Seneca and Plutarch provide us with the first explicit description of God as τὸ ὄν in Greek literature. Precisely what Seneca and Plutarch (let alone their probable source, Eudorus) meant by "God" is of course still a problem. As a Stoic, Seneca ought, it seems, to equate God with the designing fire. But as we noted with respect to Cleanthes, this did not necessarily mean that a personal deity had been replaced by an abstract principle. The same holds true for Plutarch, although he is not working in the Stoic framework. It may be that by equating Apollo and τὸ ὄν he is trying to say, "what you call God is really the world of Forms discussed by Plato." This would fit, perhaps, with his reading of the Isis and Osiris myth. But it is important to note that Apollo is not only a personal god, he is particularly the god of the oracle at Delphi, who speaks to humanity. It is hard to imagine a more personal act than speaking. The convergence of Jewish, Christian, and Greek thought concerning τὸ ὄν and ὁ ὤν is not merely an accident of grammar.

If the full implication of what Seneca and Plutarch meant by God and Being remains an open question, it is still of the utmost importance for our investigation that they are the first to demonstrate the equation of the two. On the one hand, this means that it *cannot be demonstrated* that the translators of the Septuagint had at their disposal Greek texts in which God and τὸ ὄν were interchangeable terms. On the other hand, this also indicates that *Philo* would almost certainly have known of a (Middle) Platonic doctrine in which God could be described as τὸ ὄν, and that some of the readers of the book of Revelation may have been aware of the doctrine. Since the traditional formulation of τὸ ὄν= the Forms was still a viable option, as well, there was ample opportunity for a fusion of Jewish or Christian thought with Platonic.[167]

Finally, if the equation of God and τὸ ὄν was made at some point in the 1st century BCE, we must ask: why did it happen at this particular time and not before? The key may lie in the resurgence of interest in Aristotle

---

[166] Whittaker, *God, Time, Being*, p.13. (Sorabji, *Time*, p.106, disagrees that this is the first appearance of timelessness, but he does believe (p.121) that the present passage denies duration.) In his article "Ammonius on the Delphic E," (p.189) Whittaker points out that Apollo is also identified with the Form of the Good by Plutarch (*De Def. Orac.* 433d–e).

[167] On this topic, see especially Whittaker, "Plutarch, Platonism, and Christianity," pp.50–63.

which accompanied the editing of his works in Rome c. 50 BCE.[168] One of Aristotle's doctrines was that the intellect is identified with the object of thought. Since God, for Aristotle, is nothing but intellect, "God is identical with the object of his thought."[169] Now, it appears that Middle Platonist thinkers often identified the Platonic Forms as the "thoughts of God" (see, e.g., Seneca, Ep. 65).[170] Moreover, these same thinkers tended to harmonize the "ancient" schools of thought (Academic, Peripatetic, Stoic).[171] Plato, as we know, had referred to the Forms as τὸ ὄν. If one accepted this identification, then added the Aristotelian precept that the thinker is identified with the object of thought, one could easily emerge with the teaching that *both* God and the Forms could be called τὸ ὄν.

The *Dreizeitenformel* in Greek Literature

One of the most striking things about John's interpretation of the name YHWH is that he combines the present participle ὁ ὤν with verbs that look towards the past and the future. As we have seen, this would have been quite at odds with Parmenides' and Plato's descriptions of ultimate reality. Such *Dreizeitenformeln*, however, also had a rich literary and philosophical pedigree, and they were to leave a lasting mark on the Jewish and Christian traditions. The first extant parallels we have for John's formula ὁ ὤν καὶ ὁ ἦν καὶ ὁ ἐρχόμενος come in the texts of Homer and Hesiod. While their works were subject to intense criticism for their portrayal of the gods (cf. the critiques of Xenophanes and Plato), they remained at the heart of Greek education through the hellenistic period and beyond.[172]

Homer

The *Iliad* opens with a scene that *mutatis mutandis* would fit well in the book of Revelation: Apollo (cf. Ἀπολλύων, Rev.9:11) is spreading "foul

---

[168] This was suggested to me by Professor Richard Sorabji. See also the discussion in Guthrie, 6: 59–65.

[169] Sorabji, *Time*, pp.146. Cf. *Met.* Λ 9. God "thinks of himself, therefore, and his thought is thought of thought." Translation and discussion in Guthrie, 6: 260–2.

[170] See Dillon, esp. pp. 29,48,95,138. He believes this idea may go as far back as Xenocrates (c.350 BCE; see p.29), and almost certainly to Antiochus of Ascalon (c.100 BCE; see p.95).

[171] Dillon, pp. xiv–v; 43–51,57.

[172] See, e.g., van Unnik, "A Formula Describing Prophecy," *NTS* 9 (1962), p.91. See also Weinreich, "Aion in Eleusis," *ARW* 19 (1919): 174–90. The New Testament itself bears the traces of the *Theogony* in the accounts of the imprisoned angels in 2 Pet. 2:4 and Jude 6, and some of the imagery from the battle of Zeus and Typhoeus may have been drawn upon in the composition of Rev. 12.

pestilence" through the Greek camp, and they are helpless to stop it.[173] Agamemnon has seized the daughter of Apollo's priest Chryses, and the god is wreaking his vengeance. Achilles requests that they find "some holy man, some prophet, even an interpreter of dreams" to determine what has made Apollo so angry. At this point Calchas stands up: He is described as an οἰωνοπόλος, an interpreter of bird omens, and it is said that ἤδη τά τ' ἐόντα τά τ' ἐσσόμενα πρό τ' ἐόντα. The phrase is generally taken to be a tripartite temporal formula indicating that Calchas understands "the present, the past, and the future."[174]

Calchas' ability to understand the past, present, and future is clearly a gift from the gods (cf. *Il*. 1.71). The gods, who are ἀθάνατοι, make known τά τ' ἐόντα τά τ' ἐσσόμενα πρό τ' ἐόντα.[175] While the particular elements of the formula may change, Homer's tri-partite description of Calchas' prophetic activity is the foundation for subsequent uses of the *Dreizeitenformel* in Greek literature.

Hesiod

According to the *Theogony*, Hesiod was tending his sheep in Boeotia when he received a call from the Muses to proclaim things normally hidden from mortal minds: the earliest days of the universe, and the births and battles of the gods long ago (*Th*.1–115). Although one could adduce similar instances in ancient literature (e.g. the call of the prophet Amos), comparisons with John's call on Patmos, and Moses' call at the burning bush, do spring to mind. Such promptings become more urgent when we read that

---

[173] Richard Lattimore, trans., *The Iliad of Homer* (Chicago: University of Chicago Press, 1951). Unless otherwise stated, English quotations will be taken from Lattimore. Greek text is from *Homeri Ilias*, ed. Thomas W. Allen (Oxford: Oxford University Press, 1931).

[174] See the translations adduced by Walter Belardi, "Omero, A 70," *Maia* 3 (1950): 54. Belardi himself argues that τά τ' ἐσσόμενα πρό τ' ἐόντα is meant to be taken as a whole, since the τά is lacking in the final part of the clause. He believes this emphasizes Calchas' extraordinary ability to see into the past and the future. Jenny Strauss Clay (in "What the Muses Sang," *Greek, Roman, and Byzantine Studies* 29 (1988): 330 n) takes a similar approach and suggests that *Il*. 1.70 ought perhaps to be rendered "...(who) knew both the divine and the human things." Cf. William G. Thalmann's *Conventions of Form and Thought in Early Greek Epic Poetry* (Baltimore: Johns Hopkins University Press, 1984), p.230; Kahn, *The Verb Be*, pp.350–1,454–5. Kahn believes Homer is exploiting the veridical aspect of the verb here.

[175] We may compare this with Euripedes *Helen*, ll.13–4, where the prophetess Theonoë is described as knowing τὰ θεῖα .../ τά τ' ὄντα καὶ μέλλοντα. Text in Euripedes, *Works*, vol. I, trans. by A. S. Way LCL (London: Wm. Heinemann/NY: Macmillan, 1912). Cf. also ll.922–3.

Hesiod is to celebrate τά τ' ἐσσόμενα πρό τ' ἐόντα (*Th*.32) just as the Muses sing of τά τ' ἐόντα τά τ' ἐσσόμενα πρό τ' ἐόντα (1.38).[176]
The Muses confirm Hesiod in his calling with these words:

...[the Muses] gave me a branch of springing bay to pluck for a staff, a handsome one, and they breathed into me wondrous voice, so that I should celebrate things of the future and things that were aforetime. And they told me to sing of the family of the blessed ones who are for ever, and first and last always to sing of themselves.

But what is my business round tree or rock? Come now, from the Muses let us begin, who with their singing delight the great mind of Zeus the father in Olympus, as they tell of what is and what shall be and what was aforetime, voices in unison...(*Th*. 30-39)

The words τά τ' ἐόντα τά τ' ἐσσόμενα πρό τ' ἐόντα at the conclusion of our selection (1.38) are a fairly straightforward appropriation of *Il*. 1.70. Only now it is the Muses rather than Calchas who are in the prophetic role.[177] The problems arise when one considers the earlier lines in which Hesiod is to speak of "things of the future and things that were aforetime." The idea that Hesiod considers his poetry as comparable to prophecy should not surprise us, especially given the grand and religious nature of his theme.[178] The question is, why does Hesiod include the formula twice, (apparently) omitting τά τ' ἐόντα in the first instance? The change could simply be a matter a matter of style. Hesiod's song mirrors that of the Muses, and he varies the formula to make the poem more aesthetically pleasing.[179] If this is the case, no more need be said. But such a departure from a traditional phrase catches one's attention, particularly when that traditional phrase is repeated in full a few lines later.

We return then to ll.32ff. The Greek reads:

...ἐνέπνευσαν δέ μ' ἀοιδὴν

---

[176] Translations for all passages, unless otherwise noted, are from M.L. West, *Hesiod: Theogony; Works and Days* (Oxford: Oxford University Press, 1988); Greek text in *Hésiode*, ed. Paul Mazon (Paris: Société d'Édition, 1967).

[177] See Herwig Maehler, *Die Auffassung des Dichterberufs im frühen Griechentum bis zur Zeit Pindars* (Göttingen: Vandenhoeck & Ruprecht, 1963), p.41; Eduard Meyer, "Hesiods Erga und das Gedicht von den fünf Menschengeschlechtern," in *Hesiod*, ed. Ernst Heitsch (Darmstadt: Wissenschaftliche Buchgesellschaft, 1966), p.472.

[178] Those arguing for a connection between Hesiod's poetry and prophecy include: West, in his commentary on v.32; Maehler, p.41; Thalmann, pp.146-7; Pietro Pucci, *Hesiod and the Language of Poetry* (Baltimore: Johns Hopkins University Press, 1977), p.1. W.J. Verdenius denies this and takes τά τ' ἐόντα τά τ' ἐσσόμενα πρό τ' ἐόντα "as a circumlocution for 'everything'."("Notes on the Proem of Hesiod's *Theogony*," *Mnemosyne* 25 (1972): 238-9; cf. Wilfried Stroh, "Hesiods lügende Musen," in *Studien zum antiken Epos* eds. Herwig Görgemanns and Ernst A. Schmidt (Meisenheim am Glen: Anton Hain, 1976), p. 89.)

[179] Cf. West's commentary, and the authors (with whom she disagrees) cited by Clay, p.330 n.

θέσπιν, ἵνα κλείοιμι τά τ' ἐσσόμενα πρό τ' ἐόντα,
καί μ' ἐκέλονθ' ὑμνεῖν μακάρων γένος αἰὲν ἐόντων,
σφᾶς δ' αὐτὰς πρῶτόν τε καὶ ὕστατον αἰὲν ἀείδειν (Th.32–34).

I would argue that, contrary to appearances, the middle element of the *Dreizeitenformel* has not disappeared. Hesiod has instead *shifted* it to the following line in the form of αἰὲν ἐόντων. If τά τ' ἐσσόμενα πρό τ' ἐόντα refers to past and future events (as in West's translation), the lines would indicate that Hesiod, like Calchas, speaks of the past and the future. But rather than just speaking about "the things that are," Hesiod speaks about the gods who *always* are – μακάρων γένος αἰὲν ἐόντων.[180] Of course Hesiod's gods are not strictly speaking eternal, but rather everlasting after their birth. But one could argue that he is groping towards some such concept by the implicit contrast between the Homeric "things that are" and the "blessed race of the gods who always are." There is a permanence about the gods which gives them a different manner of existence than things on earth.

It is more likely, however, that τ' ἐσσόμενα πρό τ' ἐόντα is in *synonymous* parallelism with μακάρων γένος αἰὲν ἐόντων and that both phrases refer to the gods themselves.[181] One point in favor of this reading is that Hesiod singularly fails to discuss the future in the *Theogony*, which leaves τ' ἐσσόμενα without a clear referent.[182] Heinz Neitzel goes on to ask the very pertinent question: Can one "praise" (κλείοιμι) the future?[183] One can more easily imagine "praising" that which is divine – and this is precisely how Hesiod speaks in ll.44, 66ff., and 105.[184] Furthermore, because "what will be" and "what was" constitute a grammatical unity, one must search for something that *both* "will be" and "was" to set alongside μακάρων

---

[180] Renate Schlesier, ("Les Muses dans le prologue de la 'Theogonie' d'Hésiode," *Revue de l'Histoire des Religions* 199 (1982): 164), Pucci (p.22), and Clay (pp.330–1) all suggest that Hesiod omits τὰ ἐόντα because he intends only to speak of what is eternal and not the contemporary affairs of humanity. But Hesiod does mention human matters in ll.80ff, 569ff.

[181] Heinz Neitzel, "Hesiod und die lügenden Musen," *Hermes* 108 (1980): 397–8.

[182] This has troubled commentators since Lucian. See, e.g., Meyer, p.471 n. Meyer himself suggests that Hesiod has simply lifted the phrase from Homer without troubling himself about the fact that it does not quite match his material. But this does not take into account Hesiod's careful adaptation of Homer. Thalmann (pp.41–2) says that Hesiod does make good on his promise to speak of τά τ' ἐσσόμενα, because he is describing the formation of a world order under Zeus which will continue into the future.

[183] He is apparently not the only one troubled by this word, since some commentators have suggested emending it to κλύοιμι, "hearken." See the discussion against emendation in Verdenius, p.238. Neitzel's main objection is that the future, unlike the past and present, is unknown and thus cannot be praised.

[184] Neitzel, pp.397–8. See, e.g., l.105 (of the Muses): κλείετε δ' ἀθανάτων ἱερὸν γένος αἰὲν ἐόντων.

γένος αἰὲν ἐόντων.¹⁸⁵ This can refer to nothing else, says Neitzel, than "das ewige Göttliche."¹⁸⁶ Hesiod is to sing of divine things in his poem, the births and deeds of those who both were and will be. If this is correct, Hesiod would be raising the Homeric formula to new levels. While Calchas might speak of the things which were, are, and will be on earth, Hesiod himself will speak of the gods who were, are, and will be.

Such a reading of Hesiod provides us with interesting parallels to Rev. 1:4. Hesiod, in this view, describes the immortal beings as both τά τ' ἐσσόμενα πρό τ' ἐόντα (although strictly speaking this may refer to *the things associated with* the immortal beings – their deeds, histories, etc.) and μακάρων αἰὲν ἐόντων. This has important formal similarities to John's linking of ὁ ὤν with ὁ ἦν καὶ ὁ ἐρχόμενος. That which pertains to eternity, or at least to everlasting-ness, can be described either as τὰ αἰὲν ἐόντα/ὁ ὤν or as τά τ' ἐσσόμενα πρό τ' ἐόντα/ὁ ἦν καὶ ὁ ἐρχόμενος.¹⁸⁷

Presocratic Thinkers

We have already examined the negative use of the *Dreizeitenformel* by Parmenides, along with the correction/clarification offered by Melissus. In the remainder of the Presocratic fragments we possess, the *Dreizeitenformel* is usually employed as it is in Anaxagoras fr. 12, as a dramatic way of saying "all things" or "all events."¹⁸⁸ Anaximenes (6th c. BCE) said that from air come τὰ γινόμενα καὶ τὰ γεγονότα καὶ τὰ ἐσόμενα καὶ θεοὺς

---

¹⁸⁵ As emphasized by Clay, p.330 n.

¹⁸⁶ Neitzel, p.398; Clay concurs, p.330 n. Note that a similar parallelism is present in the Muses' song in ll.36ff. In l.38, they are said to "tell of what is and what shall be and what was aforetime." We then read in ll. 43–4: "Making divine utterance, they celebrate first in their song the august family of gods..." Cf. Ernst Siegmann, "Zu Hesiods Theogonieproömium," in *Hesiod*, ed. Heitsch, p.316 n. See also the quotations in Verdenius, p.239 n which affirm the same point. Verdenius himself disagrees, saying that "the eternal aspect of the gods...does not dominate Hesiod's point of view in the *Theogony*." But there are enough references to their immortality in the proem to make it a central feature, and thus I believe Neitzel's point remains valid.

¹⁸⁷ Verdenius (p.239 n) quotes Heitsch as follows: "Hesiod im Gegenwärtigen, Zukünftigen und Vergangenen *nicht* das Verschiedene und immer Neue, sondern gerade das durch alle Zeiten hindurch Identische sieht. Sein Thema ist das Geschlecht der ewig gegenwärtigen Götter." Thalmann (p.147) writes in a similar vein: "The 'truth' that the Muses can speak, then, has the value accorded memory in mythic thought; it is a means of transcending time and of understanding what is stable and coherent and beyond the limits of ordinary experience."

¹⁸⁸ One could do the same with a two part formula, cf. Hippocrates' statement that "the warm...knows all things, what is and what will be." *KRS*, p.199 n. The three part formula seems to be preferred, since it probably seemed more "complete" to Greeks; cf. the comment attributed to Pythagoras, "the whole world and all things in it are summed up in the number three; for end, middle and beginning give the number of the whole, and their number is the triad" (in Arist. *De Caelo* 268a10, quoted from Guthrie 1: 193).

καὶ θεῖα γίνεσθαι, τὰ δὲ λοιπὰ ἐκ τῶν τούτου ἀπογόνων (ap. Hippolytus *Ref.* I,7,I). The three-fold formula may, however, be a part of Hippolytus' "wordy expansion" of his sources.[189] Empedocles attributes a similar role to Love and Strife. From these two principles, he says :

> comes all that was and is and will be in the future (ἐκ τῶν πάνθ' ὅσα τ' ἦν ὅσα τ' ἔστι καὶ ἔσται ὀπίσσω) – trees have sprung up and men and women, beasts and birds and water-bred fish, and long-lived gods, too, highest in honor.[190]

We may also compare the Orphic Derveni Theogony, where Zeus/Moira/Air/Breath (the terms appear to be interchangeable) is said to determine:

> τὰ ἐόντα καὶ τὰ γινόμενα καὶ τὰ μέλλοντα,
> ὅπως χρὴ γενέσθαι τε καὶ εἶναι καὶ παύσασθαι (XV.6)[191]

At first glance, Heraclitus (6th/5th c. BCE) fr. 30 appears to fit into the same category: κόσμον τόνδε [τὸν αὐτὸν ἁπάντων] οὔτε τις θεῶν οὔτε ἀνθρώπων ἐποίησεν, ἀλλ' ἦν ἀεὶ καὶ ἔστιν καὶ ἔσται πῦρ ἀείζωον, ἁπτόμενον μέτρα καὶ ἀποσβεννύμενον μέτρα.[192] Heraclitus' words might indicate nothing more than the everlasting existence of the universe. But at the time of Heraclitus, the word κόσμος would have retained a strong emphasis on the arrangement of things in the world rather than simply the stuff of the universe *per se*. Thus both *KRS* and Guthrie render it here "world-order," and we may say that the emphasis lies on world-order.[193] The idea that order is primarily in mind here is reinforced by the equation of the κόσμος with fire in the second half of the fragment. Fire represents the measure or proportion in which the opposites are kept in a creative tension.[194] It is fire which makes the world a true κόσμος.[195] This

---

[189] *KRS*, p.145.

[190] *KRS*, p.293.

[191] The similarities with the thought of, for example, Anaxagoras (cf. fr.12 above), are evident. See West's comments, *Orphic Poems*, p.80. In the Orphic hymn concerning Proteus mentioned above, Proteus is invoked as παντιμός, πολύβουλος, ἐπιστάμενος τά τ'ἐόντα ὅσσα τε πρόσθεν ἔην ὅσα τ' ἔσσεται ὕστερον αὖτις (Orphic Hymn 25.4–5). For Proteus as a prophet, see Virgil, *Georgics* IV, 392-3 (reference in van Unnik, "Formula," p.92).

[192] *KRS*, pp.197–8.

[193] Guthrie, 1: 454; *KRS*, p.198; Jaeger, p.115; see also Klaus Held, *Heraklit, Parmenides, und der Anfang von Philosophie und Wissenschaft* (Berlin/New York: Walter de Gruyter, 1980), pp.395–6.

[194] See especially fr. 90: "All things are an equal exchange for fire and fire for all things, as goods are for gold and gold for goods," *KRS*, pp.197–8.

[195] The language also has affinities with Heraclitus' Logos (cf. Guthrie, p.459; Fränkel, p.385; *KRS*, pp.198–9), which he may have conceived of as everlasting. See Guthrie's rendering of fr. 1 (see 1: 424–5; cf. Jaeger (pp. 228–9n)) : "Although this Lo-

is obviously not the same as saying *God* "was, is, and will be," but it is perhaps a first step in that direction.

Plato and Beyond

Although we have seen that Plato eschews the words "was" and "will be" for true being, he is happy to employ the three-times formula in other contexts. In the *Charmides*, he makes use of the Homeric motif that the prophet knows about the past, present, and future.[196] He sometimes uses the motif as the Presocratics did, as another way of saying "all things." In *Laws* 888e, he argues that chance did not bring about τὰ πράγματα γιγνόμενα καὶ γενόμενα καὶ γενησόμενα. In the Myth of Er (*Rep.* 617c), the *Dreizeitenformel* is used to describe the work of the three Fates, who may be said to hold sway over the world. Lachesis sings of τὰ γεγονότα, Clotho of τὰ ὄντα, and Atropos of τὰ μέλλοντα. Especially interesting is the appearance of the *Dreizeitenformel* in *Tim.* 38b–c. He reiterates the distinction between the eternal model and the temporal image with these words:

τὸ μὲν γὰρ δὴ παράδειγμα πάντα αἰῶνα ἐστιν ὄν, ὁ δ' αὖ διὰ τέλους τὸν ἅπαντα χρόνον γεγονώς τε καὶ ὢν καὶ ἐσόμενος....

for whereas the pattern is existent through all eternity, the copy, on the other hand, is through all time, continually having existed, existing, and being about to exist...[197]

The text, apart from its philosophical interest, is one of the few *Dreizeitenformeln* outside of Rev. 1:4 which actually employs ὤν as its present tense element.

While Plato is obviously reluctant to say that true Being was, is, and will be, he does begin the address to the new colonists of Magnesia in *Laws* 715e ff. with a reference to ὁ...θεός...ἀρχήν τε καὶ τελευτὴν καὶ μέσα τῶν ὄντων ἁπάντων ἔχων. According to Plato, this is a παλαιὸς λόγος (cf. the Orphic Theogony cited in our section on etymology). Its popularity was to prove enduring, as we will see when we examine Josephus' appropriation of the phrase in *Ap.* 2:190.

By the hellenistic era, it had become common to describe time as consisting of three parts.[198] The *Dreizeitenformel* continued to serve as a grand

---

gos exists forever..." Note that *KRS* (pp.186–7) translate the ἀεί of the text with men ("men *always* prove uncomprehending") rather than the Logos.

[196] *Charmides* 173c–174b; e.g. 174a εἴ τις πρὸς τοῖς μέλλουσι καὶ τὰ γεγονότα πάντα εἰδείη καὶ τὰ νῦν ὄντα, καὶ μηδὲν ἀγνοοῖ; Text in LCL, trans. W.R.M. Lamb, 1927.

[197] Text and trans. in LCL.

[198] E.g. Sextus Empiricus., *Outlines of Pyrrhonism* 3.142 ff.; Seneca, *De Brev. Vit.* 10.2; Philo, *Leg. All.* 3: 42–3.

way of speaking about history (whether human[199] or cosmic[200]). The Homeric use of the *Dreizeitenformel* for prophecy was also still operative.[201] A particularly interesting use of the three tenses is ascribed to the Epicureans by Sextus Empiricus. The Epicureans, he says, explained the human concept of the divine thus:

> And again, having formed an impression of a long-lived man, the men of old increased the time-span to infinity (εἰς ἄπειρον) by combining the past and the future with the present (προσσυνάψαντες τῷ ἐνεστῶτι καὶ τὸν παρῳχημένον καὶ τὸν μέλλοντα); and then, having arrived at the conception of the everlasting, they said that god was everlasting too (ἀίδιον εἶναι τὸν θεόν).[202]

The appearance of εἰς ἄπειρον indicates that we have moved beyond Hesiod's conception of gods who are deathless after birth. The gods in question here are truly everlasting.

The most important texts for our purposes are those in which the *Dreizeitenformel* is explicitly used with respect to a god or gods. We will examine three such occurences which pre-date or are contemporary with the composition of the book of Revelation: an oracle from Dodona cited by

---

[199] E.g. Cicero, *Oratio post reditum ad Quirites* 7, where he describes Cn. Pompeius as *vir omnium qui sunt, fuerunt, erunt*. For further examples see van Unnik, "Formula," p.91.

[200] See, e.g., Aristocles (1 century CE) on the Stoics:, "But the primary fire is as it were a sperm which possesses the principles of all things and the causes of past, present, and future events (τὰς αἰτίας τῶν γεγονότων καὶ τῶν γιγνομένων καὶ τῶν ἐσομένων)... (ap. Eusebius, *Pr. Ev.* 15.14.2; in Long and Sedley 1: 276, 2: 274); Epictetus (c. 55–135 CE): "For such was, is, and will be the nature of the universe ("Ότι τοιαύτη ἡ τοῦ κόσμου φύσις καὶ ἦν καὶ ἔστι καὶ ἔσται), and it is not possible for the things that have come into being to come into being otherwise than they do now..." Epictetus, fr. 8. Text and translation (with slight modifications) from Epictetus, *Works* trans. W. A. Oldfather 2 vols. LCL (London: Wm. Heinemann/NY: Geo. Putnam's Sons, 1925–8) 2: 448–9.

[201] See *Contest of Homer and Hesiod*, ll.97–8 (Hesiod (*sic!*) quotes *Il.* 1.70); Virgil (of Proteus), *Georgics* IV, 392–3; Ovid, *Metamorphoses* 1.517–8; see van Unnik, "Formula," p.92. We may compare also a note in Diodorus Siculus 9:3.2. There he tells of a time in ancient Greece when a certain tripod was to be given to one ὃς σοφίᾳ τά τ'ἐόντα τά τ' ἐσσόμενα προδέδορκεν. The "formula describing prophecy" has been transmuted to a "formula describing wisdom." Plutarch's character Theon argues in a similar vein when he declares in *De E* 387a–b that Apollo is a kind of μάντις, who speaks about the future by virtue of his knowledge of the past and present. He goes on to say that Homer was right to put the present first in *Il.* 1.70, because the philosophical man reasons from the present to the future ("if this is happening now, as a result, this will happen later") and from the present to the past ("if this is happening now, this is a result of what was happening before") (387b). For Theon, insight into what "was, is, and will be" may be a divine gift, but it is the result of dialectical reasoning rather than ecstatic revelation.

[202] Sextus Empiricus, *Adv. Math.*, book 9. Translation in Long and Sedley, 1: 143; text in Long and Sedley 2: 150.

Pausanias; an inscription to Aion from Eleusis; and an inscription to Athena in Saïs cited by Plutarch.

Pausanias (X.12.10) reports that the prophetesses at the prestigious oracle at Dodona[203] were the first to sing:

> Zeus was, Zeus is, Zeus shall be. O mighty Zeus! (Ζεὺς ἦν, Ζεὺς ἔστι, Ζεὺς ἔσσεται, ὦ μεγάλε Ζεῦ)[204] Earth sends up fruits; therefore call her Mother Earth.

Pausanias' quotation has received relatively little attention from scholars, which makes the task of assessing its date and significance all the more challenging. Martin Nilsson notes that "Der Vers bei Paus. X 12,10 ist selbstverständlich jungen Ursprungs," though he does not tell us just how young he believes it to be.[205] One scholar who has examined the matter in some detail is H. W. Parke, for whom the oracles of Greece were a lifetime study. In his book, *The Oracles of Zeus*, he proposed that these lines were "pious ejaculations" rather than answers to a consultation. He suspected that the lines were of Eastern provenance (perhaps from Persia) and that they may have been composed during the time of Pyhrrus (King in Epirus, 306–302,297–273 BCE). The proposal of a Persian origin is supported with reference to *Bundahisn* 1.3, which reads in part, "...Ahura Mazda and the region, religion, and time of Ahura Mazda were and are and ever will be..."[206] He also noted a connection with the Stoicism of the time.[207] A few years later, in his article "Mighty Zeus," he modified his proposal and suggested that the oracle may have been composed as part of the "war of propaganda" between Dodona and Delphi. Since it was alleged that the Greek gods had originated in Egypt, Parke suggests these verses were composed as part of an answer to the question, "Should we use these new (i.e. Greek) names for the gods?" The affirmative answer included a brief description of each god. We have in Pausanias the first two lines of what is

---

[203] For the prestige of Dodona in antiquity, see H.W. Parke, *The Oracles of Zeus* (Oxford: Basil Blackwell, 1967), 1ff. On Pausanias' knowledge of oracles, see Parke, "Mighty Zeus," *Hermathena* 111 (1971): 24–33.

[204] Text in van Unnik, "Formula," p.93. He notes the affinities with an item in the Tübingen Theosophy, ἦν Ζεὺς ἔστι τε νῦν Ζεὺς κ' ἔσσεται.

[205] Martin P. Nilsson, *Geschichte der griechischen Religion*, 2 vols. (Munich: C.H. Beck'sche, 1961), 1: 427 n.

[206] Translation in E.W. West, *Pahlavi Texts Part 1: The Bundahis; Bahman Yast, and Shâyast Lâ-Shâyast*, Sacred Books of the East, Vol. V (Oxford: Oxford University Press, 1880). (I have substituted Ahura Mazda for West's Aûharmazd for the sake of consistency). R. C. Zaehner gives an almost identical translation in his book *Zurvan: A Zoroastrian Dilemma* (Oxford: Oxford University Press, 1955). He also provides a transliteration of the text. The "was, is, and ever will be" portion reads 'but 'ut 'hast 'ut hame 'bavet.

[207] Parke, *Oracles of Zeus*, pp.158–61.

presumably a longer poem. Parke reiterates his theory of Persian influence, and proposes that the verses may in fact pre-date Plato.[208]

I am wary of following Parke too closely on the details of his proposals, although they do give much fodder for thought. The lines may be derived from Persia, but much of this interpretation hangs on the assumption that the use of the *Dreizeitenformel* of Ahura Mazda in the *Bundahisn* is quite early. This is not to my knowledge demonstrable. It must be remembered that the *Bundahisn* in their present form postdate the Muslim conquest of Persia (651CE).[209] Moreover, as R. C. Zaehner notes, religious influence did not simply flow from East to West: "There can...be little doubt that during the Seleucid and Parthian epochs hellenistic influences made themselves felt which may even then have penetrated into the Zoroastrian religion itself."[210] A more pertinent question is whether we can account for the phrase as it stands in Pausanias from native Greek sources. Given the numerous examples of *Dreizeitenformeln* we have seen in Greek literature, the answer is "yes." Parke himself admits that this near eastern formula may have been mediated by other Greek sources (e.g. Heraclitus) en route to Dodona.

When might these verses have been first written? In theory, it could have happened at any point in the post-Homeric period. Parke's statement that the phrase "Zeus was, Zeus is, Zeus will be" indicates a "being without beginning or end"[211] may be debated (compare the description of the gods in the *Theogony*). But it does sound more philosophical than what we find in Homer and Hesiod, and I am inclined to think Parke is correct in his assessment. Thus it is most likely the verses originated in a milieu where a fairly exalted or philosophical view of Zeus was present, along with a knowledge of the *Dreizeitenformel*. This need take us no further than the Presocratics or Plato. As we have seen, Heraclitus said the cosmos "was, is, and will be an ever-living fire," while Plato employs both the apparently traditional etymology of Zeus as "the one through whom all things have life" (*Cratylus* 396a), and the "old saying" that God holds the beginning, middle, and end of all things (*Laws* 715e ff.). Parke's suggestion for a pre-Platonic date cannot be dismissed out of hand.

---

[208] Parke, "Mighty Zeus," pp.24–33.

[209] West, *Pahlavi Texts*, p. xli.

[210] Zaehner, p.7. The fact that the author of this text (whenever it was written) could describe Ahura Mazda in this way is of course still of great interest for a general comparison of religions in the ancient world. This is especially true when one notes that the passage continues, "...while Ahriman in darkness, with backward understanding and desire for destruction, *was in the abyss, and it is he who will not be* [cf. Rev. 17:8–10] and the place of that destruction, and also of that darkness, is what they call the 'endlessly' dark..." (trans. West; italics mine).

[211] Parke, "Mighty Zeus," p.28.

I believe, however, that a Stoic origin is more likely. The idea that "Zeus was, Zeus is, Zeus will be" could quite easily find a home in Cleanthes' theology. We may venture an even more precise connection. We know that the Stoics were influenced at least somewhat by Heraclitus. As we have just seen, he said that the world-order "was, is, and will be an ever-living fire." We also know that the Stoics identified the primal world-fire with Zeus (see especially Epictetus Book 3, 13.4 ff., following earlier Stoic teaching). With these two elements in place, it does not take a great deal of imagination to substitute "Zeus" for "fire" in Heraclitus' formula, and to emerge with the verses we have at Dodona. Parke's earlier suggestion of a date in the late fourth or early third century thus seems the most likely. I would not rule out an even later date in the hellenistic era, in keeping with Festugière's assessment of the Isis inscription from Saïs (see below).

A second occurence of the *Dreizeitenformel* may be found in the Aion inscription at Eleusis.[212] Based on the style of the engraving, the inscription may be dated with some confidence to the Augustan period.[213] The value of this inscription for our investigation will be evident. We print a full transcription and translation below:

a. 1   Κόϊντος Πομπήϊος Αὔλου υἱός /
       ἐποίει καὶ ἀνέθηκε /
  3   σὺν ἀδελφοῖς Αὔλωι καὶ Σέξτωι /
       ΑΙΩΝΑ /
  5   εἰς κράτος Ῥώμης /
       καὶ διαμονὴν / μυστηρίων. /
b. 1   Αἰὼν ὁ αὐτὸς ἐν τοῖς αὐτοῖς αἰεί /
       φύσει θείαι μένων
  3   κόσμος τε εἷς / κατὰ τὰ αὐτά·
       ὁποῖος ἔστι καὶ ἦν / καὶ ἔσται
  5   ἀρχὴν μεσότητα τέλος / οὐκ ἔχων
       μεταβολῆς ἀμέτοχος /
  7   θείας φύσεως ἐργάτης αἰωνίου πάντα.[214]

---

[212] For overviews of αἰών in Greco-Roman culture, see Günther Zuntz (several small works, referred to below); Otto Weinreich, "Aion in Eleusis," *ARW* 19 (1919): 174–90; Nilsson, *Geschichte* 2: 498ff.; and the articles under "Aion" by W. Fauth, *Der Kleine Pauly: Lexikon der Antike*, eds. Konrat Ziegler and Walther Sontheimer (Stuttgart: Druckenmüller, 1964–75), 1: 185–7 (with good bibliography) and Wernicke in *PW* 1: 1042–3.
[213] See Zuntz, *Aion: Gott des Römerreichs* (Abhandlungen der Heidelberger Akademie der Wissenschaften, Philosophisch-historische Klasse 1989/2), pp.38–42; Weinreich, p. 175; Nilsson, *Geschichte* 2: 348.
[214] I have given the inscription as it stands in Zuntz (1989/2), p.37, in which he has tried to represent the structure of the inscription. The slashes (/) represent the line endings of the inscription itself. See also Wm. Dittenberger, ed., *Sylloge Inscriptionum Graecorum* 3rd .ed. (Leipzig: Hirzel, 1920), #1125; Weinreich, pp.174ff.

Quintus Pompeius son of Aulus made and dedicated (this) along with his brothers Aulus and Sextus: AION, for the power of Rome and the continuance of the mysteries:

Aion, who by his divine nature remains always exactly the same and who all together is the unique Cosmos, of such a nature that he is and was and will be, not having beginning, middle, or end, who does not partake of change, who produces the absolutely eternal divine nature.[215]

The inscription and the accompanying statue of Aion (which has not been found) would presumably have been standing at the time of the composition of Revelation. Whether the veneration of Aion would have been known to John is a matter to which we shall return shortly.[216] In the meantime we must look at the content of the inscription itself.

While the identity of the brothers who set up the statue to Aion is uncertain, they are obviously loyal Roman citizens who desire the continuance of Roman might as well as the maintenance of the Eleusinian mysteries.[217] The dedication proper (b1 ff.) betrays the influence of Greek philosophy at every turn. Lines b1,2, as has been noted by most commentators, bear comparison with thoughts in Parmenides, Xenophanes, and Plato (see esp. *Tim.* 37d6: μένοντος αἰῶνος ἐν ἑνί).[218] Aion, like Parmenides' "what is" and Plato's world of Forms, is always the same (cf. also l. b6). Aion's "divine nature" (l. b2) almost certainly derives from the previously mentioned passage in Aristotle's *De Caelo* (279a28), where it may be called ἀθάνατος καὶ θεῖος.[219] We have examined the numerous parallels to ll. b4–5 throughout the course of our investigation. Van Unnik

---

[215] The translation, which makes no claim to elegance, is based mainly on the French version by A.J. Festugière in *La Révélation d'Hermès Trismégiste* 4 vols (Paris: Lecoffre, 1944–54); vol. 4, *Le dieu inconnu*, p.181. See also Zuntz' German version, (1989/2,p.43); and H. W. Parke's English rendering, in "Mighty Zeus," p.30. (All of the above versions translate only the latter portion of inscription, omitting "Quintus...mysteries.") Zuntz' warning is well heeded: "Lassen Sie aber den griechischen Text nicht aus den Augen!" (1989/2, p.43).

[216] Nilsson (2: 348) says that the statue is not so much an object of worship as a way of showing the accord of the Eleusinian mysteries with Rome. This may be true, but the very fact that Aion is depicted as a god surely has religious significance. I have used "veneration" as an attempt to recognize Nilsson's point without losing the religious sentiment.

[217] C. Cichorius identified "Quintus" with Quintus Pompeius Auli filius, Quaestor in Bithynia in 74 BCE, but see the arguments against this in Zuntz (1989/2), pp.38–42.

[218] See e.g. Zuntz (1989/2), p.43; Weinreich, pp.175ff.; Festugière, *Le dieu inconnu*, p.181.

[219] Cf. Fauth, "Aion," pp. 185ff. Cf. Max Zepf, "Der Gott Αἰών in der hellenistischen Theologie,"*ARW* 25 (1927): 225ff. Note too the use of the archaic form αἰεί, which is not attested in Attic after 361 BCE. See Festugière, *Le dieu inconnu*, p.181; Zuntz (1989/2), p.43.

points out that ἀρχὴν μεσότητα τέλος οὐκ ἔχων is a *negative* form of the traditional formula found in, e.g., *Laws* 715e ff.[220]

The text as a whole exudes the spirit of the hellenistic *dieu cosmique*, which is so thoroughly described by Festugière in his book of the same name. Not surprisingly, this type of all embracing cosmic theology/philosophy is not always completely comprehensible. As we pointed out, Aion is identified with the cosmos in l. b3,[221] but he is at the same time (if "time" is the word we want here) creating or at least orchestrating the unfolding of this cosmos. This last point is drawn from l. b7, assuming that the "eternal divine nature" is likewise a reference to the cosmos – a point which some might also wish to debate. In terms of the *Timaeus*, which influenced so much of hellenistic cosmology, Aion could correspond either to the Demiurge, the World Soul, or the Eternal Living Creature.[222] If we wish to state what appears to be the underlying principle of the inscription, we might say that Aion is depicted as an unchanging divine entity which (who?) pervades the universe and confers divinity and everlastingness upon the cosmos. The lesson to be learned, of course, is that this Aion, who is preserver of the cosmos as a whole, is certainly capable of preserving the Roman state and the Eleusinian mysteries.

We cannot be certain whether John was aware of this use of the *Dreizeitenformel* for Aion, but it is possible. In our concluding chapter we will argue that John employs the Iao version of the divine name in Rev. 1:8. Scholars have pointed out the formal affinities between *Iao* and *Aion*. Eleusis itself lay at the heart of Greek religion, and so even in the absence of other testimony about Aion, it must at least be admitted that John could have heard about this inscription from people who had visited the site. The veneration of Aion was to continue for centuries after John, although the extent and influence of the cult have been debated.[223]

---

[220] Van Unnik, *Het Godspredikat "Het Begin en Het Einde" bij Flavius Josephus en in de Openbaring van Johannes* (Amsterdam: Noord-Hollandsche Uitgevers Maatschappij, 1976), pp.47–9. He notes a connection with the *apeiron* of Xenophanes, which likewise has no beginning, middle, or end (p.49). Probably the inscription is playing upon the ambiguity of ἔχων ("hold" or "have") in the well-known traditional formula.

[221] Festugière, *Le dieu inconnu*, p.181; Zepf, p.237.

[222] See esp. *Tim.* 34a. Dillon (pp.45–6) points out that the relationship of the Demiurge and the World Soul becomes a source of some debate in Middle Platonism. It is therefore hardly surprising that we cannot make a clear correlation of Aion to one or the other (or to the world of Forms) in a work of popular philosophy such as the Aion inscription.

[223] The literature on Aion veneration in later centuries is vast. Zuntz' works (see esp. *AIΩN in der Literatur der Kaiserzeit* (Wien: Österreichische Akademie der Wissenschaften, 1992), pp.11–25) remain the most thorough treatment of the subject, and I would concur with his conclusion that the importance of the Aion cult has been exaggerated by some scholars. For a general overview from a similar standpoint see also A.D.

As it happens, there is evidence for the worship of Aion much closer to home, in the Asia Minor city of Aphrodisias, which is situated on a tributary of the Maeander about fifty kilometres southwest of Laodicea. In 1956, four large relief-plates were uncovered.[224] Upon one of them, there is an image of Aion, appearing in profile as (in Zuntz' words) "ein schöner, bärtiger Mann, nicht jung doch kraftvoll, unbestimmten doch wohl mehr als mittleren Alters..."[225] Aion is flanked by ANΔPHA (=ἀνδρεῖα, courage) and the goddess Roma.[226] Zuntz' interpretation of the piece seems sound: "Also, symbolisch ausgedrückt: durch VIRTUS ewige Dauer des augusteischen Reichs."[227] The appearance of G. Iulius Zoilos on one of the associated plates points towards a date in the Augustan era for this depiction of Aion.[228] Assuming the plates were still in place in the latter part of the first century, it is certainly possible that John may have been aware of the role of Aion as guarantor of Roman rule. It is furthermore possible that the

---

Nock, "A Vision of Mandulis Aion," *HTR* 27 (1934): 53–104, esp. pp.83ff. A. Alföldi, ("From the *Aion Plutonios* of the Ptolemies to the *Saeculum Frugiferum* of the Roman Emperors," in *Greece and the Eastern Mediterranean in Ancient History and Prehistory*, ed. K. H. Kinzl; Berlin/New York: Walter de Gruyter, 1977, pp.1–30) sees the Aion cult as much more far reaching in its influence, particularly in Alexandria. Nilsson (2: 502ff.) also affirms the existence of the Aion cult in Alexandria. Cf. N. Belayche, "Aïôn: vers une sublimation du temps," in *Le temps chrétien de la fin de l'antiquité au moyen âge, IIIe–XIIIe siècles* (Paris: Éditions du Centre National de la Recherche Scientifique, 1984), pp.11–29. One item that may be of interest is PGM IV 1167–1206, which, reads ὁ τῶν ὅλων δεσπότης, ὁ Αἰὼν τῶν Αἰώνων σὺ εἶ ὁ κοσμοκράτωρ, Ῥα, Πᾶν. (Aion is likewise called παντοκράτορα in the "vision of Mandulis" recorded in a temple on the southern fringes of Egypt. See Nock, 61–3 for a transcript and translation of the vision.) Festugière (*Le dieu inconnu*, pp.182–199) provides translation and commentary for 18 such magical texts containing Aion.

[224] Zuntz, *AIΩN im Römerreich: Die archäologischen Zeugnisse* (Abhandlungen der Heidelberger Akademie der Wissenschaften, Philosophisch-historische Klasse 1991/3), p.22. A full description may be found in A. Alföldi, *Aion in Mérida und Aphrodisias* Madrider Beiträge 6 (Mainz am Rhein: Zabern, 1979).

[225] Zuntz, (1991/3), p.23.

[226] Zuntz, (1991/3), p.22. The inscription for Roma is missing, but Zuntz feels the identification is certain. Aphrodisias had a long history of loyalty to Rome, and was consequently well-treated by the emperors. See Joyce Reynolds, *Aphrodisias and Rome* (London: Society for the Promotion of Roman Studies, 1982), pp.1ff.

[227] Zuntz, (1991/3), p.22.

[228] Zuntz, (1991/3), pp.22–3; cf. Reynolds, pp.156ff. for more on Zoilos. Zuntz (p.23) suggests it may have been set up in the year 17 or 16 BCE to commemorate the celebration of the *Ludi saeculares* in Rome. This is a part of his larger hypothesis that Augustus himself introduced the worship of Aion as a Greek counterpart to the introduction of the "golden age" in Rome. (See Zuntz (1989/2), pp.56–67.) The suggestion is interesting, although the evidence is somewhat scanty. If Aion were seen as the god who brings in the golden age, the potential for conflict with Christianity would only be heightened.

Dreizeitenformel followed Aion to Asia Minor, though we have no direct evidence for this.

Our final text comes from Plutarch's *De Is.* 354c. There he mentions an inscription found on the base of a statue to Athena/Isis/Neïth in the city of Saïs.²²⁹ In the midst of a discourse about the hidden wisdom of Egyptian religion, he says that this statue bears the words:

ἐγώ εἰμι πᾶν τὸ γεγονὸς καὶ ὄν καὶ ἐσόμενον καὶ τὸν ἐμὸν πέπλον οὐδείς πω θνητὸς ἀπεκάλυψεν

I am all that has been and is and will be; and no mortal has lifted my mantle.

The inscription appears in slightly different form in Proclus' *Commentary on the Timaeus*. Since it is unlikely that he used Plutarch as a source, this may indicate that the dedication had some currency in educated circles.²³⁰ As to its origin, Festugière reasonably concludes that it is a fragment of an Isis aretalogy, something well-known to New Testament scholars.²³¹ Our text fits well with similar statements which describe Isis as κυρία of all, the one who divides the skies and the earth, and fixes the courses of the stars.²³² Is it then of Egyptian origin? The phrase has some affinities with a statement made by Seth to Horus, "I am Yesterday, I am Today, I am Tomorrow which has not yet come."²³³ It is possible that, in Griffith's words, Isis "is arrogating to herself the kind of power originally ascribed to Atum ('the All') or Re' as creator gods."²³⁴ Festugière, however, (in agreement with Nock) argues that the form and much of the content of the aretalogies point rather towards a Greek provenance. The Egyptian priests, he believes, were trying to present the "gospel" of Isis to the hellenistic world in terms familiar to that audience.²³⁵ With respect to our text, he concludes that the idea of a god who *is* all things "ne peut être antérieure au panthéisme stoïcien, ou même plutôt à la diffusion de ce panthéisme dans la religiosité populaire."²³⁶

I am inclined to agree with Festugière. This is not to deny that the description of Isis may fit with Egyptian conceptions of deity. But, at least in

---

²²⁹ Neïth was the ancient goddess of the city, later equated with Isis and Athena. Griffiths, p.283.

²³⁰ The first line reads τὰ ὄντα καὶ τὰ ἐσόμενα καὶ τὰ γεγονότα ἐγώ εἰμι. For text and translation see Proclus, *Commentaire sur le Timée*, trans. and notes A. J. Festugière (Paris: Librairie Philosophique J. Vrin, 1966), 1: 140 n. Weinreich, p.179, believes Plutarch's version is more faithful to the original. See also Griffiths, pp.283-4.

²³¹ Proclus, *Commentaire*, p.140 n.

²³² See Festugière, "À propos des arétalogies d'Isis," *HTR* 42 (1949): 222-3.

²³³ Griffiths, p.284 n.

²³⁴ Griffiths, p.284.

²³⁵ See Festugière, "À propos," esp. p.230; and A. D. Nock, review of Harder's *Karpocrates von Chalkis*, in *Gnomon* 21 (1949): 221-28.

²³⁶ Proclus, *Commentaire*, p.140.

the form in which we have this saying – which is of course *in Greek* – her appearance is being tailored for the hellenistic marketplace. Festugière concludes that Isis is here "nulle autre que l'Aiôn," and he then cites the inscription from Eleusis which we have already examined.[237] Elsewhere in the aretalogies, Isis takes up the prerogatives of Zeus, and so one also thinks of the oracle from Dodona.[238]

The original intent of the statue at Saïs was probably to present Isis as a world-ruler or creator figure. Plutarch uses the inscription in a somewhat different way. Isis is to him primarily the giver of wisdom. The context of the quotation, as well as the association with Athena, makes this clear. Immediately before the citation of the inscription, Plutarch makes his statement about the Egyptian priests having a "teaching about the gods [which] holds a mysterious wisdom" (354c). Immediately after, he gives an etymology for the god Amûn as "what is concealed... since they address him as one invisible and concealed, and exhort him to become manifest and clear to them. So great was the concern of the Egyptians for wisdom in religion" (354c–d). Plutarch seems to interpret the inscription to mean "*I am able to make known* all that has been and is and will be." One recalls the role of the Muses in Hesiod.[239] Note especially that the word for "lifted" in the Saïs inscription is ἀπεκάλυψεν. The appearance of the *Dreizeitenformel* for Isis alongside ἀπεκάλυψεν offers an interesting formal correspondence to the appearance of the *Dreizeitenformel* for God in the ἀποκάλυψις Ἰησοῦ Χριστοῦ (Rev. 1:1).

Summary of the Dreizeitenformel

In his invaluable article "A Formula Describing Prophecy," W. C. van Unnik suggests that "[t]he differently worded formula 'that which was, is, and shall be' does not only express the eternal duration ('ewige Dauer'), but something that surpasses the merely temporal aspect, the mystery of existence, of history in its totality."[240] The statement needs to be clarified in a few particulars. Van Unnik himself acknowledges that some uses of the *Dreizeitenformel* are not strictly religious, but refer to the broad scope of human history.[241] We might also question the implicit contrast between "eternal duration" and "that which surpasses the merely temporal aspect." Van Unnik is not arguing, I think, that the *Dreizeitenformel* indicates

---

[237] Proclus, *Commentaire*, p.140.
[238] Festugière, "À propos," p.230.
[239] Whether Plutarch really believes "no mortal has ever lifted my mantle" is also open to question. The whole point of the *De Is.* is to show that the Egyptian myths do contain hidden wisdom. Again, we might gloss the inscription, "*Few mortals* have ever lifted my mantle." The imagery of the mantle is sexual, as Griffiths (p.284) points out.
[240] van Unnik, "Formula," p.93.
[241] van Unnik, "Formula," p.91.

"timeless eternity." This is flatly denied, of course, by Parmenides and Plato. It is *precisely* "eternal duration" that lifts "the totality of history" beyond the merely temporal. Finally, some instances of the *Dreizeitenformel* (e.g. that used by Isis in Plutarch's *De Is.*) may speak about "the mystery of existence," but this can hardly be said of the *Dreizeitenformeln* as a group. The fact that Cicero writes that Cn Pompeius was one of the greatest men who ever "was, is, or will be" does not really tell us anything about the mystery of existence.[242]

But van Unnik's statement does point out something of immense interest for the interpretation of our formula in Rev. 1:4. If one wanted to make a grand, sweeping statement about the nature of God or reality or history, the *Dreizeitenformel* was an effective way of doing this. Its poetic sound gave the formula a grandeur which might transcend bare statements about "existing forever." This is particularly evident when it is used of deity. The *Dreizeitenformel* used in this capacity does lift the figure in question beyond the realm of ordinary mortals. In this regard, at least, John's description of God as "the one who is and who was and who is to come" fits in smoothly with the religious tenor of the times. We will examine later the important ways in which his formula differs from those of his hellenistic counterparts.

---

[242] Cicero, *Oratio post reditum ad Quirites* 7, see van Unnik, "Formula," p.91.

Chapter 2

The Use of the Name YHWH

The stage has now been set for our investigation of the use and understanding of the name YHWH in early Judaism. We have seen that Greek thinking would have posed a considerable challenge to a reflective Jew or Christian in the hellenistic era. The Greeks were in control of the world, which might raise the question as to whether their gods were likewise in control of the world. What is more, the chief of their pantheon, Zeus, had undergone a transformation which rendered him a considerable foe for any god claiming supremacy over the universe. No longer simply the lustful tyrant of Homeric days, he now came as the embodiment of the Stoic designing fire, or as "the one through whom all things have life." As they sang at Dodona, "Zeus was, Zeus is, Zeus will be." The name YHWH, we will see, was ready to enter the etymological fray as "the One who is." But this in turn led back to the questions posed by Greek philosophers about the nature of Being, and its relationship to time and space. YHWH's confrontation with the "gods of the nations" was taking a new turn.

Yet at this crucial juncture YHWH (as a name) becomes strangely quiet. The name did not disappear entirely, but it did become noticeably withdrawn. In this chapter we will undertake a detailed examination of what happened to the tetragrammaton, both written and spoken, during the hellenistic period. We conclude with some proposals as to why Jews were reluctant to use the name at this time.

Septuagint

Writing the Name

We will examine the Septuagint translation of Ex. 3:14 in chapter 3. For the moment we will concentrate our efforts on the variants of the name YHWH that appear in the MSS of the Greek bible from the New Testament era. We will follow this with an examination of two passages that (apparently) warn against speaking the divine name, Lev.24:10–16 and Am.6:10.

The Greek manuscripts contain a number of variations on the MT's YHWH. IAΩ appears in place of the tetragrammaton in the late first century BCE/early first century CE papyrus from Qumran, pap4QLXXLev[b].

At fr. 20:4 we find των εντολων ΙΑΩ.[1] As we will see, this form of the name is well attested in Judaism during our period. We will discuss below these other instances of Iao and the various proposals which have been offered for the history of this form. Although pap4QLXXLev[b] constitutes the only direct MS evidence for this reading, Skehan adduces Origen's use of Iao in his explanation of the name Ιερεμιας (μετεωρισμος Ιαω) in his commentary on John 1:1 as another example of this textual tradition.[2] A roughly contemporary text, P. Fouad 266 (Rahlfs 848), consistently uses the square (Aramaic) script to render the tetragrammaton, and nowhere does it employ κύριος.[3] The unusual form ΠΙΠΙ, which is an obvious attempt to use Greek letters to produce something that looks like the tetragrammaton (written in Aramaic script), occurs in a fragment of Ps.22 from the Hexapla in the Cairo Genizah.[4] Jerome also mentions such a variant.[5] In the Syrohexaplar, the name appears as *Pypy* in Syriac script.[6]

We also have evidence for YHWH in the paleo-Hebrew script of the tenth to sixth century BCE. The Scroll of the Minor Prophets (8HevXIIgr) contains this form of the tetragrammaton. It was written between 50 BCE

---

[1] *Discoveries in the Judaean Desert IX*, eds. Patrick W. Skehan, Eugene Ulrich, and Judith E. Sanderson (Oxford: Oxford University Press, 1992), pp.163,168. 4QLXXNum has a lacuna where the divine name should appear, and the editors of *DJD IX* (p.188) believe that either YHWH (in square Hebrew script) or κύριος could fill the gap. ΙΑΩ and the abbreviation KC do not seem to fit the size requirements of the space, and YHWH in paleoscript, and the form ΠΙΠΙ are judged to be developments prior to the copying of 4QLXXNum. For dating see Patrick W. Skehan, "The Divine Name at Qumran, In the Masada Scroll, and in the Septuagint," *Bulletin of the International Organization for Septuagint and Cognate Studies* 13 (1980): 28-29. For a good survey of the use of divine names in early Greek texts, see Leslie John McGregor, *The Greek Text of Ezekiel: An Examination of its Homogeneity*, Septuagint and Cognate Studies 18 (Atlanta: Scholars Press, 1985), pp.85-90.

[2] Skehan, "Divine Name," pp.30-31. The etymology of Jeremiah in turn appears to have been drawn from an onomasticon of LXX names. Origen employs the form Ιαη in his commentary on Ps.2:2.

[3] Mid-first century BCE Greek MS containing the second half of the book of Deuteronomy. See Albert Pietersma, "Kyrios or Tetragram: A Renewed Quest for the Original Septuagint," in *De Septuaginta*, eds. Pietersma and Claude Cox (Mississauga, Ontario: Benben Publications, 1984): 86,89-90; George Howard, "The Tetragram and the New Testament," *JBL* 96 (1977): 63ff.; Skehan, "Divine Name," pp.31ff. The text was first brought to attention by W.G. Waddell in "The Tetragrammaton in the LXX," *JTS* 45 (1944): 158-61.

[4] Pietersma, p.88.

[5] In Ep.25 *Ad Marcellam*; see Baudissin, 2:9; Skehan, "Divine Name," p.32.

[6] Baudissin, 2:.8; Skehan, "Divine Name," p.32. Skehan also mentions (p.32) the use of *Popi* as a substitute for the divine name in the gemara to y. Nedarim XI, 1.

and 50 CE.⁷ The form is also evidenced in the translation of Aquila, in a palimpsest from the Cairo Geniza.⁸ W. Baudissin believes that Origen may have been referring to such texts of Aquila (or possibly Symmachus) when he made his much-discussed remark: "In the more accurate exemplars [of the LXX] the (divine) name is written in Hebrew characters; not, however, in the current script, but in the most ancient."⁹ We find a paleo-Hebrew abbreviation of the divine name, consisting of two paleo-Hebrew *yods*, in a third century CE text of Genesis (P. Oxy. 7:1007).¹⁰

When one picks up a modern LXX text, of course, one does not find these variants. Κύριος (with or without the article) is the preferred rendering of the tetragrammaton. Since the textual evidence for this comes in MSS copied by Christians, however, it has been argued that this is a later development and may even post-date the New Testament itself.¹¹ While we have already noted in the introduction that we intend to avoid discussing κύριος *per se*, a brief discussion of this particular issue is appropriate here.

The view that κύριος did not appear in the LXX until after the advent of the Christian era is implausible. Albert Pietersma has undertaken a very detailed analysis of the translation technique of the Greek Pentateuch and has concluded that the evidence strongly suggests that κύριος was the original reading of the text.¹² Even more persuasive is the testimony of Philo and the NT itself. Philo consistently uses κύριος as a designation for God. But might this not be, as Howard suggests, simply another instance of Christian scribes inserting κύριος in place of the tetragrammaton?¹³ Such an objection is countered when one considers that Philo does not merely employ κύριος as a title for God in his texts – he frequently interprets the word itself and even derives significance from its etymology.¹⁴ In *Leg. All.* 95, for example, he comments on the use of the compound form κύριος ὁ

---

⁷ Pietersma (pp.88–9) stresses that while it is a Greek MS, it is not properly speaking LXX: "A hebraizing recension of the LXX it is, but a representative of the LXX itself it is not." Cf. Skehan, "Divine Name," pp.32–3.

⁸ Baudissin, 2: 7.

⁹ Quoted in Pietersma, p.87. Pietersma notes a similar statement by Jerome in *Prologus galeatus* (*PL* 28: 594–95). See the discussion in Baudissin, 2:6ff.

¹⁰ Skehan, "Divine Name," p.33; Howard, p.74.

¹¹ See especially Howard's article for a detailed argument of this position. Cf. Hartmut Stegemann, "Religionsgeschichtliche Erwägungen zu den Gottesbezeichnungen in den Qumrantexten," in *Qumran: Sa piété, sa théologie et son milieu*, ed. M. Delcor (Paris: Duculot, and Leuven: University Press, 1978), pp.204ff.

¹² Pietersma, pp.93–101. See also McGregor, pp. 57–92.

¹³ Howard, pp.70–71.

¹⁴ Stegemann, among others, dismisses the evidence from Philo, saying that while he may have *heard* κύριος, a Hebrew tetragrammaton was written in the actual text (Stegemann, p.206). While this is possible, the only tangible evidence we have is that Philo read κύριος in his LXX (see below).

θεός in Genesis: "This is in order that, should he obey the exhortations, he may be deemed worthy by God (θεοῦ) of His benefactions; but that, should he rebel, he may be driven from the presence of the Lord (κυρίου) who has a master's authority over him."[15] In *Quis Her.* 22ff., Philo discusses the distinctions between God as κύριος and God as δεσπότα.[16] Κύριος, he says, comes from κῦρος meaning "power," and it indicates that which is secure (while δεσπότα derives from δέος, "fear," and indicates a "terrible lord" – Gk. φοβερὸν κύριον).

As for the NT, we must first note the fact that there is no known evidence of the tetragrammaton in any surviving MS of the NT. If it were ever there, it has vanished without a trace. Secondly, as in the case of Philo, the presence of κύριος in the LXX is crucial to the interpretation of certain NT passages. Foremost among these is Ro. 10:9ff, where Paul states that salvation rests upon believing in the resurrection of Christ and *confessing Jesus as Lord.*[17] He then cites some OT texts which he believes support his assertion: Is.28:16, "No one who believes in him will be ashamed" (Ro.10:11); and Joel 3:5, "All who call upon the name of the Lord will be saved" (Ro.10:13). The latter is a direct quotation from the LXX: πᾶς...ὃς ἂν ἐπικαλέσηται τὸ ὄνομα κυρίου σωθήσεται. Even if one wishes to make God the Father and not Christ the antecedent of these verses (and this is by no means certain),[18] the passage only makes sense based on LXX texts containing κύριος. How else does one account for the phrase "for the same is Lord of all" (ὁ γὰρ αὐτὸς κύριος πάντων) in v.12, just before the Joel quotation? The tetragrammaton would not make grammatical sense here. It is far more likely that Paul is making a Christological statement through a deliberate juxtaposition of κύριον Ἰησοῦν and LXX references concerning the saving power of God, ὁ κύριος.[19]

It is safe to say that, even if κύριος were not the original LXX reading, there were certainly Greek MSS containing this rendering of the divine name during the NT era. This should not obscure the fact, of course, that *some* Greek manuscripts did contain variations of the tetragrammaton

---

[15] Trans. in LCL Philo, vol.I. This is a recurrent theme in his writings. See *Op.* 125; *Cher.* 83; *Sac.* 87; *Gig.* 45; *Quod Deus* 110; *Plant.* 85f.; *Sob.* 55; *Mig.* 168–9; *Quis Her.* 166. Pietersma (p.93) is convinced that Philo read κύριος in his Greek bible, and the case is also made by N.A. Dahl and Alan F. Segal in their article, "Philo and the Rabbis on the Names of God," *JSJ* 9 (1978): 1–28.

[16] He is commenting on the unusual use of Δέσποτα in Gen.15:2.

[17] Gk. ...ἐὰν ὁμολογήσῃς ἐν τῷ στόματί σου κύριον Ἰησοῦν.

[18] It would certainly not be abusing the text to think that since κύριος designated Christ in v.9, it designates him still in vv.11–13. See the comments by C.E.B. Cranfield, *The Epistle to the Romans* ICC, 2 vols. (Edinburgh: T.&T. Clark, 1979), 2:529.

[19] See Cranfield, 2: 527f.; Peter Stuhlmacher, *Paul's Letter to the Romans*, trans. Scott Hafemann (Louisville: Westminster/John Knox, 1994), p.157.

rather than κύριος. These variations must be kept in mind in our investigation of Rev. 1:4.

Saying the Name

We will confine ourselves here to two LXX texts: Lev.24:10–16 and Amos 6:10. In the story of Leviticus 24, the son of an Israelite mother and an Egyptian father fights with an Israelite. In the midst of the fight, the man "blasphemes (or 'utters')[20] the Name and curses (v.11)." After a time in prison, he is executed after a word from the Lord declares that anyone, whether native or alien, who blasphemes the name should be stoned by the entire community (vv.15–16). Our primary concern is with the first part of v.16, "whoever blasphemes the name of the Lord..." The Hebrew reads נקב שם יהוה, while the LXX gives the somewhat surprising reading ὀνομάζων δὲ τὸ ὄνομα κυρίου. At first glance, it appears that an edict against blasphemy has been transformed into a more general provision against uttering the name of the Lord. No less an authority than A. Marmorstein believes this is the meaning of the Greek text.[21]

On closer inspection, however, it becomes clear that the LXX has given a very reasonable translation of a difficult Hebrew original. The Hebrew verb נקב can simply mean "specify" or "designate" as well as "curse."[22] Moreover, one could (with Brown-Driver-Briggs) take יקב in Lev.24:11

---

[20] Heb. יקב. For a thorough discussion of this passage (particularly the verbs יקב and קלל) see J. Weingreen, "The Case of the Blasphemer," *VT* 22 (1972): 118–123. Far less satisfying is the treatment of J. B. Gabel and C. B. Wheeler, "The Redactor's Hand in the Blasphemy Pericope of Leviticus XXIV," *VT* 30 (1980): 227–9. They believe the prohibition against merely uttering the name lies in the MT itself. They write (p.227) : "Obviously the Priestly writer or redactor of the passage read back into the earlier period a custom from his own time that he felt required Mosaic authority." The redaction makes "the uttering of the divine name for any purpose a sin" (p.229). The latter statement ("...for any purpose...") is particularly problematic – would a priestly redactor really have believed that the high priest in the temple was sinning when he pronounced the name according to its letters on the day of atonement? There is also the serious problem that, as far as I can determine, Lev. 24:16 is not used in later tradition as a justification for not saying the tetragrammaton. In short, there is no compelling reason to adopt Gabel and Wheeler's proposal.

[21] Marmorstein, *The Old Rabbinic Doctrine of God* (London: Oxford, 1927), pp.17–18; Samuel S. Cohon, "The Name of God: A Study in Rabbinic Theology," *HUCA* 23, Part 1 (1950–51): 591.

[22] E.g. Is.62:2, which uses נקב to refer to God "designating" the new name (שם) of the restored Zion. Cf.s.v. נקב in William Holladay, *A Concise Hebrew and Aramaic Lexicon of the Old Testament* (Grand Rapids, MI: Eerdmans, 1971). Holladay lists Prov.11:26 "the one who hoards grain is cursed" under נקב, while Evan-Shoshan in his concordance lists this under נקב. If Evan-Shoshan is correct in his estimation, this would leave only the examples in Leviticus 24 as possible uses of נקב for "curse." See also Weingreen, pp.118–119.

as a qal imperfect of קבב, which does properly mean "curse" (as frequently in the Balaam narratives in Numbers 22–24).²³ The LXX translators appear to have derived the forms in Leviticus 24 from נקב, and then consistently rendered them in the sense of "designate" or "name,"²⁴ leaving the reader to realize from the context and the use of קלל/καταράομαι (vv.11,14) that the offense in question is in fact cursing God and not merely speaking His name. The translation could, of course, be *used* to support a prohibition against saying the divine name, but this does not mean the translators intended it to be taken that way.²⁵

Amos 6:10 presents similar problems. The context is not entirely clear, but Andersen and Freedman suggest that two men have come to bury their relatives – the relatives may perhaps have died in an epidemic after a siege.²⁶ After they have removed the corpses, the man outside asks the one inside if there is anything left. "No! Nothing!" he replies. The one outside answers, "Silence! For we must not invoke Yahweh's name."²⁷ The last line, according to Andersen and Freedman, refers to the fact that the normal funeral rites, including the invocation of YHWH's blessing on the dead, should not take place. The nation has been justly punished by YHWH, and it is therefore inappropriate to mourn in the usual manner.²⁸

Our primary concern is v.10, "Silence! For we must not invoke Yahweh's name!" The Hebrew reads הס כי לא להזכיר בשם יהוה, which the LXX renders Σίγα, ἕνεκα τοῦ μὴ ὀνομάσαι τὸ ὄνομα κυρίου. In the Greek bible, the *hiphil* of זכר is usually translated by the verb

---

²³ This will not work as well with the participle in v.16, though, and so the likelihood that יקב is derived from קבב in v.11 is lessened. Weingreen (p.119n) notes that the rabbis debated this very point, although he believes the derivation from יקב is certain and that the rabbis knew this. The "debate" was intended only to make the matter clear.

²⁴ ἐπονομάσας in v.11; ὀνομάζων and ὀνομάσαι in v.16.

²⁵ For further discussion, see Baudissin, 2:174–175.; cf. George Foot Moore, *Judaism in the First Centuries of the Christian Era* (Cambridge: Harvard University Press, 1927), pp.424–5. We would stress as well that even if one sees a prohibition against speaking the divine name in the LXX here, it is clearly in a context of cursing, and so should be linked with the prohibitions against swearing/cursing by the name which appear elsewhere in early Judaism. It does not necessarily inform us about the use or non-use of the name in greetings, prayer, etc. Weingreen (p.121) connects this passage with Ex.20:7 and Dt.5:11 and concludes that the offense in Lev.24:16 is using the divine name "for no reason." He also believes it is a "later development" than the surrounding material in Leviticus 24, although how much later he does not say.

²⁶ See F.I. Andersen and D. N. Freedman, *Amos*, AB (New York: Doubleday, 1989), pp.569–74.

²⁷ I have used Andersen and Freedman's translation.

²⁸ See Andersen and Freedman, pp.572–4. Their suggestion seems quite plausible, particularly in light of the parallels they cite in the careers of Jeremiah (chap. 16) and Ezekiel (chap. 24).

μιμνήσκομαι or its compounds.²⁹ This is quite fitting, since the Greek verb can mean "to make mention of" as well as "to remember."³⁰ The use of ὀνομάσαι would be something of a departure from the norm. It might even appear that the translator (perhaps influenced by Lev. 24:16 LXX) has made a tendentious translation to support a pre-existing practice of not "naming the name" of YHWH.

Before we conclude this, however, we must examine a very relevant set of parallels in Ex. 23:13 and Josh. 23:7. The passages teach, in *almost* identical language, that the Israelites are not to "mention" or "invoke" the names of other gods (Joshua has "their gods"):

Ex. 23:13: ושם אלהים אחרים לא תזכירו
Josh. 23:7: ובשם אלהיהם לא תזכירו

In both cases, the Hebrew uses the verb תזכירו. But the Greek text of Exodus translates this with ἀναμνησθήσεσθε, while Joshua has ὀνομασθήσεται. We cannot assume that the translator of Joshua is depending on Lev. 24:16 here. If anything, the context implies that one *would* "mention" or "invoke" the name of YHWH, as opposed to the names of other gods. The difference is best accounted for by grammar. Note that the Joshua text has a *beth* before the word "name," while the Exodus text lacks it. Our text in Amos likewise has the *beth* and translates with ὀνομάσαι. The same idiom may be witnessed in Jer. 20:9.³¹ It would appear that the translator of Joshua quite rightly distinguished his text from that of Exodus by using a conventional translation idiom in which זכר coupled with בשם would be rendered with a combination of ὀνομάζω and ὄνομα.³² If, as Andersen and Freedman suggest, להזכיר בשם יהוה in Am. 6:10 (and by extension, in Josh. 23:7) means to *invoke* the name of YHWH, we must say further that "naming the name" captures this just as well, if not better, than

---

²⁹ See, e.g., Gen. 40:14, 41:9; 1 Sa. 4:18; Is. 66:3; Ezek. 21:28, 29:16. An exception is Is. 49:1, which uses the verb ἐκάλεσεν.

³⁰ See LSJ, Bauer.

³¹ Note, however, that Jeremiah has a *qal* rather than a *hiphil*. The LXX reads Οὐ μὴ ὀνομάσω τὸ ὄνομα κυρίου for the the MT אזכרנו. What is important for us is that in the next strophe ("...or speak again in his name") the MT has בשמו. Thus it appears that the LXX has a slightly different *Vorlage*, or it has simply taken בשמו with both clauses. In either case, the grammatical point is evident. As in Joshua, "naming the name" is not seen as a bad thing here: despite his personal anguish over his message, Jeremiah knows he *must* "name the name of the Lord." (The LXX of Jer. 23:36 also employs ὀνομάζω for זכר.)

³² The idiom also appears in the MT of Is. 48:1. Unfortunately, the Greek appears to be translating a different *Vorlage* which makes it unhelpful for comparison.

"remembering the name." All in all, there is no evidence that the Greek gives us a tendentious translation of the Hebrew.[33]

On a final note, we should point out that in the rabbinic writings, the word זכר often occurs in the context of pronouncing the tetragrammaton (see examples below). It is thus *possible* that the language of Am. 6:10 influenced later discussion concerning the pronunciation of the divine name. It is equally likely, however, that this was simply the usual way to speak about pronouncing the name, and no explicit connection is intended. In support of this we may cite the fact that, as far as I am aware, Am. 6:10 is not introduced in later Judaism as a "proof-text" for supporting the prohibition against saying the name.

Qumran

Writing the Name

The Dead Sea Scrolls display a great diversity in their handling of the tetragrammaton. We find the conventional YHWH in square Hebrew characters (יהוה); YHWH in square characters but in red ink;[34] YHWH in paleo-Hebrew script; and the aforementioned transliteration ΙΑΩ in pap4QLXXLev[b].[35] The scribes also employed a number of substitutions for the tetragrammaton: other divine titles like El or Adonai, pronouns like "I" or "He," or even four dots inserted in the text where the name was to appear.

The majority of the Qumran texts employ the square or Aramaic script, although there are some which are entirely written in paleo-Hebrew

---

[33] We may also point out that in the New Testament, the phrase "naming the name" is nowhere associated with "not pronouncing the tetragrammaton." 2 Ti. 2:19 states, "Let him turn from unrighteousness, everyone naming the name of the Lord (πᾶς ὁ ὀνομάζων τὸ ὄνομα κυρίου)." The author appears to have merged Numbers 16:26 and some text containing "naming the name" (Lev. 24:16? Josh 23:7?). What is important is that naming the name is a good thing; it seems equivalent to "call upon the name of the Lord." (Cf. Joseph and Aseneth 11:17 for a similar use of "naming the name.") Whether the author is thinking of God or the Lord Jesus is not quite certain, although I would tend towards the former. This would be in contrast to Acts 19:13, where some Jewish exorcists attempt to "name the name of the Lord Jesus" over people with evil spirits.

[34] Joseph Fitzmyer, "The Semitic Background of the New Testament *Kyrios*-Title," in *A Wandering Aramean: Collected Aramaic Essays* (Missoula, MT: Scholars Press, 1979), pp.127,141 n. He notes that these are from as yet unpublished fragments from caves 4 and 11.

[35] See *DJD IX*, pp.163,168. For an overview of divine names at Qumran, see Stegemann, pp.195–217.

script.³⁶ In the *pesher* MSS from Qumran, for instance, we find the tetragrammaton written out in the conventional square lettering.³⁷ Skehan concludes that the "bulk of the strictly Biblical MSS from Qumran" follow this pattern.³⁸ It should be noted, however, that in the orthography of the period, the letters *yod* and *waw* were quite similar in appearance. Depending on a particular scribe's handwriting, the tetragrammaton could easily look like והוה rather than the modern יהוה. This is significant in that it accounts for the later use of the Greek letters ΠΙΠΙ for the tetragrammaton.

Although the appearance of the divine name in Aramaic script is less conspicuous than its appearance in paleo-Hebrew, there is some indication that even here the name was treated with special care. Yadin notes that in col. 17, l. 13 of the Temple Scroll, the scribe inadvertently omitted the *waw* from YHWH and inserted it later. He did not follow his usual practice of correcting above the line, however. The *waw* pokes its head up between the two *he's* from the bottom – Yadin describes it as "camouflaged." This is one of only two instances in the scroll where such a technique was used, and it argues for the special status of the divine name in the eyes of the scribe.³⁹

Such a high view of the name is obvious in those texts which write the tetragrammaton in paleo-Hebrew.⁴⁰ Skehan believes this was a later development within the community, beginning with 4Q171 (Herodian era) and 1QpHab (early first century CE).⁴¹ In any case, the use of paleo-Hebrew for the divine name soon became widespread, and is evidenced in, for example, 4QpPs^a; 1Q14,15; 11QPs^a; and 4QIs^c.⁴² The last two texts are worthy of special mention. 11QPs^a shows that scribes working at roughly the same time could treat the name in different ways: a contemporary copy, 11QPs^b, writes everything including YHWH in conventional square script. 4QIs^c, meanwhile, marks the final stage of the process by which divine names other than the tetragrammaton were also written in paleo-Hebrew. As Skehan puts it: "...the initial purpose of avoiding unwarranted utterance

---

³⁶ See Yigael Yadin, *The Temple Scroll: The Hidden Law of the Dead Sea Sect* (London: Weidenfeld and Nicolson, 1985), p.68.

³⁷ E.g. 4Q163, which Strugnell dates to the early 1st century BCE; the pre-Herodian 4Q162; and 4Q166–170, which date from the late Hasmonean to the later Herodian periods. See Skehan, "Divine Name," p.21.

³⁸ Skehan, "Divine Name," p.22.

³⁹ Yadin, p.68.

⁴⁰ See Stegemann, p.206.

⁴¹ Skehan, "Divine Name," pp.22–3; Jonathan P. Siegel, "The Employment of Paleo-Hebrew Characters for the Divine Names at Qumran in the Light of Tannaitic Sources," *HUCA* 42 (1971): 161.

⁴² Skehan, "Divine Name," pp.2–28.

of the divine name by his readers has given way to a kind of partly reverential, partly decorative, fetish."[43]

Twice in the Psalms scroll, one finds the name in paleoscript with four dots both above and below it.[44] It is noteworthy that in both instances, the tetragrammaton is found before אלוהו or אלוהים, and it is not found in the Masoretic text of the psalm being transcribed (Ps. 145:1 and Ps. 138:1). M.H. Segal notes that in the transmission of the Hebrew bible, doubtful readings were marked by dots above and below (cf. b. Ber. 9c).[45] It appears that the scribe, being familiar with the reading preserved in the MT, was doubtful of the reading in the text he was copying. It is also possible that he inadvertently wrote the name and employed the dots as a way of indicating his error rather than erasing the name.[46]

Shemaryahu Talmon believes that the tetragrammaton in paleo-Hebrew was written in after the rest of the text was completed, a further sign of the special treatment accorded to the name.[47] At times, this special treatment extended to prefixes and suffixes which were attached to the tetragrammaton. In 4QIs^c, both prefixes and suffixes attached to the tetragrammaton were written in the old script, an indication that they somehow shared in the holiness of the name.[48] That this was not the universal practice is shown by 11QPs^a, where one finds the prepositions *lamed, beth,* and *kaph* in square script, even though they are attached to YHWH in paleoscript.[49] Siegel relates this to the rabbinic rule (y. Megillah *1:* 9 [71d]) which permitted the erasure of prefixes but not suffixes when writing the divine name.[50]

The matter of when one used paleo-Hebrew script is open to question. Yadin argues that the older script was used when quoting the Bible, while actual biblical texts employed the square script. The fact that the Psalms at Qumran depart from this pattern, he says, is certainly a matter of controversy, but the general rule still holds.[51] Siegel, on the other hand, asserts that the biblical or non-biblical context is not necessarily the criterion for

---

[43] Skehan, "Divine Name," p.28. For the text of 11QPs^a see *Discoveries in the Judaean Desert of Jordan IV,* ed. James Sanders (Oxford: Oxford University Press, 1965).

[44] *DJD IV,* p.13. The occurrences are in 16:7 and 21:2.

[45] M.H. Segal, "The Promulgation of the Authoritative Text of the Hebrew Bible," *JBL* 72 (1953): 42.

[46] Siegel emphasizes the permanence of the divine name in his article on paleo-Hebrew at Qumran, p.171.

[47] Siegel, p.161; Stegemann, p.204.

[48] Siegel, p.161.

[49] See the discussion in Skehan, "Divine Name," pp.24–5.

[50] Siegel, p.164.

[51] Yadin, pp. 67–8.

the employment of paleo-Hebrew for the divine name. He cites simple scribal preference as the determining factor for its use or non-use.[52] In light of the use of paleo-Hebrew in the Psalter, it is perhaps best to speak of a tendency to use this script in biblical quotations, without solidifying it into an actual rule.

Respect for the divine name is equally evident in texts which omit it altogether. The scribes of 1QS, 4Q175-6, 4QSam[c] and 1QIsa[a], for instance, substitute four dots in place of YHWH.[53] In Is.42:6 of 1QIsa[a], however, the יהוה of the MT has been left out, and a different scribe has added *five* dots above the line. Skehan concludes quite reasonably that this represents the *plene* spelling of Adonai (אדוני), which illustrates the use of this *qere* at this time.[54]

At times scribes tendentiously substituted pronouns for the divine name. The Temple scroll regularly substitutes "I said" for "the Lord said," although this is probably less an indication of a concern to avoid writing the name than it is of the scribe's intention to elevate the Temple Scroll to the status of an authoritative promulgation of doctrine for the community.[55] In CD 9:5, the tetragrammaton is twice removed in a quotation from Nah.1:2 and replaced with הוא.[56] We find an elongated form of הוא in 1QS 8:13; the text has הואהא.[57] The substitution of יהוה with הוא may derive from Is. 42:8 אני יהוה הוא שמי. Rather than reading it as "I am YHWH, this [i.e. YHWH] is my name..." they apparently understood it as "I am YHWH, 'Hu' is my name." Perhaps this was interpreted to mean that 'Hu' was the acceptable substitute for the tetragrammaton.

---

[52] Siegel, p.164.

[53] Emile Puech, "Une apocalypse messianique (4Q521)," *RQ* 60 (Oct.1992): 516; Skehan, "Divine Name," pp.14–15, 25. Examples of this include 1QIsa[a] col. 33, above line 7; 1QS 8:14; 4QSam[c] fragment 1, line 3; and col. 3, line 7; and 4Q175, lines 1 and 19. Stegemann (pp.204-5 n) suggests that the practice may derive from those Greek MSS of the Bible wherein four dots were used to mark the place where the tetragrammaton in Hebrew would later be inserted.

[54] Skehan, "Divine Name," p.25. The MT reads אני יהוה קראתיך, while the scroll has אני קרתיכה with the dots above the line. See also Howard, p.66. This substitution of Adonai for the tetragrammaton naturally invalidates W. Bousset's claim that this practice was not in place in the time of Jesus (*Kyrios Christos*, trans. John Steely; Nashville: Abingdon, 1970, p.128).

[55] See Yadin, pp.65ff.; he notes quotations from Dt.12:26 and Nu.30:2. Recall that elsewhere the scribe has no compunctions about writing the name in the square script.

[56] Joseph M. Baumgarten, "A New Qumran Substitute for the Divine Name and Mishnah Sukkah 4.5," *JQR* 83 (1992): 2. Baumgarten (p.3) notes that this occurs in a blessing formula, although the את ברוכ is written above the line. On the same page he lists examples of other substitutions for YHWH in blessing formulae.

[57] Puech, p.516; Baumgarten, "Qumran Substitute," p.2.

Baumgarten isolates a related substitution in 4Q266 (cf. 1QS 11:15).⁵⁸ We find there a blessing formula ברוכ את אונ הו הכול.⁵⁹ Baumgarten renders this "Blessed are you, אונ הו of everything..." He feels that the writer is "disguising the divine name by blending it with the invocative אנא," and that this is parallel to the use of אני והוא in the Palestinian Targum and אני והו in *m. Suk.* 4:5 (see below).⁶⁰ I believe this is a reasonable explanation of a difficult text. It is true that "the All" could function independently as a divine epithet (see Sir. 43:27), such that 4Q266 might be read "Blessed are you, אונ הו, the All..." But this still leaves us with the strange phrase אונ הו. As Baumgarten himself suggests, the phrase אונ הו הכול could be a corruption of אדון הלוכ, "Lord of all," a phrase which appears in 11QPs 28:7 and 4Q409 1, ll.6,8.⁶¹ "Blessed are you, Lord of all..." would be a very natural blessing formula.

Is Baumgarten, then, still correct to say that אונ הו is a substitute *for the tetragrammaton*, since it seems to function as a substitute for Adon? I would say yes. In *m. Suk.* 4:5, for instance, the very similiar phrase אני והו is clearly a substitute for YHWH in Ps. 118:25. The substitution of Adon/Adonai for YHWH is of course a commonplace in early Judaism, and would have occured in blessing formulae (see e.g. 4Q408, discussed below). It appears that the writer of 4Q266 wished to return to the biblical blessing formulae, which generally employ the tetragrammaton. Yet his scruples against actually pronouncing the tetragrammaton led him to use the substitute form אונ הו. This may seem like a somewhat unusual procedure, but 4Q266 is an unusual text.⁶²

More common was the practice of using other divine designations such as El or Adonai in place of the tetragrammaton. El occurs over 50 times in 1QS and its appendices, and according to Skehan, it is manifestly a spoken replacement for YHWH in 1QSa 2:4 (cf. Dt.23:2–4) and 1QSb 5:25 (in a

---

⁵⁸ Baumgarten, "Qumran Substitute," pp.1–5.

⁵⁹ Baumgarten argues against the suggestion that the text ought to be read "You are the all," (*sic*; הכול expected) את הו הכל in his article " אונ הו - את הו הכול הכול: A Reply to M. Kister" *JQR* 84 (1994): 485–87). He provides a very clear photograph of the text to prove his point. He notes that the presence of a medial *nun* in final position poses no problem, since this is a characteristic of this particular scribe.

⁶⁰ We might also mention here the proposal by Baillet (accepted by Puech, p.516) that 4Q511, fr.10 substitutes יוד for the divine name in the phrase "the judgments of ירוד" (cf. the "judgments of YHWH" in Ps.19:10). But G. Wilhelm Nebe argues convincingly that this is simply a scribal error for "the judgments of his hand" – "his hand" being ידו. See Nebe, "Der Buchstabenname Yod als Ersatz des Tetragramms in 4Q511, Frag.10, Zeile 12?" *RQ* 12 (1986): 283–4.

⁶¹ "Reply to Kister," pp.485–7; cf. "New Qumran Substitute," p.3 n.

⁶² Baumgarten himself relates 4Q266 to the rabbinic teaching that the name was "swallowed up" by the elders of Israel in former times (tBer. 7:23). I am not completely convinced of this association, but it is possible.

paraphrase of Is.11:1–5).⁶³ In 1QH and 1QM, El is again used frequently of God. We have already alluded to the presence of the more familiar *qere* of Adonai at Qumran in the five dots of 1QIsaᵃ. Strugnell notes that in 4Q134, the tetragrammaton (in square script) is preceded by two dots (like an English colon), which he believes is an indication to substitute the *qere* – presumably Adonai – and to avoid pronouncing the name itself.⁶⁴ More explicit evidence is found in 1QH 7:28, where Adonai replaces YHWH in the text of Ex.15:11. It was also the designation of choice for the scribe of 1QSb in his descriptions of God as the source of blessing.⁶⁵ It is inserted in place of YHWH in Ps.129:4 and Ps.130:1 of 11QPsᵃ; usually the scribe wrote the tetragrammaton in paleoscript.⁶⁶ The case for the *qere* of Adonai is cemented by the recently published text of 4Q408. Line 6 contains the familiar OT blessing formula ברוך יהוה. But the scribe has corrected himself and inserted above the line אדני אתה .⁶⁷ The most likely explanation of this is that the manuscript has been thus altered to prevent someone reading the name YHWH aloud.⁶⁸

Greek and Aramaic Texts

We have already noted the presence of IAΩ in pap4QLXXLevᵇ. As for the Aramaic material, 4QEnᵇ employs מרא in 1 En. 9:4⁶⁹ and מריא in 10:9.⁷⁰

---

⁶³ Skehan, "Divine Name," p.16. We must also be aware, however, that some of these "substitutions" may simply represent textual traditions which diverge from the MT. James Davila isolates one such instance in 4QGenExodᵃ, where Elohim appears in Gen. 22:14 for the MT's YHWH. He notes that the Syriac Peshitta appears to have a *Vorlage* of מלאך אלהים. See Davila, "The Name of God at Moriah: An Unpublished Fragment from 4QGenExodᵃ," *JBL* 110 (1991): 577–82.

⁶⁴ Siegel, p.171.

⁶⁵ Skehan, "Divine Name," pp.16–17.

⁶⁶ Skehan ("Divine Name," pp.23–24) concludes, "This lapse from his usual style shows clearly what the scribe of 11QPsᵃ was pronouncing when he encountered the divine name."

⁶⁷ See Annette Steudel, "4Q408: A Liturgy on Morning and Evening Prayer – Preliminary Edition," *RQ* 63 (1994): 313–334. She states on p.316 that the correction appears to be by the same hand that wrote the text. On the basis of paleography she dates the text to the Hasmonean period (perhaps early in that era, see pp.318–9).

⁶⁸ Steudel suggests (pp.332–3) that the scribe actually had a *Vorlage* of אתה אדני, but "fell back into the style of the biblical psalms" while copying the text. This may be, but the *kethib/qere* solution seems more obvious. Cf. the brief study by Steven Byington, in which he concluded after a comparison of 1QIsaᵃ and the MT that "some passages indicate that יהוה was pronounced אדני at the time and place of the writing of 1QIsaᵃ; no passage indicates the contrary." See Byington, "יהוה and אדני," *JBL* 76 (1957): 58–9.

⁶⁹ For text, see Klaus Beyer, *Die aramäischen Texte vom Toten Meer* (Göttingen: Vandenhoeck and Ruprecht, 1984), p.337.

The relevant text for 4QEn^b 9:4 has מרנא רבא [הו]א מרא עלמא extant,[71] while the latter has מ]ריא] (with the *resh* being only somewhat legible). We also note the presence of מרי, "my Lord" in Prayer of Enoch 10.[72] Although the reading in 10:9 could correspond to a *Vorlage* of YHWH (if indeed there is a Hebrew *Vorlage*), the fact that the two other readings would translate as Adon/Adonai make it likely that "Lord" (Adonai/κύριος/ מרא) was already functioning as an independent divine epithet at the time of the composition of this portion of Enoch.

Saying the Name

The Qumran texts contain only one passage which directly discusses the use of the name YHWH:1QS 6:27–7:2.[73] It presents problems in text, translation, and interpretation. For the purpose of discussion, we will first present Vermes' complete English translation:

> If any man has uttered the [Most] Venerable Name {col. 7} even though frivolously, or as a result of shock or for any other reason whatever, while reading the Book or

---

[70] The Greek equivalent in 1En.10:9 is ὁ ΚΣ. See Joseph Fitzmyer, "New Testament Kyrios and Maranatha and their Aramaic Background," in *To Advance the Gospel: New Testament Studies* (NY: Crossroad, 1981), p.22.

[71] Matthew Black renders the Ethiopic, "...our great Lord, Lord of the ages, Lord of Lords..." and we can plausibly posit the use of מרא in the portion of the verse immediately following עלמא (Black, *The Book of Enoch or 1 Enoch*; Leiden: Brill, 1985). This is significant because there is an extant fragment of this verse in Hebrew in 1Q19, and there "Lord of Lords" is rendered [את] אדון אדונים (see Beyer, p.337; *Discoveries in the Judaean Desert I*, eds. D. Barthélemy and J.T. Milik (Oxford: Oxford University Press, 1955), p.152).

[72] Beyer, p.266; cf. Stegemann, pp.210ff.

[73] CD 15:1 refers to not swearing by El/Elohim or Adonai. Although this does not directly concern YHWH, the notion of *not swearing* by the name is a quite significant one. The background for this passage is Lev.19:12, which states that "You shall not swear falsely by my name, and profane the name of your God. I am YHWH." In CD, the notion of not swearing falsely (לשקר) has been expanded to a general prohibition against the swearing of oaths by any of the names of God. (The fact that YHWH is not mentioned does not, of course, imply that one *can* swear by that name. CD avoids the use of YHWH altogether, using El as the designation for God.) Instead, one is to swear by the curses of the covenant. The following line makes the rationale clear, although here the prohibition is extended even to the Law of Moses: "He shall not mention the Law of Moses for...were he to swear and then break (his oath) he would profane the Name (Vermes)." That is, swearing by God, or even by the Law which was so closely associated with him, could entail making God party to a falsehood should the oath not come to pass. Since this could result from lack of information, change of circumstances, etc., as well as from deliberate falsehood, it was thought best to avoid such oaths altogether. If one followed the prescribed formula of swearing by the curses of the covenant, however, God's reputation was kept free from blemish. See the discussion in Lawrence Schiffman, *Sectarian Law in the Dead Sea Scrolls* (Chico, CA: Scholars Press, 1983), pp.136ff.

praying, he shall be dismissed and shall return to the Council of the Community no more.[74]

The crucial textual question lies in the junction of the end of column 6 and the beginning of column 7. The Hebrew reads:

שר יזכיר דבר בשם הנכבד על כול ה] (6:27)

[75]ואם קלל או להבעת מצרה או לכול דבר (7:1)

The editors of *Die Texte aus Qumran* feel that the small lacuna at the end of column 6 justifies a full break, and thus in their translation they begin a new sentence with 7:1.[76] Vermes, on the other hand, carries on in full stride from 6:27 to 7:1. This raises the question of what relationship exists between the uttering of the name (6:27) and the cursing which results in expulsion from the community. Unfortunately, textual analysis alone will not give us the answer.

One must first decide how to render יזכיר דבר בשם הנכבד. The verb is a hiphil of זכר, thus, "cause to remember," or more idiomatically, "utter," "mention." This is the interpretation of יזכיר given in all the translations noted thus far. Lawrence Schiffman and P. Wernberg-Møller, however, both understand it as "swear."[77] Even if one takes it as "utter," the translation "whoever utters a word by (or "in") the glorious name against anyone..."(cf. *Die Texte aus Qumran*) seems to imply something more than simply speaking the name. It appears that someone could be in-

---

[74] Geza Vermes, *The Dead Sea Scrolls in English*, 3rd Edition (Sheffield: JSOT Press, 1987), pp.70–71. Florentino García Martínez renders it: "Whoever enunciates the Name (which is) honoured above all [...] (Col. 7) whether blaspheming, or overwhelmed by misfortune or for any other reason, {...} or reading a book, or blessing, will be excluded, and shall not go back to the Community council." García Martínez, *The Dead Sea Scrolls Translated*, trans. by Wilfred G.E. Watson (Leiden: Brill/Grand Rapids, MI: Eerdmans, 1996), p.11. Cf. Skehan (p.15): "Whoever invokes the glorious Name in a statement... [he then states that the text does not preserve the circumstances] but if he has uttered a curse either because he was shaken by some crisis, or whatever may have prompted him to it, then reads from the Book or offers a blessing, they shall exclude him from the community."

[75] *Die Texte aus Qumran* 3rd ed.; ed. Eduard Lohse (Darmstadt: Wissenschaftliche Buchgesellschaft, 1981), p.24. The translation is: "[W]er etwas erwähnt im Namen dessen, der hochgeehrt ist, gegen jemanden, [...]." Col. 7 begins: "Und wenn er einen Fluch ausgesprochen hat, etwa er durch eine Notlage verängstigt war, oder welchen Anlaß er auch haben mag..."

[76] There is a small tear in the lower left hand corner of col. 6 after the *he*. Only one or two words would be able to fit in the gap. See the photographs of the MS in *The Scrolls from Qumran Cave 1*, photographs by John C. Trever (Jerusalem: Albright Institute and Shrine of the Book, 1972).

[77] Schiffman, p.133; P. Wernberg-Møller, *The Manual of Discipline* (Leiden: Brill, 1957); see his translation and notes on pp.112–3. Holladay (s.v. זכר) notes the use of the hiphil of זכר with בשם as an idiom for swearing in Is.48:1 and Am.6:10.

voking God *against* someone. An oath or curse would provide a natural setting for this.[78] As for בשם הנכבד, "the glorious Name" is quite fitting. Schiffman argues convincingly that in light of the parallels elsewhere in Jewish literature (e.g. Dt.28:58, Sir.47:18), this must refer to the tetragrammaton.[79]

As for column 7, I would prefer the translation "if he has uttered a curse..." (cf. Skehan and *Die Texte aus Qumran*) for ואם קלל rather than Vermes' "even though frivolously."[80] The only other major question is how one renders the clause אשר לו הואה קורה בספר או מברך. Skehan translates, "(but if he has uttered a curse)...*then reads from the Book or utters a blessing...*"[81] Vermes has "(If any man has uttered the...Name)...*while reading the Book or praying...*" The latter seems a more natural rendering of the participles קורה and מברך, and it seems more likely that the name would be read *while* reading or blessing rather than *prior to* such activity.

My own summary translation would run: "If a person invokes the glorious name against anyone...or if he utters a curse whether from being overcome by distress, or anything else which might happen to him; while reading in the book or blessing; then let him be separated and not return again to the council of the community." It does not seem coincidental that elsewhere (e.g. OT, rabbinic literature), *oaths/curses* (cf. Jewish interpretation of the third commandment; exegetical tradition of Lev.24:10ff.); *Scripture reading* (as witnessed in the scribal habits at Qumran); and *blessings* (cf. employment of the name in the temple blessing) constitute the major categories around which debate about the use of the divine name centered.

It is difficult to know what to make of all this, but I would propose the following tentative explanation. The possibility that the offense in 6:27 involves an oath of some kind would make a transition to curses (7:2) quite

---

[78] Even if one follows García Martínez and has the על כול modify the Name ("honoured *above all*), the idea of swearing could still be supported by the Old Testament parallels.

[79] Schiffman, p.133; Skehan points out ("Divine Name," p.16) that the scribes' avoidance of YHWH throughout 1QS is further evidence that the "glorious Name" is YHWH.

[80] We might compare in this regard the phrase אשר יחלל את שם, "one who curses (or "profanes") the name," which occurs in a list of other transgressors (e.g. necromancers) in fragments from 4Q of the Damascus Document, 4Q270, fr.9, 1:11 (cited by Baumgarten, "Qumran Substitute," p.5.) Unfortunately, the precise context of this phrase is lost to us. We must also reckon with the fact that "profanation of the name" was not necessarily a matter of saying the name at the wrong time or in the wrong way. The name was usually seen as being profaned by the sinful *actions* of people. What is in question here is more likely to be moral offense rather than ritual offense.

[81] The translation in *Die Texte aus Qumran* is essentially the same, employing *und* instead of "then."

plausible. The end of column 6 and the beginning of column 7 would thus appear to list a number of circumstances under which one might intentionally or unintentionally utter the divine name YHWH. These would include oaths, curses, "crises," Scripture reading, or prayers/blessings. The penalty for such is expulsion from the community. If such a reconstruction is correct, it would provide evidence for a thoroughgoing ban on the pronunciation of the tetragrammaton at Qumran, at least at some point in the history of the community. Even if this precise reconstruction is faulty, the text suggests some type of prohibition with regards to uttering the name under certain circumstances.[82]

Apocrypha and Pseudepigrapha[83]

Writing the Name

Since most of the manuscripts we have of the Apocrypha and Pseudepigrapha significantly post-date the New Testament era, orthography *per se* is of little interest to us. We do find the tetragrammaton in square script in fragments of the book of Jubilees found at Qumran.[84] One does not want to make too much of this evidence, but it does indicate that those writings which did have Hebrew originals may have employed the tetragrammaton in the text.[85] This does not mean, of course, that the name was pronounced.

The closest thing we have to an actual use of the name YHWH outside of these fragments in Jubilees is the aforementioned transliteration *Iao* and variants such as *IHU* and *Iaoel*. In verse 8 of the Prayer of Jacob we find, "you who sit [upon] the s[er]pen[t] gods/the [God who s]i[t]s [upon the

---

[82] A possible exception to this prohibition *may* be in the case of exorcisms (e.g. 11Q11, 1:2–4, which includes the name YHWH). One would imagine that the powerful name of YHWH would be the most effective weapon in conflict with demons. It may be that even here the tetragrammaton was substituted for by Adonai, but there is a genuine possibility that on these (presumably) rare occasions YHWH itself was pronounced.

[83] A note on the editions used. The general translation for the Apocrypha used is the Revised Standard Version, as found in the *Oxford Annotated Apocrypha*, ed. Bruce Metzger (NY: Oxford University Press, 1965). For the Pseudepigrapha, I have generally used *The Old Testament Pseudepigrapha*, ed. James H. Charlesworth, 2 vols. (NY: Doubleday, 1983; henceforth *OTP*). Other translations will be cited as relevant.

[84] See, e.g., 4Q216, fr.1, col.I:3: "by the word of YHWH" for an extent witness. García Martínez restores YHWH frequently to the Jubilees texts based on the non-Hebrew witnesses, pp.238–245. See *DJD* XIII, eds. Harold Attridge, et al. (Oxford: Oxford University Press, 1994).

[85] Skehan likewise argues from the discrepancies between the Cairo MS B and the Masada scroll of Sirach that YHWH stood in the original text of that book. The avoidance of the tetragrammaton in the Masada scroll is in his eyes a later development. The Cairo MS substitutes ייי for the divine name. Skehan, "Divine Name," pp.18–20.

s]un, Iao."⁸⁶ In the Ladder of Jacob (extant only in the Slavonic Explanatory Palaia) 2:17-18, Jacob sings of God: "Twelve-topped, twelve-faced, many-named, Holy, Holy, Holy, Yao, Yaova, Yaoil, Yao, Kados, Chavod, Savaoth...fiery one! Lightning-eyed holy one!" The Testament of Solomon contains apparent variations of Iao in its list of names which overcome the thirty-six "world rulers of the darkness of this age": "Angel, Eae, Ieo, Sabaoth" (18:15) and "Iae, Ieo, sons of Sabaoth" (18:16) are said to be effective against the spirits of fights and feuds in the home, and dissensions. In The Life of Adam and Eve (Vita) 14:2, we read: "And Michael himself worshipped [Adam] first, and called me [the devil] and said, 'Worship the image of God, *IHU*.'" One should probably take *IHU* as modifying God, but it could perhaps refer to Adam himself.⁸⁷ Finally, we note the presence of compound names like Iaoel in the Apocalypse of Abraham 10:3,8 (where it refers to an angel) and 17:13 (where it appears as a name for God);⁸⁸ and Iael in Apocalypse of Moses 29:4,33:5.⁸⁹ We will deal with the latter passages in our section on the significance of the name.

It is not surprising to find that the Apocrypha and Pseudepigrapha in their Greek exemplars frequently use substitutions for the name YHWH, primarily κύριος.⁹⁰ It would be tedious to multiply examples.⁹¹ One could look for representative purposes at the Wisdom of Solomon, which follows in the wisdom tradition of Proverbs. The latter uses YHWH frequently as its designation for God, and this is reflected in the use of κύριος in the

---

⁸⁶ Charlesworth (*OTP* 2: 721) notes that the Greek could also be rendered "upon the Sun-god Iao" or "upon Helios Iao."

⁸⁷ Some manuscripts omit the name *IHU* altogether, indicating the scribes may have felt *IHU* was, or at least appeared to be, applied to Adam. In the absence of other evidence for Adam actually being called by the divine name, it is best to understand *IHU* as pertaining to God himself. See M.D. Johnson's notes in *OTP* 2: 262, and the discussions in Baudissin, 2: 190-91, and Fossum, pp.277-8.

⁸⁸ D.J. Harrington (*OTP* 2: 338) notes that the name Jahel in LAB 26:12 ought to refer to Solomon, since Jahel is described here as the one who will build a house in God's name. He also suggests that this could be a reference to the angel Iaoel as in Ap. Abr. 10:4, 9. Ginzberg is more emphatic in affirming that this is Solomon. In *Legends of the Jews* 7 vols. (Philadelphia: Jewish Publication Society of America, 1946), 6:183 n, he says that the problem is easily solved when one renders the passage back into Hebrew, employing the name Ithiel (אתיאל) for Solomon (cf. Prov. 30:1). A scribe, not understanding this, wrote Jahel.

⁸⁹ The Gk. form of the latter is Ἰαήλ. Text in Daniel A. Bertrand, *La vie grecque d'Adam et Ève* (Paris: Adrien Maisonneuve, 1987). A variant form Ἰοὲλ appears in texts C,R,E,F; Bertrand (p.132) cites a parallel in the *Gospel of the Egyptians* (NH III,2), p.44, 1.27, and p.65, 1.23.

⁹⁰ We can include the *Dominus* of the Latin texts and מרא in the Aramaic in this same discussion.

⁹¹ Foerster provides a summary and statistics of the use of κύριος in the Apocrypha and Pseudepigrapha in his article "κυριος" in *TDNT*, 3:1082-3.

Wisdom of Solomon. Another interesting appearance of this designation comes in the Greek additions to the book of Esther, especially in the prayers of Mordecai and Esther (AV 13:8–14:19; LXX 4:17a–17z). Here κύριος appears so frequently (18 times in these verses) it almost seems like a deliberate attempt to somehow counterbalance the notorious absence of God's name in the Hebrew original. Also worthy of note are those phrases which correspond to Hebrew phrases containing the tetragrammaton. Thus we find "the Lord our God" (Bar.1:10ff.; cf. "Lord my God" Bel 25); and "O Lord Almighty, God of Israel" (Bar.3:1; cf. 4 Ezra 1:15; Pr. Man. 1). Baudissin concludes from his study of the post-biblical Jewish literature that these writers employed κύριος in place of the *Vorlage* YHWH (for those books with Hebrew originals) or on the model of the written or spoken tetragrammaton with which they were familiar.[92]

There are also instances where κύριος itself appears to be avoided. This might indicate an aversion to using even this derived divine title on the part of the author or translator. Foerster notes that the Sibylline Oracles, III and IV Maccabees, and the Letter of Aristeas all avoid κύριος.[93] An even more striking example is the absence of this term in I Maccabees. God is not even referred to until 2:61, and there only as a pronoun without an antecedent.[94] Thereafter, the preferred designation for God is "Heaven" (οὐρανός), as in 4:24: "On their return they sang hymns and praises to Heaven, for he is good, for his mercy endures forever."[95] One also finds designations such as "the God of Heaven" and "the Most High"[96] (Tob. 1:3,4,13;4:11, etc; Sir. 4:10; 7:9,15; 24:23,etc..).[97]

The Apocrypha and Pseudepigrapha sometimes employ ὄνομα as a substitute for YHWH. A clear example is the mention of the "name of God, ineffable in glory" engraved on the mitre of the high priest (Ep. Arist. l.98).[98] One must observe instances of "the name of God" with caution,

---

[92] Baudissin, 2:190.

[93] Foerster, 3:1082. The introduction to the book of Baruch in the Oxford Annotated Apocrypha points out that κύριος occurs only in the first part of the book (1:1–3:8) and is lacking in the distinctive second section (3:9–5:9).

[94] "...none who put their trust in him (ἐπ᾽ αὐτον) will lack strength."

[95] This usage, and the related designation "God of Heaven" (cf. Dan. 2:19), may have contributed to the idea held by certain Greek and Roman authors that the Jews worshipped heaven. Cf. Diodorus Siculus *Bibliotheca Historica*, XL,3; Juvenal *Saturae*,XIV, 97; *Contra Celsum* V,6. for references and discussion see Menahem Stern, ed., *Greek and Latin Authors on Jews and Judaism* 3 vols. (Jerusalem: Israel Academy of Sciences and Humanities, 1974), 1: 20–29; 2: 102,132–3,253,283; and Hengel, *Judaism and Hellenism*, 1: 255ff.

[96] See, e.g., Ep. Arist. 19; 4 Ezra *passim*, 2 Baruch 6:6,17:2; Ap. Zeph. A. For further examples and discussion, see Hengel, *Judaism and Hellenism*, 1: 296–8.

[97] This does not preclude his use of κύριος, cf.2:2.

[98] Cf. 1 Esdras 1:48; Sir. 45:15; Jud. 9:7.

however, since it does not always refer to the tetragrammaton. As often as not, the "name" suggests the reputation or fame of God rather than an appellation. The context alone determines whether or not "the name" is an actual surrogate for YHWH.[99]

Saying the Name

There are many references in the Apocrypha and Pseudepigrapha to God's name being "unutterable" or shrouded behind a veil of secrecy. "Or who will be able even to hear only the name of the great heavenly God who rules the world?" asks the Sibylline Oracle (3:18–19). The Apocalypse of Zephaniah (A) describes him as "the ineffable (Gk. ἄρρητος) most high God,"[100] and Ap. Abr. 10:4 speaks of the "ineffable name" of God.[101] In a similar vein, a Jewish interpolation in a poem by Diphilus speaks of "God, the Lord of all...whose name is awesome, and I would not utter it."[102] In the Lives of the Prophets 2:16, Jeremiah is said to have put the ark and other holy things inside a rock and sealed it with the name of God. The mystery was heightened when "a cloud covered the Name, and no one knows the place, nor is able to read the Name to this day and to the consummation."[103]

Closely related to this idea of the mysterious nature of the name is the concept of man's inability to fully grasp the nature of God, which can be

---

[99] A special case involves texts where the name is said to be "upon" or "in" Israel, or Israel is "called by the name" of God. It is unclear in the texts from the Apocrypha and Pseudepigrapha whether the name YHWH is directly in view. I tend to think the phrase has been taken from the Old Testament and used in a general way to describe God's presence with his people. In the Targums, however, there is more explicit mention of the name YHWH in this respect (see below in our section on the significance of the name). Examples of the name being on Israel in the Apocrypha and Pseudepigrapha include 2 Macc.8:15 (which could refer to the name YHWH with its phrase, "his holy and glorious name"); Bar. 2:15 (the "name" is quite prominent throughout this chapter); Sir. 36:12; 4 Ez.4:25, 10:22; 2 Bar.48:23; T12P, TDan 6:7 (God's name will be throughout Israel); Pss. Sol. 9:9; cf. Odes of Sol. 8:19, 22:6; Ap. Elijah 1:9.

[100] Note, too, Ap. Zeph.6:7, where the seer calls upon "Eloe, Lord, Adonai, Sabaoth"; and Sib. Or. 3:11. The juxtaposition of Adonai and Sabaoth could be a reflection of the *qere* of Adonai for YHWH. But as O.S. Wintermute points out in his notes (*OTP* 1: 512), "...it would appear that the author of this text was not well acquainted with Hebrew." Both Adonai and Sabaoth functioned as independent divine epithets elsewhere (e.g. in the magical papyri), and so their appearance here together could be coincidental.

[101] The Ascension of Isaiah 1:7 reads, "As the LORD lives whose name has not been transmitted to this world and as the Beloved of my LORD lives, and as the Spirit...(cf.7:37)" The Ascension is a Christian work, but it may preserve earlier Jewish tradition.

[102] Preserved in Clement, *Stromata* 5.14.121,1–3. See *OTP* 2: 828–9.

[103] Trans. D.R.A. Hare, *OTP* 2: 388. There is also mention of a hidden name in 1 En. 69:14. We will reserve discussion of this for the following chapter.

expressed by saying that God is essentially nameless.[104] O.S. Wintermute's comments on the use of ἄρρητος in the Apocalypse of Zephaniah summarize the matter neatly. "[It] may be used of God in two senses: (1) one who is indescribable because he is beyond comprehension, and (2) one whose name ought not to be spoken outside of a limited cultic setting." He admits that it is difficult to know which applies in the Apocalypse of Zephaniah.[105] (The same might be said for Sib.Or. 3:18-19, quoted above.)

The restrictions against using the divine name in oaths which we noted in our discussion of Qumran has parallels in the Apocrypha and Pseudepigrapha, most notably in Sir.23:9-10. In his "instruction concerning speech" Sirach declares: "Do not accustom your mouth to oaths, and do not habitually utter the name of the Holy One; for as a servant who is continually examined under torture will not lack bruises, so also the man who always swears and utters the Name[106] will not be cleansed from sin." The following verse goes on to describe the unforgivable iniquity of the one who utters many oaths. The offense thus consists not in speaking the name *per se*, but rather in using it in frequent oaths. This would be objectionable for at least two reasons. First, the violation of such oaths would drag the name into disrepute. Second, one presumes that these oaths would often be for relatively petty concerns. If so, this might be viewed as taking the name in vain, contrary to the third commandment.[107]

---

[104] Hengel, *Judaism and Hellenism*, 1: 266-7; C.H. Dodd, *The Bible and the Greeks* (London: Hodder and Stoughton, 1935), p.3. It is generally said that this is a Greek idea (see, e.g. Marmorstein, *Old Rabbinic Doctrine of God*, pp.17ff.). See below in our discussion on namelessness in Philo.

[105] In the first instance, God's name cannot be known (or indeed he has no name) and therefore *cannot* be uttered. In the second, it can be known but *ought not* to be uttered. See Wintermute, in *OTP* 1: 508 n. Hengel (*Judaism and Hellenism*, 1:266-7), believes that the Jews developed the idea of the "essential namelessness of God" after the cultic prohibition of pronouncing the name was already well established, "making a virtue of necessity," as he puts it. Cf. Wis. 14:21, where idolaters give wood and stone "the name that ought not to be shared" (τὸ ἀκοινώνητον ὄνομα), although this is properly more a statement about God's uniqueness than his incomprehensibility. 4 Bar. 6:13 speaks of "the great name which no one can know," but S.E. Robinson believes this is a Christian interpolation (*OTP* 2: 415).

[106] Gk. ὁ ὀμνύων καὶ ὀνομάζων, lit. "the one swearing and naming..." (A,Sc add τὸ ὄνομα κυρίου.)

[107] Sir.23:12 may allude to someone actually cursing the name of God: "There is an utterance which is comparable to death; may it never be found in the inheritance of Jacob." But this is not certain. This passage may be in part a reflection upon the case of the blasphemer in Lev.24:10ff. In Jub. 36:7, Isaac makes his sons swear by the "great name," surely the tetragrammaton. This may simply be a biblical motif not reflective of contemporary practice - although Schiffman (p.140) does think the early Tannaim used the tetragrammaton in oaths. (We will discuss the Jubilees passage again in our discussion of the significance of the name.)

The only clear indication in the Apocrypha and Pseudepigrapha that the tetragrammaton may have been pronounced (under certain circumstances) comes in Sir.50:20.[108] After the service in the Temple, the High Priest Simon son of Onias descends "to pronounce the blessing of the Lord with his lips, and to glory in his name." That this is a reference to the actual uttering of the tetragrammaton is clear not only from the biblical (Num.6:24–27) and rabbinical (b. Sot. 37a–38b) parallels, but also from the discussion in Sir.45:15 about Aaron being commissioned to bless the people "in the name" (ἐν τῷ ὀνόματι). Since there is no mention made of any specific day, such as Yom Kippur, we cannot necessarily restrict this blessing to one time of the year.[109] As for the identity of Simon, the majority of scholars identify him as Simon II, who flourished c. 200 BCE.[110] James VanderKam has recently challenged this consensus, arguing that there is good reason to think that the man in question is Simon I, fl. 300 BCE.[111] I am inclined to agree with VanderKam. If, however, the figure in question is in fact Simon II, this would only inform us that the tetragrammaton was pronounced in the temple at least until 200 BCE.

Philo

Before turning to Philo's awareness, or lack of awareness, of the name YHWH, it is essential to realize that for him God is essentially name-less, and any names God gives to people are a concession to their weakness.[112]

---

[108] There *may* be a reference to the practice of saying the name in the temple in Jub. 23:21. It says of the "future evil generation": "...and they will pronounce the great name but not in truth or righteousness. And they will pollute the holy of holies with their pollution and with the corruption of their contamination." Trans. Wintermute, *OTP* 2: 101. The mention of the holy of holies makes one wonder if it is corrupt priests (perhaps of the Antiochene era) who are "pronouncing the great name but not in truth or righteousness."

[109] *Contra* the note in the Oxford Annotated Apocrypha. See especially Fearghas Ó'Fearghail, "Sir. 50, 5–21: Yom Kippur or The Daily Whole Offering?" *Biblica* 59 (1978): 301–316. He argues convincingly that the passage in fact refers to the daily whole offering, and thus cannot be cited as evidence that the name was only said on the day of atonement. See also Patrick W. Skehan and Alexander A. DiLella, *The Wisdom of Ben Sira* AB (New York: Doubleday, 1987), pp.550–51.

[110] See, e.g. Skehan and Di Lella, p.9; see discussion in James C. VanderKam, "Simon the Just: Simon I or Simon II," in *Pomegranates and Golden Bells*, eds. David P. Wright, David Noel Freedman, and Avi Hurvitz (Winona Lake, IN: Eisenbrauns, 1995), pp.314–16.

[111] VanderKam, *passim*.

[112] For discussion, Harry A. Wolfson, *Philo*, 2nd printing revised; 2 vols (Cambridge, MA: Harvard University Press, 1948), 2: 110–126; Ronald Williams, *Jews in the Helle-*

Since God is ultimately incomprehensible (particularly to those still in mortal bodies, see *Som.* 1:232), and hence inexpressible (note his use of ἄρρητον of God in both *Quis Her.* 170 and *Mut.* 15), no name can give an accurate indication of who he is.[113] God cannot have a "proper name" (ὄνομα κύριον; cf. *Mut.* 12f.), and so he provides substitutes for people to use.[114] These substitutes occupy a rough hierarchy in his view, and we will treat them accordingly.

The closest one can come to an accurate designation for God in Philo's thinking is ὁ ὤν (and its counterpart τὸ ὄν). This is indicated by his frequent use of these terms, and also by his statement in *Abr.* 121 that ὁ ὤν is God's "proper name."[115] Taken at face value, this is in contradiction to the assertion in *Mut.* 12f. that God has no proper name. There is certainly some terminological imprecision here, but we need not conclude that Philo is hopelessly muddled with respect to the name. God remains inherently unnamable, but the designation ὁ ὤν does capture the idea that God is the one who is "essentially existent" (the Loeb translator's rendering of ὄντως

---

nistic World: Philo (Cambridge: Cambridge University Press, 1989), pp.38–42,94–5; David Runia, *Philo of Alexandria and the Timaeus of Plato* (Leiden: Brill, 1986), p.438. Wolfson (*Philo*, 2: 110–126) has argued that the idea of God's namelessness actually goes back to Philo, but he neglects Cicero, *De Natura Deorum* 1:31, where the Epicurean Velleius speaks of Plato "qui in Timaeo patrem huius mundi nominari neget posse." (See Runia, *Timaeus*, p.111). Velleius' selective quotation of *Tim.* 28c omits εἰς πάντας, thus making the impossibility of declaring him "to all" a more general statement on the mysterious nature of God. See Whittaker, "Plutarch, Platonism, and Christianity," pp.50–1.

[113] See esp. *Spec Leg.* 41; *Quis Her.* 170; *Mut.* 11,15; *Mos.* I, 75; *Som.* I, 67,230; on man's general inability to embrace the reality of God's being, see *Post.* 15–16; *Quod Deus* 62; *Fug.* 141; *Praem.* 39–40. Philo held that the name and the thing were coterminous; see *Cher.* 56, *Mut.* 14. See also Wolfson, 2: 110–126 and Williamson, pp.38–42. David Runia, in "Naming and Knowing: Themes in Philonic Theology" (in *Knowledge of God in the Graeco-Roman World*, eds. R. van den Broek, T. Baarda, and J. Mansfeld; Leiden: Brill, 1988), sees a philosophical background: "Implicit at this point [i.e. *Change of Names* 11–15] is the Platonist argument, derived from the theological reflection on the first and second hypotheses of the *Parmenides*, that any name or attribute adds to Being (p.77)."

[114] This requires him to provide an interesting interpretation of episode at the burning bush. According to Philo, the text should not be read, "my name, Lord (taking κύριος as a proper name) I did not make known to them"; but rather, "my proper name (taking κύριος as an adjective corresponding to our English "proper") I did not make known to them" – the words, he believes, are out of order in the present text of the LXX. For an excellent discussion of this matter, see V. Nikiprowetzky, *Le commentaire de l'Écriture chez Philon Alexandrie* (Leiden: Brill, 1977), pp.59–62, 85–7. Cf. *Mut.* 12f.; Runia, *Timaeus*, p.438, "Naming," pp.76–91. Runia ("Naming and Knowing," p.78) notes that "mortality does not need a 'substitute for the divine name,' [Colson's translation of *Mut.* 13] for any name applied to God is substitutionary."

[115] Gk. κυρίῳ ὀνόματι καλεῖται.

ὄντος in *Abr.* 124). As such, it can be viewed as a "proper" or "fitting" name for God.[116]

A key passage in this regard is *Mos.* 1:74–76, where Philo discusses the passage of the burning bush. God replies to Moses' request for a name by saying ἐγω εἰμι ὁ ὤν – a direct quotation from the LXX of Ex. 3:14. But Moses is to tell the people this "that they may learn the difference between what is and what is not, and also the further lesson that no name at all can properly be used of Me, to Whom alone existence belongs."[117] Thus while ὁ ὤν may be a designation – indeed for Philo, *the* designation – for God, it is not strictly speaking a name, at least in this passage. In fact it is not even a title (πρόσρησιν). In this same text God tells them to use "the God of Abraham, Isaac, and Jacob" as their title for him (cf. Ex.3:15). Again, one must acknowledge that this stands in tension with the statement in *Abr.* 121.

Lest we stray too far into the realm of the meaning of this designation ὁ ὤν, which we will explore in the next chapter, let us move to the designation which occupies the next rung on Philo's ladder. According to *Abr.* 124, God presents himself to "the best" as ὁ ὤν, and to the next level of people as θεός. This is in keeping with Philo's understanding that θεός designates God's merciful power (δύναμις) while κύριος represents his judicial or ruling power (see e.g. *Cher.* 27–8).[118] Κύριος is the designation by which the third class of men know God. They are the ones who experience him as ruler and judge (*Abr.* 124).[119]

As for YHWH itself, we must ask whether Philo actually knew the tetragrammaton in Hebrew.[120] The extent of Philo's general knowledge of Hebrew has been the subject of much debate, but certainly he knew some

---

[116] Nikiprowetzky (p.59) suggests that κυρίῳ ὀνόματι...ὁ ὤν in *Abr.* 121 ought to be rendered, "...que Dieu est nommé l'Etre...*au sens propre* ou en *termes appropriés*." See also the discussion in Runia, "Naming," pp.76ff. Although he is speaking of the title κύριος ὁ θεός, his conclusion (p.77) is relevant:: "God therefore grants the improper use of a name, κύριος ὁ θεός (the Lord God) *as if it were a proper (i.e. legitimate) name*...(italics his)"

[117] Loeb translation.

[118] This, as has been amply noted, is the opposite of the later rabbinical formulations. For complete discussions, see A. Marmorstein, "Philo and the Names of God," *JQR* 22 (1931): 295–306; and Dahl and Segal, *passim*. See the notes above in the discussion of the LXX use of κύριος for a list of the relevant passages in Philo.

[119] It is at least of passing interest that at one point Philo identifies the λόγος as the name of God. *Leg. All.* 3: 207: "We may be content if we are able to swear by His Name, which means the interpreting word (τοῦ ἑρμηνέως)" (Loeb translation).

[120] For detailed discussion, see Baudissin, 2:175–181; Nikiprowetzky, pp.58–62, 85–88.

words, and one would presume that the name of the God of Israel might be among them.[121]

We can begin by stating that Philo apparently knew something about the tetragrammaton – in fact, he uses the very word in *Mos.* 2:114 (τετραγράμματον δὲ τοὔνομά). He is discussing the array of the high priest, which includes the gold plate on which are "four incisions showing a name..." Later in the passage (*Mos.* 2:132) he again speaks of "the graven shapes of four letters, indicating, as we are told, the name of the self existent."[122] It is possible that Philo knew that the name had four letters but did not know what they were, but this strikes me as exceedingly unlikely. It is hard to imagine a Jew of Philo's status and learning not bothering to find out the letters of the traditional name of the Jewish God. He may not have known the pronunciation of the tetragrammaton, but he almost certainly knew what its letters were.[123]

In *Mig.* 103, he indicates that the plate reads in full, "Holy to the Lord" (cf. Ex.28:36 and 39:30).[124] The last example shows that Philo not only knew of a name of God with four letters, he also probably knew that this name of God was rendered κύριος in his Greek Old Testament.[125] A simple comparison between Ἁγίασμα κυρίου in Ex.28:36 and the four-lettered name engraved on the golden plate would make the matter clear. Note, too, that the graven letters in *Mos.* 2:132 represent the name of the *"self-existent"* (τοῦ ὄντος). While Philo may simply be using this as a favored designation of God, it is probably not coincidental that this form is derived from the LXX of Ex. 3:14, where the meaning of YHWH is discussed in the Hebrew text.

Philo also knows of the restrictions which accompany this name. The quotation from *Mos.* 2:114 continues "(showing the name) which only

---

[121] Cf. Nikiprowetzky, pp.63ff.; Wolfson, 1: 88–9.

[122] Loeb translation. Gk.: τῶν τεττάρρων αἱ γλυφαὶ ἐξ ὧν ὄνομα τοῦ ὄντος φασὶ μηνύεσθαι.

[123] Nikiprowetzky (p.59) thinks it is certain that Philo knew the tetragrammaton.

[124] This does not necessarily stand in contradiction to the two other instances where only the name is mentioned. Since it appears that the name of the Lord was already treated in a special manner at the time of Philo, it is only natural that its appearance on the golden plate would attract his attention and that he might neglect to mention the other words upon it. It is of course possible, but unlikely, that he knows of a (perhaps erroneous) tradition that the plate only had the name YHWH on it, while in *Mig.* he simply quotes the Exodus text. See also the note to *Mos.* 2:114 (p.504) and the appendix (pp.608–9) in the Loeb edition. For a thorough discussion, see Nikiprowetzky, pp.87–8. Cf. Josephus, *Bell.* 5: 235.

[125] Nikiprowetzky (p.62), thinks it is only probable that Philo knew the equivalence κύριος = YHWH.

those whose ears and tongues are purified[126] may hear or speak in the holy places, and no other person, nor in any other place at all."[127] It is noteworthy, however, that Philo does *not* cite the case of the blasphemer in Leviticus 24 LXX as a support for this practice. He discusses the latter passage shortly thereafter, in *Mos.* 2:192ff. Philo understands the Leviticus text to involve two prohibitions: not blaspheming God and not "naming the name of the Lord" (24:15–16). He concludes that θεόν in v.15 refers to the gods of the nations and not to the God of Israel. They are not to be cursed lest a general disrespect for the word "God" ensue.[128] As for uttering the name of "the Lord of gods and men,"[129] the offense consists in saying it ἀκαίρως, "at the wrong time," "unseasonably" (*Mos.* 2:203–4). That this is closely related to Philo's understanding of the third commandment (where the prohibition is against saying the name "in vain," ἐπὶ ματαίῳ, cf.*Quis Her.* 170) becomes apparent in *Mos.* 2:208, where the offense of "naming the name" consists in making "the most holy and divine name an expletive."[130] Merely saying the name is not the offense in question.

We may summarize as follows: For Philo, God is essentially nameless. The most fitting designation for human beings to use of him is ὁ ὤν. The latter is a "proper name" *in some sense*, with the recognition that God remains ultimately unnamable. He certainly knows about the *existence* of the tetragrammaton, and he may have seen it as underlying the LXX terms ὁ ὤν and κύριος. He may well not have known how this tetragrammaton was pronounced, and if he did, he does not appear to want to share it with his readers. Finally, he believed the tetragrammaton was only spoken and

---

[126] Note that the Loeb ed. does not translate the σοφίᾳ of the Greek; thus we should read "purified by wisdom" or something similar. A similar phrase, "those whose ears are purified," appears in *Gig.* 54, where it refers to those who hear the "mysteries" expounded by Moses.

[127] Loeb translation. Gk. text: ᾧ μόνοις τοῖς ὦτα καὶ γλῶτταν σοφίᾳ κεκαθαρμένοις θέμις ἀκούειν καὶ λέγειν ἐν ἁγίοις, ἄλλῳ δ'οὐδενὶ τὸ παράπαν οὐδαμοῦ. Nikiprowetzky (pp.59,86–7) believes that Caligula uttered the name (*Leg.* 353), but all the text asserts is that the emperor uttered something offensive. It is not at all clear that Philo intends us to understand the tetragrammaton here. Caligula may have simply been declaring his own divinity, which would have been blasphemous enough for a faithful Jew.

[128] Cf. Josephus, *Ant.* 4: 207; *Ap.* 2: 237. The prohibition derives from the LXX of Ex. 22:27, which renders the Hebrew אלהים לא תקלל "do not curse God" as θεοὺς οὐ κακολογήσεις "you will not revile gods." This is a curious translation of אלהים, since nothing in the context indicates that it should refer to anyone but the God of Israel. Nonetheless, one can see how it would admirably serve Philo's (and Josephus') purpose of showing that Judaism is not a misanthropic, xenophobic religion.

[129] Gk. εἰς τὸν ἀνθρώπων καὶ θεῶν κύριον.

[130] Gk. τὸ ἁγιώτατον καὶ θεῖον ὄνομα...λόγων ἀναπλήρωμα. In *Dec.* 82ff., Philo interprets the third commandment in terms of not swearing oaths, since if one swears falsely he is making God party to a lie.

heard in the temple. It seems Philo knew of a restriction on the utterance of the name YHWH, and that he respected this restriction.

Josephus

Josephus also affords us valuable information concerning the use of the divine name. Baudissin makes the very important point that, as a priest, Josephus would likely have known the tetragrammaton, and known it according to its correct pronunciation.[131] He mentions the letters engraved on the high-priest's crown on a few occasions. In *Ant.* 3:91, he speaks of the plate of gold ὅς ἱεροῖς γράμμασι τοῦ τὴν προσηγορίαν ἐπιτετιμημένος ἐστι.[132] These letters are described as "vowels" in *Bell.*5:235: τὰ ἱερὰ γράμματα ταῦτα δ' ἐστὶ φωνήεντα τέσσαρα. Since the Hebrew letters in the tetragrammaton could not be represented by Greek consonants, the designation "vowels" would make the most sense to his readers. (Thackeray suggests that he may be thinking of the Greek form Ιαυε.[133]) That Josephus had a high regard for this name is evidenced by the story he tells of Alexander the Great bowing before the divine name on the high priest's crown (*Ant.* 2: 331–2). The account is naturally of dubious historical value, but it does illustrate the idea that for Josephus, the name was worthy of peculiar respect.

The name appears in a different context in *Ant.* 3:270 where Josephus relates traditions concerning the test of the adulterous woman (Nu.5:11f.). Josephus, in agreement with rabbinic tradition (see b.Sot. 7a,b) gives special attention to the writing of the *name of God* on the skin which is to be washed into the "waters of bitterness."[134] In the biblical text, there is mention only of the curses being written on the skin, although YHWH is included thereon in the formula "The Lord make you a curse and an oath

---

[131] Baudissin, 2:181.

[132] Thackeray points out in his note in the Loeb edition that the ἱεροῖς γράμμασι refer to the paleo-Hebrew characters of the name YHWH (cf. Ep. Arist. 98). In *Ant.* 3:187, Josephus explicitly states that it is the "name of God" (τὸ ὄνομα τοῦ θεοῦ) on the crown. All texts and translations unless specified are from the LCL edition of Josephus (9 vols.; trans. H.St.J. Thackeray, Ralph Marcus, Allen Wickgren, and L.H. Feldman; London: Wm. Heinemann/NY: Geo. Putnam's Sons/Cambridge: Harvard University Press, 1926–65).

[133] LCL, note to 5:235.

[134] For an overview of the similarities and differences between Josephus and the later rabbinic writings, see Louis Feldman's "Introduction," in *Josephus, Judaism, and Christianity*, eds. Louis H. Feldman and Gohei Hata (Detroit: Wayne St. University Press, 1987), pp.37–42; and in the same volume, David M. Goldenberg, "Antiquities IV: 277 and 288 Compared with Early Rabbinic Law," pp.198–211.

among your people..." (Nu.5:23). According to Josephus, after oaths are sworn, the name is expunged (ἀπαλείψας)[135] from the skin and wrung into a bowl along with some soil from the temple. The woman then drinks this. If she is guilty, the water will poison her, and if she is innocent, she will remain healthy.

We see here that the name of God is closely associated with oaths and curses, just as it was in much of the Jewish literature already surveyed. The terrifying consequences of swearing a false oath by the name are vividly seen in the physical distress of the convicted adulteress. One can easily see how traditions such as these would have led a Jew to think twice about invoking the name of God in this way, and indeed to abstain from such swearing altogether.

The most significant passage in which Josephus discusses the use of the name is his account of the burning bush episode in *Ant.* 2:275. Moses wants to know "how he (i.e. God) should be addressed, so that, when sacrificing, he might invoke him by name to be present at the sacred rites."[136] He then states: "God revealed to him his name, which ere then had not come to men's ears, and of which I am forbidden to speak."[137] The phrase rendered "forbidden" is οὐ θεμιτόν. Θεμιτός hovers between the meanings "proper, reasonable" and "necessary, required."[138] Elsewhere Josephus uses it with regards to the High Priest (for whom alone it is θ. to see the holy of holies, *Ant.*14:72); a judge (who deems it not θ. to judge a man's sons since he himself is a father, *Bell.*1:541); of men who had sworn solemn oaths to Josephus (and hence it was not θ. for him to disbelieve them, *Vita* 275); and, most interestingly, of the Decalogue (which it is not θ. for Josephus to relate "to the letter," *Ant.*3:90).[139] The sense in *Ant.* 2:275

---

[135] Nu.5:23 uses ἐξαλείψει, which is the same verb used in Rev. 3:5 "their name will not be expunged from the book of life..."

[136] Trans. by Thackeray. The idea that Moses wanted the proper ritual name is a noteworthy gloss on the story. It may well be that Josephus is indirectly indicating here that he thought of the name YHWH primarily (or even exclusively) as a designation restricted to the cult.

[137] Trans. Thackeray. Gk. ὁ θεὸς αὐτῷ σημαίνει τὴν αὐτοῦ προσηγορίαν οὐ πρότερον εἰς ἀνθρώπους παρελθοῦσαν, περὶ ἧς οὐ μοι θεμιτὸν εἰπεῖν.

[138] See the definitions in Karl H. Rengstorf, *A Complete Concordance to Flavius Josephus* (Leiden: Brill, 1975), s.v. θεμιτός.

[139] For other instances see Rengstorf. Thackeray says that there is no known rabbinic parallel to the restriction against speaking about the Decalogue. It is possible that here θεμιτὸν means something like "convenient." In any case, the idea of "convenience" does not apply in the context of the prohibition about the divine name in *Ant.* 2:275. Jacob Jervell, in his essay "Imagines und Imago Dei: Aus der Genesis-Exegese des Josephus," accepts the sense of "prohibition" or "reluctance" in both *Ant.* 2:275 and *Ant.* 3:90 (in *Josephus-Studien*, eds. Otto Betz, Klaus Haacker, and Martin Hengel; Göttingen: Vandenhoeck and Ruprecht, 1974; p.199). He also notes that Josephus has a certain inhibition

would appear to be "proper." While Thackeray's "forbidden" is perhaps a bit strong, it is likely that Josephus is speaking of some cultic prohibition against speaking the name, at least to foreigners.[140]

Mention might also be made of the somewhat curious paucity of references in Josephus to κύριος as a word for deity. Josephus overwhelmingly prefers θεός, employing κύριος for the God of Israel on only two occasions, both of which are prayers addressed to ὦ δέσποτα κύριε (*Ant.* 13:68; 20:90).[141] While there is a remote possibility that this indicates a reluctance on his part to employ even the Greek surrogate for the name YHWH, it is far more likely that Josephus is attempting to use the most generally accepted term for God possible.[142]

We conclude with Josephus' observations on two of the OT passages we have discussed earlier. With respect to the case of the blasphemer (Leviticus 24), Josephus speaks only of the punishment of one who blasphemes God (ὁ δὲ βλασφημήσας θεόν, *Ant.*4:202). He does not mention the LXX phrase about "naming the name." Like Philo, he explains that this injunction includes not blaspheming the gods of other nations, out of respect for the word "god" (*Ant.*4:207; *Ap.*2:237).[143] Finally, Josephus takes the third

---

about revealing the Scriptures to non-Jews (*Ant.* 1:9), although the fact that the Septuagint had already been translated made him more open to sharing his perspective with Greeks (*Ant.* 1:10; Jervell, p.199).

[140] The last point is mentioned by Baudissin, 2:181. It appears reasonable, even though no specific reference is made in the text of speaking the name *before pagans*. In *Ap.* 2:82, Josephus speaks of the Jewish religion, "the secrets of which we may not reveal to aliens" – *de qua nihil nobis est apud alios effabile* (LCL). Thackeray notes that Reinach emends *effabile* to *ineffabile*, because the entire thrust of this section is to dismiss the charge that the Jewish temple ritual involves offensive mysteries such as the eating of Greeks (cf. *Ap.* 2:94,106 – 106 states outright that no "ineffable mysteries" occur in the temple). The emendation seems reasonable in light of the context, but the possibility remains that in the earlier verse Josephus is referring to (legitimate) mysteries which may not be revealed, while later he refutes the idea that these consisted of gruesome anti-Gentile rites. It is of interest that in the Eleusinian mysteries, the personal name of the Hierophant was to remain unknown and unuttered until his death. See George E. Mylonas, *Eleusis and the Eleusinian Mysteries* (Princeton: Princeton University Press/London: Routledge and Kegan Paul, 1961), p.155 n.

[141] This is the common LXX rendering of MT אדני יהוה. See Foerster, 3: 1058ff. for discussion and examples.

[142] For discussion, see Louis H. Feldman, "Josephus' Portrayal of the Hasmoneans" in *Josephus and the History of the Greco-Roman Period*, eds. Fausto Parente and Joseph Sievers (Leiden: Brill, 1994), pp.65ff.; Gohei Hata, "The Story of Moses Interpreted within the Context of anti-Semitism" in *Josephus, Judaism, and Christianity*, pp.180–197; and Adolf Schlatter, "Das Verhältnis Israels zu den Völkern" (written in 1932) in *Zur Josephus-Forschung*, ed. Abraham Schalat (Darmstadt: Wissenschaftliche Buchgesellschaft, 1973), pp.157–203.

[143] Cf. LXX Ex.22:27, and the note above on Philo's use of the same verse. This does not prevent Josephus from proceeding to offer a critique of idolatry in the following

commandment specifically as a command against swearing false oaths: ὁ τρίτος δὲ ἐπὶ μηδενὶ φαύλῳ (*Ant*.3:91; cf. Philo, *Decalogue* 82f.).

Greek and Roman Writers

The Greek and Roman writers of our period provide scattered and tantalizing information about the name of the God of the Jews. That the information is scattered is not surprising, given that Judaea was a small and rather distant colony amidst the vast empires of the day. References increased as Rome was forced to intervene militarily in Jewish affairs of state, and as the Jewish diaspora spread throughout the empire. The evidence is tantalizing not only because of its paucity, but also because of the worrisome inconsistency of the sources.

We will treat the material in three categories: 1) Accounts which state that the Jews worshipped an unknown or nameless god; 2) Accounts which link Jewish worship with the worship of pagan gods (particularly Dionysus); and 3) Accounts which describe the Jews as worshipping a god named "Iao."

There was much uncertainty among non-Jews as to the name of the Jewish God. In the 102nd book of his history (now lost to us), Livy apparently stated that the Jewish God had no name or image.[144] The key reference for this is *Scholia in Lucanum* 2:593, which reads:

> Incerti Iudea dei.[145] Livius de Iudaeis "Hierosolimis fanum cuius deorum sit non nominant, neque ullum ibi simulacrum est, neque enim esse dei figuram putant.[146]

Later, J. Lydus (in *De Mensibus* 4:53), states that Livy held that the God worshipped in Jerusalem was "unknown" – ἄγνωστος. But M. Stern points

---

verses. See Hata, pp.192–4, Schatter, pp.198–9; and Feldman, "Josephus' Portrayal," pp.65ff. All these authors point out that this verse was used as a defense against the charges of misanthropy leveled against the Jews.

[144] This conclusion is affirmed by both Stern (1: 331) and P.W. van der Horst, "The Unknown God," in *The Knowledge of God in the Graeco-Roman World*, p.37. For the idea of "unknown god" in antiquity, the classic text is Eduard Norden, *Agnostos Theos* (Leipzig: B.G. Teubner, 1913); see esp. pp.60ff. for a discussion of the passage from Livy. (Note that van der Horst's article is largely a critique of some of Norden's central ideas.) See also Hengel, *Jews, Greeks, and Barbarians* trans. John Bowden (London: SCM, 1980), p.102.

[145] Cf. the phrase *incerti Iudaea dei* in Pompey's speech concerning his conquests in Lucan's *Pharsalia* 2:593.

[146] Text in Stern, 1: 330. His translation runs: "And Judaea given over to the worship of an unknown God. Livy on Jews: 'They do not state to which deity pertains the temple at Jerusalem, nor is any image found there, since they do not think the God partakes of any figure.'"

out that Livy does not use *ignotus* with respect to the Jewish god. He believes this is a later Neoplatonic term put in Livy's mouth by Lydus.[147] Indeed, even Lucan (c.39–65 CE) with his "incerti dei" goes beyond what is found in the actual quotation from Livy. This represents his interpretation of the historian's words.[148] Thus, while the idea that the Jews believed in a God who was "beyond naming" (cf. our discussion of Philo above) may have been known to the Greeks and Romans, the citation from Livy may only tell us that the Jews in Jerusalem were unwilling to state the name of their God to foreigners.[149]

As Martin Hengel notes, "For non-Jews, it seemed...natural to identify the God of the Jews with a known divine figure..."[150] Zeus or Jupiter, as the supreme gods of the Greek and Roman pantheons, might seem like logical choices. Augustine reports that Varro (116–27) "thought the God of the Jews to be same as Jupiter."[151] An even more common identification, however, was Dionysus.[152] Tacitus (*Hist.* 5.5:5),[153] Lydus (*De Mensibus* 4:53), and Cornelius Labeo (ap. Macrobius, *Saturnalia* 1:18:18–21) all make this association, and a coin from 55 BCE of the curule aedile A. Plautius shows a kneeling king who is labeled BACCHIVS IVDAEVS. E. Babelon argues that this must be the high priest, "the priest of the Jewish Bacchus."[154] This identification may have been based on more than mere speculation. According to 2 Macc. 6:7, the Jews "were compelled to walk in the procession in honor of Dionysus, wearing wreaths of ivy" on the day

---

[147] Stern, 1:331 n.

[148] Van der Horst, p.37. See also the statement in Cassius Dio (c.160CE–230CE) that the Jews had no image of God and that they believed him to be "unnamable and invisible" (ἄρρητον δὲ δὴ καὶ ἀειδῆ). Stern, 2: 350–51. Dio is supposed to rely on Livy for this portion of his history (Stern, 2: 347). It is quite possible that Livy's description is intended to portray the Jews as a philosophically minded people, since *nominant* recalls Cicero's reference to the *Timaeus* in *De natura deorum* 1:31: qui in Timaeo patrem huius mundi *nominari neget posse*.

[149] The *Scriptores Historiae Augustae* (*Divus Claudius* 2:4) report that Moses was told by an "unknown god" (*ab incerto*) that no man would live for more than one hundred twenty years (Stern, 2: 635). But the *Scriptores* are probably late (perhaps end of the fourth century CE) and one should not lean too heavily upon them for evidence of usage during our period. See the introduction (with extensive bibliography) in Stern, 2: 612ff; and van der Horst, p.37.

[150] Hengel, *Jews, Greeks, Barbarians*, p.102.

[151] *De Consensu Evangelistarum* I, 22:30 (cf.I, 23:31); in Stern, 1: 209–10.

[152] Hengel, *Jews, Greeks, Barbarians*, p.102.

[153] Tacitus actually mentions the Roman god Liber, who was identified with Dionysus. He discounts the identification of Liber and the God of the Jews, since "Liber established festive rites of a joyous nature, while the ways of the Jews are preposterous and mean." (Stern, 2: 26–7.) Nonetheless, he still serves a witness to the belief among some Romans that the two were the same.

[154] Cited by Andrew Alfödi, "Redeunt Saturnia Regna," *Chiron* 3 (1973): 138–9.

of the god's feast.[155] It is possible that some participated willingly. L. Feldman cites an inscription which states that a Jew named Niketes contributed to the festival of Dionysus.[156] In any event, an outside observer might simply observe that Jews were involved in the worship of Dionysus.

Plutarch gives special attention to this matter in his *Quaestiones Convivales*, and he provides us with an item which may be of interest for our study of the divine name. In *Quaest. Conviv.* IV, 6:1-2, Moiragenes reports that the Hebrews hail their god – Dionysus, in his view – with the cries "Euoe" and "Sabi."[157] We also have evidence from Demosthenes (384–322 BCE) that some Asiatic cults cried "Euoe Saboe" to invoke the Phrygian deity Sabazius (of whom more anon) along with Dionysus.[158] It seems possible that someone who knew of the designation "Iao (or Yahweh) Sabaoth" (whether from magical texts or direct contact with Jews) might easily confuse these two phrases and conclude that Jewish worship was some version of the Dionysus cult.[159] Once such a view was propagated, a traveler armed with such information might easily pick out something that sounded like "Euoe" in the various Hebrew or Aramaic words uttered during festival times,[160] and so the cycle of misinformation would continue.

The cry of "Sabi" might also call to mind the Jewish "sabbath," an ordinance which was quite familiar to Greek and Roman authors.[161] Since

---

[155] Cf. 2 Macc.6:7. See Stern's discussion, 1: 560; Hengel, *Jews, Greeks, Barbarians*, pp.102ff. Alfödi notes the presence of the vine leaf, grape cluster, cup, and amphora on the coins of the Maccabees. He argues that they are symbols of divine sovereignty, but one can easily see how they might be confused with symbols of Dionysus.

[156] Feldman, *Jew and Gentile in the Ancient World* (Princeton: Princeton University Press, 1993), p.74.

[157] See Molly Whittaker, *Jews and Christians: Graeco-Roman Views* (Cambridge: Cambridge University Press, 1984), pp.126–8 for translation and discussion.

[158] *De Corona* 260, as cited by Whittaker, *Jews*, p.128.

[159] Franz Cumont, *Les religions orientales dans le paganisme romain* 4th ed. (Paris: Librairie Orientaliste Paul Geuthier, 1929), p.60, says that Sabazius was linked "par une audacieuse étymologie" with Iahwé Zabaoth. See also Eugene N. Lane, "Sabazius and the Jews in Valerius Maximus: A Re-examination," *Journal of Roman Studies* 69 (1979): 35–38.

[160] It would be tempting to speculate as to whether "Iao," "Yahweh," or some other version of the divine name might have been uttered and confused with "Euoe," but this is not demonstrable. It could just as easily be "All*eluia*" or some such thing. The possibility is still worth keeping in mind.

[161] E.g. Ovid, *Art of Love* 1.75–6,413–16; Horace, *Satires* 1.9.67–72; Tacitus, *Hist.* 4.11–18; Juvenal, *Saturae* 5.14.105–6. For texts on the sabbath and commentary, see Whittaker, pp.63–73. Nilsson argues that it was the Sabbath, rather than the designation Sabaoth, which led to the identification with Sabazius. He says that the Sabbath was a feast day around the time of Christ, replete with ample amounts of wine, and that in the

Sabazius was identified with Dionysus,[162] Moiragenes seized upon the cry as another correlation between the Jews and the Bacchus cult. Nor was he the only one to associate the Jews with Sabazius. Valerius Maximus (early first century CE) wrote that in 139 BCE, the praetor Cornelius Scipio Hispalus "compelled the Jews, who attempted to infect the Roman customs with the cult of Jupiter Sabazius (*Sabazi Iovis cultu*), to return to their homes."[163] The passage has attracted much attention as a proof text both for Jewish missionary activity at this period and for possible Jewish syncretism.[164]

Leaving aside the general question of Jewish proselytism, we must still ask whether this passage indicates that Jews were proselytizing in Rome for "Jupiter Sabazius." Eugene Lane, among others, has pointed out that there is a long lacuna in this portion of Valerius, and the passage in question is found only in an epitome inserted by Julius Paris, c.400 CE. He suggests that the passage in Julius Paris may reflect a conflation of three separate edicts involving Chaldeans, Sabazius worshippers, and Jews.[165] There is another piece of evidence, however, which may link the Jews and Sabazius. The grave of a certain Vincentius, which might appear at first glance to be Christian, contains the inscription *numinis antistes Sabazi*, and the heavenly banqueting scenes depicted on it show some of the revel-

---

heavily syncretistic area of Asia Minor (which had a large number of Jews), this was bound to lead to confusion with Sabazius-Dionysus cults.(Nilsson, *Geschichte*, 2: 662.)

[162] Whittaker, *Jews*, p.128 n; Stern, 1: 560.

[163] Alfödi (in the article in *Chiron* cited above) makes an interesting case, largely from numismatic evidence, that the events described by Valerius reflect a situation of great social turmoil and much apocalyptic speculation – indeed, it was seen as the cataclysm which was to precede the return of the Golden Age. He cites coins from the period which depict astral symbols of rule, abundant fruit, and other signs of such a restoration. He reaches his conclusion by comparing these with signs of social unrest, such as the activities of the groups mentioned by Valerius and the dire predictions of the third Sibylline Oracle, most of which he dates to this time (he notes esp. Sib. Or. 3:192–4,608–25). (For a discussion of dating and provenance, see J.J. Collins' introduction to Sib. Or. 3 in *OTP* 1: 354–5.) The expulsion of (supposed) Sabazius worshippers is also explicable in light of the Bacchanalia scandal of 186 BCE. Amidst charges of ritual murder and general lewdness, the authorities set out to destroy the cult and killed many of its adherents. Cumont provides a helpful summary of this and other aspects of Dionysus worship, pp.195ff.

[164] For extensive bibliography, see Stern, 1: 358–9. For a recent discussion of the Sabazius controversy, see Paul Trebilco, *Jewish Communities in Asia Minor* (Cambridge: Cambridge University Press, 1991), pp.140–2. For a survey of the evidence on Jewish proselytism, see Scot McKnight, *A Light among the Gentiles: Jewish Missionary Activity in the Second Temple Period* (Minneapolis: Fortress Press, 1991).

[165] Lane, pp. 36–7. He also notes that the record of this same event in the epitome of Januarius Nepotianus makes no mention of Sabazius. Cf. Trebilco, p.141. Note, however, that the Jews could be referred to as "Chaldeans," e.g. Jud. 5:6.

ers wearing the Phrygian cap associated with Sabazius. At the same time, the escort into heaven is labeled an *angelus bonus*, which appears to derive from Judaism.[166] Cumont believes that the Sabazius worshippers' concern with ritual purity may also have been derived from the Jews.[167]

This leaves us with several options. It is possible that some Jews could have blended their traditions with the worship of foreign gods,[168] or used the designation Jupiter Sabazius to make their name Iao Sabaoth "comprehensible and sensible to pagans."[169] But other explanations offer themselves to us. Like Varro, the Romans may have simply equated the Jewish high God with their own supreme deity, and then added the epithet Sabazius from their observation of the Jewish concern with "sabbath." One might also argue from the evidence presented by Nilsson that a cult of Jupiter Sabazius with strong Jewish elements had in fact developed in Asia Minor and then been carried to Rome. Its pagan adherents were incorrectly labeled as "Jews" and expelled from the city.[170] I would favor the explanation offered by Hengel that the Roman authorities (or the historians who passed the tradition along) may have confused the Jewish name Iao Sabaoth with the more familiar divine names Jovis and Sabazius, rather than that the Jews adopted this name themselves.[171] Careful, precise investigation was not the watchword for Greeks and Romans writing on Jewish religion, and thus such confusion is a distinct possibility.

For all their misunderstanding of the Jews, some of the Greeks and Romans did know of a term which at least approximated the Old Testament name of God: Iao. The word shows up first in Diodorus Siculus' *Bibliotheca Historica* I,94:2 (first century BCE). In the course of discussing the lawgivers and gods of various peoples, he mentions "among the Jews Moyses [who] referred his laws to the god who is invoked as Iao."[172] But Lydus records the words of an even earlier historian in his *De Mensibus*

---

[166] Nilsson, *Geschichte* 2: 662ff.; Cumont, p.60. See also Nilsson, "À propos du tombeau de Vincentius," *Revue archéologique* 31-2 (1949): 764-9. Trebilco (p.141) does not believe the Vincentius tomb is relevant to the discussion of the decree.

[167] Cumont, p.61.

[168] Thus Cumont, cited in Stern, 1: 359. The reverse could also be true: Hengel notes a Phrygian cult of *Theos Sabathikos*, which may have been a pagan adaptation of the Jewish God. Hengel, *Jews, Greeks, Barbarians*, p.106. Nilsson (*Geschichte* 2: 665) notes that the members of the group were known as "Sabbatists" (Sabbatistoi). He believes they are clearly a heathen association.

[169] The suggestion of Marcel Simon, in Lane, p.37.

[170] The identification of them as "Jews" may have resulted from their purity concerns and possible sabbath observance (although the latter is simply an inference from the presence of Sabbatist cults in Asia Minor).

[171] Hengel, *Jews, Greeks, Barbarians*, p.106.

[172] Gk. παρὰ δὲ τοῖς Ἰουδαίοις Μωυσῆν τὸν Ἰαὼ ἐπικαλούμενον θεόν. Stern, 1: 171-2

(IV,53): "The Roman Varro (116–27 BCE) defining him [scil. the Jewish God] says that he is called Iao in the Chaldean mysteries."[173] Lydus follows this statement by citing Herennius (to be identified with Philo Byblius, b. 64CE)[174], who gave a Phoenician etymology for Iao.[175]

The question naturally arises as to where they received their information. In the case of Varro, Norden does not rule out the possibility of written sources on Jewish religion, such as may have been used by Alexander Polyhistor and Posidonius.[176] Baudissin concurs, suggesting that in addition to the mystery literature mentioned in the text of Lydus, Varro may have drawn upon Greek travel literature.[177] As for the "Chaldean mysteries," Baudissin is probably correct in equating them with the sort of literature known to us in the magical papyri from Egypt. There is, however, the possibility that Varro drew on sources familiar with Greek versions of the Old Testament itself. The Jews are described as the descendants of the *Chaldeans* in Judith 5:6. We have already noted the presence of Iao in the late first century BCE/early first century CE pap4QLXXLev^b. Juvenal (*Saturae* XIV, 102) speaks of "all that Moses handed down in his secret tome" – *tradidit arcano quodcumque volumine Moyses*.[178] If Varro had a similar view of the Jewish writings, he could conceivably be using "Chaldean mysteries" as a term for the Jewish scriptures. The abundant use of Iao in the magical papyri, however, makes the first case more likely.

---

[173] Gk. Ὁ δὲ Ῥωμαῖος Βάρρων περὶ αὐτοῦ διαλαβών φησι παρὰ Χαλδαίοις ἐν τοῖς μυστικοῖς αὐτὸν λέγεσθαι Ἰάω. In Stern, 1: 211–12.

[174] See Baudissin, 2: 204–5.

[175] He takes it to mean ἀντὶ τοῦ φῶς νοητόν. Baudissin (2: 204) points out that the following part of the quotation from Philo – καὶ Σαβαὼθ πολλαχοῦ λέγεται – makes it clear that he is talking about the Jewish God. Cornelius Labeo (third century CE) lies outside our period (for dates see Nilsson, *Geschichte* 2: 477; A.D. Nock, "Oracles théologiques" *Revue des études anciennes* 30 (1928): 288), but it is worth noting that he identifies Iao with other gods: "Then ponder that Iao is the supreme god among all/In winter he is Hades, at the beginning of the spring he is Zeus/In summer he is Helios, while in autumn he is the graceful Iao." (*ap*. Macrobius, *Saturnalia* I, 18:20; Nilsson notes that the final Iao is corrupt in the text and should be read Ἴακχον, another name for Dionysus. In any case, Iao itself certainly occurs elsewhere in the passage.) The thrust of the passage is to make the equation between Liber and Iao, and he introduces the above quotation (supposedly derived from Apollo of Clarus) as evidence of his point. Text in Stern, 2: 410–11. He notes (2: 412) that "at Claros there was a systematic tendency towards the unification of creeds that could include even the God of Judaism."

[176] Norden, pp.61–2. He doubts whether Varro received his information directly from Pompey, despite his friendship with the latter. The fact that Livy speaks of the nameless God of the Jews in connection with Pompey strengthens this argument. Elsewhere Norden theorizes that Varro may have drawn upon Nigidius Figulus, *De Diis* (see Baudissin, 2: 202 n).

[177] Baudissin, 2: 202–3.

[178] Stern, 2: 102–3.

As for Diodorus, Posidonius has also been put forward as his source.[179] Other scholars reach back as far as Hecataeus, upon whom Diodorus relied in his first book. This view has been sharply criticized by E. Schwartz and W. Aly.[180] But we cannot rule out that Hecataeus may have been Diodorus' source. The form יהו is in evidence in Egypt as early as the fifth century BCE,[181] and references to Iao are common in the magical papyri. The matter cannot be decisively settled, but an origin with Hecataeus should not be excluded.[182]

The Greeks and Romans we have been discussing did not have the Jews at the center of their thoughts. They were a marginal people, interesting to some writers, strange and distasteful to others. This very fact makes the testimony we do find about the name of God all the more interesting. Through their works we can confirm some of what has already been suspected from the Jewish sources. The Jews were, at least at times, reticent to proffer the name of their God to foreigners; they were given to substitute for the divine name, e.g. with "the God of Heaven"; and when they did communicate something resembling the tetragrammaton, it was under the form Iao.

Magical material

The name Iao also appears on a number of magical texts, inscriptions and amulets from the ancient world. Although much of this material postdates the composition of Revelation, there is good evidence that the name Iao was in circulation quite early.[183] Morton Smith dates *PGM* 4: 1217–1226 and 4: 3007–86 before 70 CE, based largely on the mention of the "unquenchable light in the Holy Place," a reference he feels would be out of

---

[179] By, e.g., I. Heinemann and G. Pfligersdorffer, in Stern,1: 172 n. Willy Theiler includes this portion of Diodorus in *Poseidonios: Die Fragmente* 2 vols (Berlin: De Gruyter, 1982). He says in his commentary that the *Grundlage* for the passage is Hecataeus (2: 98).

[180] E. Schwartz, "Diodorus" in *PW* 5: 670; Wolfgang Aly, *Strabonis Geographica: Band 4 Strabon von Amaseia* (Bonn: Rudolf Habelt, 1957), pp.200–2; Stern, I:172.

[181] For texts see A. Cowley, *Aramaic Papyri of the Fifth Century* (Oxford: Oxford University Press, 1923).

[182] Baudissin (2: 203–4) is cautious here, but he argues that Hecataeus may have provided the information reported by Diodorus. He also observes that while Diodorus might have learned of the name Iao on his own journey to Egypt (*Bib. Hist.* I, 44:1), the composition of the present passage makes it likely that he is dependent on a literary source.

[183] In his introduction to the magical papyri, Betz says that the documents range from the second century BCE to the fifth century CE. See H. D. Betz, ed., *The Greek Magical Papyri in Translation* 2 vols (Chicago: University of Chicago Press, 1986), 1: xli.

place after the destruction of the Temple. Both texts mention Iao.[184] An amulet from Emesa in Syria, to be dated to the first century BCE, begins with the words: IAO IAO IAO SABAOTH ADONAI.[185] If Varro's "Chaldean mysteries" are in fact magical texts, this would provide further support for an early date for at least some of the "Iao" material.

It is a commonplace in the literature on magic that names hold a particular potency.[186] The magicians apparently also held to the idea that "more is better," and hence we often find names of divinities piled up on top of one another in considerable number. Some may have been working with the idea that the true God had many names or was essentially nameless.[187] Others were probably hedging their bets by invoking as many powerful beings as possible.[188] In any event, they seemed especially eager to employ names connected with the Jewish God, and in particular the name Iao.

We begin with occurrences in the magical papyri. To assemble all the references to Iao we would have to replicate virtually the whole of Betz' volume, so we must be content with selective examples. At times, the Iao form may have resulted from the random combination of vowels, which is common in our texts.[189] But it is likely that in many of these instances, the

---

[184] Morton Smith, "The Jewish Elements in the Magical Papyri," *SBL Seminar Papers* 25 (Atlanta: Scholars Press, 1986), pp.460–1. Smith notes that the petition in 4:1217–1226 is "markedly different from the syncretistic material that precedes it."

[185] Roy Kotansky, *Greek Magical Amulets* Part 1 (Opladen: Westdeutscher Verlag, 1994), pp.248–56. It also appears on another 1 century BCE amulet from Macedonia (Kotansky, pp.211–15). Marc Philonenko has dated a magical amulet containing what appears to be the name Iao to the end of the Seleucid era. See Philonenko, "Une intaille magique au nom de Iao," *Semitica* 30 (1980): 57–60. See also the illustrations and discussion in Philonenko's article "L'Anguipède alectorocéphale et le dieu Iao," in *CRAI* (1979): 297–304.

[186] See, *inter alia*, Burkhard Gladigow, "Götternamen und Name Gottes" in *Der Name Gottes*, ed. H. von Stietencron (Düsseldorf: Patmos, 1975), pp.19ff.; Ganschinietz, "Iao" *PW* 9: 712,715; Bilha Nitzan, "Hymns from Qumran – 4Q510–4Q511," in *The Dead Sea Scrolls: Forty Years of Research*, eds. Devorah Dimant and Uriel Rappaport (Leiden: Brill, 1992): 54,56–7; Hengel, *Judaism and Hellenism*, 1: 241ff.

[187] Thus E. R. Goodenough, *Jewish Symbols in the Greco-Roman Period* 13 vols. (NY: Pantheon, 1953–68), 2: 200–201,294–5. He points out that the two can work together: the many-namedness can in fact indicate that God has no true name. See also Gladigow, pp.25–30; Ganschinietz, p.715; *PGM* 4: 605f.; 5:115; 12:237–8; 13:424f.

[188] E.g. *PGM* 4:1460–1495, where a host of gods and goddesses including Hekate, Pluto, Anubis, Isis and Zeus are mentioned before the invocation of Iao Sabaoth.

[189] Smith, pp.456–7. He also notes that "Ia" and "Io" represented cries in Greek, and hence "we should expect IAO to turn up almost everywhere and, especially in lists of vowels or isolated cries, to be, normally, without specific theological reference." I would emphasize that the similarity of Iao to the crying noises may in fact have contributed to

writer was already aware that Iao was a divine name and was playing with its vowels as another means of securing power from the name.[190] More often, the combination of Iao with other divine names derived from Hebrew or Aramaic gives a more certain indication that the word is referring to the God of the Jews, although even here one cannot always be sure if a given writer is fully aware, or aware at all, of the Jewish origin of the word.[191] We can select among many examples *PGM* XXXVI: 35f.: "IAO SABAOTH ADONAI ELOAI ABRASAX ABLANATHANALBA..."[192]. Occasionally we find variants. Thus *Iaweh* appears in *PGM* 23:31[193]; *Iabas* in *PGM* 5:102; and *Iabai* in *PGM* 12:5.[194]

These are obviously Jewish epithets, and so it is reasonable to conclude that at some point there was contact between Jews and these magicians. As Goodenough suggests throughout his work, many of the spells may in fact have been Jewish in origin. But this point must be sharply qualified. Even if the writers of these spells (whether Jewish or pagan) knew these divine names, there is abundant evidence that many of them knew little else. Perhaps the most telling example of this is the previously mentioned *Prayer of Jacob*, which contains more explicitly Jewish elements than most of the papyri. Yet even here it is likely that Iao is identified with the sun-god.[195] In *PGM* 3:145, the writer identifies Iao, Adonai, Michael, Gabriel, and others all as angels or subordinate deities. There are also instances of gross misspellings which indicate that the words were half-known syllables thought to have some magical potency. Thus we find "...MISAEL IRRAEL ISTRAEL" in *PGM* 4:1815[196]; "OSRAEL" in *PGM* 4:3034; and

---

the name's popularity, as here one had a bona fide divine name which could be perfectly wedded to the magicians' penchant for long vocalic cries.

[190] E.g. *PGM* III: 572; *PGM* II: 15

[191] For statistics on the use of Iao in the papyri, see the article by Smith.

[192] Cf. *PGM* III:75. *Abrasax* and *Ablanathanalba* are two very common examples of *voces*, magical titles that often accompany the name Iao (and sometimes occur independently). See Smith, p.457.

[193] *Iaweh* is the transliteration in Betz, 1: 262-4. This presumably corresponds to a Greek form Ιαουε (as in Clement of Alexandria *Strom.* V,6,34; see Baudissin, 2: 116,215ff.) The Betz reference comes from Kestos 18 of Julius Africanus, a Christian writer of the third century CE. He is in turn quoting an earlier unnamed poet. The passage may lend support for the modern idea that the proper pronunciation of the tetragrammaton was "Yahweh," but ironically it is a peripheral form in the papyri, appearing only here.

[194] The latter two are identified in Betz, 1: 335, as Samaritan enunciations of the divine name.

[195] See the reconstructed text in Betz, *PGM* XXIIb:1-26 and the notes by Charlesworth in *OTP* 2: 721.

[196] Ganschinietz (in "Israel," *PW* 9: 2233-4) says that here Israel is the name of a demon, and notes that it occurs in a seven-numbered scheme. This may reflect a planetary motif.

"ASSTRAELOS" in *PGM* XXXVI:259.[197] The name Iao could also be combined with pagan deities, as in *PGM* 1:14–18, where Iao is an angel of Zeus.[198]

All of this makes it unlikely that the magicians were generally aware that Iao was connected with the "secret" tetragrammaton, and that this is the reason it appears so frequently in the magical texts. Iao itself was one of the worst kept secrets in the Mediterranean world, appearing as it does in the writings of Egyptian magicians, Roman historians, Jewish translators of the bible, and on multitudes of amulets from all over the Empire. While at certain points in the tradition (particularly in its early development) the name Iao *may* have been linked with the tetragrammaton and acquired an air of mystery, at other times it was simply regarded as a potent name for the God of the Jews, if not indeed the name of some subordinate deity. If Ganschinietz goes too far in declaring that "Iao was for the magicians not a God but a name,"[199] Goodenough seems equally mistaken in elevating the references to Iao to the level of sophisticated religious terminology.[200] We must instead recognize a broad spectrum of usage. Iao can be the random collection of vowels noted by Smith, or a "word of power" (so Ganschinietz), or a designation for some lower deity of angel, or a conscious invocation of the God of the Jews.

An examination of magical amulets serves only to make the picture more complex.[201] One could imagine some gems enjoying popularity among a wide spectrum of Jews, their magical overtones notwithstanding. An amulet found at Caernarvon in Wales (date: c.75–140 CE), for exam-

---

[197] There is always the possibility, of course, that such alterations are deliberate (perhaps to create angel names that sound like "Israel." Cf. Gershom G. Scholem, *Jewish Gnosticism, Merkabah Mysticism, and Talmudic Tradition* (NY: Jewish Theological Seminary, 1960). He notes (p.95 n) that Asrael appears in the Testament of Solomon. The name also figures in 1 Enoch. But in light of the "amazing mistakes" (Smith's term, p.459) made about Judaism elsewhere in the papyri, it is equally likely that the writer simply did not know the exact designation or spelling for (in this case) Israel. Cf. "ISAK" in *PGM* I: 216 and the idea in 4:1376 and elsewhere that Basym (the Hebrew for "in the name of") is the name of an angel. (The last point I owe to Smith, p.459.)

[198] Discussion in Goodenough, 2: 194–5. Cf. Baudissin, 2: 198–9.

[199] Translation (in Goodenough, 2: 252) of his statement in "Iao," p.715.

[200] Goodenough is not an absolutist about this, and he does recognize some uses of Iao which might correspond to Ganschinietz' description. But he is a bit too effusive in his apologetic for the use of Iao when he says, for instance, "Image after image on these stones is given the name Iao...with the result that Iao remains essentially aniconic." Goodenough, 2: 252. One imagines a flustered amulet-wearer attempting to explain this to his local rabbi.

[201] For a general overview of amulets, see Campbell Bonner, *Studies in Magical Amulets: Chiefly Graeco-Egyptian* (Ann Arbor: University of Michigan Press, 1950), pp.1ff. He discusses the name Iao on pp.26ff.,134–5.

ple, contains fragments of Jewish liturgy written in Greek letters.[202] This could serve a Jew or a non-Jew equally well. On the other hand, we have a plethora of amulets bearing the divine name Iao which seem to clash head on with the anti-iconic stance of the Hebrew scriptures. Foremost among these are those bearing the anguipede, a snake-legged figure (usually having a cock's head and bearing a shield and a whip in its arms) which shows up time and again on magical amulets.[203] The figure has attracted much attention, but no firm conclusions have been reached as to its provenance or its significance.[204] For our purposes, it is sufficient to point out that the appearance of the name Iao with such a figure constitutes a fairly egregious violation of the common Jewish prohibition of divine images. This would not of course preclude their use by non-Jews, who may have felt the names associated with the Jewish God had a particular potency. We may only conclude that many Hebrew names, including Iao, were in circulation amongst magicians from at least the first century BCE onwards. But it remains uncertain how much they knew about the Jewish faith, and whether they connected the name Iao with the tetragrammaton.

New Testament

The name YHWH, as is well known, does not occur explicitly in the New Testament.[205] In quotations from the OT, for instance, where the MT reads יהוה, the NT generally speaking has κύριος.[206] There is also evidence for

---

[202] We will discuss this in detail in the following chapter under the meaning of the name.

[203] Far less often, Iao is depicted as having an ass' head. This has led some to derive the name Iao from *io*, the Coptic word for "ass" (Ganschinietz, p.716). The view is generally dismissed, see e.g. A. Procopé-Walter, "Iao und Set," *ARW* 30 (1933): 34 n.. Although the derivation is dubious, the linguistic similarities may have played a role in the development of the ancient legend that the Jews worshipped an ass' head in the temple. Cf. Josephus Ap. 2: 79–80 (Stern, 1: 409–10); Ap. 112–114, (Stern, 1: 99–100).

[204] See, e.g., C. Colpe, "Geister (Dämonen)," in *Reallexikon für Antike und Christentum* 9 (1976): 618–19. See also Marcel Le Glay, "Abrasax," in *Lexicon Iconographicum Mythologiae Classicae*, I/1, pp.6–7; Procopé-Walter, pp.39f.; Martin P. Nilsson, "The Anguipede of the Magical Amulets," *HTR* 44 (1951): 61–64; Philonenko, "L'Anguipède," pp.297ff. For illustrations, see Goodenough, vol. 3, figs.1061f; and *Lexicon Iconographicum Mythologiae Classicae*, I/2 (Zurich and Munich: Artemis, 1981), pp.6–14.

[205] As we have argued above, Howard's theory (and in fairness to him, it is only presented as a theory) that the tetragrammaton may have appeared in the original NT texts has no MSS support, and furthermore rests on dubious assertions about the (non-) use of κύριος.

[206] Among numerous examples, see Mt. 1:22,3:3; Mk.12:29; Lu.4:19; Ac.2:21; Ro.4:8.

the corresponding Aramaic title מרא in 1Cor. 16:22 (Gk. μαραναθά, "Our Lord, come!), although this likely has particular reference to Jesus Christ. As we have indicated, the substitution of Adonai/κύριος/מרא for YHWH is a matter of great intrinsic interest, particularly for New Testament Christology. For this very reason, we have chosen to avoid the topic and concentrate on the usage and meaning of YHWH itself. We will only note here that κύριος appears not only in Paul's letters to Jewish and Gentile Christians, but also in letters which appear to be addressed to strictly Jewish audiences, such as the book of James. Thus, while Jewish Christians could possibly have used the name YHWH when (and if) they spoke Hebrew, when they wrote (and presumably spoke) in Greek, they used κύριος. This at least is what the concrete evidence of the New Testament suggests. Furthermore, the admittedly slight evidence of 1Cor.16:22, when combined with the use of מריא for God in 4QEn^b, suggests that they may have used מרא in place of the name YHWH in their Aramaic discourse.[207]

Rabbinical Literature

Writing the Name

In light of the extraordinary care with which the written name was handled in the Qumran scrolls, it is appropriate to look briefly at rabbinic teachings on this matter.[208] In our discussion of Josephus we alluded to b.Sota 7a,b, where the accused woman is adjured to confess before the name was blotted out from the scroll into the water. In m. Sotah 1:4 it is reported that they used to say to the suspected adulteress, "do thou behave for the sake of his great Name, written in holiness,[209] that it be not blotted out through the water [of bitterness]." This reflects both the belief that bad behavior disgraced the name, while good behavior honored it, and the belief that there was something special about the written name which made its blotting out in the water a serious matter indeed.[210]

---

[207] See the two essays by Fitzmyer, "New Testament *Kyrios* and *Maranatha*" and "The Semitic Background of the New Testament *Kyrios*-Title"; and Richard Bauckham, *Jude and the Relatives of Jesus in the Early Church* (Edinburgh: T.&T. Clark, 1990), ch. 6.

[208] See especially Siegel's article (cited above) "The Employment of Paleo-Hebrew"; cf. Urbach, 2: 738 n.

[209] I.e., upon the scroll which was to be wrung out into the water.

[210] Some scholars are skeptical about the historical value of judicial discussions in the Mishnah. See especially E.P. Sanders, *Judaism: Practice and Belief 63 BCE–66 CE* (London: SCM/Philadelphia: Trinity Press International, 1992), pp. 420ff. This skepticism stems from questions about how much power the rabbis actually held under the pre-destruction judicial system, and whether the discussions involve actual practice or are

In b.Yoma 8a, we are told that a person who has the divine name inscribed on him should not bathe, presumably again lest the name be blotted out.[211] In b.Sanh. 102b, Ahaziah is censured because he erased the divine name from the Scriptures and substituted the names of idols. Even the accidental writing of the name was an issue with which to be reckoned. If someone inadvertently left the *daleth* off "Judah" and thus produced the tetragrammaton, R. Judah was willing to accept this — but the Sages declared that this "was not of the most preferable" (b. Shab. 104b). The parallels with Qumran indicate that the practice of treating the written tetragrammaton with special care was an ancient practice.[212]

Saying the Name

We begin with the discussions in the Mishnah concerning the use of the tetragrammaton in Temple practice.[213] The sources for this are in the tractates Tamid and Yoma. These are generally acknowledged to be fairly reliable indicators of Second Temple practice, although Sanders is skeptical about the masterly role played by the Pharisees vis-a-vis the Sadducees in the proceedings.[214] As always, a question mark hangs over the information, but we can have more confidence here perhaps than elsewhere. While it is true that, like Ezekiel's vision of the temple in Ezek. 40–48, we have in the Mishnah a blend of historical remembrance and idealistic blueprinting for

---

merely reflections upon biblical texts. In this particular case, however, we have external attestation (Josephus) for the importance of the divine name in the trial of the adulteress.

[211] If there was a practice of inscribing the name on one's person, I am unaware of it. (But cf. the Baraita in b.Shab. 120b, which teaches that there should be no nudity in the presence of the name. This also presupposes that the name is written on someone.) Perhaps some over-zealous people took the thought of God's name being "on" or "in" his people to its literal conclusion. It is equally likely that the discussion is purely theoretical.

[212] Also worthy of note is the engraving of the name on amulets in b. Shab 61b. The archaeological evidence surveyed in our section on magic suggests that this too had its roots in the Second Temple period.

[213] For overview, see the introductions to the translations of Hebert Danby (*The Mishnah*; Oxford: Oxford University Press, 1933)and Jacob Neusner (*The Mishnah: A New Translation*; New Haven/London: Yale University Press, 1988); Samuel Safrai, ed. *The Literature of the Sages, Part 1* Compendia Rerum Iudaicarum ad Novum Testamentum (Assen/Maastricht: Van Gorcum; Philadelphia: Fortress, 1987), pp.211ff.. For application of Mishnaic texts to the NT, see e.g. Neusner, "The Use of the Mishnah for the History of Judaism Prior to the Time of the Mishnah." *JSJ* 11 (1980): 177–85; Sanders, *Jewish Law from Jesus to the Mishnah* (London: SCM, 1990), *passim*; Craig A. Evans, "Mishna and Messiah 'in Context': Some Comments on Jacob Neusner's Proposals." *JBL* 112: 267–89; Neusner, "The Mishna in Philosophical Context and out of Canonical Bounds." *JBL* 112 (1993): 291–304.

[214] Sanders, *Judaism: Practice and Belief*, pp.11,80; cf. Marmorstein, *Old Rabbinic Doctrine*, p.29.

the future, it seems likely that there would be a good deal of interest in preserving the memory of how things were done in the cult. In the case of the divine name, the argument for the authenticity of the traditions is strengthened not only by the parallel passages in Philo,[215] but by the nature of the discussion itself. While in general the rabbis wished to curtail the use of the divine name, here is it affirmed that the name was spoken openly in the temple.

We now turn to the individual passages. The material in m. Yoma is central to our investigation. While the substitution "the name" (השם) is said to have been used in certain portions of the ceremony of the day of atonement (cf. m. Yoma 3:8,4:2; cf. בשם 6:2), this is likely a substitution for the tetragrammaton on the part of the Mishnah.[216] In any case, elsewhere in Yoma it is explicitly stated that the high priest uttered the tetragrammaton itself. In the latter portion of 3:8, during the prayer of confession given between the porch and the altar, he quotes Lev.16:30: "For on this day shall atonement be made for you to cleanse you; from all your sins shall you be clean before the Lord." The people respond by saying "Blessed be the name of the glory of his kingdom for ever and ever!"[217] Similarly, when the lots are cast for the two goats, he declares that one is a "sin offering to the Lord,"[218] and the people again respond, "Blessed be the name of the glory of his kingdom for ever and ever!" (4:2).

That this is a response to the uttering of the tetragrammaton itself becomes apparent in 6:2, where it is emphasized (after a repetition of the quotation from Lev. 16:30 in the confession over the scapegoat) that this is the "Expressed Name," the שם המפרש.[219] The response of the priests and

---

[215] e.g. *Mos.* 2:114.
[216] Gedalyahu Alon, *Jews, Judaism, and the Classical World* trans. Israel Abrahams (Jerusalem: Magnes Press, 1977), pp.237,243. For Hebrew text see Johannes Meinhold, *Die Mischna: Joma* (Giessen: A. Töpelmann, 1913).
[217] Danby translation, as throughout. The Hebrew for "before the Lord" reads לפני יי, with the two yods being a substitute for the tetragrammaton.
[218] Heb. לירי. R. Ishmael is quoted here as saying that he only needed to say "to the Lord."
[219] Rashi did not identify the שם המפרש with the tetragrammaton, but Maimonides did, and the latter is surely correct here. See the discussion in Cohon, p.587. The phrase derives from the verb פרש, which indicates "make distinct" or "declare," although it may also have the sense of "separated" or "distinguished" (thus Brown-Driver-Briggs). The verb only occurs five times in the OT, six if we include the Aramaic of Ezra 4:18 (e.g. Lev.24:12 and Num. 15:34 where the people need a word from God to *make clear* what they ought to do with the blasphemer and the sabbath breaker, respectively). מפרש itself (admittedly in Aramaic) actually appears in Ezra 4:18, but its use there is ambiguous. One cannot say for certain why the word became attached to the tetragrammaton – it could either be that YHWH was a "distinguished" (i.e. "special") name, or that it was a name whose "express" (or "explicit") pronunciation attracted attention.

the people in the temple court reaches a crescendo at this point, and it is said that on hearing the name "they used to kneel and bow themselves and fall down on their faces and say, "Blessed be the name of the glory of his kingdom for ever and ever!"

It seems unlikely that such a crucial part of such a major festival would be fabricated by the rabbis out of whole cloth even generations after the temple was destroyed. The case for the basic reliability of the tradition is strengthened by its appearance in the tractate m. Tamid. In an admittedly fantastic list of "things that could be heard from Jericho," one reads that "they say even the voice of the High Priest (could be heard) when he pronounced the Name on the Day of Atonement."[220] This is not meant to be taken literally, of course. It is presumably a way of saying that the High Priest uttered the name distinctly, or that he uttered it in a loud voice.

It is sometimes asserted that the name was only uttered clearly on the Day of Atonement. But this is not at all certain. In m. Tamid 7:2 (cf. m. Sotah 7:6, which is an almost verbatim parallel) there is a contrast between the twice-daily blessing of the priests in the holy place and the blessing in the "provinces" (מדינה). In the holy place, it is said, the name in the blessing is said "according to its writing" – ככתבו, while in the provinces it is given with a "substitute" – בכנויו.[221] The contrast is between the expressed tetragrammaton and the substitute, here almost surely Adonai. Traditions contained in the Talmud, as we will see, imply that the name was somehow "swallowed up" during the blessing. It is perhaps noteworthy that the mention of the name on the Day of Atonement drew such a dramatic response and stuck so firmly in the memory, making it seem like a unique event. But in terms of hard evidence *from the Mishnah*, there seems to be no reason to exclude the pronunciation of the tetragrammaton from the daily blessing.[222]

We must also mention here the much-discussed t. Sot. 13:8: "After Simon the Righteous died, his brethren refrained from blessing people with the Divine Name."[223] Even if this were historically accurate, it would have

---

[220] M. Tamid 3:8. It is interesting to note that the phrase rendered "pronounced the name" is מזכיר השם. We saw the hiphil of זכר used with שם used earlier in 1QS 6–7 with regards to the "invocation" of the name against someone; cf. also Ex. Rab.1:29, which speaks of Moses slaying the Egyptian by pronouncing the name over him: הזכיר עליו את שם. For text and discussion of the latter see Jakob Petuchowski, "Judaism as 'Mystery' – The Hidden Agenda?" *HUCA* 52 (1981): 141–152.

[221] See also b.Sot. 37a–38b; Sifre on Numbers 6:23,27; b.Yoma 69b.

[222] The new Schürer accepts the evidence of the Mishnah and affirms the name was pronounced according to its letters in the priestly blessing. See Emil Schürer, *The History of the Jewish People in the Age of Jesus Christ (175 B.C.–A.D. 135)*; revised and edited by G. Vermes, F. Millar, and M. Black; vol. 2 (Edinburgh: T.&T. Clark, 1979): 306–7.

[223] Trans. J. Neusner, *The Tosefta: Nashim* (New York: KTAV, 1979).

to be weighed against the assertion in m. Tamid that the name *was* used in the blessing. As it happens, the problems with the passage are many. The identity of Simon the Righteous is uncertain. Most assume he is the Simon II mentioned in Sir. 50:1–6, who lived c. 200 BCE.[224] VanderKam, we have seen, has argued that the Simon in Sirach is Simon I, c. 300 BCE. Alon, meanwhile, believes "Simon the Righteous" is a figure from the *end* of the Second Temple period. (He cites t.Sot. 8:6 where a Simon hears about the death of Gaius Caligula.)[225]

Although I favor the identification of "Simon the Righteous" in the Tosefta with Simon I, the historicity of the passage is in any case questionable. The teaching is set within a passage whose aim is to teach that "when righteous people come into the world, good comes into the world and retribution departs from the world. And when they take their leave from the world, retribution comes into the world, and goodness departs from the world" (t.Sot. 10:1). Thus there is not necessarily any more historical grounding in the statement that the name ceased to be used in the blessing after his death than that "conscientious students" ceased after the death of Ben 'Azzai (15:4), or that "the glory of the Torah" ceased after the death of R. Eliezer (15:3). Moreover, this passage could have been influenced by the text about Simon in Sir. 50:20, which may have been understood to indicate a cessation of the name in the temple. Most likely it stems from a distant remembrance of the time when a substitution for the tetragrammaton began to come into general use,[226] or from a tradition that the priests, in grief over Simon's death, temporarily stopped using the name in the benediction.[227] Given the importance Marmorstein attaches to this passage, we conclude by quoting Urbach's judgement: "At any rate, we must not regard this tradition as fundamental and infer from it, in contradiction of all other sources, that a law was promulgated forbidding the use of the Name in the priestly benediction in the Temple."[228]

The pronunciation of the name is mentioned outside the context of the temple in m. Sanh. 7:5, which contains a summary of the proceedings against the blasphemer, המגדף. He is not guilty, according to the Mish-

---

[224] See Schiffman, p.147 n.

[225] Alon, p.242 n.

[226] Thus Schiffman, p.134.

[227] Urbach, 1: 128.

[228] Urbach, 1: 128. Before we leave the temple setting, we also mention briefly the teaching that during the blessing the High Priest did not raise his hands above the mitre on which the name of God was inscribed (m. Tamid 7:2). R. Judah disputed the tradition, however, and thus it may be that certain rabbis had imagined it based on their understanding of the sanctity of the name, while actual temple practice was in accordance with R. Judah.

nah, unless he "pronounces the Name itself."[229] Euphemisms were used during most of the trial, and the name would only be expressly pronounced at the end of the trial by the chief witness, after all the people had been sent out. The judges then tore their garments, and the charge was affirmed by the other witnesses. There is nothing here which goes against the tenor of the times as described in the earlier sections of our inquiry. It would be quite in keeping with what we know of the Judaism of the day to spare the court and audience from a series of blasphemies of the name YHWH, even though they were merely being repeated as evidence in a trial.

Another passage in m. Sanh. appears to make pronouncing the tetragrammaton a matter of (eternal) life and death. M. Sanh. 10:1 begins by stating that all Israelites have a share in the life to come. Then it lists the exceptions to this rule. Among these exceptions we read, "Abba Saul says: Also he that pronounces the Name with its proper letters."[230] Abba Saul, it should be noted, was a third generation Tanna, flourishing c. 130–160 CE,[231] and such a severe judgement on the bare pronunciation of the Name (if that is indeed what this is referring to) is not met with before his time.[232] Like many items in rabbinic literature, this is not "Jewish law," or even "Jewish belief." It is the opinion of one rabbi, with whom others may well have disagreed. The custom of not using the tetragrammaton is certainly well attested in earlier documents, but this particular theological statement about what happens to those who do so is not.

If the statement is read in context, it becomes evident that Abba Saul himself (or at least the redactor of the Mishnah) may not even be referring to someone who simply pronounces the tetragrammaton. His teaching follows the condemnation (by R. Akiba) of "he that reads the heretical books, or that utters charms over a wound and says, *I will put none of the diseases upon thee which I have put upon the Egyptians: for I am the Lord that healeth thee.*" Given the well-documented use of divine names in magic,

---

[229] Heb.: אינו חיב עד שיפרש את השם (some eds. substitute הי for השם). Text in Samuel Kraub, *Die Mishna: Sanhedrin, Makkot* (Giessen: A. Töpelmann, 1933). Kraub notes the connection between the verb for "pronounce," יפרש, and the שם המפרש discussed above.

[230] Heb. ההוגה את השם באותיותיו.

[231] Hermann L. Strack and Günter Stemberger, *Einleitung in Talmud und Midrasch*, 7th ed. (Munich: Beck'sche, 1982), p.84.

[232] A similar assertion is made in Abot de-R. Nathan (Recension 1, xii; see Urbach, 1: 130); cf. R. Levi, "He who pronounces God's name is guilty of death," Pesiqta R. K. 148a, as cited by Marmorstein, *Old Rabbinic Doctrine*, p.19. It was recorded that R. Hanina b. Teradion was killed by the Romans because he uttered the name in public (b. 'Aboda Zara 18a) – but even this is not the same as forfeiting life in the world to come.

we can concur with Urbach when he suggests that the statement by Abba Saul may refer to the pronunciation of the name in charms.²³³

M. Ber. 9:5 reads: "And it was ordained that a man should salute his fellow with [the use of] the Name [of God]; for it is written, *And, behold, Boaz came from Bethlehem, and said unto the reapers, The Lord be with you.*" There are two basic approaches to this passage. The first sees this whole discussion as simply a rabbinical reflection upon Ruth 2:4. Since the text explicitly mentions the use of YHWH in the greeting of both Boaz and the reapers, the use of the tetragrammaton in greetings was seen to be "ordained."²³⁴ Yet at the time of the rabbis, such a greeting was not practiced. Thus an explanation had to be given for the discontinuation of the practice. This explanation appears to be that because the people had neglected the Torah, it was necessary to "make void the Law," i.e. retract the practice of greeting with the name (cf. t. Ber. 7:23).

One can also take the passage as expressing actual historical circumstances. Urbach links this Baraita with the one which immediately precedes it, and takes the time of this ordination to have been "after the heretics [var. the Sadducees] had taught corruptly and said there is but one world."²³⁵ But this would tell us very little indeed, since we cannot be sure who the heretics are. Even if we do identify them with the Sadducees, they were in power long enough to make precise dating impossible. We must also deal with the possibility that the name in question may have been not the tetragrammaton but the substitute Adonai.²³⁶ Thus even if one is inclined to take our passage in a straightforward historical sense, it is still too obscure for us to draw any firm conclusions. It is possible that at some point in the late second temple period, and perhaps even beyond, the name YHWH was used in greetings, but this cannot be established with any certainty.

Our final Mishnaic passage is m. Suk. 4:5, which we have mentioned previously in our discussion of the Qumran text 4Q266.²³⁷ During the Feast of Booths, the Mishnah reports, celebrants would recite Ps. 118:25 as they marched round the altar:

אנא יהוה הושיעה נא אנא יהוה הצליחה נא

---

²³³ Urbach,1: 130.
²³⁴ Cf. Ruth Rab. 4:5.
²³⁵ Urbach, (1:129). He says that the decree was instituted to bolster the teaching of Divine Providence, which was denied by the Sadducees. See also the discussion in Alon, pp.248ff.
²³⁶ Schiffman, p.135, thinks it is "probable" that Adonai was used, and suggests that the practice may have arisen to counter the severe restrictions against saying divine names by sectaries like those at Qumran. Graetz held that the greeting was re-instituted during the Bar Kochba period to distinguish Jews from Christians; see Cohon, p. 588.
²³⁷ See Baumgarten, "A New Qumran Substitute," pp.1–5.

O YHWH save us! O YHWH rescue us!

According to R. Judah, however, they said:

אני והו הושיעה נא   אני והו הושיעה נא
O "I and He" save us! O "I and He" save us![238]

R. Judah flourished c. 150 CE. If we assume that the attribution is accurate, this tradition would be close enough to the destruction of the temple to warrant serious consideration, and yet far enough away to make one suspect there could have been an embellishing of the tradition. There would, of course, be a clear reason for re-interpreting this particular account of the Feast of Booths. Post-destruction rabbis were obviously concerned to safeguard the sanctity of the name YHWH, and it would be somewhat awkward to find the name pronounced aloud during the festival, as is implied by the citation of Ps. 118:25. R. Judah may have catered to contemporary sensibilities by saying a substitute for the name was used.

But there are problems with this view. The foremost among them is that this particular substitution is so strange that one wonders why R. Judah would have chosen it. Later rabbis were able to draw a theological lesson from the curious formula "I and He": God shared with Israel in their pain and captivity.[239] It seems more likely that the formula came first and this ingenious (and theologically powerful) interpretation came later. In any case, if R. Judah had simply wanted to deny that the name was pronounced at the Feast of Booths, one would have expected him to say something like, "The name was not said according to its vowels" or "A substitute was used," rather than that they said, "'I and He' save us!" The suspicion that this substitution may in fact constitute Second Temple practice is confirmed by the appearance of ברוך את אונ הו הכול in 4Q266.[240]

This may also tell us something about *how* the name was pronounced in this period. As we will see below, it is evident that some Jews used "Iao" or "Yahu" as divine epithets. It must be admitted that אני והו sounds more like אנא יהוה when יהוה is pronounced "Yahu" instead of "Yahweh." It could be that "Yahu" was *already* a substitute for the "genuine" pronunciation "Yahweh," so that the formula אני והו is a doubly substitutionary phrase. It would blend a secondary pronunciation with the invocative אנא. But it remains possible that "Yahu" was the authentic pronunciation of the

---

[238] See Baumgarten, "A New Qumran Substitute," p.4; Urbach, 1: 128.

[239] E.g. y.Suk. 54c, cited by Baumgarten, "A New Qumran Substitute," p. 1; for further examples, see C.H. Dodd, *The Interpretation of the Fourth Gospel* (Cambridge: Cambridge University Press, 1953), pp.94–5; and Philip B. Harner, *The 'I Am' of the Fourth Gospel* (Facet Books, Biblical Series; Philadelphia: Fortress, 1970), pp.19ff.

[240] See Baumgarten, "A New Qumran Substitute," p.1.

tetragrammaton in the Second Temple period.²⁴¹ This question will be treated more fully in a discursus below.

We turn now to the Talmuds. Again, we will begin with what the Talmuds say about practice regarding the name in the temple. Some passages in the Talmuds simply reinforce what we already know about temple practice from the Mishnah. B. Hag. 16a adds one interesting detail. It notes that one ought not to look upon three things: the rainbow, because it is the appearance of the likeness of the glory of the Lord (cf. Ez. 1:28); the Prince, because God's honour will be put upon him;²⁴² and the priests *when they give the blessing and speak the divine name*. This is a vivid example of the respect with which the name was held. Like the Prince and the rainbow, it was believed to share in the very glory of God.

It also seems to imply that the name was said explicitly during the daily blessing. There is another tradition ascribed to R. Tarfon, however, which reports that the priests "swallowed up" the name during the temple service. The history of this tradition is quite complicated and requires extended discussion. We begin with t.Ber. 7:23, despite the fact that it does not directly concern temple practice. We read there: "In former times, when the Torah was being forgotten from Israel, the elders used to cause it [the Name] to be swallowed up (Heb. מבליעין); for it is written (Ruth 2:4): 'And behold Boaz came.'"²⁴³ The rest of Ruth 2:4 of course reads "...and said unto the reapers, 'The Lord be with you'," which we have just seen was raised with respect to the question of greeting with the name. This sentence, then, appears to refer to the non-pronunciation of the tetragrammaton.

The Palestinian Talmud, in y.Yoma 3:7 (40d), also discusses "swallowing the name" but in a very different context:

> At first he (the High Priest) used to utter it aloud; when unruly men increased, he used to utter it softly. R. Tarfon said: "I was standing among my brother priests in the line and I inclined my ear towards the high priest and I heard him muffle (or "cause to be swallowed," מבליע) it [the Name] in the melody of the priests. At first it was entrusted to all men; but when unruly men increased, it was confided only to those who were worthy.²⁴⁴

The Baraita appears in slightly different form in *Sifre Zuta*, where the context is made the priestly benediction,²⁴⁵ and in b.Qidd. 71a, where the

---

²⁴¹ For the question of whether אני והו represents the "swallowing" of the name in rabbinic texts, see below.
²⁴² Cf. Num. 27:20, as noted by the editors of the Soncino Talmud.
²⁴³ Translation (with Hebrew text) in Baumgarten, "A New Qumran Substitute," p.4.
²⁴⁴ Translation in Urbach, 1:127.
²⁴⁵ Sifre Zuta on Numbers 6:27; see Urbach, 2: 736.

introduction is changed to, "Once I went up after my mother's brother to the priests' platform..."[246]

Even if we only deal with the Palestinian Talmud the going is fairly rough. The identity of the "unruly" – the פרוצין – is no more certain than is the identity of the "heretics" in m.Ber.9:5. Urbach suggests that they are "none other than people who used the Name irresponsibly,"[247] and it is best not to say much more than that. The passage may simply be reminiscing about "the good old days" before you had to hide the name of God from people. As for R. Tarfon, he was a second generation Tanna (according to Neusner, c. 50–120 CE) and the teacher of R. Judah b. Ilai.[248] If the attribution is accurate, it is likely that Tarfon would have been in a position to know what Temple practice was. Unfortunately, even if this is the case, what he meant by "swallowing" (or "mixing," as Marmorstein renders it[249]) is not clear. Is it the same as "uttering it softly," presumably while the priests were singing?[250] Or could "mixing" refer to the same phenomenon evinced in m.Suk. 4:5, where אני והו, is substituted for the tetragrammaton? We saw that this may well represent actual Second Temple practice, at least for the Feast of Booths. But R. Tarfon's report concerns the *high priest*, and there is no reference to the Feast of Booths.[251] I tend to believe, on the basis of the Mishnah, that the name *was* pronounced according to its letters in the daily blessing, and that the Tarfon story is a later embellishment. Even if the story is accurate, we must remember that the name was at least said on the Day of Atonement.

---

[246] Urbach, 2: 736. The Baraita in b.Qidd. follows directly after mention of the "12-lettered name," but Urbach does not think the two must be taken together. Certainly the other versions of the tradition are speaking of the tetragrammaton.

[247] Urbach,1: 129.

[248] Strack-Stemberger, p.79.

[249] Marmorstein, *Old Rabbinic Doctrine*, p.21. Although I have found no mention of textual variants in these passages, it is worth noting that בלל means "to mix," and according to Jastrow, בלע itself can also have this meaning. It is possible that there was some confusion in the transmission of the text, with בלע eventually becoming the established form in the tradition.

[250] Cf. the comment by Eduard Baneth, who says that the name was spoken twice daily "aber nicht so klar wie heute durch den Hohenpriester; denn der Priestersegen wurde gesungen, und im vielstimmehen Gesange kommen die Worte nicht so deutlich zu Gehör." Baneth, *Mishnajot: Teil II, Ordnung Mo'ed.* (Basel: Victor Goldschmidt, 1968), p.320 n. Meinhold makes an almost identical statement in his *Joma*, p.60 n.

[251] It may be of interest that the account of R. Tarfon in b.Qidd. follows a Baraita about the name YHWH being taught to the Sages' disciples only once (or twice, according to other rabbis) in a septennate. Could it be that the Tarfon tradition was devised as a poetical way of describing this restriction on the use of the name by the rabbis? That is, the "swallowing" referred originally to the reluctance of the Sages to say the name, and this "swallowing" was then given fabular expression in the chanting of the priests.

We can now leave the temple and consider the relevant rabbinic teachings on pronouncing the name outside the cult. Not surprisingly, saying the name YHWH under ordinary circumstances is frowned upon.[252] The Sages, according to b.Qidd. 71a, taught the name to their students only once every seven years. We have cited above instances where the pronunciation of the name is associated with the forfeiture of life in the world to come. We might add *haggadot* such as b.Hag. 49b, where Isaiah, after pronouncing the name, is said to have been swallowed by a cedar and sawn in half.[253] While it is possible that such a belief was prevalent during the New Testament era, it may well be a later development. Perhaps more representative is the story of Rabbi Huna, who heard a woman say the name and banned her, but later released her from the ban (b.Ned. 7b). This may indicate an earlier belief in which saying the name was indeed considered a serious offense, but not so dire as was held by (or ascribed to) Abba Saul. One cannot exclude the possibility that different views circulated during the late Second Temple period.

We can be more confident about the antiquity of traditions concerning the use of the name in blasphemy, oaths, and curses, since we have many parallel passages extant from the Second Temple period. The first receives attention in b. Sanhedrin (e.g. b.Sanh. 60a), which affirms the mishnaic teaching (m.Sanh. 7:5) that the blasphemer is not to be executed unless he has pronounced the tetragrammaton itself (Mishnah: "pronounces the Name"; Talmud: "'blesses' the name of four letters").[254] This is no doubt a very ancient tradition based on Lev. 24:11ff. As for oaths, Schiffman asserts that "there can be no question that early tannaitic practice required that judicial oaths be taken by the Tetragrammaton," although the practice

---

[252] Witness the curious exegesis of Ex. 3:15 in b.Pes. 50a, where שמי לעלם , "my name forever" is interpreted as "my name to conceal" (reading לעלם as an infinitive of the verb עלם). Moore (1: 428) is probably correct to see this as justification for a pre-existing practice of not saying the name. We must also mention here b. Rosh Hashanah 18b, which speaks of a decree promulgated by the Greek government (מלכות יון) forbidding the Jews to mention the name of God ("Heaven") in their documents – להזכיר שם שמים. This presumably took place just before the Maccabean era (cf. Cohon, p.588). The use of זכר is interesting (cf. 1QS 6–7; Ex. Rab. 1:29; y.Tam. 3:8), but it appears from the rest of the Baraita that the designation is "the Most High God" and not the tetragrammaton.

[253] Compare the tradition noted above about R. Hanina b. Teradion being killed by the Romans (b. 'Aboda Zara 18a).

[254] This leads on to a discussion of whether one must rend one's garments when a Gentile blasphemes the name (answer: no) and the wistful remark of R. Hiyya that one needn't rend one's garments since there is so much blasphemy nowadays that one's garments would be completely in tatters! The Talmud goes on to say that it is hardly likely that Gentiles would have known the secret name of God, and so the references must be to the use of substitutes in blasphemy.

likely died out by the end of the tannaitic era.[255] Curses by the divine name, on the other hand, are explicitly forbidden in b.Tem. 3a, b.Mak. 16a, b.Shev. 21a, and y.Shev. 3:10.[256] Such a practice was not only unseemly, it was viewed as deadly. Y.Yoma 3:7 records the story of Samuel hearing a man cursing his son by the divine name, whereupon the son dies. Another story (or perhaps another version of the first) in Eccl. R. tells of a Persian woman who cursed her son with "one word" of the divine name.[257] He, too, dies. Artapanus records a similar tale of Moses knocking Pharaoh unconscious with a mere whisper of the name.[258] There is abundant use of divine names for cursing in magical texts. The underlying tradition of the extraordinary cursing power of the name YHWH may well go back quite far, back to the days when it first became a hidden name, or even earlier.

Targums[259]

Throughout our study of the divine name in early Judaism we have noted the frequent allusions made to blasphemy, swearing falsely, and the taking of oaths.[260] The Targums are no exception. In the case of the blasphemer in Lev. 24:11ff., both Ps-Jon. and Neofiti emphasize that the man *blasphemed*[261] the *great and glorious* name, thus relieving the ambiguity of the

---

[255] Schiffman, p.140; on p.151 he cites Sifre Num. 14, Mekilta de-Rabbi Ishmael 16 and b.Shev. 35b in this regard. This section of Schiffman (pp.136ff.) provides a very good overview of the divine name and oaths. We would add that the bitter water test of m.Sotah amounts to an oath by the tetragrammaton, since this was written on the scroll.

[256] See Schiffman, p.141.

[257] Eccl. R. 3:11, see Schiffman, p.141.

[258] Ap. Eusebius, *Praeparatio Evangelica* 9.27.1-37; in *OTP* 2: 901.

[259] The Aramaic Bible series (T.&T. Clark) provides helpful introductions to individual Targums. For general overview see Le Déaut, *Introduction à la Littérature Targumique*. Part I (Rome: Pontifical Biblical Institute, 1966) and *The Message of the New Testament and the Aramaic Bible*. Subsidia Biblica 5 (Rome: Pontifical Biblical Institute, 1982). *The Aramaic Bible: Targums in their Historical Context*, eds. D.R.G. Beattie and M.J. McNamara (Sheffield: JSOT, 1994) contains many helpful articles by Targumic scholars. See also Bernard J. Bamberger, "The Dating of Aggadic Material," *JBL* 68 (1949): 115–123; Etan Levine, "The Biography of the Aramaic Bible," *ZAW* 94 (1992): 353–379; McNamara, *The New Testament and the Palestinian Targum*; and Anthony D. York, "The Dating of Targumic Literature," *JSJ* 5 (1974): 49–62.

[260] The significance of the Targumic term *Memra* is a special case and will be dealt with in our chapter on the meaning of the name. Nor are we concerned here with the abbreviations used for the divine name (often a *he* or three *yods*) since the actual manuscripts we have for the Targums are quite late (excluding the Qumran Targums of Job and fragments of Leviticus).

[261] In keeping with the practice of Targum translations, we will italicize those words which are added or altered in the Targums. All Pentateuchal texts are my renderings of Le Déaut's French translation (*Targum du Pentateuque*, in the Sources Chrétiennes series, Paris: Cerf, 1978–80) unless otherwise noted. For the Aramaic text of Ps-Jon., I

Hebrew text (cf. our discussion above on Lev. 24:11ff. in the LXX).[262] They likewise make the general principle clear at the end of the passage. Anyone who utters the name *with curses* (Neof., v.16) or *offends the proper name* (Ps-Jon. v.16) is to be killed.[263] The grave offense of swearing falsely by the name is also emphasized in the Targums. Both Tg. Onqelos and Ps-Jon. on Ex. 20:7 understand taking the name in vain to be *swearing* in vain by the name. In Ps-Jon. Dt. 5:11 this is lengthened to the name *of the Memra* of YHWH, and at the close of the verse we read that he will not go unpunished who takes in vain the *holy* name *of YHWH*.[264] Note too Ps-Jon. Ex. 21:17, where the one who curses his father or mother *by the explicit name*[265] will be put to death. Like Josephus, Ps-Jon. highlights the role of the name in the bitter water test of Numbers 5. Ps-Jon adds in v.19 that the woman must swear an oath *by the great and glorious name* (whereas Josephus stresses the writing of the divine name on the scroll). The idea of swearing *by the name* is also added in Tg. Jer. 4:2, 12:10 and Tg. Zeph. 1:5.

Ps-Jon shows its awareness of traditions concerning the pronunciation of the name on the day of atonement in Lev. 16:21. Aaron is to confess the sins of the people and put them on the goat's head *with an oath spoken and expressed*[266] *by the great and glorious name*. The Targumic addition immediately calls to mind the emphasis on the explicit pronunciation of the name in m.Yoma. There is no direct mention in the Targums of whether the name was expressed with its letters in the daily blessing, but it is interesting that in keeping with rabbinic practice (m.Meg. 4:10) the priestly

---

have used *Targum Pseudo-Jonathan of the Pentateuch: Text and Concordance*, ed. E.G. Clarke (Hoboken, NJ: KTAV, 1984).

[262] "Great and glorious" in Aramaic is שמא רבא ויקירא. This is a stock phrase in Ps-Jon. which will appear regularly in the texts we discuss. Note the similar description of the name of God as "glorious and honored and great and splendid and amazing and mighty" in Jub. 36:7.

[263] For translation and text variants see Le Déaut. We find an interesting tradition preserved in both Neofiti and Ps-Jon. of Dt. 32:3. According to Neofiti, Moses, after calling down a curse upon the impious who mention the Lord's name with blasphemies, goes on to explain that not even the angels of the service say the divine name until they have thrice said "holy, holy, holy." Neofiti then says that this is how Moses learned not to pronounce the name until he had sanctified his mouth with twenty-one words (that is, the twenty one words that precede the first mention of YHWH in the MT of Deuteronomy 32; see the note in Le Déaut). Ps-Jon preserves this last item but omits the mention of angels. I have found no parallels to this in any earlier sources, and so the tradition cannot really be pressed into service for our investigation.

[264] Cf. Tg. of the Minor Prophets, Zech. 5:3, "everyone who swears *falsely by my name is punished...*"

[265] Aram. שמא מפרש.

[266] "Spoken and expressed" is אימירא ומפרשא.

blessing of Num. 6:24-26 was not translated in Onqelos and Neofiti. (Ps-Jon, true to its idiosyncratic nature, does retain the Hebrew but adds an interpretive Aramaic paraphrase.)

Why was the use of YHWH restricted in Early Judaism?

Our survey of the use of the name YHWH in early Judaism confirms that the tetragrammaton was treated with great reverence at this time. The rabbinical strictures concerning the writing of the name are borne out by the evidence of the documents from Qumran. We have evidence from Philo, Josephus, and the rabbinical literature that the pronunciation of the tetragrammaton was restricted to the temple. The widespread use of substitute forms like κύριος or Adonai also attests to the reticence of Jews to use the name YHWH. We have seen, however, that the name YHWH had not completely disappeared. There is strong evidence that the name was pronounced according to its letters on the day of atonement, which means that its proper pronunciation would have been known to a large number of people. Stories about the illicit use of the name in curses and magic add further confirmation that some people did know the name. The tetragrammaton continued to have a rich underground life even after its public profile lessened.

But why all the mystery? Why did the Jews feel it improper to use the name which their ancestors had employed quite freely? It will not do to say that it was out of "superstition" or "reverence." These words are quite vague. More to the point, they beg the question of why Jews in the second temple period expressed their "superstition" or "reverence" in this particular way. Surely there were both superstitious and reverent people at the time of David or Jeremiah. But they saw nothing wrong with saying the name. It may well be the case that people in the second temple period thought that they were being respectful by not saying "YHWH," and that others were afraid to say it lest something terrible happen to them. We are left with the question of why the practice arose in the first place, and whether any rationale was offered for it.

We must say from the outset that we have no direct evidence to tell us precisely when and why the practice of not using YHWH was introduced. While portions of the Hebrew bible seem reticent to use the tetragrammaton (e.g. the "Elohistic psalter"), these are difficult to date and offer no explicit information as to why they are avoiding the divine name. If, as seems likely, the original LXX read κύριος for YHWH, this would indicate that by at least the mid-third century BCE some people were substituting for the tetragrammaton under certain circumstances. Beyond this, the evidence for early second temple Judaism dries up.

There is, however, still a way forward. We have seen numerous texts from the *later* second temple period which do address the issue of the divine name. At the very least, we may suggest some reasons why the custom of not using the name was maintained in early Judaism. Moreover, it is likely that these same factors were involved in the institution of the practice in the first place.

The best-documented reasons for the disuse of the name YHWH cluster around blasphemy, curses and oaths, and magic. Although it has been suggested by some that the LXX of Leviticus 24 treats the mere utterance of the name as a sin, we saw that this goes far beyond the evidence of the LXX itself. Moreover, later exegesis of these verses stressed only that no one was to *blaspheme* the name of God, and for some exegetes, the names of other gods (see Philo, *Mos.* 2:192ff.; Josephus, *Ant.* 4:202; m.Sanh. 7:5; Targums to Leviticus 24). If the intent of the MT or the LXX of this passage were to prohibit any pronunciation at all of the tetragrammaton, it is remarkable that we have no record of anyone using them for this purpose. Although *oaths* probably *were* taken by the tetragrammaton at some point in the tannaitic era, there is still abundant evidence that taking oaths by the name was considered to be an unwise practice. Sirach indicates that frequent oaths taken by the name will lead to ruin, while Philo (*Dec.* 82ff.), Josephus (*Ant.* 3:91), and the Targums (on Ex. 20:7) all hold that the third commandment refers to the swearing of false oaths by God's name. The one who swears falsely, as Philo points out (*Dec.* 82ff.), makes God party to a lie and thus disgraces the name. It is easy to see how a reticence to make God a liar might lead to a full scale prohibition against any oaths using the divine name. There is also much positive evidence regarding the prohibition of *cursing* with the name. 1QS 6:27–7:2 seems to threaten expulsion from the community for those who curse with the name, and the Talmuds are full of denunciations of the practice (see b.Tem. 3a, b.Mak. 16a, b.Shev. 21a, y.Shev. 3:10).

There is a fine line, of course, between cursing and *magic*, since much of the latter consists precisely of cursing one's enemies. Thus the prohibitions against cursing may apply equally to magical practices employing the name. The widespread use of variations of the divine name in magic shows that this was a very real problem in the Jewish community. Certainly many of the spells we possess come from pagan sources who have at best a passing knowledge of some Jewish names and beliefs. But it is equally certain that some, and perhaps many, Jews were involved in one way or another with practices which could be classified as magic. We have proposed that Abba Saul is likely referring to magical practices when he denounces those who say the tetragrammaton in m.Sanh. 10:1. Even a cursory glance at the magical papyri and amulets shows why the rabbis and other Jews would be opposed to the use of the divine name in this way. Magical practices were forbidden in the Pentateuch, so the whole enterprise was suspect from the start. One would not need to be overly pietistic to suspect that using the name of God to smite one's enemy, or to win a horse race, was grossly inappropriate for a member of the covenant community. (One could reasonably subsume this under the third commandment, although I know of no actual text where this connection is made.) Finally, magical spells were a hotbed of syncretism and hence a threat to Jewish monotheism. When the God of Israel (usually in the guise of "Iao") became just another name to be tossed into the mix along with Zeus and Apollo and Isis, the center of the tradition was at stake.

As we have said, we have no direct evidence as to why the name initially fell into disuse. But the evidence presented above is quite suggestive. In each of the areas discussed – blasphemy, oaths and curses, and magic – there were compelling theological and sociological reasons to restrict the use of the divine name. It is easy to see how restrictions imposed within this matrix of issues might easily be extended to include any use of the tetragrammaton in speech. We would submit that the misuse of the name in these areas was the engine which pushed forward more wide-ranging restrictions on the name.[267] When we read in rabbinic texts that the name was taken from Israel because of their "unworthiness,"[268] this may reflect the abuse of the name in the ways we have discussed.

There were doubtless other factors at work which contributed to the withdrawal of the name YHWH. Here we leave the explicit evidence and rely more on inference. The connection of the *temple* and the name has been well documented, especially by Hayward. Equally well-documented is the central importance of the temple for early Judaism. Thus when we read that "the name was said according to its letters in the temple, but with a substitute in the provinces," we must see this in the light of the overall consolidation of power by the temple authorities. It is one piece of the larger puzzle. Having the exclusive rights to say the name would have been of inestimable value for the powers in Jerusalem. If the wealth and splen-

---

[267] A word must be said here about the use of the name in Scripture readings and blessings. While these are also well attested (cf. especially the evidence from Qumran), it is difficult to see how they would constitute *reasons* for the disuse of the name. We can see how abuse of the name in blasphemy, oaths, curses, and magic might lead people to withdraw it from common use. It is difficult to fit Scripture reading or blessings into this same category. It seems far more likely that the withdrawal of the name in these areas was the result of a pre-existing prohibition.

[268] See t.Ber. 7:23; y.Yoma 3:7; cf. Targums Neofiti and Pseudo-Jonathan Ex. 32:25ff., 33:6.

dor of the temple were not enough of an attraction, now it had become the repository of the sacred name itself. (Comparisons to the holdings of a museum might be appropriate.) The process would have been self-perpetuating. As people began to view the temple as the center of a series of concentric circles of holiness, it would seem increasingly sensible to keep the holy name in the holy place. This would in turn further enhance the prestige of the temple, and so the cycle would go. The temple authorities, no doubt, would have told themselves that they were thereby guarding the name from the various misuses noted above. They could also legitimately argue that the Lord had chosen to "put his name" in the temple (see Dt. 12:5,11; 1 Ki. 8:16–19; 9:3). This should not be dismissed out of hand. But neither should a consideration of power politics.

The increasing importance of the temple was itself a part of the broader question of Jewish identity. The temple was a place where one could be relatively free of Gentile interference and practice the ancestral customs. It was a visible boundary between Us and Them. In a similar way, *not* speaking the name YHWH openly was a way of distinguishing oneself from the broader hellenistic culture. Josephus in particular seems to treat it as a national (or perhaps a priestly) secret, as Judaism's answer to the Eleusinian mysteries. As we will see below in our discursus on the pronunciation of the name, it is possible that some Jews did share the name with foreigners. (This is on the admittedly questionable assumption that "Iao" was the, or at least a, way of pronouncing the tetragrammaton). Yet it is certain that some Jews, and probably most Jews, did keep the name hidden from those outside the community. One might say that as the national borders of Israel dissolved, the borders around the name were tightened in compensation.[269]

But this immediately raises a problem. For when we consider what the tetragrammaton was replaced with – most notably κύριος – we must admit that this signaled an engagement with Greek culture, not a retreat. "Lord" on its own might be a rather strange epithet for God,[270] but everyone knew what the word meant, and they could presumably understand something of what the Jews were getting at by using it. Substitutions like this were far better suited for communication with foreigners than the more exotic (and nationalistic) YHWH. They would also be useful for engaging the philosophically minded – although as we will see, this could also be done with *interpretations* of the name YHWH.

These last two points are clearly in tension, but they are certainly not mutually exclusive. One of the central threads of Old Testament theology is that YHWH, the covenant God of Israel, is also Elohim, the God who

---

[269] I am grateful to Prof. Philip Esler for this suggestion.
[270] It was of course familiar enough as a modifier in divine names, e.g. "Lord Serapis."

created the world. This reality could be expressed in the relationship of the titles YHWH and κύριος. The Jews' unique relationship with God was reflected in the restriction of the name YHWH to the covenant community. At the same time, YHWH's claims on all humankind were expressed in the title of κύριος. In any event, both the maintenance of Jewish boundaries, and effective communication with foreigners, fostered the same thing: the restriction of the spoken name YHWH.

Before we conclude, we should add that once this custom was in place, the Jews (as Hengel says[271]) "made a virtue of necessity," and exploited the theological potential of the now hidden name. Philo made the idea of God's namelessness a pillar of his whole intellectual enterprise, and the "ineffable" God became a regular feature on the landscape of Jewish literature (e.g. Ap.Abr. 10:4, Ap.Zeph. A). It was an effective way of communicating God's otherness, his transcendence. We need not conclude that the imminent God had disappeared from Judaism, as is sometimes suggested. The hymns at Qumran, to cite but one example, give ample testimony that the nearness of God was still cherished by his people. One could still speak of God's imminence using other names.[272] YHWH became almost exclusively a vehicle of God's transcendence. It was also ideally suited for speaking about eschatology. As the rabbis reflected on the phrase in Zechariah 14, "in that day my name will be one," they wondered how it was that God, who was already one, would be one at some future date. R. Nahman b. Isaac answered this by referring to the practice of substituting Adonai for YHWH. "In this world," he said, "His name is written with a *yod he* [i.e. YHWH] and read *alef daleth* [i.e. Adonai]; but in the future world it shall all be one; it shall be written with *yod he* and read as *yod he*."[273]

We may end by reiterating our first point: it is probably impossible to establish a clear history of when and why the name YHWH largely disappeared from use. We might venture to say that the restriction of the name was precipitated by its abuse in blasphemy, oaths, etc., and that this restriction was furthered by social factors such as the consolidation of power in the temple, and the preserving of national identity in a new cultural and

---

[271] Hengel, *Judaism and Hellenism*, 1: 266–7.

[272] We might also question whether the loss of the "personal" name YHWH had a profound effect on Jewish theology. Warm, personal relationships can thrive in the absence of personal names. This is most evident in families, where the use of "mother" and "father" hardly betrays distance – quite the opposite. Loving husbands and wives often omit their personal names altogether when addressing one another. Examples could be multiplied. Since the case cannot be decided on *prima facie* grounds, one would have to prove that Jewish prayers and writings from the second temple period show a conspicuous absence of a personal God. I have not been convinced that this is the case.

[273] See b.Pes. 50a.

political environment. In any case, we cannot simply say that it was the result of "reverence" or "superstition," although no doubt these two factors were important in perpetuating the restrictions on saying the name in everyday life. We have seen that there were some compelling reasons for taking the name out of general circulation, and that once this practice was established, Jewish theologians were able to reflect on it in quite interesting ways. If we may be allowed a paradox: the name, though silenced, was still speaking.

Discursus: The Pronunciation of the Tetragrammaton

We have seen in our discussion that "Iao"[274] was widely reported in the sources as being the name of the Jewish God. This gives rise to the following question: Was "Iao" the way people, or at least some people, actually pronounced the tetragrammaton during the Second Temple period?

Although we can avoid the specialized problems that attend the study of the name in ancient Israel, it is important to note that the origins of the Iao designation go far back.[275] We encounter it most commonly in the יהו -ending of personal names which abound in the Old Testament.[276] This יהו form is generally thought to be an abbreviated form of the name YHWH.[277] In these theophoric names, in the Elephantine papyri and ostraca,[278] and in the Greek and Roman witnesses, we meet with a trigram rather than a tetragram (e.g. Iao, IAO, יהו, יהה). Nonetheless, some scholars have argued that it had an independent status quite early on. The geographical designation *Yhw* (perhaps in the vicinity of Seir) has been found inscribed on two temples in Nubia (modern Sudan), one dating from c.1400 BCE

---

[274] For the sake of convenience, we will use "Iao" as an all-encompassing term for the similar variants (יהו, יהה, IAO, and so on) which crop up throughout our period of concern.

[275] The article by Freedman and O'Connor, "YHWH," in *TDNT* 5: 500–21, provides an excellent overview of this highly technical material. See also Parke-Taylor, pp.18ff.

[276] See Freedman and O'Connor, p.501. Note that the precise form Ιαω does *not* go back to the Septuagint, which renders theophoric divine names with the endings -ια and -ιου. See Stig Norin, "Die Wiedergabe JHWH-haltiger Personnamen in der Septuaginta," *SJOT* 1 (1988): 76–95.

[277] Baudissin, 2: 194ff.

[278] We should also note the variant form יהה which occurs once in the papyri, but quite frequently in Samaritan ostraca. See two articles by André Dupont-Sommer: "'Yaho' et 'Yaho Seba'ot' sur des ostraca araméens inédits d'Éléphantine." *CRAI* (1947): 175–191; and "Le syncrétisme religieux des Juifs d'Éléphantine d'après un ostracon araméen inédit," *Revue de l'histoire des religions* 130 (1945): 17–28; B. Porten in Anchor Bible Dictionary, II, pp.445–55; Parke-Taylor, pp.81–4.; Rose, pp.16ff.

and the other from c.1250 BCE.[279] *If* this place name also served as the name of the deity (not an unknown phenomenon; cf. Ashur[280]) and *if* this name in fact formed the basis for the later Israelite *Yhwh*, then the Iao form could date back quite far indeed. But the evidence is tenuous, and M. Rose's contention that *Yhw* was the original form can hardly be considered proven.[281]

We now turn to the question of how the personal name of the Jewish God may have been pronounced in early Judaism. We must emphasize from the start that a final resolution of the problem of *precisely* how the name was said is impossible. We have no tape recordings of people saying the tetragrammaton; and even if we had one from, say, Jerusalem, there would still be the possibility that there were significant local variations elsewhere in the Mediterranean. The somewhat mysterious status of this divine name during our period exacerbates the problem. At best, we can raise the question of whether the name may have been said *something like* Yahu or Yaho, or *something like* the currently favored pronunciation Yahweh – or we may conclude that both forms were current among different groups.

We begin with the evidence for the pronunciation Yahweh. Old Testament scholars over the last century are generally agreed that this is how the name would have been said in ancient Israel.[282] G. J. Thierry, among others, has asserted that יהוה should be understood as a verbal form, in parallel with אהיה in Ex. 3:14. While "Yahweh" does not correspond to a Qal imperfect of היה (which would be יהיה), the form can be accounted for by: a) the existence of an early form of the verb to be הוה; b) by the retention of the original *pathah* of the first syllable; and c) the tendency to treat divine names conservatively and preserve the archaic form.[283] Freedman and O'Connor come to a similar conclusion about pronunciation, but they base it more on parallel forms in Amorite.[284] The discussion is difficult to follow for those without a deep knowledge of comparative Semitics, but one must admit that the virtual unanimity of the *cognoscenti* on the matter counts for something.

---

[279] Mettinger, p.26.

[280] Mettinger, p.26.

[281] Rose, *passim.*; Werner Schmidt, "Der Jahwename und Ex 3,14," in *Textgemäss: Aufsätze und Beiträge zur Hermeneutik des alten Testaments* (Göttingen: Vandenhoeck and Ruprecht, 1979), p.126; Freedman and O'Connor, pp.506ff.

[282] Freedman and O'Connor, p.500.

[283] G.J. Thierry, "The Pronunciation of the Tetragrammaton," *Oudtestamentische Studiën*, Deel V (1948): 39–41.

[284] Freedman and O'Connor, pp.512-3. They are also of the opinion that Yahweh may originally have represented a Hiphil rather than a Qal.

Unfortunately, there is no direct evidence from the late Second Temple period which supports such a pronunciation. One can find occasional epithets in the magical papyri which come close to it, but these are of uncertain date, and more importantly, such a reading was bound to come up given the magicians predilection for vocalic combinations. The absence of this form, however, should not be taken as absolute evidence against its use at this time. Many within Judaism appear to have been less than eager to say the name aloud, and it is possible, albeit unlikely, that they could have proffered the form Iao to outsiders while retaining the "true" pronunciation within their own community (see below).

For the earliest concrete testimony to the pronunciation "Yahweh" we must turn to Clement of Alexandria, Diodorus of Tarsus (late fourth century CE) and Theodoret (fifth century CE). In *Stromata* 5,6,34, Clement cites the form Ιαουε.[285] Diodorus gives the tetragrammaton as *ioth, alph, ouau, he*,[286] while Theodoret says that the Samaritans said the divine name Ιαβε or Ιαβαι.[287] (He says that the Jews, by contrast, pronounced it Αια.[288]) Baudissin makes a case for the reliability of Clement's testimony by saying that he probably received it from his teacher in Palestine, who may have been a converted Jew.[289] This is possible, but it reads quite a bit into the available evidence.[290] Nonetheless, it remains a fairly early attestation for this reading of the divine name. Diodorus seems either to be citing a (perhaps deliberately) corrupted version of the tetragrammaton as יאוה or, as seems more likely, to be giving a phonetic rendering of the pronunciation "Yahweh." As for Theodoret, like Diodorus he is obviously writing at some distance from the first century. His Αια seems to be either a version of אהיה from Ex.3:14 (cf. Hos. 1:9) or of יה, neither of which represents the tetragrammaton proper.[291] While the evidence he gives from the Samaritans cannot be dismissed out of hand,[292] neither can it be accorded the status of reliable ancient tradition.[293] At best, the testimony of

---

[285] Baudissin (2: 216–7) Ganschinietz, p.700. B.D. Eerdmans, "The Name Jahu," *Oudtestamentische Studiën*, Deel V (1948): 5.

[286] Fr. 64 in Deconinck's ed., as cited by Le Boulluec and Sandevoir, pp.111–12.

[287] *Quaest. in Exod.* interr. 15, Ιαβε; *Haeret. fab.* 5,3 Ιαβαι.

[288] Alternate reading Ια. See Baudissin, 2: 222.

[289] Baudissin, 2: 217.

[290] Marcel Caster (In *Les Stromates* I, Sources Chrétiennes 30; Paris: Cerf, 1951) by contrast renders *Strom.* I, 1,11 "l'autre de Palestine, juif de naissance." On this matter, see the note on p.163 of Theodor Zahn's *Forschungen zur Geschichte des neutestamentlichen Kanons und der altkirchlichen Literatur*, vol 3 (Erlangen: Deichert, 1884).

[291] Baudissin (2: 222) makes a strong case that Theodoret has lifted this form from Jerome's *Lib. Interp. Heb. Nom.*

[292] As Eerdmans does, pp.2–3.

[293] Thus Thierry, pp.34–6. He cites other instances where the Samaritans have preserved older forms of spelling, orthography, etc.

the latter two individuals can serve as supplements to the scholarly reconstruction and the earlier witness of Clement. They cannot serve as the centerpieces of an argument for "Yahweh."

The case can hardly be considered closed, and so we turn to the Iao form. There have been linguistic arguments advanced for reading the tetragrammaton as "Yaho" or "Yahu," although the majority of scholars have obviously not been convinced by them. The final *he*, which causes the most obvious problem for the supporters of "Iao," has been variously explained as :the "explosion of breath" which accompanied the name when it was shouted in worship;[294] a vowel letter representing "o";[295] and as a plural ending to an original יהו.[296] One can hardly blame scholars for not embracing such questionable alternatives. A more plausible suggestion is that the *he* simply functions as a consonant, giving us the possible vocalizations *Yahôᵃh* or *Yahûᵃh*. The Greek transliteration would be 'Ιαώ.

In any case, grammatical considerations are secondary in light of the attested usage of a Iao form throughout much of Israel's history. There is also the witness of Jerome, who explicitly states that the tetragrammaton *legi potest Iaho*.[297] If the adherents of the "Yahweh" version may present Clement and Theodoret as witnesses, surely it is not out of court for the Iao party to do the same with Jerome.

One could take an *ad hominem* approach and object that those who said Iao or something similar were not "real" Jews. As Thierry says of the Jews at Elephantine, "they stood in principle on the side of Jeroboam, son of Nebat, 'who made Israel to sin'."[298] But this approach is of limited use. One could put the appearance of Iao in the magical papyri, on the Abrasax amulets, and perhaps even in the Jewish text the Testament of Solomon in this category, but there are numerous cases where this does not apply. B. Porten has argued against the commonly held view that the Jews at Elephantine were syncretistic.[299] The Apocalypse of Abraham may be tainted by Bogomil glosses, but these do not necessarily include the presence of the Iaoel name in the text. We must also ask whether the pagan and later Christian sources received their version of the name from "heretical" or genuine Jews. Most impressive of all, of course, is the presence of Iao in pap4QLXXLev^b. It is admitted that many of the sources may fall outside the "mainstream" of Judaism. But this does not mean it was relegated only to the dark corners of magical practice and heretical belief.

---

[294] A. Lukyn Williams, "Yaho," *JTS* 28 (1927): 282.

[295] D.D. Luckenbill, cited in Eerdmans, p.15.

[296] H. Grimme, cited in Eerdmans, p.14.

[297] Eerdmans, p.6.

[298] Thierry, p.42. It should be said that his article is on the whole very well-balanced and thorough.

[299] Porten, pp.453–4.

One final possible argument against Iao as a pronunciation of the *tetra*grammaton is its consistent appearance as a *tri*gram. Hebrew personal names and the texts at Elephantine both employ יהו, and the Greek texts generally employ 'Ιαώ. In the case of the Greek, one can argue that there is no way to represent the "h" of "Yaho." But given the ancient predilection for assigning great importance to numbers, and even the number of letters in a word,[300] the presence of only three letters in the name is significant.[301] At least some of the people who employed this form in writing must have been aware of the discrepancy between their version and the four-lettered reading. But this argument is not unanswerable. All it shows is that Jews would not have equated the Greek or Latin form "Iao" with the Hebrew tetragrammaton itself. It is does not necessarily imply that the tetragrammaton did not *sound* like "Iao" (cf. *Yahô^{a}h/Yahû^{a}h* above).

We are now faced with the unenviable task of trying to sort through this collection of often contradictory data. One option is to posit a "public" and a "private" expression of the divine name by ancient Jews. That is, when outsiders inquired about the name of their God, the Jews told them "Iao," when they told them anything at all. In the temple and in their private usage, they employed a different pronunciation – presumably "Yahweh." In other words, Iao was a *conscious substitution* for the true divine name. If this appears to reek of a "conspiracy theory" of history, one can recall Josephus' statement that he was not permitted to speak the divine name to outsiders (*Ant.* 2:276). This comes from a man who went out of his way to explain Jewish customs and history to a gentile audience. A fitting analogy would be the Eleusinian mysteries, the secrets of which were kept well guarded despite the world-wide interest in the rites. Jews like Josephus may have regarded the name of God an even greater mystery, a secret well worth keeping. At the same time, Josephus' priestly background may have made him more sensitive to this issue. Hence, his failure to mention "Iao" in his writings. Other Jews, however, may have felt this (hypothetically) secondary pronunciation was suitable for Gentile ears.

While such a view is possible, a more nuanced approach seems preferable. The following is offered as a tentative solution. It is difficult, albeit not impossible, to believe that the name Iao was the equivalent of the secret name which was pronounced in the Temple, and which the rabbis later passed along amongst themselves. All the indications are that there was very little secret about Iao at all. While the rabbis could have simply re-

---

[300] Cf. the passage from Clement's *Strom.* V discussed above. He even goes on to make an association between the four-lettered name for God in Hebrew and the fact that the Greek θεός also has four letters. See also Philo's use of the word "tetragrammaton" in *Mos.* 2:114.

[301] As stressed by Thierry, pp.30–32.

Discursus: The Pronunciation of the Tetragrammaton 121

fused to admit that their "secret" name was in fact a matter of public record, it seems more probable that their version of the name, if not actually "Yahweh," was something different from Iao.

But the matter cannot be dropped there. We have stressed that the divine name Iao did have widespread currency before, during, and after our period of concern. While it does tend to crop up on the margins of Jewish society, or on the sometimes hazy border between Judaism and paganism, it was respected enough to find its way into a Greek biblical text at Qumran and to be passed on as a divine epithet by later Christian scholars conversant with Judaism. It probably originated either as an early (perhaps pre-exilic) and independent version of the name YHWH, which continued to enjoy some popularity among the people; or as a derived, shortened form of the tetragrammaton, which became a divine epithet based on its appearance in Hebrew theophoric names.[302] (One might account for the appearance of יה as an independent divine name in the same way.) I would tend to favor the latter view, mainly because the evidence for יהו in theophoric names is more widespread and certain than the evidence for ancient near eastern parallels to Iao. But I would also contend that for many Jews, this "shortened" form functioned *for them* as the personal name of their God. Indeed, it is not out of the question that, being accustomed to using this form in their everyday speech, they then *read* the tetragrammaton as "Iao." It was this form that then "leaked" out into the pagan world. Presumably, Jews who used the Iao form *and* did not feel constrained by custom replied honestly to pagan inquiries and said that "we call our God 'Iao'." Is it unthinkable that some Jews may have rejected the custom against speaking the name and shared it with their neighbors?[303]

The point is worth elaborating. We must ask whether many ordinary Jews in Egypt or Asia Minor would have known precisely how the name was pronounced in the temple or in rabbinic circles, or whether they would have necessarily used that form had they known of it. Religious pilgrims could supply the information to some people, perhaps, but this did not guarantee that changes in pronunciation would not have occurred as the name came into more general circulation. And if the pronunciation of "Iao" was a popular designation for God in other pockets of the diaspora, as well as at Elephantine, would they necessarily have changed this at the report of what was going on in Jerusalem? The temple may indeed have been the focal point of Jewish religion, but the priestly hierarchy was hardly the subject of universal admiration even (or perhaps especially) in Palestine. Might the "Iao" adherents have rejected the (putative) Jerusalem

---

[302] Baudissin has a good discussion in 2: 193–202.

[303] This is not to mention the possibility that they could have come by the name via apostate Jews, Jewish magicians, LXX manuscripts with Iao, etc.

pronunciation, or else have regarded it as a local variation which did not diminish the significance of their own rendering?

In sum, then, I would suggest that there were two streams of tradition with regards to the pronunciation of the divine name in Judaism. The "official version," presumably passed along by the temple hierarchy and the rabbis, may well have been "Yahweh" (although this is not provable from the existing evidence), and was likely *not* Iao. At the same time, a more popular version of the name, Iao, flourished among some Jews, perhaps especially in the diaspora. Iao originated, it is true, from a shortened version of the tetragrammaton, but it eventually gained independent status as the designation for the Jewish God. This form was more widely dispersed among the pagans, since its adherents were less attentive to the traditions restricting the usage of the divine name.

Chapter 3

The Significance and Meaning of the Name

The restrictions imposed on pronouncing the name YHWH did not obviate the need to understand what the name meant. If anything, such restrictions may have encouraged people to consider what lay behind this mysterious designation for God. This much, at least, might be suitable for public discussion. God's words in Exodus, "I am who I am," cried out for further explanation, and Jewish thinkers took up the task with vigor. The need for providing a creditable elucidation of the divine name became especially acute in light of the challenges of hellenization, which we have examined in chapter 1.

Since our primary concern is with purported etymologies for YHWH and their effect upon Rev. 1:4, we will spend most of our time discussing the exegetical traditions surrounding Ex. 3:14 and related texts. But our survey of the tetragrammaton in the New Testament era would be incomplete without some mention of the broader *significance* of the name YHWH in early Judaism. We realize that the terms "meaning" and "significance" are the source of unending debate among philosophers of language. Rather than entering into that debate, we will simply define the terms for our own discussion: "meaning" will refer to etymological reflection on the name, while "significance" will refer to the other attributes associated with the name (its power, activity, etc.). We will begin with a brief survey of the latter, then move on to an extended treatment of the former.

The Significance of the Name

Any assessment of the significance of the name must have some clear boundaries. "The Name" could stand for any or all of the activities and attributes of the God of Israel, which would give rather too large a scope for our inquiry. Firstly, then, we will only concern ourselves with texts where the name YHWH itself is clearly under consideration. Secondly, even in those texts which do refer to YHWH, we cannot fully examine all the relevant theological points raised. An excellent example of this is the name residing "in" the angel of the Lord. Fossum has already explored this issue at length in *The Name of God and the Angel of the Lord*, and his work has in turn sparked a lively debate. In cases like this we must be content with a summary and perhaps a few critical comments. Finally, we are not interested in the significance of *substitutes* for the name YHWH. In particular, we will avoid insofar as possible the significance of κύριος, which is not an etymology of the tetragrammaton but a substitute for it.

The name in or on people, angels, and things

The name YHWH was often said in the OT to be in or on people, angels, or things.[1] This tradition was maintained in later Jewish literature.[2] We have already seen how Philo and Josephus allude to the inscription of the name YHWH on the mitre of the High Priest. When we recall that the temple appears to have been the only place where the name was "lawfully" uttered, one can see how the temple would have been closely connected with the name YHWH.[3] It was its repository. Whether the apparent restriction of the name to the temple was a conscious act based on the OT teaching that the Lord would "put his name" there (e.g. Dt.12:5,11; 1 Ki.8:16–19; 9:3), or whether it was simply a factor of the increasing power of the temple hierarchy, is uncertain (see the discussion in our previous chapter).

Israel is said to be called by the name of the Lord in Dt.28:10. Ps-Jon. Dt. 28:10 takes this quite literally, reading: "And all the people of the earth will see that the name of YHWH *is inscribed on the phylacteries that you have* on you and they will fear you." The wilderness generation, according to Neofiti and Ps-Jon., wore not phylacteries but golden crowns inscribed with "the great and glorious name" (though they were stripped of them after the incident of the golden calf, Ex. 32:25ff.; cf. Ex. 33:6).

Finally, there has been much speculation in both ancient and modern times concerning the angel in Ex.23:21, who leads God's people and in whom God's name resides. Although the Exodus text does not say explicitly that this is the name YHWH, later interpreters understood the text that way. The designation of Metatron as the "lesser YHWH" (3 En. 12:5) seems to be the product of such interpretation. But the uncertainty of the date of this tradition makes its value for our investigation limited. Perhaps

---

[1] See Fossum, pp.87–106.

[2] Examples of the name being on Israel in the Apocrypha and Pseudepigrapha include 2 Macc.8:15 (which could refer to the name YHWH with its phrase, "his holy and glorious name"); Bar. 2:15 (the "name" is quite prominent throughout this chapter); Sir. 36:12; 4 Ez.4:25, 10:22; 2 Bar.48:23; T12P, TDan 6:7 (God's name will be throughout Israel); Pss. Sol. 9:9; cf. Odes of Sol. 8:19, 22:6; Ap. Elijah 1:9.

[3] See Robert Hayward, *Divine Name and Presence: The Memra* (Totowa, NJ: Allanhead, Osmun, and Co., 1981), pp.99–113.

more relevant is the name Iaoel in Ap. Abr.10:3,8; 17:13.[4] Baudissin regards this as an angel name like Michael or Gabriel, giving the sense "Iao is God."[5] But while it certainly sounds like an angel name (a significant point, as we will see below) it appears in a hymn to God in Ap. Abr.17:13 along with Eli; eternal, mighty one; Sabaoth; and El.[6] This is quite close to its usage in the Ladder of Jacob 2:17-18. The analogous name Iael in Ap. Moses 29:4 and 33:5 is also addressed directly to God.[7] Moreover, while Iaoel is described as an angel in Ap. Abr.10:3, he is particularly described as "Iaoel of the same name," who is to consecrate Abraham "through the mediation of my ineffable name." Iaoel, it appears, is the name of God which is then put "in" the angel (10:8).

I would argue that the compound designation "Iaoel" is a sophisticated interpretation (perhaps "illustration" is a better word) of Ex.23:21. The Iaoel name is the *same* as God's – Iao and El are two divine names with widespread attestation, and one could also view them in combination as a short-hand version of the OT designation YHWH Elohim. This preserves the sense of the Exodus passage: it is the name of God which is in the angel. At the same time, Iaoel *sounds* like the name of an angel. It makes the identification of God and the angel more obvious than in the case of Michael in The Testament of Abraham, without threatening to deify the angel as might happen with the designation of Metatron as the "lesser YHWH."[8]

Finally, in both the OT and early Judaism, the name served as a way of emphasizing both God's presence with his people and his transcendence of any particular place. In the narrative of Exodus 33, God declares that he

---

[4] Ap. Abr. 10:8 includes the variants (in Slavonic): *iaolu* (MS L); *iloilu* (SP); *ioilu* (M); *aolu* (A); *idolu* (N). See Belkis Philonenko-Sayar and Marc Philonenko, *Die Apokalypse Abrahams*, JSHRZ 5.5 (Gütersloh: Mohn, 1982), note on 10:8. For a detailed discussion of the figure of Iaoel, see Fossum, pp.318-321; Larry Hurtado, *One Lord, One God* (Philadelphia: Fortress Press, 1988); Margaret Barker, *The Great Angel* (London: SPCK, 1992), pp.77ff.; Christopher Rowland, *The Open Heaven* (London: SPCK, 1982), pp.101 ff.

[5] Baudissin, 2: 218-9 n. See also Ganschinietz, "Iao," p.704, who cites parallels in magical papyri and Ethiopic magical texts.

[6] R. Rubinkiewicz, in his introduction in *OTP* 1: 684, states that these verses (17:8b-19), could be a Bogomil addition, but he does not press the point or elaborate on why he believes this. In the absence of further testimony to the contrary, we will treat them as part of the Apocalypse proper.

[7] "Iael, eternal king..." (29:4); "Holy Iael, pardon him, because he is your image..." (33:5). See the texts in Bertrand. It is perhaps impossible to say what relationship Iael bears to Iaoel. Either form could have given rise to the other, or they could have arisen independently (although this is less likely given their similarity). Both Iao and Ia (cf. Heb. יה) are of course well attested divine names. The variant Iōēl, on the other hand, would appear to be a corruption of Iaoel (suggested by Baudissin, 2: 218 n).

[8] See Philonenko-Sayar and Philonenko, p.418. They note that Iaoel plays the same role as does Michael in the Testament of Abraham and Metatron in the Hebrew 3 Enoch.

will send his angel before the people, since if he himself goes he would destroy them. If this angel is the same angel as in Ex. 23:21 – and surely later commentators could have made such a connection – we would have evidence that the name could signify that God was with his people, but not in direct contact with them. The prayer of Solomon in 1 Kings 8 expresses a similar thought. The temple is for the name of the Lord (8:20) – it is here that he will listen to the prayers of his people. At the same time, Solomon declares that "heaven and the heaven of heavens cannot contain him; how much less this house which I have built!" (v.27). He repeatedly says to God, "Hear *from heaven*" (vv.30,34,36, etc.), which is his dwelling place.

Jesus and the Name

In two places in the NT, Heb.1:4 and Phil.2:9, Jesus is said to have been given or to have inherited a special name. One finds a similar thought in Eph.1:21, where Christ is set above every name that is named.[9] This motif has been connected with the traditions concerning the name-bearing angel in Ex. 23:21, and so it is appropriate to make some brief comments here. Again, we stress that our discussion will be of a summary nature and will not attempt to resolve the heated debates that surround this issue.

The name given to Christ in the Philippians passage is generally agreed to be κύριος/YHWH, and thus we will devote particular attention to this text. Phil 2: 5–11, as is well known, forms a hymn or portion of a hymn which is almost universally regarded as a pre-Pauline piece. The passage raises all sorts of exegetical and theological problems, and the literature on it is correspondingly quite exhaustive.[10] For our purposes, we need only note from the context that the hymn traces the career of Christ from pre-existence, through his incarnation and death, and concludes with his exaltation and universal acclamation.

V.9 follows immediately upon the mention of Christ's death on the cross. It will helpful to cite this in full along with vv.10–11, since they too factor heavily in the discussion:

διὸ καὶ ὁ θεὸς αὐτὸν ὑπερύψωσεν
καὶ ἐχαρίσατο αὐτῷ τὸ ὄνομα
τὸ ὑπὲρ πᾶν ὄνομα

---

[9] We may also mention here Jesus "manifesting" the name of the Father to his disciples in the gospel of John (17:6ff.). This name is said to be "given" to Jesus in 17:11. This may well be the name YHWH.

[10] In addition to the commentaries, see especially Ralph P. Martin, *Carmen Christi: Philippians 2:5–11 in Recent Interpretation and in the Setting of Early Christian Worship* Rev. Ed. (Grand Rapids: Eerdmans, 1983); Takeshi Nagata, *Philippians 2:5–11: A Case Study in the Contextual Shaping of Early Christology* (diss. Princeton, 1981); and Otfried Hofius, *Der Christushymnus Philipper 2:6–11* (Tübingen: J.C.B. Mohr (Siebeck), 1976).

ἵνα ἐν τῷ ὀνόματι Ἰησοῦ
πᾶν γόνυ κάμψῃ
ἐπουρανίων καὶ ἐπιγείων καὶ καταχθονίων
καὶ πᾶσα γλῶσσα ἐξομολογήσηται ὅτι
κύριος Ἰησοῦς Χριστὸς
εἰς δόξαν θεοῦ πατρός.

As we have said, the name in question here is generally seen as the κύριος of v.11; and it is further argued that behind this κύριος stands the name YHWH itself.[11] The relationship of this κύριος to the tetragrammaton will occupy us below. For the moment, we will look at the arguments in favor of the identification of the "highest name" with κύριος/YHWH. The highest name in the Old Testament would presumably be YHWH, and so there is an immediate predisposition to think that this might be the name in question in the hymn. This is supported by the culmination of the acclamation of Christ, where every tongue confesses κύριος Ἰησοῦς Χριστός. Jesus Christ *is* κύριος. The phrase, "every knee shall bow and every tongue confess..." is taken directly from the LXX of Is.45:23, where it is asserted that every knee will bow to *God*, and every tongue confess that righteousness and glory belong to Him. This is a remarkable assertion, and it is even more remarkable when one considers that Isaiah 45 is at pains to say that YHWH alone is God, and there is no other. For the early Christians to use the text of Jesus indicates both their high view of Jesus and their conviction that worshipping him was compatible with the monotheism of the Old Testament.[12]

The argument that the "name above every name" is connected with the κύριος of v.11 seems fundamentally correct, but it needs further refinement. Some older scholars, for instance, argued that the name in question was Jesus.[13] It is true that v.10 declares that at the name of *Jesus* every knee shall bow. But there are two strong arguments against this: 1) The name *Jesus* does not seem to be a new name bestowed on him at his exaltation; and 2) ἐν τῷ ὀνόματι Ἰησοῦ can easily be understood as the name Jesus *bears*, i.e. κύριος/YHWH. The mention of Jesus is still significant, however, in that it emphasizes, in the words of Gerald Hawthorne, that the "lordly power has been put into the hands of the historical person of Jesus of Nazareth." The Emptied one is now Lord.[14]

---

[11] Martin provides a very thorough list of commentators who interpret the phrase this way on p.245 of *Carmen Christi*.

[12] On this see Hurtado, *One Lord, One God*.

[13] Martin, p.235.

[14] Hawthorne, *Philippians* WBC (Dallas: Word, 1983), p.92. Cf. the similar comments by Nagata, p.279; and Peter O'Brien, *The Epistle to the Philippians* (Grand Rapids: Eerdmans, 1991), p.240. It is interesting to compare the similar scene of acclamation in

The question remains as to whether Jesus is portrayed as identical with YHWH, subordinated to Him, or in some relationship not clearly defined. Some degree of subordination seems implied by the closing expression: the worship of Jesus[15] is *to the glory of God the Father*.[16] Could κύριος, then, be simply a functional title expressing the fact that Jesus rules over the universe? This seems to be excluded by the earlier statement that he has received the name that is above every name. The bare designation κύριος, which in its weakest form could simply mean "sir," would of course be shared by any number of people. It is κύριος *as a rendering of the tetragrammaton* that is in view here. If the phrase "to the glory of God the Father" forbids an *Identifizierung* of the Father and Jesus, the use of κύριος as surrogate for YHWH demands at least a *Gleichsetzung* of the two.[17] Whether the early Christians would have felt comfortable addressing Jesus directly as YHWH (that is, without employing κύριος or מרא) is difficult to ascertain since our materials are in Greek. We must be content to say that Philippians 2:9 asserts that Jesus received the κύριος name as a rendering of the tetragrammaton at his exaltation.

The Power of the Name

In our previous chapter we noted the *power* of the divine name in oaths and curses. In the Targums, the uttering of the name brings forth water from the rock (Ps-Jon. Num. 20:8) and even raises the dead (Ps.-Jon. Dt. 9:19). It is surely no coincidence that Moses' wonder-working staff is said to have the "grand and glorious name" inscribed on it (Ps-Jon. Ex.2:21, 4:20). Phinehas even uses the name to fly off in pursuit of Balaam (Ps-Jon. Num. 31:8).[18]

Of far greater importance is the association of the name and the creation of the world.[19] This *topos* first appears in Prayer of Manesseh 3: "...who hast confined the deep and sealed it with thy terrible and glorious name." The Prayer may be as early as the last two centuries BCE,[20] and so the

---

Rev.4–5, where it is precisely as the "Lamb having been slain" (5–6) that Christ is worshipped.

[15] Again there is a general consensus that the worship is directed to Jesus himself and not through Jesus to the Father; see Martin, pp.249ff.; O'Brien, pp.239–40.

[16] This point is emphasized by Käsemann and affirmed by Martin; see Martin, pp.274–5. The key parallel is 1Cor. 15:28.

[17] See Fitzmyer, "The New Testament *Kyrios*-Title," p.130.

[18] For other rabbinical passages on the power of the name, see Petuchowski, pp.141–147.

[19] See Fossum, pp.82ff., 245ff., noting that Fossum includes much later material in his discussion; and Ginzberg, 1: 7.

[20] Cf. Introduction to P. Manasseh in the Oxford Annotated Apocrypha.

connection of the name and creation appears to be quite old. Similar themes appear frequently in later rabbinical literature.[21]

In some instances, the creative name is associated with an oath. In Jubilees 36:7, Isaac says to his sons: "And now I will make you swear by the great oath – because there is not an oath which is greater than it, by the glorious and honored and great and splendid and amazing and mighty name which created heaven and earth and everything together – that you will fear (God) and worship him."[22] The connection between name and oath is of central importance for understanding 1 En. 69:13–26. We read:

> And it was he (Kasdeya') who reckoned up the gematria (lit. the number) of the Chief of Days for Kasbeel, who revealed the sum of the oath to the angels when he dwelt above in glory, and its name is BIQA. This (satan) told Michael to show him the hidden Name, that they might pronounce it in the oath, so that those who revealed all that was secret to the children of men might tremble before that Name and oath (1 En.69:13–14).[23]

The passage is plagued with difficulties. Even if we take Black's translation at face value, there is some question as to the meaning of BIQA and the oath "'AKA'" in v.15. These names have the same gematria value as the names יהוה האלהים and אדני יהוה respectively, but it is unclear what their actual meaning (if any) might be.[24] Perhaps they are neologisms whose only significance lies in their association by gematria with יהוה האלהים and אדני יהוה. What is clear is that the name is secret, and that it is associated with the oath which created the world and which continues to sustain it.[25] In light of the frequent association of the name YHWII and the creation elsewhere in Jewish literature, it seems safe to say that this name and oath are somehow related to the tetragrammaton.

The association of an oath with the ordering of the world is not unique to Judaism. The Presocratic philosopher Empedocles, for example, said

---

[21] Cf. Ps-Jon. Ex.28:30; y. Sanh. 29; b. Suk. 53b and b.Mak. 11a; Fossum, p.250.

[22] Trans. Wintermute, *OTP* 2: 124. See Fossum, pp.254–6.

[23] Trans. by Black, *The Book of Enoch*, p.65.

[24] Black, pp.247–8; A. Caquot and P. Geoltrain, "Notes sur le texte éthiopien des 'Paraboles' d'Henoch," *Semitica* 13 (1963): 39–54. Siegbert Uhlig (*Die Äthiopische Henochbuch, JSHRZ* 5: 6; Gütersloh: Mohn, 1984) provides a summary of views in his note to 69:15; Fossum, p.258.

[25] The implication of the passage seems to be that the technological innovations introduced by the fallen angels (69:6 ff.; cf. 8:1 ff.) were accomplished by the illicit use of the name/oath. The author of this portion of Enoch appears to view such innovations as a type of creative activity, which had to be initiated by divine power (comparisons with Prometheus' stolen fire are appropriate). His ambivalence to technology is quite evident. There may also be an undercurrent of anti-magical polemic. See also Black, p.248. Note, too, that the fact that Michael is somehow entrusted with the name in 1 Enoch 69 does *not* make him a demiurgic figure in this passage. (Fossum raises this possibility on p.259.) The most natural reading of the text is that God is seen as the creator.

that the cosmic cycles of change initiated by the contest of "Love" and "Strife" are marked "by a broad oath" (fr. 30: πλατέος...ὅρκου).[26] Fossum makes the crucial observation that for Jews, the creative and sustaining oath would almost certainly have been the יהי, "let it be..." of Genesis 1.[27] God says יהי, and the world order comes to be. The expression "let it be..." is easily seen as a kind of oath. As it happens, we have confirmatory evidence of this in b. Men.29b, where *yod* and *he* are said to be involved in the creation of this world and the future world. While different letters of the alphabet are elsewhere said to be involved in the creation of the world, the *yod* and *he* here appear to refer to the יהי of Genesis 1.[28]

Fossum makes the further observation that this oath יהי should be connected with the name YHWH.[29] Again, I would agree with him.[30] The close visual resemblance between יהי and יהוה provides us with our first clue. We have more concrete evidence in the Targums Neofiti and Ps-Jon.to Ex. 3:14. Both begin their explanation of the name YHWH with the words "The one who spoke and the world was..." This designation for God appears elsewhere in Jewish literature as well.[31] What God spoke, of course, was יהי. It could be that the name יהוה and the oath יהי were associated solely because of the similarity of their letters, and because one generally associates oaths with names ("I swear by X"). It seems more likely, however, that the two words were believed to have a closer etymological link. Some modern scholars (notably Albright, Cross, and Freedman) believe the original meaning of YHWH Sabaoth was, "He who causes the hosts to be..."[32] Some ancient Jews may have understood the

---

[26] *KRS*, p.295.

[27] Cf. Fossum, p. 78. Although Fossum is commenting on Samaritan texts of late date, his observation on the link between the name YHWH and the command יהי in Genesis 1 is a valid and important one.

[28] This seems far more likely to me than that this text refers to the designation יה. Even if this were the case, we would have a reference linking a divine name to creation, and we would have to ask why this designation in particular was chosen. The answer would again be: because it contains the letters of the divine command יהי.

[29] Fossum, pp.78 ff.

[30] As indicated above, I would nonetheless disagree with him on the extent to which the name was viewed as a hypostasized demiurge in the New Testament era.

[31] See especially Mekilta de Rabbi Ishmael, *passim*; Fossum, pp.79–80.

[32] W.F. Albright, "Contributions to Biblical Archaeology and Philology: The Name Yahweh," *JBL* 43 (1924): 370–78; F.M. Cross, *Canaanite Myth and Hebrew Epic* (Cambridge: Harvard University Press, 1973), pp.60–75; D.N. Freedman, "The Name of the God of Moses," *JBL* 79 (1960): 151–56; Freedman-O'Connor, pp.513–6. In the last article, Freedman gives examples of other OT phrases where he believes the meaning "he causes X to be" is present; e.g. Judges 6:24, "he creates peace"; Ex.34:14, "he creates zeal"; Ex.17:15, "he creates my refuge." Parke-Taylor (pp.58ff.) notes that this thesis was proposed by LeClerc as early as 1700.

name YHWH in the same way: He is the one who causes things to be.[33] Another alternative is that they understood YHWH to mean, "He is" (cf. Ex. 3:14 LXX) and then drew the logical implication that he is thereby the one who brings all else into being. There is obviously little difference in the end between these two options.

The Meaning of the Name

The association of the name YHWH and creation was thus enhanced, or perhaps even engendered by, the *etymology* of the name. This leads us quite naturally to a more thorough investigation of what Jews in the Second Temple period thought the name meant. We have just mentioned the two most likely explanations of the name YHWH: "He is" and "He causes to be." As in our previous chapter, we will examine the relevant material from early Judaism, c.150 BCE to 100 CE. In light of the extraordinary importance of the LXX translation of Ex. 3:14 for our discussion, however, we will make an exception to our *terminus a quo* and deal with this earlier text in some detail. We will also examine the use of ὁ ὤν in three verses of Jeremiah LXX, and give a brief survey of the use of אני הוא/ἐγώ εἰμι in Is.40–55.

The LXX Translation of Ex. 3:14

The description of God as ὁ ὤν may ultimately be traced back to the LXX rendering of Ex. 3:14. As is well known, the LXX translates אהיה אשר אהיה as ἐγώ εἰμι ὁ ὤν : "I am the one who is." It also replaces the אהיה at the close of the verse with Ὁ ὤν (ἀπέσταλκέν με). This translation has met with much criticism. H.D. Preuß labels the LXX rendering a "False translation."[34] Von Rad says: "Nothing is further from what is envisaged in this etymology of the name of Jahweh than a definition of his nature in the sense of a philosophical statement about his being (LXX ἐγώ εἰμι ὁ ὤν) – a suggestion, for example, of his absoluteness, aseity, etc."[35] Elias Bicker-

---

[33] This is not to suggest, of course, that they travelled the same intellectual path at the above named scholars. The question of whether the verb to be ever had a *hiphil* form is secondary; we are solely concerned with what theologians *might* have done. I see no reason they could not have invented a *hiphil* to make a theological point. The frequent connections between the name and creation suggest they might have done this very thing.

[34] Preuß, *Theologie des Alten Testaments*, Band 1 (Stuttgart: Kohlhammer, 1991), p.161.

[35] Von Rad, *Old Testament Theology*, Vol. 1, trans. by D.M.G. Stalker (Edinburgh: Oliver and Boyd, 1962), p.180. Cf. the comments by André Lacocque, who objects to the translation "celui qui est" (*Le devenir de Dieu*; Encyclopédie Universitaire; Paris: Éditions Universitaires, 1967, p.100).

man talks of the Seventy "Platonizing the Lord Himself."³⁶ We will argue here that the LXX gives a plausible reading of a very difficult Hebrew text. We will then examine the possible influence of hellenistic thought on the translation.

Our first task is to assess the translation on linguistic grounds. One of the foremost authorities on the LXX, J. W. Wevers, says of the translators: "Theirs was a holy task, not to be taken lightly...This meant that the translators pondered their task, tried to give their work an inner consistency..."³⁷ If Wevers is correct in his assessment, we would imagine that they would have treated the translation of a crucial text like Ex. 3:14 with special care. It was not the sort of thing one dashed off at the end of the day. We may assume that they believed they were giving a faithful rendering of the Hebrew. Our sympathy for the translators should increase when we consider the difficulties this verse presents. One could try and treat the verse straightforwardly, as do Aquila and Theodotion.³⁸ But their reading ἔσομαι ὅς ἔσομαι is at best vague, and at worst an "absurd tautology" for the Greek reader.³⁹ While it has been argued that the Hebrew is intended to be vague, one can hardly blame the translators for trying to bring out some positive meaning from the text.

But why this particular reading? Wevers concludes, "It is doubtful whether one should understand ὁ ὤν as anything more than this straightforward attempt to make an acceptable Greek version of the Hebrew; it is not a philosophic statement; it is rather a religious affirmation."⁴⁰ We will take up the latter part of this quotation in a moment. For now, we may confirm Wever's opinion that the translators have given "an acceptable Greek version of the Hebrew." A noteworthy article in this regard was published by E. Schild in 1954.⁴¹ He gives a detailed view of the grammatical problems associated with the phrase אהיה אשר אהיה, and cites parallel Old Testament passages, particularly 1 Chr. 21:17, which might help us to understand the Exodus text. In the Chronicles verse, David responds to God

---

³⁶ Quoted in Hengel, *Jews, Greeks, Barbarians*, p.96. Cf. the comments by Morton Smith in his article "The Image of God: Notes on the Hellenization of Judaism" (*Bulletin of the John Rylands Library* 40 (1957–8): 473–512): "...there is no doubt that we are looking at a hellenization of the Biblical religion [in the LXX rendering of Ex.3:14] (p.474)." In his mind it is a "clear Platonism." The commentaries on Exodus generally mention the LXX rendering only in passing.

³⁷ Wevers, xiv. Cf. the similar comments by Le Boulluec and Sandevoir, pp.31 ff.

³⁸ See W.R. Arnold, "The Divine Name in Ex. 3:14," *JBL* 24 (1905): 114. This article is also helpful for the detail it provides on the ancient versions of Ex.3:14, particularly those in Latin.

³⁹ This is Wever's assessment, pp.33–4.

⁴⁰ Wevers, pp.33–4.

⁴¹ Schild, pp.296–302.

The Meaning of the Name 133

with the phrase, אני הוא אשר חטאתי, "I am the one who has sinned." If we took the Hebrew literally, we would have "I am he which I have sinned." This sounds peculiar in English, and apparently it would have sounded peculiar in Greek to the Septuagint translators. They translate it ἐγω εἰμι ὁ ἁμαρτών, "I am the one who sins." It is the same construction that we find in Ex. 3:14. It is true that the Chronicles verse does not have a verb in the first clause, as does the text in Exodus. But the two are still very close.

The key grammatical point which Schild illustrates from 1 Chr. 21:17 and is this: whereas in Hebrew a first person verb or noun in the main clause may be followed by a verb in the first person in the subordinate clause (I am he *that I have sinned*), in English (and Greek) the verb is rendered in the third person (I am he who has sinned; or I am the one who is sinning). We can see another instance of this in the very important phrase "I am the Lord who led you out of Egypt," which shows up frequently in the Old Testament. The Hebrew in Lev. 19:36, for example, reads: אני יהוה אלהיכם אשר הוצאתי אתכם מארץ מצרים. The LXX translates this ἐγώ εἰμι κύριος ὁ θεὸς ὑμῶν ὁ ἐξαγαγὼν ὑμᾶς ἐκ γῆς Αἰγύπτου.[42] Again, this is not precisely the same as Ex. 3:14, since ὁ ὤν functions there as a substantive and not as a simple participle, but it is very close.

After considering such parallel phrases, Schild concludes that the Hebrew of Ex. 3:14 should be read, "I am the one who is" or "I am he who is." Rather than being an *idem per idem* idiom which gives a "noncommittal, circular definition" of God,[43] the verse instead gives a positive affirmation of God's existence, his reality.[44] Although Schild never mentions the LXX, his understanding of Ex. 3:14 is obviously compatible with that of the ancient translators. He is not the only scholar to uphold the reasonableness of such a translation. R. de Vaux, J. Lindblom, and H. Cazelles have all given support to it.[45]

---

[42] Cf. the parallels in Gen. 15:7; Ex.20:2, Lev.11:45, 20:24.

[43] Cf. the words of Mettinger (p.33), who says that the repeated use of the same root "can endow an expression with a suspicion of haziness." He cites as examples Ex. 4:13, "Send the one you will send"; 1 Sam. 23:13, "And they went where they went"; and 2 Ki. 8:1, "Dwell where you will dwell."

[44] Schild, p.301. See also Mettinger, p.34, although he does not in the end embrace this interpretation.

[45] See de Vaux, pp.51ff.; Lindblom, "Noch einmal die Deutung des Jahwe-Namens," *Annual of the Swedish Theological Institute* 3 (1964): 4–15; Cazelles, *Autour de L'Exode* (Paris: LeCoffre, 1987), pp.269–287.; Cazelles, *Autour de L'Exode* (Paris: LeCoffre, 1987), pp.269–287. Nahum Sarna, while not explicitly endorsing the translation, notes that YHWH "either...expresses the quality of Absolute Being, the eternal, unchanging, dynamic presence, or it means, 'He causes to be'." See Sarna, *Exodus*; JPS Torah Commentary (Philadelphia: Jewish Publication Society, 1991), pp.17–8.

Schild's view has met with criticism in some quarters.⁴⁶ The criticisms (e.g. the fact that 1 Chr. 21:17 is not an exact grammatical parallel to Ex. 3:14⁴⁷) may keep us from saying that Ex. 3:14 *must* be translated ἐγω εἰμι ὁ ὤν. The fact remains that it *could* legitimately be translated in this way.

Before turning to the Greek background, we should make one final note on the appearance of ὁ ὤν in v.14c: Ὁ ὤν ἀπέσταλκέν με for MT אהיה שלחני. This reading cannot be defended in the same way as the earlier portion of the verse. One could then introduce it as evidence that the LXX translators were tendentiously bringing Greek philosophy into the text after all. Before we conclude this, we must return again to Wevers. He points out that a first person subject for ἀπέσταλκέν would have been a "grammatical absurdity," and the translators were therefore "driven to a participial form."⁴⁸ This explanation makes a good deal of sense. It does change the perspective of the verse somewhat, in that a declaration of the name אהיה (*I am* has sent me) has been transformed into a declaration of the name יהוה (*The one who is* has sent me). The translators might well argue that they had preserved the essential sense of the text while making some necessary grammatical adjustments.⁴⁹

The fact remains, however, that ἐγω εἰμι ὁ ὤν does sound very philosophical. Certainly later exegetes (particularly Philo) understood it in this way. Has Greek philosophical speculation crept into the LXX? We have already seen one important argument against such a contention: the plausibility of the translation as a rendering of the Hebrew. It should also be noted that J. Freudenthal has demonstrated that the LXX in general exhibits little or no influence from Greek popular philosophy.⁵⁰ Ex. 3:14 would be the exception, not the rule. As for the purported distinction between the Hebrew "dynamic" use of the verb to be and the Greek "static" use, we would concur with James Barr that such a distinction, even if valid, cannot

---

⁴⁶ See esp. Albrektson, pp.15–28.

⁴⁷ Albrektson, pp.21–2.

⁴⁸ Wevers, pp.33–4. He believes this problem in 14c may have contributed to the rendering ἐγω εἰμι ὁ ὤν earlier in the verse.

⁴⁹ It remains true that a possible nuance of the text has been lost, namely the sense that אהיה (I am) is God's name for himself, while יהוה (He is) is the name given to God's people to use. As Hayward points out, God declares "I am (there)," and his people joyfully respond, "He is (there)." See Hayward, *Divine Name*, pp.99–113, discussed in full below. But the LXX translators may have felt they had no choice but to alter this aspect of the verse.

⁵⁰ Freudenthal, "Septuagint: Are there Traces of Greek Philosophy in the Septuagint?" *JQR* 2 (1890): 205–222. This is confirmed by Hengel, *Judaism and Hellenism*, 1: 162. See also Marguerite Harl, Gilles Dorival, and Olivier Munnich, *La Bible greque des Septante* (Paris: Cerf, 1988), p.232; Feldman, *Jew and Gentile*, pp.52–3; Le Boulluec and Sandevoir, pp.31ff.

be deduced from linguistic usage.[51] There is no *prima facie* reason for thinking ὁ ὤν automatically conveys a "static" sense of being rather than a "dynamic" one.[52] It is worth asking in this regard whether a translation using the word γίνομαι, for example, would be in any way more accurate than the LXX as it stands.[53] Did the author of Exodus wish to imply that God has come into being, and might presumably pass away as well? This would certainly be the implication of "becoming" for an educated Greek.

Finally, we may adduce two crucial pieces of evidence gathered from our survey of Greek uses of τὸ ὄν. 1. The earliest evidence for the description of God as τὸ ὄν comes from the source behind Seneca's Ep. 58 and Plutarch's E at Delphi, and thus cannot be dated before the first century BCE;[54] and 2. There is no evidence for the use of ὁ ὤν for deity in non-Jewish literature before Numenius (2nd c. CE) – and this reference, if valid, may be traced back to the LXX itself.[55] This does not mean that the Septuagint translators were unaware of the philosophical implications of τὸ ὄν or ὁ ὤν. It does mean that the translation must be seen as an original contribution to religious thinking, not a passive reception of pre-existing ideas.

A controlling Greek influence on the LXX translation is thus not demonstrable, and it is almost certain that the use of ὁ ὤν for deity was a Jewish innovation. We may, however, suggest a few possibilities as to how the LXX translation related to its hellenistic environment. It is possible that the translators were attracted to ὁ ὤν because of its similarities to the

---

[51] Barr, *The Semantics of Biblical Language* (Oxford: Oxford University Press, 1961), pp.58–72. Lacocque's counterarguments (pp.100–1, 105 n.) do not overturn Barr's thesis.

[52] Childs' comments on the "history of exegesis" are general, but have a particular relevance to the LXX translation: "In the contemporary period it has become a hallmark of theology to reject, by and large, the history of exegesis as being misled by philosophical interests...However, it remains a real question to what extent one philosophical system has been substituted for another. Surely, it is not a self-evident historical fact that the ancient Hebrews had no concept of being, but only action...A similar oversimplification to be avoided would be constructing a history of development from the early Hebrew meaning of God's name as 'becoming' to a later growth of a concept of being caused by the infiltration of Greek elements." Childs, p.87.

[53] See the comments by Childs above, and note the title of Lacocque's book, *Le devenir de Dieu*.

[54] M. Delcor, in his article "La signification de l'E delphique et Exode 3,14–15" (in *De la Tôrah au Messie*, eds. M. Carrez, J. Doré, P. Grelot; Paris: Desclée, 1981, pp.361-8), asks whether Plutarch is actually *polemicizing* against the LXX claim that the Jewish God alone is ὁ ὤν. He rightly answers "no" (p.367), although he does not give a reason for Plutarch's equation of τὸ ὄν and deity. As we have seen, the simple answer is that this was a common doctrine of Middle Platonism.

[55] See John Whittaker, "Moses Atticizing," *Phoenix* 21 (1967): 196–201. He argues that the text of Numenius fr.22 does include ὁ ὤν (a point questioned by some scholars) and that he depends on the LXX for this designation.

Platonic τὸ ὄν. Even if this is true, their rendering of Ex. 3:14 must be considered a radical transformation of the Platonic term.[56] The substitution of a personal deity for an impersonal world of Forms is hardly a genuflection to the Academy. It is more of a *coup d'état*. It is also significant that God speaks and reveals himself in the Exodus passage – in the LXX no less than the MT. While there is certainly an element of revelation in Parmenides and Plato (most clearly in the *Phaedrus*), one does not find a self-revelation of τὸ ὄν. The Goddess speaks to Parmenides, and Socrates speaks to his interlocutors, but τὸ ὄν remains passive and silent, the object of investigation. Not so with the God of the burning bush.

Another possibility is that the LXX is engaged in a tacit polemic against the well-known etymology for Zeus which we studied in our first chapter: he is the one "through whom (δι' ὄν) all beings have life (ζῆν)."[57] As we pointed out, this was known among Jews as well as Gentiles; and interestingly enough, it appears precisely in Jewish accounts of the translation of the LXX (Ep. Arist. 15/16; Josephus, *Ant.* 12:22). Might the translators have reflected on this pagan etymology as they pondered the etymology for YHWH in Ex. 3:14? Did they wish to say that their Lord, YHWH – not Zeus – is ὁ ὤν, the one who is, and the one who is by implication, the source of everything else that is?

I find the latter alternative quite appealing, although it cannot be demonstrated conclusively. In any event, because this Jewish etymology is rooted in the Pentateuch, the final word as to the significance of ὁ ὤν must be drawn from these Scriptures themselves. What might a reader of the Pentateuch find there to fill in the meaning of ὁ ὤν? One might reasonably see in the words "I am the One who is" a statement of God's eternity: "I am the one who *always* is." Recall "the eternal God" spoken of by Abraham in Genesis. Or, one might relate ὁ ὤν to God's truth, particularly in contrast to the idols, the false gods of Egypt and elsewhere: "I am the God who *really is* God."[58] A reader with an eye for the immediate context might see in the words the idea: "I am the God who *is with* my people," just as he was with Moses (Ex. 3:12). Finally, one might understand the words in the sense that God is the source of all being: "I am he who is *absolutely*, who exists without depending on anything or anyone else for existence." This would be a reasonable extrapolation from the creation account in Genesis.

---

[56] This applies yet more strongly to the other possible meanings of τὸ ὄν. The switch to the masculine from the neuter precludes any explanation such as, "God is *whatever is the case*" or "God is *existence*" or "God is *what the universe essentially is*." The God who speaks to Moses cannot be simply another name for everything that exists.

[57] E.g *Cratylus* 396a. See above.

[58] J. Philip Hyatt sees this as a possible meaning of the Hebrew text itself (*Exodus*, NCB; London: Marshall, Morgan, and Scott, 1971, p.77).

The LXX version, then, is a reasonable translation of a troublesome text. The translators might well have had one eye on Greek philosophical and religious conceptions. Their translation may be an invitation to consider the ontological possibilities wrapped up in the enigmatic "I am who I am." But if this was the case, their formulation of God as ὁ ὤν was a radical innovation. It would constitute the first evidence we possess for an identification of God and Being (or God as *the* Being). Moreover, the substitution of a personal God for the impersonal world of Forms would be a significant departure from Platonic philosophy. Of course, what the translators may have intended by ὁ ὤν, and what later generations drew from ὁ ὤν, are two different things. The subsequent understanding of ὁ ὤν will occupy a significant portion of the investigation which follows.

Ὁ ὤν *in the LXX of Jeremiah*

The phrase ὁ ὤν appears as a divine epithet three times in the book of Jeremiah (1:6, 14:13, 39:17). We cite the instances below:

LXX	MT
καὶ εἶπα Ὁ ὤν δέσποτα κύριε...(1:6)	ואמר אהה אדני יהוה (1:6)
καὶ εἶπα Ὁ ὤν κύριε...(14:13)	ואמר אהה אדני יהוה (14:13)
λέγων Ὁ ὤν κύριε...(39:16–7)	לאמר אהה אדני יהוה (32:16–7)

What has happened seems fairly obvious. The translator read אהה as אהיה. Since Jeremiah is speaking, אהיה could not simply be the verb to be, and so the translator drew upon the substitution of אהיה with ὁ ὤν in Ex. 3:14 (esp. v.14c, Ὁ ὤν ἀπέσταλκέν με).[59] Thackeray suggests that the solution was encouraged by the likenesses between the call of Moses and the call of Jeremiah.[60] The God known as ὁ ὤν called Moses; why not the same for Jeremiah?

These passages are not simply of interest as examples of translators' ingenuity. If we assume that Jeremiah was put into Greek in the first century BCE[61] – and certainly after the translation of Exodus – we have perhaps our earliest evidence for the acceptance of ὁ ὤν as a divine epithet within Greek speaking Judaism. Secondly, we find formulae similar to Ὁ ὤν δέσποτα κύριε in later Jewish and Christian liturgy. Apostolic Constitutions 8.5.1ff. (to be discussed in more detail below) begins ὁ ὤν, δέσποτα

---

[59] See H.St.J. Thackeray, *The Septuagint and Jewish Origins*, British Academy Schweich Lectures 1920 (Oxford: Oxford University Press, 1921), pp.33–4; Emanuel Tov, *The Septuagint Translation of Jeremiah and Baruch* (Missoula, MT: Scholars Press, 1976), p.24.

[60] Thackeray, p.34.

[61] See Tov, "The Literary History of the Book of Jeremiah," in *Empirical Models for Biblical Criticism*, ed. Jeffrey H. Tigay (Philadelphia: University of Pennsylvania Press, 1985), p.214.

κύριε ὁ θεὸς ὁ παντοκράτωρ... It seems most likely that the phrase ὁ ὤν, δέσποτα κύριε was lifted from the LXX of Jer. 1:6 and made part of a liturgical formula. What began as an attempt to patch up a (presumably) corrupt Hebrew *Vorlage* ended up as an important element of worship for Greek speaking Jews and Christians.

אני הוא and ἐγώ εἰμι in Is. 40–55

It has been suggested that the phrase אני הוא in Is. 40–55 (43:10,13; 46:4; 48:12; 52:6; cf. 43:25; 51:12) is the functional equivalent of the self-proclamation of God as אהיה in Ex. 3:14. This is believed to be borne out by the usual LXX rendering of אני הוא in these chapters as ἐγώ εἰμι.[62] Since our primary concern is with the form of the divine name ὁ ὤν, and since there is already a vast amount of scholarship on אני הוא and ἐγώ εἰμι, we may be content with a short survey of this topic.[63] The connection with Ex. 3:14, however, makes some discussion essential. This will also give us an opportunity to touch upon the importance of Is. 40–55 for the development of the traditions found in Ex. 3:14. As we have stressed, our emphasis is on the early Jewish and hellenistic backgrounds to Rev. 1:4. But it will be salutary to take a brief diversion here and remind ourselves of the importance of the OT itself for gaining a fully orbed perspective on Revelation 1:4.

The motif of the "second Exodus" permeates Is. 40–55, as is universally recognized by commentators. We would not be surprised, then, to find some reference to the divine name as revealed in the burning bush episode.[64] The first hint that the author does have Exodus 3 in mind comes from the recurrence of pairs like "first and last" (particularly important because it is used of God: 41:4, 44:6; 48:12); "old and new" (42:9; 43:18–9; 48:3ff.); and "former and future" (41:22–3; 44:7; 46:3–4,9–10). We also have statements and allusions about God's everlasting existence (40:28; 51:6,12–3; cf. 43:10,13; 45:17). As we will see, later Jewish exegetes often elucidate אהיה אשר אהיה in terms of past/future or God's eternity. This may mean nothing more, of course, than that these exegetes read Ex. 3:14 *in the light of* Is. 40ff. – as doubtless they did. But it is equally possible

---

[62] An exception is 43:12–3, where the LXX lacks any equivalent for both אני הוא and ואין אל earlier in the sentence.

[63] Recent accounts, in addition to Harner's *The 'I Am' of the Fourth Gospel*, include David M. Ball, *'I Am' in John's Gospel* (Sheffield: JSOT, 1996), esp. pp.24–45;177–203; and Delbert Burkett, *The Son of Man in the Gospel of John* (Sheffield: JSOT, 1991), pp.142–60. See also Dodd, pp.93–6; and Raymond Brown *The Gospel according to John* 2 vols. (Garden City, NY: Doubleday, 1966–70), 1: 533ff.

[64] I am not assuming the author of Is. 40–55 necessarily knew Exodus 3 in the form in which we know it. But as our discussion indicates, he appears to be familiar with the tradition of "I am who I am."

that the later interpreters fused these two portions of scripture because they saw an integral connection between the two passages. The idea that God comprehends history as past creator and future deliverer could have developed independently of the traditions concerning the divine name. But it seems more likely that even at this early date אהיה אשר אהיה was understood as a statement about God's eternal existence and his consequent ability, and availability, to save his people.

This is not to say that אני הוא itself is equivalent to אהיה in the MT of Isaiah 40–55. It is of interest that on three occasions אני הוא occurs in close conjunction with references to God's enduring existence (43:10, 12–13;46:4;48:12).[65] This has led some scholars to argue that it ought to be rendered "I am" at least in certain verses of Is. 40ff.[66] This is possible, but it is not strictly necessary. I cannot see that any of the uses of אני הוא in these texts demands any translation other than "I am he" or "I am the one," i.e. I am YHWH, or I am God. Because Exodus traditions, and particularly allusions to Ex. 3:14, suffuse these texts, אני הוא may at times take on "coloring" from Ex. 3:14. But this is based on the context of Is.40–55 as a whole. It is not a function of the grammar.

An especially apposite example for us is Is. 48:12. Delbert Burkett has suggested that there is a three-fold temporal reference to God in Is. 48:12. He writes as follows:

> In v.12...the speaker declares his existence in present, past, and future: 'I Am, I (was) first, and I (will be) last.' This threefold declaration is undoubtedly an interpretation of the divine name *ehyeh* (Exod. 3.14), which as a Qal imperfect verb has three possible time references: 'I am', 'I was', or 'I will be'. The speaker thus identifies himself as the one who revealed his name and nature to Moses as 'I am who I am' or 'I am, I was, I will be'.[67]

The MT and LXX of the relevant portion of the verse read:

אני הוא אני ראשון אף אני אחרון
ἐγώ εἰμι πρῶτος, καὶ ἐγώ εἰμι εἰς τὸν αἰῶνα

This is of obvious interest for our study. There is, however, no compelling reason to translate the verse as Burkett suggests. It is perfectly natural to take אני הוא as "I am he" in the sense of "I am YHWH," realizing that the (implicit) "am" functions solely as the copula, and is not a statement of

---

[65] I say "enduring existence" because these particular texts do not specify that God's life is everlasting, though the author surely believed this to be the case. One should also note that 43:12-3 is only included if גם מיום אני הוא is rendered "from everlasting I am (He)." Some scholars object and believe it should be read "henceforth I am (He)." See Ball, p.196.

[66] See Burkett, p.144.

[67] Burkett, p. 156.

existence, in the present tense or otherwise.⁶⁸ (The rendering "It is I" might capture this best.) This is confirmed by reference to the parallel texts in אני ראשון ואת אחרנים אני הוא 41:4; and 44:6 אני ראשון ואני אחרון. The phrase אני הוא serves as a stylistic variation on the theme that "I, YHWH, am first and last."⁶⁹ I do not then consider Is. 48:12 to be a bone fide *Dreizeitenformel*. The genuinely temporal element is bipartite ("first and last"), as is reflected in the LXX version.⁷⁰

Of course, we must reckon with the fact that later Jewish interpreters of Is. 48:12 could have read the verse in the way Burkett suggests. While I know of no direct evidence for this, one could submit that the Targumic interpretation of Dt. 32:39 as "I am he who is and who was and I am he who will be" is based on Is. 48:12. This is no small point, since Dt. 32:39 itself contains the phrase אני אני הוא. But as we will argue below, it is more likely that this is a conflation of traditions surrounding Ex. 3:14, seen through the prism of Is. 40–55 as a whole.

What *is* certain is that אני הוא was at times translated in the LXX as ἐγώ εἰμι, and that this move virtually ensured that readers of the Greek bible would see some correlation between the ἐγώ εἰμι of Is. 40ff. and the ἐγώ εἰμι ὁ ὤν of Ex. 3:14. One cannot base too much on a comparison of the LXX and the MT of Is. 40–55, since it is apparent that the LXX is often translating a different Hebrew *Vorlage* with respect to divine names.⁷¹ But the repeated translation of אני הוא by ἐγώ εἰμι does draw one's attention. The most provocative text for our purposes is Is. 43:25 (cf. 51:12):

אנכי אנכי הוא מחה פשעיך

---

⁶⁸ The translation suggested by Burkett works no better if one takes הוא itself to be a copula linking the אני to the remainder of the statement. As T. Muraoka notes, the biblical Hebrew use of the pronoun as "copula" must be distinguished from Indo-European usage where the "copula is provided by a verb of existence." See Muraoka, *Emphatic Words and Structures in Biblical Hebrew* (Jerusalem: Magnes Press/Leiden: Brill, 1985), p.69; more generally pp.67–77. See also B. Waltke and M. O'Connor, *An Introduction to Biblical Hebrew Syntax* (Winona Lake, IN: Eisenbrauns, 1990), p.131 n. They write that the linking pronoun (e.g. הוא) is "often called a *copula* or binder; this usage should not be confused with the more regular description of *hayā* as a copula(r verb)."

⁶⁹ Cf. Harner, p.14: "Second Isaiah regarded the phrase 'I am he' as an abbreviated form of other expressions, especially 'I am Yahweh,' summing up in concise terms everything represented by the longer terms."

⁷⁰ It may be, of course, that the LXX is translating a different *Vorlage* (see note below). But it is equally likely that they have simply smoothed out the reading represented by the MT.

⁷¹ E.g. Is. 42:8,45:3,5: κύριος ὁ θεός for MT יהוה; 41:4: θεός (no article) for יהוה;43:11: ὁ θεός for יהוה. For this reason I am somewhat wary of introducing Is. 45:18 into the discussion, where the LXX reads Ἐγώ εἰμι for MT אני יהוה. It seems more likely that this is a textual problem rather than a theologically tendentious rendering of "I, YHWH" by "I am." Dodd (p.94) is duly cautious.

ἐγώ εἰμι ἐγώ εἰμι ὁ ἐξαλείφων τὰς ἀνομίας.

Again, it is not necessary to take ἐγώ εἰμι as a divine title in this verse. The translator may simply have thought that repeating ἐγώ εἰμι was more elegant than repeating ἐγώ alone. But the explicit appearance of the copula serves as an invitation to associate this verse with Ex. 3:14. Thus Dodd, followed by others, renders the LXX: "I am 'I AM', who erases your iniquities."[72] The same holds true for 43:10 (cf. 46:4), where ותבינו כי אני הוא is translated καὶ συνῆτε ὅτι ἐγώ εἰμι. It would be natural to take this as a divine title, with the implication that ἐγώ εἰμι says something about God's everlasting or even "absolute" existence.

To summarize, neither the MT nor the LXX of Is.40–55 demands an absolute equation of אני הוא or ἐγώ εἰμι with אהיה. But the possibility of making such an equation is there. Indeed, in the case of the LXX, it was almost inevitable that it would be made. We will follow up on the implications of this for John's gospel in our section on the meaning of the name YHWH in the NT. We conclude by reiterating the importance of Is. 40–55 for shaping the developing traditions surrounding the revelation of the name in Ex. 3:14. While the association with Ex. 3:14 is not made explicit, there are strong hints that the author of these chapters understood אהיה אשר אהיה as a statement about God's everlasting existence, and his willingness and ability to help his people in their distress.

Qumran

The sectaries at Qumran, as we noted in Chapter 1, were both ingenious and prolific in their depiction (or non-depiction) of the name YHWH. Their variations fairly leap off the scrolls. The case of the meaning of the name is quite different. There are no texts which to my knowledge openly address this question, as do Philo, the rabbis, or (implicitly) the LXX.. We find only a few allusive references which may or may not reflect a particular understanding of the name YHWH. There are passages, however, which feature noteworthy uses of the verb "to be," and as such fit into our general discussion of "Being" and ὁ ὤν/τὸ ὄν. These texts will occupy the greater part of our discussion.

We begin, however, with an orthographic note which may be of interest. In our previous section on Qumran, we noted that *yod* and *waw* were indistinguishable in a number of the scrolls. Thus the name YHWH, when it was written, would appear as והוה (see e.g. 11QT 63:8, among numerous instances). Now, the 3rd person Qal imperfect masculine singular of היה, which would be יהיה in modern Hebrew script, also appears as והוה (see e.g. 11QT 63:4, only a few lines up from our previous example) The words

---

[72] Dodd, p.94; Burkett, p.144.

for "YHWH" and "He is, He will be" are written in exactly the same way. When we recall the care with which the name YHWH was treated at Qumran, it is quite possible that they were aware of this connection. Thus they may well have understood at least one meaning of the name YHWH to be "He is" or "He will be."[73]

We begin our discussion of the verb "to be" with the appearance of הווא ונהיה,[74] the Qal and Niphal participles of היה, in texts like 1QS 3:15, 1QM 17:5, 4Q180:1f.; 4Q418, fr.43:2. If one were to translate these as free-standing entities, "Being" and "Becoming" would be natural equivalents. The significance of these two words for Greek thought need hardly be emphasized. That they should appear together at Qumran leads Martin Hengel to make the following comment:

> We may see here [i.e. in 1QS 3:15–4:26] the concern for a systematic, indeed almost 'philosophical' conceptuality which had not appeared earlier in Hebrew thought. This applies, for example, to the pair of concepts 'being and happening' (הווה ונהיה), which is used elsewhere on a number of occasions in Essene writings. E. Kamlah is probably right when he observes that here 'the Jewish belief in creation' is, among other things, wrestling with an 'understanding of the world which has developed the abstract terms of being and becoming, in other words, Greek. One might translate the...sentence by πάντα τὰ ὄντα καὶ τὰ γινόμενα'.[75]

Hengel may be correct in his general assessment of a new concern for systematic conceptuality, but we must not be too quick in imagining that the sectaries at Qumran were whole-hearted Platonists on the basis of this text alone. 1QS 3:15, for example, seems to contrast *what is going on now* (הווא) with *what will take place in the future* (נהיה). In the present, the sons of justice are led by the Prince of Lights, and the sons of deceit are led by the Angel of Darkness (3: 20 ff.). In the future, the former group will receive eternal blessing, the latter eternal destruction (4:6 ff.). The emphasis does *not* lie in the reliability and stability of הווא compared with the unreliability and flux of נהיה (which would be the classic Parmenidean/Platonic formulation).

---

[73] We may also note that the verb to be appears fairly frequently in texts associated with creation. See e.g. 4Q402, fr.4:12;1QH 18:2;4Q511, fr.10: 10–11;1QS 3:15;CD 2: 9–10;4Q180:1–2;4Q418, fr.43:2;1QS 11:11;1QS 11:18. It is impossible to say whether this predilection for היה has a direct connection with the name YHWH, or whether it is an extrapolation from the יהי of Genesis 1.

[74] The spelling of the verbs varies with different texts. We are giving the "standard" version as it appears, e.g., in Armin Lange, *Weisheit und Prädestination* (Leiden: Brill, 1995), p.57 n.

[75] Hengel, *Judaism and Hellenism*, 1: 219. For additional discussion of the 1QS 3:13ff., see Jean L.-Duhaime, "L'Instruction sur les deux esprits et les interpolations dualistes à Qumrân (1QS III, 13–IV, 26)," *Revue biblique* 84 (1977): 566–594; and Hartmut Stegemann, "Zu Textbestand und Grundgedanken von 1QS III, 13 – IV,26," *RQ* 13 (1988): 95–131.

The case is even clearer in 1QS 11:11, where the two are used in parallel: "By his knowledge everything *shall come into being* (נהיה) and all that *does exist* (הויה) he establishes with his calculations..." נהיה and הויה here are not ontologically distinct categories. The difference is between those things that exist or happen now, and those things that will exist or will happen in the future.[76] It is, of course, possible that in earlier times some philosophically minded Jews had developed the phrase הווא ונהיה as a strict translation of "Being" and "Becoming" in the Platonic sense, and that the Qumran usage is a distant echo of a past attempt at hellenization. (We will argue below for just such a phenomenon with regards to 1QS 10-11 and 1QH 20.) But even if this is so, it appears that many of these associations had been lost by the time the phrase made its way into the Scrolls.

The verb נהיה also appears in the formula רז נהיה, "the mystery of becoming/what will be," which appears several times in the scrolls.[77] Armin Lange gives a thorough discussion of the phrase and comes to the following conclusion:

> רז נהיה bezeichnet somit ein Phänomen, das ethische, historische, nomistische, eschatologische und urzeitliche Komponenten in sich vereinigt. Es handelt sich um eine Welt- bzw. Schöpfungsordnung, die ethische und historische Komponenten enthält und sich dereinst im Eschaton erfüllt. Es beginnen sich also im Begriff רז נהיה die ethisch-sittlichen Elemente der weisheitlichen Urordnung mit der Vorstellung einer prädestinatianischen, auf das Eschaton zulaufenden Geschichtsordnung zu vereinigen.[78]

Lange's summary makes good sense of the phrase as we find it in the Scrolls. The רז נהיה is best understood as God's "plan for the ages," the strictly determined sequence of events which will unfold throughout his-

---

[76] See Lange, p.57. He does say נהיה indicates *Werden* rather than *Sein*. For the future orientation, he cites Sir. 42:19, where the Greek equivalent of נהיות is τὰ ἐσόμενα. In the OT, the Niphal is far rarer than the Qal, and usually means "occur, come to pass, happen." See, e.g. Ex.11:6, Joel 2:2, and the discussion in BDB.

[77] See 1Q26, fr.1, 1:1,4; 1Q27, fr.1, 1:3,4; 4Q416, fr.2, 1:5 (=4Q417, fr.1); 4Q416, fr.2, 3:14,18,21; 4Q417, fr.2, 1:6,21; 4Q417, fr.2, 2:3 (=4Q18, fr.43); 4Q418, fr.123, 3:4.

[78] Lange, p.60; see his discussion of רז נהיה, pp.57-61. He gives sound arguments against the theory of Wacholder and Abegg that the "Mystery of Existence" may have been the title of a text or texts used by the Qumran community. (Cf. D.J. Harrington, who translates the phrase "the mystery that is to be/come," but affirms that it "seems to be a body of teaching concerning behavior and eschatology." "The *Raz Nihyeh* in a Qumran Wisdom text," *RQ* 65-8 (1996): 549-53.) Lange's translation "Geheimnis des Werdens" serves as reminder that the phrase is not about an abstract inquiry into "Being" as such (as one might infer from the rendering the "mystery of existence"; see e.g. García Martínez in 4Q416,4Q417). For a discussion of "mystery" at Qumran, and related concepts, see also Hengel, *Judaism and Hellenism*, 1: 221-224.

tory into the eschaton. As such, it has significant parallels in other early Jewish literature.[79]

Perhaps the most noteworthy instance of this phrase for our purposes comes in 1Q27, fr. 1, 1: 3–4, which reads as follows:

ולוא ידעו רז נהיה ובקדמוניות לוא התבוננו ולוא ידעו מה אשר יבוא עליהמה ונפשמה לוא מלטו מרז נהיה

> And they do not know the future mystery, or understand ancient matters. And they do not know what is going to happen to them; and they will not save their souls from the future mystery (García Martínez)

This text highlights the eschatological aspect of the רז נהיה. It also features the word יבוא. We might render the phrase more literally "that which *will come upon* them." This is somewhat reminiscent of Rev. 1:4, at least insofar as we have a look back at the past (ובקדמוניות) and a look towards the future which specifically employs the word "come" (cf. Is. 41:22). This is not, of course, to suggest that 1Q27 constitutes an exegesis of the divine name, but it may help us better understand the final element in John's formula in Revelation.

The רז נהיה is important to our discussion not only because it offers a somewhat unusual use of the verb "to be." More importantly, it introduces us to the idea of the *Schöpfungsordnung*, which appears throughout the Scrolls, although not always under the description רז נהיה. This *Schöpfungsordnung*, as it turns out, is sometimes described in terms usually reserved for God himself. In particular, it can be called "that which always is" (see below). The idea of a pre-existent plan of creation and history which "always is" recalls the τὸ ὂν ἀεί of the *Timaeus*, and for this reason alone it is worth pursuing. We will examine two crucial texts in some detail: 1QH 20: 9–11 and 1QS 11: 3 ff.

We begin with 1QH 20. If we take 20:4 ("[For the Instruc]tor, praises and prayers," etc.) as our launching off point, the poem begins with a call to worship God at the appropriate moments of the day and year. Given the intensity of debates about the calendar at this time, one should not underestimate the importance of this matter of the proper times and seasons.[80] The "wonderful secrets" of God that are revealed to the Instructor (ll.11–13) include not only the knowledge of God's character, but also of "the positions of the day, according to their regulation...the appointed moment of the night...the positions of the stations in the commands of their signs...(ll.5,6,8)." The order of creation established by God, and revealed by God to the hymn writer, is the foundation of his religious practice. The

---

[79] See, e.g., 1 En. 39:11; 2 Bar. 21:5–8,17; 48:2ff.; Ap. Abr. 22:1–5.
[80] See the comments by Svend Holm-Nielsen in *Hodayot: Psalms from Qumran* (Aarhus: Universitetsforlaget, 1960), p.203; and L.-Duhaime, p.574.

eschatological dimensions of God's plans, which are explicitly linked with the heavenly bodies in 1QS 11 (see below), are here mostly reserved for ll. 14 ff. (albeit in fragmentary form).

The translation of ll.9–11, our primary concern, is no easy matter. Compare the renderings of García Martínez and Vermes:

Hebrew

ותעודת הווה והיאה תהיה ואין אפס וזולתה לוא היה ולוא יהיה עוד
כי אל הן[ד]עות הכינה ואין אחר עמו

García Martínez
(...in accordance with the decree established through God's mouth), and through the witness of what is. And this will be, and nothing more; besides him there is no other, nor will there ever be another. For the God of knowledge has established it and no-one else with him.

Vermes
(...by the certain law from the mouth of God), by the precept which is and shall be forever and ever without end. Without it nothing is nor shall be, for the God of knowledge established it and there is no other beside Him.

It is clear that by his decree God alone has established the world, and in particular the appropriate occasions for worship (which are of course determined by the observation of the heavenly bodies). But the details remain obscure. תעודה is notoriously difficult to translate, and the problem is compounded by its appearance in construct with the verb to be.[81] While Vermes' "precept" makes sense, García Martínez' "witness of what is" is not as strained as it might first appear. The writer is stressing the accuracy of his knowledge about the cosmos and the proper times for worship, and he states that this is in accordance with the hidden decree of God and with the witness, or testimony, of the cosmos itself. Both of these (at least in his mind) are in line with his religious practices.[82] Such a reading may also fit the construct chain תעודת הווה better than Vermes' "precept which is..."

M. Delcor takes a completely different approach. He renders the phrase "le statut fixé par celui qui est..."[83] He suggests that הווה may be "une déformation intentionelle du tétragramme divin jamais employé dans les textes de Qumran."[84] His suggestion for the translation is intriguing, particularly because of the precedent of ὁ ὤν in the LXX. Attractive as this

---

[81] See the comments by Carol Newsom, *Songs of the Sabbath Sacrifice* (Atlanta: Scholars Press, 1985), p.161. She rejects the traditional rendering "witness" and notes that in many cases in the scrolls it is synonymous with מועד, "appointed time." Cf. Lange, p.152.

[82] Cf. the use of τὰ ὄντα for the created order in Wis.7:17.

[83] Delcor, *Les hymnes de Qumran: Hodayot* (Paris: Letouzey et Ané, 1962), pp.248–9. Millar Burrows gives a similar rendering in his translation. See the discussion in Holm-Nielsen, pp.203–4.

[84] Delcor, pp.248–9.

translation might be for our purposes, however, the context dictates that הורה indicates the created order.⁸⁵ As Svend Holm-Nielsen points out, the thought here is that God's word (the "decree") gives the "theoretical expression" and the universe the "actual expression" of the "regular changing of times."⁸⁶ While Delcor's interpretation cannot be ruled out completely, the rendering "the witness of *what* is" is to be preferred.

The problems continue as we move to the next clause (if indeed it is a separate clause). If one takes היאה as an enclitic, this would yield "the witness of what was, what is, and what will be," which would have obvious attractions for our study of Revelation 1:4. But this seems rather forced, and it would violate our understanding of "the witness of what is" as a complete thought meaning something like "the testimony of the universe." It seems better to take היאה as a simple feminine pronoun. Both García Martínez' and Vermes' renderings are compatible with this view. The immediate antecedent appears to be תעודת, but the writer may also have the "fixed decree" (תכון נאמנה) in mind as the verse proceeds. The latter may be more in the forefront of the author's thinking when he says, "without it nothing is or will be." Nothing exists apart from the decree of God. It is also possible that "what is" is in view: apart from the created order nothing (else) is or will be. (This may be the sense of García Martínez' version.) ואין אפס could either be "and nothing more" or "forever and ever," but the former is to be preferred because of the parallels to Is.45:6 (see below).

Finally, we come to וזולתה לוא היה ולוא יהיה עוד. García Martínez takes this to refer to God, but this is extremely unlikely. While the final *he* might theoretically have a masculine antecedent, it is more natural to take it as a feminine referring back, like היאה, to תעודת or תכון נאמנה. This conclusion is also justified by the use in the following clause of a *waw* for "him" in עמו, and of a *he* in the verbal form הכינה, "he established *it*," where God can obviously not be intended as the object. Furthermore, Vermes' version "without it...established it" flows more smoothly than García Martínez' "besides him...established it." As we will see, the question of whether this refers to God or the precept (or something else) is a crucial one.

We may summarize our discussion of the translation by offering a "Targum" of the text (italicizing our additions in good Targumic fashion):

---

⁸⁵ Holm-Nielsen (p.204) argues that the text cannot mean "the one who is" because this would be too close to the Yahweh name. But as Delcor correctly recognizes, this is precisely why one *could* argue for the meaning "the one who is" – it would be a play on the meaning of the divine name. The context alone argues against the translation "the one who is."

⁸⁶ Holm-Nielsen, p.204.

The Meaning of the Name 147

...in accordance with the decree established through God's mouth, and through the witness of what is, *that is, the testimony of the universe*, and *this decree and this testimony*[87] will *continue to* be, and nothing else *will take their place*, and apart from *this decree and this testimony* there was nothing nor will anything ever be, because the God of knowledge has established *this decree and testimony*, and there is no one else with him.

We gain a deeper appreciation of the passage by comparing it with the Old Testament text with which it interacts, Is. 45:3ff.[88] We will summarize the points of contact below, and then discuss their significance for interpreting 1QH 20:9-10:

1QH 20:9-10

ותעודת הווה והיאה תהיה ואין אפס וזולתה לוא היה ולוא יהיה עוד
כי אל הן[ד]עות הכינה ואין אחר עמו

Is.45:3ff.

³ונתתי לך אוצרות חשך ומטמני מסתרים למען תדע כי אני יהוה
הקורא בשמך...אני יהוה ואין עוד זולתי אין אלהים...
⁴כי אפס בלעדי אני יהוה ואין עוד

The verbal parallels appear to be deliberate. אפס and זולת are found relatively infrequently in the OT (אפס 43x in MT; זולת 16x), and their uses in Isaiah – and particularly in Isaiah 45 – are the closest parallels to their uses in 1QH. אפס is used in conjunction with אין only in Is.41:12, 45:14 and 46:9. זולת is used with the negative outside Isaiah,[89] but the sequence ואין עוד זולתי אין אלהים (Is.45:5) shows the closest affinities to 1QH's ...וזולתה לוא היה ולוא יהיה עוד כי אל הן[ד]עות.... The formula אחר עמו does not occur in the OT, and indeed אחר (אין) (in the singular) is never used to describe the uniqueness of the God of Israel.[90] Once again, the closest parallel we have is in Isaiah: God declares in Is.42:8 and 48:11, "My glory I will not give to another" – כבודי לאחר לא אתן.

The connections between 1QH 20:9-10 and Isaiah 45 extend to the context, hence our citation above of the verses concerning Cyrus in Is.45:3.

---

[87] I have kept both "decree" and "witness/testimony" in the rendering because it is unclear which the author might have had in mind. "Testimony" lies nearest to the pronoun היאה, but "decree" makes more sense in the phrase "nothing is nor will be."

[88] Holm-Nielsen (p.207) notes that Isaiah is used frequently in 1QH. As we hope to demonstrate, however, he is mistaken to say "...what is especially remarkable about this psalm [which includes our text, 20:9-10, although he uses the old numbering system in which 20=12] is the surprising small extent to which Is. is used – if it is used at all." Is. 45:3ff. suffuses our portion of the text.

[89] Cf. esp. Hos.13:4, 2 Sa. 7:22, 1 Chr. 17:20. The only use of the precise form זולתה occurs in 1 Sa. 21:10, where it refers to the sword of Goliath.

[90] The Israelites are commanded not to worship "other gods" (Ex.34:14), nor even mention their names (Ex.23:13), but this is a slightly different matter, and the plural, not the singular, of אחר is used.

Whatever the original author may have intended by "I will give you the treasures of darkness and the hidden wealth of secret places," the writer of 1QH appears to have interpreted these words in light of his own experience of revelation from God: "And I, the Instructor, have known you, my God, [ידעתיכה, likely a deliberate contrast to the לא ידעתני of Is.45:4]...and I have listened loyally to your wonderful secret through your holy spirit. You have opened within me knowledge of the mystery of your wisdom, the source of your power..."[91]

What is most interesting, however, is that "the Instructor" has taken words originally referring to the uniqueness of God, and (with the exception of ואין אחר עמו) transferred them to God's "decree" which holds the creation together, or to the creation itself (if "the witness of what is," or simply "what is," is to be understood as the antecedent throughout the verse). In fact, not only is Is.45:3ff. concerned with the revelation of the uniqueness of God. We might also say that it is concerned with *the revelation of God's name*. All his activity is designed to reveal that אני יהוה ואין עוד.

Before we attempt to answer why the hymn writer was willing to describe God's decree, or the created order, in such terms, we must look at 1QS 11:3ff. The passage has some obvious affinities with 1QH 20. If we take 1QS 10 and 11 as constituting a single hymn, then both our passages begin with instructions concerning the proper times for worship. "At the commencement of the dominion of light, during its rotation and when retired to its appointed abode..." In 1QS, the eschatological significance of the celestial order is made clear. The description of the heavens culminates in 10: 7–8:

> ...the constellation of the harvest up to summer, the constellation of seed-time up to the constellation of the grass, the constellation of the years up to their seven-year periods. At the commencement of the seven-year periods up to the moment decided for deliverance. (García Martínez)

The cycle of feasts and jubilees will eventually issue in eschatological redemption for the faithful. We might term this arrangement a part of the *mystery* of God, and in fact mystery language is frequently used in the passage (cf. 11:3,5,19). Finally, like 1QH 20, 1QS 10–11 draws from Isaiah 40ff. the idea of the uniqueness of the God of Israel (11:11,17–18).

We will concentrate on ll.3–8. The passage consists of a lengthy chiasm extolling the wonders of God, and his faithfulness to enlighten the heart and support the steps of the author.[92] Once again, a comparison of the key

---

[91] "Secret" and "mystery" are respectively סוד and רז, but one is still struck by the appearance of מסתרים in Is.45:3.

[92] The chiasm flows as follows: A: God's judgment and the perfection of the path (l.2); B: knowledge of God/light (l.3); C: eyes observing wonders (l.3); D: light of heart be-

passages in the translations of García Martínez and Vermes will be instructive:

Hebrew

³...ובנפלאותיו הביטה עיני ואורת לבבי ברז
⁴ נהיה והויא עולם משען ימיני
⁵...בהויא עולם ⁶הביטה עיני תושיה אשר נסתרה מאנש

García Martínez
³...and my eyes have observed his wonders, and the light of my heart the mystery of the future[93] and of what it is for always. There is support for my right hand... ⁵My eyes have observed what always is, wisdom that has been hidden from mankind...

Vermes
³...my eyes have beheld his marvellous deeds, and the light of my heart, the mystery to come. He that is everlasting is the support of my right hand... ⁵My eyes have gazed on that which is eternal, on wisdom concealed from men...

"The mystery of the future/to come" (1.3), which the two translators handle in the same way, is the by now familiar רז נהיה. The difficult question is how this relates to the words which follow immediately after it, והויא עולם. One can take the two phrases as referring to the secrets of the future and "what it is for always" (García Martínez); or to "what happens and is happening forever" (Wernberg-Møller); or one can follow Vermes and make הויא עולם an epithet for God. Maurice Baillet also believes הויא עולם is a reference to God here in 1QS 11:4.[94]

The question may be resolved, I believe, by referring to the corresponding phrase in the chiasm, "My eyes have observed (הביטה) what always is, wisdom that has been hidden from mankind...(ll.5–6)" As García Martínez' translation suggests, "what always is" (חויא עולם) should be taken with "wisdom that has been hidden from mankind..." (תושיה אשר נסתרה מאנש). There is a good parallel for this in 1.19, where the hymn writer says no one but God is able "to gaze (להביט) into the abyss of your mysteries...(García Martínez)." "What always is," then, is the wisdom of God, which may also be described as the mystery of God. As we observed above, this is nothing else than God's plan for the ages.

If we ask where the writer came up with the idea that God's wisdom, a) is equivalent to his plan for the ages; and b) is "eternal" (עולם), we must begin with the book of Proverbs. As for the first matter, in Proverbs 3: 19–

---

holding what is and will be (1.3): E: support for right hand (1.4); F: steps on the firm rock (1.4); F¹: truth of God is rock of steps (1.4); E¹: support for right hand (1.4); D¹: wonderful mystery is light of heart (1.5); C¹: eyes have observed what always is (1.5); B¹: knowledge and understanding (1.6); A¹: judgement of God (ll.7–8). The chiastic structure is particulalry clear in the center of the text (C,D,E,F), which is our primary concern.

[93] The first edition of García Martínez' translation inadvertently added "and the present" at this point; this has been corrected in the second edition.

[94] In *DJD VII*, ed. Maurice Baillet (Oxford: Oxford University Press, 1982), p.227.

20, it is said: "With wisdom (בחכמה) YHWH founded the earth, He established the heavens with understanding (בתבונה). With his knowledge (בדעתו) he divided the deeps..." One may be troubled by the fact that the Qumran writer uses תושיה for wisdom, in the first instance, rather than the sapiential terms in Pr. 3:19–20. The term does appear, however, in Pr. 3:21: "My son, do not let (these things) be lost from your eyes (מעיניך), preserve prudence and shrewdness (תושיה ומזמה)." Whatever the precise nuance of תושיה might be in Proverbs, one can easily see how later interpreters could have seen it as meaning essentially the same thing as חכמה, תבונה, etc. The fact that it occurs in close conjunction with מעיניך may partly explain why the Qumran writer chose to use it here, since he wishes to speak about something that can be "gazed" upon.[95] (The "gazing" also has significant parallels in Greek thought, which we will examine in a moment.) Whatever one makes of the vocabulary employed, the passage in Proverbs does indicate that "wisdom" was somehow the instrument of God in creation. The eternity of wisdom, meanwhile, is affirmed in Proverbs 8. Wisdom is the first of God's works: "from eternity (or "from of old" – מעולם) He appointed (thus NIV) me, from the beginning of the ancient times of the earth...(8:23)" (Note that while wisdom is generally designated as חכמה, in 8:14 she is said to possess תושיה.)

In Proverbs, then, wisdom is an eternal entity (or at least an ancient one, depending on how one takes עולם) which God in some sense employs as an agent in creating the world. The vocabulary used by the writer of 1QS 10–11, as well as the content of the passage, indicates that he was well aware of Proverbs 3 and 8 while composing this piece.

We may now attempt to put all of this together. In light of the many affinities in content and style between 1QH 20 and 1QS 10–11, it seems reasonable to take them as representing an outlook on wisdom which formed a significant part of the sectaries' thinking. The most relevant tenets for us are these: God's wisdom, which serves both as instrument and blueprint for creation and history, may be called "that which always is," and indeed may be described in terms usually reserved for YHWH himself. It is theoretically possible that the writers of these pieces may have developed this teaching solely on the basis of the Old Testament and their own ingenuity. But it is hard to avoid the thought that Greek philosophy, and the *Timaeus* in particular, may have contributed to the understanding of wisdom expressed in these texts. The world of Forms in the *Timaeus* is quite similar to the type of blueprint that seems to underlie the Qumran theology. The fact that this world of Forms is called τὸ ὂν ἀεί, "that which always is," makes some sort of comparison with 1QS 11 inevitable. It should also be

---

[95] מזמה also appears in 1.6 of 1QS 11, in parallel with תושיה and דעה.

recalled that in the *Phaedrus* the gods and fortunate humans *gaze upon*[96] τὸ ὄν ὄντως (247c–d, 249c). This is strikingly similar to the language used in 1QS 11:5–6, "My eyes have observed what always is..."

Precisely how and why this connection was made remains a matter of speculation. The situation is complicated by the fact that our two central concerns – the description of God's wisdom or plan as τὸ ὄν ἀεί, and the implicit comparison between this wisdom and God himself – are so intimately bound up with one another. That is, if one calls wisdom (for whatever reason) τὸ ὄν ἀεί, one has already assigned divine attributes to it; and conversely, if one (for whatever reason) believes wisdom is in some sense like God, it is hardly surprising that one should describe wisdom as τὸ ὄν ἀεί. Despite these reservations, let us make some proposals about how Greek thought may have influenced the theology of the sectaries in this matter.

It seems doubtful, although not impossible, that the writers of 1QH 20 and 1QS 10–11 were directly influenced by the *Timaeus* or Platonic thought in general. More likely, the connections were made earlier on by Jews with a certain inclination towards Greek philosophy. The *Timaeus* is in many ways close to the account of creation in Genesis, and so this would be a natural place for such Jews to find points of comparison between their faith and Greek thought. The twenty-second chapter of the Apocalypse of Abraham provides particularly helpful comparative material. There we read:

> And I said, "Eternal, Mighty One! What is this picture of creation?" And he said to me, "This is my will with regard to what is in the light and it was good before my face. And then, afterward, I gave them a command by my word and they came into existence. Whatever I had decreed was to exist had already been outlined in this and all the previously created (things) you have seen stood before me."[97]

In modern idiom, we might say that Abraham is shown a "film" of creation and history which depicts events without actually "being" them. (The problem with this analogy, of course, is that this "film" of creation is actually the blueprint or plan for what has transpired and will transpire in the future.[98]) This already situates the Apocalypse of Abraham within a worldview which owes something to the *Timaeus*, even if the principles might conceivably be extrapolated from the Hebrew bible. Moreover, the *OTP*

---

[96] The word ἰδοῦσα is used in 247c–d.

[97] Trans. Rubinkiewicz, in *OTP* 1: 700.

[98] At Ap. Abr. 25:4, we have the remarkable statement that the temple Abraham sees is "my *idea* of the priesthood of the name of my glory... (italics mine)." Whether the putative Semitic original had any Platonic overtones in the use of "idea" is impossible to say. But this certainly seems possible, given the context of the passage.

notes that the phrase rendered "with regard to what is" might derive from an original Greek of πρὸς τὰ ὄντα.[99]

In the *Timaeus*, of course, the world of Forms (or the Eternal Living Creature, to use the language of the dialogue) is described as τὸ ὂν ἀεί. It would be quite tempting to see Plato's world of Forms performing a role analogous to that played by wisdom in biblical texts such as Proverbs chapters 3 and 8. We may also propose that Jews who had an interest in Platonic thought were probably also aware of the Septuagint's description of God as ὁ ὤν.

With these facts in hand, we may construct a few syllogisms which might reflect the development of thought in these Jewish "wisdom" circles. The following are given as examples:

Syllogism 1
The world of Forms is τὸ ὂν ἀεί (Tim. 27d)
Wisdom, as it is used in Proverbs, seems to be like this world of Forms
Therefore, wisdom may also be described as τὸ ὂν ἀεί.

Syllogism 2
God is ὁ ὤν (Ex. 3:14 LXX)
Wisdom is eternal, like God
Therefore wisdom may be described as τὸ ὂν ἀεί.

Syllogism 3
Wisdom is eternal and may be described as τὸ ὂν ἀεί
God is eternal and may be described as ὁ ὤν
Therefore Wisdom is in a fundamental way *like God*.

Other syllogisms of similar nature could be constructed. The main point is this: the description of the world of Forms in the *Timaeus* as τὸ ὂν ἀεί, combined with the description of God as ὁ ὤν in Ex. 3:14 LXX, *may* have contributed to the striking language used of wisdom in 1QS 10–11 and 1QH 20.

Finally, if Judaism already had at this time a developed "theology of the name" in which the name YHWH had cosmogonic functions, this could also contribute to the understanding of the texts as they stand. The obvious connection of YHWH and his (cosmogonic) name would help make a text like 1QH 20 more understandable.

None of this, of course, can be established with absolute certainty. We have simply laid out a few possible ways in which Jewish speculation about wisdom and creation could have led to the texts we find in 1QS and 1QH. Others might well be devised. If forced to choose, I would suggest that it is most likely that some type of influence from Platonic thinking had worked its way into the tradition prior to the composition of our texts. In

---

[99] In *OTP* 1: 700. The notes also point out that the Old Slavonic for "light" is very close to the word for "council/counsel," which would fit the context quite well.

Apocrypha and Pseudepigrapha

We will devote most of our discussion to the designation of God as ὁ ὤν. It should be noted that 1 En. 39:12 *may* contain an interpretation of the tetragrammaton. It reads "Those who sleep not bless thee; they stand before thy glory, saying: Holy, holy, holy, is the Lord of Spirits: he fills the earth with spirits."[100] This is clearly a reflection of the Trishagion of Is.6:3. Throughout this section of 1 Enoch, the phrase "The Lord of Spirits" (quite often in the form "the Name of the Lord of Spirits") is used to describe God.[101] What is striking is the use of the phrase, "he *fills* the world with spirits." God is the creator of the angelic hosts, not merely the one who rules over them. This seems quite close to the interpretation of the name YHWH favored by Albright, Cross, and Freedman, in which YHWH Sabaoth is taken to mean, "He causes the hosts to be."[102] The passage in 1 Enoch could simply be a general interpretation of the phrase "Lord of Hosts," independent of etymology. But the possibility remains that someone in the tradition did in fact take יהוה as a hiphil of the verb to be, and understood the phrase to mean that God fills the world with spirits.[103]

We now return to ὁ ὤν. At times, the understanding of God as "the One who is" is not explicit, but may help to explain certain curious turns of phrase. 2 Macc. 7:28 describes creation thus: οὐκ ἐξ ὄντων ἐποίησεν αὐτὰ (that is, the heavens, earth, etc.) ὁ θεός. This can be rendered either "God did not make them out of things that are..." or "God made them out of things that are not."[104] The gods of the nations, the idols, equally *are*

---

[100] Black's translation. See his discussion, p.191.

[101] Black (pp.191-2) suggests that this is an "interpretative transformation" (a phrase he borrows from B.H. Streeter) of the Old Testament title "Lord of Hosts." Already in the LXX we find the latter translated as κύριος τῶν δυνάμεων (3 Ki.17:1; Ps. 45:12, Nu.16:22, 27:16; cf. 1QH 10:8.), and Black suggests that either this Greek phrase or a (theoretical) κύριος τῶν πνευμάτων lies behind the Ethiopic "Lord of Spirits." Either of these Greek phrases could be taken to mean that the Lord rules over the angelic hosts.

[102] See above.

[103] This does not, of course, mean that Albright *et al.* are necessarily correct that this accounts for the origin of the name YHWH. But if these scholars were able to reconstruct such a reading from the texts at their disposal, the author of the Parables of Enoch or his source may well have done the same. This is especially true when one considers the ancients' penchant for etymological game-playing.

[104] The category of non-being could be expanded to include the dead, or those who never existed. Sir. 17:28 reads: "From the dead, as from one who does not exist (ὡς μηδὲ ὄντος), thanksgiving has perished..." Cf. Wis. 2:2.

not. The pious Esther of the LXX additions pleads with God not to give over his scepter τοῖς μὴ οὖσιν (4:17q= English 14:11). These "non-beings" are to be equated with the idols with which the enemies of the Jews have covenanted (4:17o=English 14:8). Wis. 14:13 speaks of idols in a similar vein: "for neither have they existed from the beginning nor will they exist for ever" – οὔτε γὰρ ἦν ἀπ' ἀρχῆς οὔτε εἰς τὸν αἰῶνα ἔσται.[105]

Occurences of ὁ ὤν itself are widespread enough to show that it was a "live" term among some sectors of Jews, although κύριος and ὕψιστος, for example, are far more prevalent in the Apocrypha and Pseudepigrapha than ὁ ὤν. We begin with Wis.13:1. The RSV renders this verse: "For all men who were ignorant of God were foolish by nature; and they were unable from the good things that are seen to know him who exists (τὸν ὄντα)." Although the writer avoids the Platonic τὸ ὄν and uses the more personal ὁ ὤν,[106] there is an implicit comparison here between the things that are seen and the one who *really* exists, namely God. Such a distinction between the visible world and the ideal world is of course a commonplace of Platonism. While the Platonic distinction between the visible and the ideal world may inform this text, the context of Wis. 13:1 points us back to the question of idolatry, and the non-existence of any rivals to the one true God. In 12:23ff., the author castigates the (presumably Egyptian) idolaters who worship animals, "creatures which they...thought to be gods" (12:27). The worshippers of fire, wind, and air receive fewer lashes from him (cf. 13:6, "yet these men are but little to be blamed..."), but they still are counted among those who ignorantly reverence the creation rather than the Creator, and thus "not even they are to be excused" (12:8). Most miserable of all are those who set their hope on "dead things" (ἐν νεκροῖς) and "give the name 'gods' to the works of mens' hands" (13:10). The polemic against idolatry essentially carries on through the remainder of the book, and the writer's perspective is aptly summed up in the aforementioned statement from 14:13, "neither have they existed from the beginning nor will they exist for ever."

The point of 13:1, then, is not *primarily* that God has "essential" existence as compared with the transient creation. This may lie behind the writer's thinking, but the main contrast is between the God who created the world and who acts in history –the God *who is* – and the false gods of the nations who are unworthy of worship, and who therefore *are not*. The

---

[105] The returning Nero, according to Sib .Or. 5:34, will declare himself equal to God, "but will prove that he is not" – ἐλέγξει δ' οὔ μιν ἐόντα. The text may only mean, however, that Nero will prove that he is *not God*. Cf. Sib. Or. 3:310.

[106] A point rightly emphasized by David Winston, *The Wisdom of Solomon* (Garden City, NY: Doubleday, 1979), p.249.

author of Wisdom is not hostile to philosophy, but his discussion of the God *who is* is structured more by the religious impulse to exalt the true creator than by a dispassionate concern with the nature of reality. It should also be noted that this denunciation of idolatry remains rooted in the events of the Exodus, which makes a reference to ὁ ὤν (Ex. 3:14) all the more appropriate.

The Fourth Book of Ezra provides us with our second example. 4 Ez. 8:7 reads, "For you alone exist, and we are of your hands, as you have declared."[107] The Latin for the first clause reads *Solus enim es*. This is not precisely ὁ ὤν, but it does closely resemble LXX Ps.89:2, ἀπὸ τοῦ αἰῶνος ἕως τοῦ αἰῶνος σὺ εἶ, which may have been influenced by the LXX rendering of Ex.3:14.[108] Idolatry is not in question in 4 Ezra 8. Instead, the author is lamenting the brevity and feebleness of human existence. "O my soul...not of your own will did you come into the world, and against your will you depart, for you have been given only a short time to live" (8:4–5). We might paraphrase his point in the chapter by saying that human life is derived, contingent upon the will of God, who alone is self-existent.[109]

The Sibylline Oracles are also conversant with the description of God as "the one who is." Sib. Or. Fr.1, l.35 uses ὑπάρχω rather than εἰμί, but the sense is clear enough. After extolling God as the one "who rules alone, exceedingly great, unbegotten, universal ruler, invisible" and so on, the passage concludes, "He rules heaven; holds sway over earth, he himself exists (αὐτὸς ὑπάρχει)."[110] Sib. Or. 5:173–4 (echoing Is.47:8) uses ὑπάρχω and εἰμί in parallel as it contrasts the boastful claims of Rome and the genuine majesty of God:

ἀλλ' ἔλεγες »μόνη εἰμὶ καὶ οὐδείς μ' ἐξαλαπάξει«
νῦν δὲ σὲ καὶ σοὺς πάντας ὀλεῖ θεὸς αἰὲν ὑπάρχων

---

[107] Trans. B. Metzger, *OTP* 1: 542.

[108] The MT of the verse reads מעולם עד עולם אתה אל, "from everlasting to everlasting you are God." The BHS apparatus points out that the Septuagint takes אל, "God," as אל, "not," and thus the LXX renders v.3 "do not turn man towards lowliness..." where the MT has "you return man to the dust." The MT is the more sensible reading, and so we must ask why the LXX translator felt compelled to transform in this way what is a fairly straightforward Hebrew text. The only explanation I can give is that he was captured by the idea that "God is" – a concept he would probably know either from LXX Ex.3:14 itself or from uses of ὁ ὤν derived from it – and was willing to strain the Hebrew somewhat to introduce this idea into the present text.

[109] Cf. 4 Ez. 9:18: "For there was a time in this age when I was preparing for those who now exist, before the world was made for them to dwell in, and no one opposed me then, for no one existed."

[110] All Sibylline Oracle texts are from J. Geffcken, *Die Oracula Sibyllina* GCS 8 (Leipzig: J.C. Hinrichs'sche, 1902).

The structure of the verse makes it likely that ὑπάρχω and εἰμι are synonymous here. Rome claims the divine prerogative of independent existence (or perhaps the divine prerogative of absolute authority), and God answers by destroying Rome and asserting his own eternal being.[111]

Two further examples from the Sibylline Oracles are of even more direct relevance to Rev. 1:4. Sib. Or. 1:137–146 is introduced by Collins as "A riddle on the name of God." The verses are also found in the "Tübingen Theosophy" and apparently are an intrusion into the text of the first Sibylline book. This makes dating the piece difficult. Collins believes that the Christian redaction is no later than 150 CE,[112] and thus it appears likely that this piece is also earlier than that date. The riddle begins, "I am the one who is" – εἰμὶ δ' ἔγωγε ὁ ὤν, a transparent citation of Ex.3:14, which has been altered slightly, probably for stylistic purposes. The section continues with a gematria puzzle which has baffled scholars to this day. We will make no attempt to solve it here. Suffice it to say that the designation of God in LXX Ex.3:14 appears here as shrouded in mystery. It is a part of a riddle. It is difficult to say whether the writer is aware of the mystery surrounding the pronunciation of the tetragrammaton (the gematria itself does not seem to be related to the name YHWH in any clear way), but it is certainly possible that he made such a connection.

Our final example consists not simply of an isolated reference to the designation ὁ ὤν, but a series of references to the divine name. It comes from the first section of Book 3 (ll.1–45), which Collins says could have been written anytime in the late hellenistic or early Roman periods.[113] The reference to ὁ ὤν occurs in 1.33: "you do not fear the existing God (τὸν ἐόντα θεόν) who guards all things." This much is familiar territory, since the phrase is linked with the denunciation of idols in ll.30–31. Idols are nonentities; only the true God *is*.

Things get more interesting when we go back a few verses. The writer extols God in familiar terms as the "one God, sole ruler, ineffable, who lives in the sky, self-begotten, invisible...." (ll.11ff.). At ll.15,–16 we meet with a phrase with obvious affinities to our text in Revelation: "he himself, eternal, revealed himself as existing now, and formerly, and again in the future."[114] Where, one might ask, did God reveal this about himself? It could be argued that this is simply a general conclusion of the author drawn from the Bible, mixed perhaps with a bit of Greek philosophy. But

---

[111] Collins, in *OTP* 1: 390, dates Book 5 to c.100 CE, and he notes that "all scholars date it between A.D. 80 and 130," thus making it quite relevant for our study of Revelation.

[112] In *OTP* 1: 332.

[113] In *OTP* 1: 360.

[114] Gk. ἀλλ' αὐτὸς ἀνέδειξεν αἰώνιος αὐτὸς ἑαυτόν ὄντα τε καὶ πρὶν ἐόντα, ἀτὰρ πάλι καὶ μετέπειτα.

in light of the writer's use of τὸν ἐόντα θεόν in 1.33, it seems more likely that he is reflecting on the *locus classicus* of God's revelation of himself, namely Ex.3:14. The fact that later rabbinic writings exegete the Exodus passage using a similar threefold temporal description bolsters the case for this interpretation.[115]

The mention of God's *name* follows almost immediately: "For who, being mortal, is able to see God with eyes?/or who will be able even to hear only/the name of the great heavenly God who rules the world/who created everything by a word...(3:17–20)" These verses call to mind the inutterability of God's name, and the connection of God's name with the creation of the world, which we explored in the previous chapter. There is a final tantalizing bit of evidence in 11.23–26: "Indeed it is God himself who fashioned Adam, of four letters/the first-formed man, fulfilling by his name/east and west and north and south." This acrostic, which enjoyed widespread popularity in later Jewish and Christian literature, is based on the Greek directions ἀντολίην, δύσιν, ἄρκτον and μεσημβρίην.[116] What is significant for our purposes is that l. 24 uses the very word "tetragrammaton" in its description of Adam's creation. It reads: αὐτὸς δὴ θεός ἐσθ' ὁ πλάσας τετραγράμματον Ἀδάμ. It scarcely seems coincidental that Adam, who is created in God's image (as 1.8 makes explicit), should be said to have four letters in his name, just as God does in the Hebrew Scriptures. One could say that the writer has θεός in mind here as his "tetragrammaton," but the name YHWH seems more likely.

Taking all these facts together, it seems probable that the author of this section of the Sibylline Oracles is deliberately reflecting on various aspects of the name YHWH: its inutterability; its relationship to the creation; its similarity to the four-lettered name of Adam; and its interpretation by a three-fold temporal reference and by the comprehensive expression ὁ ὤν.

We close our examination of ὁ ὤν by observing that this designation may even have been used in the liturgy of Greek-speaking Jews. The texts in question are in the so-called "Hellenistic Synagogal Prayers," found in books seven and eight of the later Christian work the Apostolic Constitutions.[117] While the precise dating and provenance of various portions of the

---

[115] See discussion later in this chapter.

[116] For details, see Dominique Cerbelaud, "Le nom d'Adam et les points cardinaux: récherche sur un thème patristique," *Vigiliae Christianae* 38 (1984): 285–301.

[117] A broad consensus has emerged that parts of books seven and eight do in fact represent the liturgy of the hellenistic synagogue. See David Fiensy, "Redaction History and the Apostolic Constitutions," *JQR* 72 (1982): p.293; Fiensy, "The Hellenistic Synagogal Prayers: One Hundred Years of Discussion," *JSOP* 5 (1989): 17–27; Marcel Metzger, *Les Constitutions Apostoliques* (3 vols., Sources Chretiennes, Paris: Cerf, 1985–87), esp. 1: 20ff.; James H. Charlesworth, "A Prolegomenon to the New Study of the Jewish Background of the Hymns and Prayers in the New Testament," *JJS* 33 (1982): pp.283–4;

"Prayers" remains contested,[118] David Fiensy has dated what he believes to be the genuine Jewish material (AC 7.33-38) to c.150–300 CE.[119] This portion of the AC, as it happens, contains a direction quotation of LXX Ex.3:14 (AC 7.33.7). The writer praises God for his faithfulness to the patriarchs, and says of Moses: "And in this way you spoke to Moses, your faithful and holy servant, in the vision at the bush: *I am the Being: this is for me an eternal name, and a remembrance to generations of generations.*"[120] "I am the Being" is the familiar Ἐγώ εἰμι ὁ ὤν. This does not tell us whether the liturgist was philosophically disposed, nor whether he was thinking of God as "essentially existent" or as the true God in distinction from idols. What it does tell us is that this phrase from the LXX was regarded as sufficiently "inspired" to be included in the worship of the community of Greek-speaking Jews (and of course in the worship of the Christians who borrowed it).

The other examples from the Apostolic Constitutions are of more questionable origin, but they are of sufficient theological interest to merit some consideration. They are found in book 8, which has a complicated redaction history.[121] The prayer of ordination in AC 8.5.1ff. begins ὁ ὤν, δέσποτα κύριε ὁ θεὸς ὁ παντοκράτωρ, ὁ μόνος ἀγέννητος καὶ ἀβασίλευσας, ὁ ἀεὶ ὢν καὶ πρὸ τῶν αἰώνων ὑπάρχων.[122] We have pointed out that the opening of the prayer appears to derive from the LXX of Jer. 1:6. God's eternity is explicitly linked with ὁ ὤν in the phrase ὁ ἀεὶ ὤν, which is elaborated in the following clause καὶ πρὸ τῶν αἰώνων ὑπάρχων. In AC 8.12.6ff. God is described as τὸν ὄντως ὄντα θεόν, "the one who is truly God," and τὸν πρὸ τῶν γενητῶν ὄντα, "the one who is before all that has been made." The use of ὄντως catches the eye, being similar to the Philo's description of God, and Plato's description of the Forms.

Phillip Sigal, "Early Christian and Rabbinic Liturgical Acculturation," *NTS* 30 (1984): 63–90.

[118] Charlesworth discusses the difficulties in dating on p.284 of his "Prolegomenon" article. Fiensy, who has studied the material extensively, is only confident in asserting the Jewish nature of AC 7.33-38 ("Redaction History," p.301; see also Metzger's notes on this section in vol. III, p.181).

[119] Fiensy, "Hellenistic Synagogal Prayers," pp.26–7.

[120] Trans. D.R. Darnell, *OTP*, 2: 678. It is also noteworthy that ὁ ὤν is seen as "the eternal name," whereas one could argue that the Exodus text presents "the God of Abraham, Isaac, and Jacob" as "the eternal (or memorial) name."

[121] See M. Metzger, 1: 17ff.; Emmanuel Lanne, "Les ordinations dans le rite copte," *L'Orient syrien* 5 (1960): 81–106; W.H. Bates, "The Composition of the Anaphora of Apostolic Constitutions VIII," *Studia Patristica* 13/II (Berlin: Akademie Verlag, 1975): 343–355.

[122] Cf. Rev. 1:8, Ἐγώ εἰμι τὸ ἄλφα καὶ τὸ ὦ, λέγει κύριος ὁ θεός, ὁ ὢν καὶ ὁ ἦν καὶ ὁ ἐρχόμενος, ὁ παντοκράτωρ.

We conclude with a brief look at the use of ὁ ὤν on the base of an altar in Pergamum, dated to the second or third century CE. It is inscribed θεὸς κύριος ὁ ὤν εἰς ἀεί.[123] Below this portion of the inscription one reads Ζώπυρος τῶ [ι] κυρίωι τὸν βωμὸν καὶ τήν φω[ι]τοφόρον μετὰ τοῦ φλογούχου. M. Nilsson attributes this altar to a God-fearer, who has perhaps mixed some elements of oriental religion (the use of fire) with worship of the Jewish God.[124] This seems reasonable enough, although a Jew could have constructed such an altar.[125] While ὁ ὤν εἰς ἀεί could conceivably be taken as a predicate ("Lord God, who exists forever...") rather than as a title, Nilsson points out that εἰς ἀεί may be drawn from Ex.3:15 LXX (...τοῦτο μού ἐστιν ὄνομα αἰώνιον...). This would make ὁ ὤν εἰς ἀεί a conflation of Ex. 3:14 and Ex. 3:15.[126] If he is correct in attributing this inscription to a God-fearer, we can say further that ὁ ὤν served well as a bridge between Judaism and hellenistic culture. Like ὕψιστος, it was a title which appealed to an international audience without sacrificing the essentials of Jewish monotheism. If on the other hand Zopyros was a Jew, this would still argue for the continued importance of ὁ ὤν in Greek speaking Jewish communities during the Common Era.

Magical material

The magical texts and materials do not provide us with a great deal of assured information about the meaning of the divine name, but there are some amulets which are of interest in this regard.[127] Campbell Bonner has published an amulet on which a mummy (presumably a sign of immortality[128]) appears with Ἐγώ inscribed on its left and ὁ ὤν on its right.[129] The

---

[123] Martin Nilsson, "Zwei Altäre aus Pergamon," *Eranos* 54 (1956): 167–173. See also the general discussion of syncretism in Asia Minor in his *Geschichte*, 1: 662ff.; Trebilco, p.163, gives second century; A. T. Kraabel, cited in Leonard Thompson, *The Book of Revelation* (NY/Oxford: Oxford University Press, 1990), p.143, gives third century.

[124] Nilsson, "Altäre," pp.169–171. He notes that lamps to θεὸς ὕψιστος were common in Asia Minor. G. Delling agrees with Nilsson that this is the altar of a God-fearer; see Delling's article, "Die Altarinschrift eines Gottesfürchtigen in Pergamon" *NovT* 7 (1964–5): 73–80.

[125] Trebilco (p.163) favors this option. He notes that the use of a lamp would not be antithetical to Jewish practice. The word βωμὸν does not necessarily imply the idea of sacrifice, since it may simply mean the *base* for the lamp.

[126] Nilsson, "Altäre," p.169. Delling (p.78) denies a connection with Ex. 3:14 because "in Ex. iii.14 wird das Sein Gottes schlechthin betont, in unserer Inschrift das unaufhörliche Sein." Delling could be right, but we cannot assume that the writer of the inscription would have interpreted Ex. 3:14 along the lines suggested by Delling. In any case, the designation ὁ ὤν appears to derive ultimately from the LXX. Aune (*Revelation 1–5*, p.30) is also skeptical of Delling's objections.

[127] See Aune, *Revelation 1–5*, pp.30–1.

[128] Thus Goodenough, 3: 275.

160 Chapter 3: The Significance and Meaning of the Name

ubiquitous Iao appears on the opposite side of the amulet amidst other names. As Bonner points out elsewhere in his book, the presence of Iao does not necessarily indicate a Jewish provenance for the work, and the same could be said for the presence of Ἐγὼ ... ὁ ὤν.[130] As with the altar at Pergamum, we are either dealing with a pagan who appropriated a mystical-sounding name for deity from (probably Egyptian) Jews, or with a Jew who felt free to employ some unconventional symbols in connection with God.[131] Aune mentions another amulet which speaks of "One God in the heavens...who exists [ὁ ὤν] and who existed before [προών], the one greater than all, who dominates all beings in midheaven."[132] As Aune points out,"...ὁ προών is a more literary grammatical choice than ὁ ἦν in Rev. 1:4."[133]

Of even greater importance is the amulet found at Caernarvon in Wales (late first/early second century CE), which we have mentioned previously. The first several lines are of immense interest to us:

Ἀδωναῖε Ἐ/λωαῖε Σαβα/ωθ ειε εσαρ ει/ε σουρα αρβαρ/τιαω ὢν ὤν/ ὢν ζῶν κα/λῶς...[134]

Kotansky is surely correct to read ειε εσαρ ειε as a Greek transliteration for the Hebrew אהיה אשר אהיה. As he points out, this formula appears in other Hebrew and Aramaic magical texts.[135] We also find the divine name Iao within the phrase σουρα αρβαρτιαω. The word αρβαρτιαω closely resembles the magical name Ἀρβαθιαω, meaning "fourfold-Iao" (likely a reference to the tetragrammaton). Kotansky argues that the shift from θ to τ, however, yields the equivalent of the Hebrew עברת יהוה, "the wrath of YHWH" (cf. Zeph. 1:18, Ezek. 7:19). Thus σουρα αρβαρτιαω may be translated, "Turn aside the wrath of Iao."[136]

Kotansky's translation of σουρα αρβαρτιαω is not certain, however. First, αρβαρτιαω is not a perfect equivalent for עברת יהוה. There is an

---

[129] Bonner, p.278. Only the obverse side of the amulet is shone in his fig.151, and so we cannot actually see the Ἐγὼ...ὁ ὤν. It does provide us, however, with a picture of the mummy, which appears on both sides of the charm.

[130] Bonner, pp.29ff.

[131] Whether the artisan or the user of this amulet would have known of the relationship of the Iao name and the phrase, "I (am) the one who is" is uncertain. I would tend to doubt it, since the Iao name does not seem to be given special prominence on the amulet. It would not be out of the question, however, for someone in Egypt to be aware of the link.

[132] Aune, Revelation 1–5, p.31.

[133] Aune, Revelation 1–5, p.31.

[134] Text (including the intermittent accentuation) in Kotansky, p.4. Slashes (/) represent the original line divisions.

[135] Kotansky, p.5.

[136] Kotansky, p.6.

extra *rho* in the first syllable. Secondly, it would be unusual, though certainly not impossible, for Adonai *et al.* to be ranged *against* Iao, as Kotansky's translation demands. This depends on his translation of σουρα as "turn aside" in the sense of "turn away." If we assume that σουρα stands for the Hebrew סורה, it is noteworthy that this particular form of the verb סור occurs only twice in the MT, in Jud. 4:18 and Ruth 4:1. In both cases, it must translated something like "Come aside" or "Come here."[137] In other words, it means precisely the opposite of "turn away." I would suggest that it makes more sense to translate σουρα as "come here," and to take αρβαρτιαω as a corrupted form of Ἀρβαθιαω, retaining the meaning "fourfold-Iao." Thus: "Come here, fourfold-Iao!" The presence of αρβαρτιαω=Ἀρβαθιαω, "fourfold-Iao" would also help explain why there are *four* divine names given in the first portion of the text: Ἀδωναῖε, Ἐλωαῖε, Σαβαωθ, and ειε εσαρ ειε. These four names may have been regarded as the four manifestations of the "fourfold" Iao.

Also of great interest to us is the tri-fold ὤν, especially since it occurs in close conjunction with ειε εσαρ ειε. As Kotansky writes: "The words ὤν ὤν ὤν would then seem to represent a somewhat imprecise Greek gloss on the transliterated Hebrew of ειε εσαρ ειε..."[138] Whether the triple ὤν is to be linked with the formula in Rev.1:4, *et al.* (as suggested by Kotansky) remains uncertain, but some connection with Ex. 3:14 LXX seems assured. In order to assess the significance of this connection, we must turn to the final phrase we quoted, ζῶν καλῶς. I would concur with Kotansky that this does not refer to God but rather to the wearer of the amulet: "Such a theme ['living excellently'] would have been appropriate for a protective amulet that must have also served to provide for the needs of the bearer's afterlife."[139] The progression would seem to be this: ειε εσαρ ειε/ אהיה אשר אהיה was a magical name in its own right. The writer of this amulet also knew that it could be rendered Ἐγώ εἰμι ὁ ὤν. Such a God, who *always is*, would be extremely useful to someone interested in prolonging life or seeking blessings after death (perhaps including eternal life, though this is not specified). The similarity in sound between ὤν and ζῶν would enhance the association.[140] We will argue below that the likeness between these two words may also have influenced John's description of Christ as ὁ ζῶν in Rev. 1:18, as a counterpoint to the description of God as ὁ ὤν in 1:4.

---

[137] Jud. 4:18: "Jael went out to meet Sisera and said to him, 'Come, my lord, come right in. Don't be afraid'..." Ruth 4:1: "...Boaz said, 'Come over here, my friend, and sit down.'" (Both translations from NIV.)

[138] Kotansky, p.6.

[139] Kotansky, p.10.

[140] Kotansky (p.12) gives another example of ὤν and ζῶν occuring together in a funerary context. This may be a coincidence, however, and I would not press the point.

Philo

Philo provides us with by far the largest body of material surrounding the designation ὁ ὤν. It is perhaps his favorite term for deity. Philo, however, is equally comfortable using τὸ ὄν for God.[141] The two expressions appear to be interchangeable. In *Mut.* 7ff., for instance, Philo refers repeatedly to God as τὸ ὄν, with an emphasis on God's inscrutability. In 1.11, however, he sums up his arguments by quoting Ex.3:14 LXX, which of course uses ὁ ὤν.[142] Before we deal with the content of ὁ ὤν/τὸ ὄν, we must examine why Philo treats the two terms as functional equivalents.

The simple answer is that Philo had most, and perhaps all, of his work done for him. Our investigation of Seneca and Plutarch revealed that Middle Platonists had already used τὸ ὄν for God by the early first century CE, and most likely by the first century BCE. Philo moved in a similar current of Middle Platonism, and so it is highly likely that he was aware of the use of τὸ ὄν for deity. If we accept the plausible thesis that the equivalence originated with Eudorus of Alexandria, the case becomes even more secure. The use of ὁ ὤν for deity, meanwhile, was staring Philo in the face at Ex. 3:14 LXX, a passage he refers to numerous times.[143]

It is difficult to overestimate the importance of this *pre-existing* convergence of God, τὸ ὄν, and ὁ ὤν for the development of Philo's thought. As Philo surveyed the contemporary religious and philosophical scene, he would have found a point of contact between Judaism (as he knew it) and Platonism (as he knew it) at the most fundamental level. Surely this would have served as an inspiration to – and a justification of – his project of reconciling religion and philosophy.[144] If the bible and Plato were essentially agreed on the nature of ultimate reality, there was undoubtedly room for harmonization on many other issues as well. The interplay of ὁ ὤν and τὸ ὄν serves as a microcosm of Philo's entire intellectual enterprise.

This does not mean the picture is entirely clear. One of the most valuable lessons we can learn about Philo from this study is how difficult it is to disentangle the Greek from the Jewish strands in his thought. Philo does work with the biblical text, and to some extent the personal aspect of ὁ ὤν

---

[141] It would be tedious to multiply examples, since the term is used thus throughout his works. See e.g. *Mut.* 27, where the phrase "I am your God" is explained in part by saying that τὸ ὄν is not "relative." Cf. *Post.*15,167.

[142] Montes-Peral, p.49.

[143] For texts and discussions see J.P. Martin, "La Primera Exegesis Ontologica de 'Yo soy El que es' (Exodo 3,14-LXX)," *Stromata* 5:102–5. We will deal with most of these texts below.

[144] We cannot exclude the possiblility that Alexandrian Jews before Philo had already made this connection, so that Philo was in fact building on a tradition rather than making an original contribution. But in the absence of contrary evidence, we may give Philo the benefit of the doubt.

may override the neutrality of τὸ ὄν. As L. Montes-Peral writes, "Das Seiende ist nur eine sprachliche Abstraktion des biblischen ὁ ὤν der Septuaginta; eine Abstraktion, die die Transzendenz Gottes herausstellen will."[145] Certainly Philo makes a clear distinction between God as ὁ ὤν and the world of Forms.[146] This is in distinction from Plato himself, who understands τὸ ὄν precisely as this world of Forms. At the same time, we will see that the Platonic conception of τὸ ὄν informs Philo's discussion at every turn.

We may now turn to the content of ὁ ὤν/τὸ ὄν in Philo's works. He draws out many nuances of meaning for the phrase in the course of his exegesis of the Pentateuch. Indeed, the flexibility of ὁ ὤν/τὸ ὄν was probably one of the factors which led Philo to employ them so frequently. Besides serving as an emblem for his fusion of religion and philosophy, they allowed him to articulate aspects of his theology both negative and positive.

Philo's "negative theology" has attracted much attention, and his understanding of Ex. 3:14 lies at the core of this theology. We have already noted his doctrine of the namelessness of God. It bears repeating that this namelessness is only one example of the utter incomprehensibility of the Creator. In *Mut.* 7 he writes, "Do not however suppose that the Existent which truly exists (τὸ ὄν, ὅ ἐστι πρὸς ἀλήθειαν ὄν) is apprehended by any man."[147] The "logical consequence" of this is that no proper name can be given to God. Philo's proof text for this is Ex. 3:14: ἐγώ εἰμι ὁ ὤν is equivalent to "My nature is to be, not to be spoken (ἴσον τῷ εἶναι πέφυκα, οὐ λέγεσθαι; *Mut.* 11; cf. *Som.* 230)." From this perspective, God's "answer" in Ex. 3:14 is in fact a refusal to answer. Whatever we might make of this interpretation, it has appealed to many later interpreters of the verse.

Philo states his point more precisely in *Fug.*165, which is also an investigation of the episode of the burning bush. Moses prays to learn τίς ἐστιν ὁ θεός; but the response is negative:

ἀλλ' ὅμως ἴσχυσε μηδὲν περὶ τῆς τοῦ ὄντος ἐρευνᾶν οὐσίας.

Nevertheless he did not succeed in finding anything by search respecting the essence of Him that is.

Here we have one of the pillars of Philo's theology: human beings can only know God's existence, not his essence. The theme appears repeatedly in his works. In *Praem.* 39, he asserts that the vision of Jacob "only showed

---

[145] Luis Angel Montes-Peral, *Akataleptos Theos: Der unfassbare Gott* (Leiden: Brill, 1987), p.51.
[146] See esp. *Cher.* 2:49; *Spec. Leg.* 1:46–9.
[147] All texts and translations are from the LCL unless otherwise noted.

that He is, not what He is" (οὐχὶ τῆς ὅ ἐστιν ἐμφαινούσης, ἀλλὰ τῆς ὅτι ἔστιν). *Virt.* 215 distinguishes God's ὕπαρξις, which can be known, from his οὐσία, which cannot. *Post.* 15ff. says that the benefit of seeking God is "to apprehend that the God of real Being (ὁ κατὰ τὸ εἶναι θεός) is apprehensible by no one, and to see precisely this, that He is incapable of being seen." God's "essential nature" (ἡ κατὰ τὸ εἶναι φύσις) is so distant from us "that we cannot touch it even with the pure spiritual contact of the understanding (*Post.* 20)."[148] The last phrase is echoed in *Som.* 1: 230: λέγεσθαι γὰρ οὐ πέφυκεν, ἀλλὰ μόνον εἶναι το ὄν, and again Ex. 3:14 is cited in connection with this assertion. Examples could be multiplied,[149] but suffice it to say that for Philo God is essentially Other.[150]

If God's essence is incomprehensible, his existence is imperceptible by sense. Philo's debt to Plato here is substantial. For Plato, τὸ ὄν is tantamount to the νοητὸς κόσμος, which stands in contrast to the world of becoming (ἡ γένεσις, or the αἰσθητὸς κόσμος).[151] Philo not only borrows Plato's ideas about τὸ ὄν, he even uses the same imagery. In *Plant.* 21-2, Philo declares that God gives "wings" to the soul who eagerly desires to "perceive the Existent One" (τὸ ὄν κατιδεῖν). Similar motifs recur throughout his works.[152] One can hardly help thinking of the ascent of the soul in *Phaedrus* 246ff., where the soul beholds τὸ ὄν (or τἀληθῆ, 247d, τὸ ὄν ὄντως 249c).[153]

But we must also recall that, as far as I can determine, Philo studiously avoids using τὸ ὄν for the Forms. In fact, Philo describes the unseen world as being created on day one (*Op.* 15ff.), in contradiction to *Tim.* 52a.[154] In *Spec. Leg.* 1: 46ff., for instance, he says that "Forms" are a reasonable description of God's *powers*, since, like the Forms, the powers give shape to the things in the world but are themselves only perceptible by the intellect. Since one of the foundational truths of Philo's system is the distinction

---

[148] Cf. e.g. *Post.* 168-9; *Som.* 1: 231; *Spec. Leg.* 1: 32ff. For secondary literature, see Runia, *Timaeus*, pp.436-7; Williamson, pp.36-42; Montes-Peral, pp.58ff.; Wolfson 2: 110-126; Esther Starobinski-Safran, "Ex. 3,14 dans l'oeuvre de Philon d'Alexandrie," in *Dieu et l'Être: Exégèses d'Exode 3,14 et de Coran 20,11-24*, ed. A. Caquot et al. Centre d'Études des Religions du Livre (Paris: Études Augustiniennes, 1978), p.54.

[149] Cf. e.g. *Quis Her.* 170 and *Som.* 1: 67.

[150] Cf. Starobinski-Safran, pp.50-51; Wolfson 2: 110-126; Whittaker, "Moses Atticizing," pp.197-8. Runia, "Naming," pp.82-3, believes that the idea of God being ἀκατάληπτος was likely a general feature of Middle Platonism rather than a distinctive of Philo.

[151] Cf. e.g. Plato, *Tim.* 27d-28a; Runia, *Timaeus*, pp.92ff.

[152] See *Post.* 167; *Leg. All.* 1: 82; *Praem.* 38; *Spec. Leg.* 1:37ff.; *Mig.* 182-3.

[153] The image of the charioteer appears in *Praem.* 37-8, which likewise treats of the souls desire to see God. The charioteer, however, seems to represent God as the one who steers the universe, rather than the soul itself.

[154] A point made by Runia, *Timaeus*, p.427; and Wolfson 1: 306.

between God as he actually is, ὁ ὤν/τὸ ὄν, and God as he is mediated to the creation in his powers, the use of τὸ ὄν solely for God appears to be deliberate. While some Middle Platonists (like Seneca's source in *Ep.* 58) may have felt comfortable using τὸ ὄν in a number of ways, Philo stays firmly with the equation τὸ ὄν = God.

Philo does not interpret ὁ ὤν in a purely negative fashion. He understands it to mean that God alone has real or genuine being. God may be described as τὸ ὄντως ὄν (*Post.* 167); ὁ πρὸς ἀλήθειαν ὤν/τὸ πρὸς ἀλήθειαν ὄν (*Mut.* 7,11); and μόνος...πρὸς ἀλήθειαν ὤν (*Mos.* 2: 100).[155] This is no real innovation on his part. Plato had already spoken of τὸ ὄν ὄντως in *Phaedrus* 249c, and we find similar phrases elsewhere in his writings.[156] Philo has transferred (and at times adapted) the Platonic titles and ascribed them to the God of the Scriptures.

This "real being" of God has at least two aspects. First, God "is" in contrast to idols. Philo brings out this traditional Jewish motif most clearly in *Decal.* 8, where he denounces idolatry saying, "throughout the cities those who do not know the true, the really existent God (τὸν ὄντα ὄντως ἀληθῆ θεόν) have deified hosts of others who are falsely so called."[157] He reads Ex. 3:14 along similar lines in *Mos.* 1: 75. The first lesson to be drawn from ἐγώ εἰμι ὁ ὤν, says Philo, is that the people "may learn the difference between what is and what is not (διαφορὰν ὄντος τε καὶ μὴ ὄντος)." (The second lesson concerns God's namelessness.) This might be an oblique reference to the false gods of Egypt, a contrast made more explicit in Wis. 13:1.

Another interpretation also suggests itself: God "is" not only in distinction from idols, but from all other things as well. In *Det.* 160, Philo offers yet another reading of Ex. 3:14. Here he says that ἐγώ εἰμι ὁ ὤν:

...ὡς τῶν μετ' αὐτὸν οὐκ ὄντων κατὰ τὸ εἶναι, δόξῃ δὲ μόνον ὑφεστάναι νομιζομένων.

...(implies) that others lesser than He have not being, as being indeed is, but exist in semblance only, and are conventionally said to exist.

While Philo does not use the term "becoming" here, he is obviously indebted to the Platonic distinction between the world of genuine being and the world of mere becoming (see e.g. *Tim.* 27d–28a; *Rep.* 485a–b,527b). The presence of δόξῃ is a further indication of his dependence on Plato.[158]

---

[155] For these, see Montes-Peral, p.48. Cf. the related phrases ἡ κατὰ τὸ εἶναι φύσις and ὁ κατὰ τὸ εἶναι θεός (*Som.* 1: 66; *Post.* 15)

[156] E.g. *Rep.* 477a,478d,490a.

[157] Cf. e.g. *Post.* 166–7, where the golden calf is contrasted with τὸ...πρὸς ἀλήθειαν ὄν.

[158] For the role of δόξᾳ in Plato's epistemology see, e.g., *Rep.* 477b ff.

Another way of expressing the same point is to say that God is *alone*, or that he has independent existence. *Leg. All.* 2:1 states that "it is good that He Who is should be alone" – τὸ μόνον εἶναι τὸν ὄντα καλόν ἐστι. Although Philo prefers to interpret this "aloneness" as God's unity or simplicity, he admits that one can also understand it to mean that "neither before creation was there anything with God, nor, when the universe had come into being, does anything take its place with Him" (*Leg. All.* 2:2). *Mut.* 27 reads τὸ γὰρ ὄν, ᾗ ὄν ἐστιν, οὐχὶ τῶν πρός τι: "for the Existent considered as existent is not relative." The phrase τὸ... ὄν, ᾗ ὄν immediately brings to mind Aristotle's *Met.* Γ 1 (1003a21), which we have examined in some detail.[159] It is not clear whether Philo uses τὸ... ὄν, ᾗ ὄν in its entirety as a designation for God (cf. Patzig and Merlan), but it is certainly possible. In any case, this unusual formulation leads one to believe that Philo has adopted it from a pre-existing source, perhaps a commentary of some sort on Aristotle. *Mut.* 27 is a pithy statement of Philo's conviction that no analogy can be drawn between God in his essence and the creation. There is a vast chasm between them.[160]

There is some indication that Philo drew out the idea of God's *necessary* existence from the epithet ὁ ὤν. In other words, God is of such a nature as to exist. Recall the words from *Mut.* 11: "My nature is to be, not to be spoken" (ἴσον τῷ εἶναι πέφυκα, οὐ λέγεσθαι). The bare existence of God or the gods had been affirmed throughout Jewish and Greek history. It is the addition of πέφυκα that catches our attention. Again, Philo has not made this step independently. Plato had already spoken of "that which by nature (πεφυκώς) is" in *Rep.* 490a. Of equal interest is the modification of one of Zeno's syllogisms by Diogenes of Babylon (c.230–140 BCE). Zeno had argued that one may reasonably honor the gods; that it is unreasonable to worship the non-existent; therefore the gods exist. Diogenes, probably responding to critiques of Zeno, tried to shore up the proof by adding the key idea that the gods *are of such nature* (πεφυκότας) as to exist (ap. Sextus Empiricus, *Adv. Math.* Book 9, 134 ff.). It has been debated whether Diogenes hereby inaugurates the Ontological Argument for the existence of God/the gods, but one could certainly read it along those lines.[161] Philo is, as usual, appropriating Greek philosophical terminology

---

[159] Runia ("Naming," p.80) does not believe Philo is referring to Aristotle here. While a direct reference indeed seems unlikely, it is still possible that Philo is quoting or adapting a slogan which ultimately stems from the Peripatetics.

[160] See e.g. Starobinski-Safran, pp.49–50; J. Martin, pp.107–8.

[161] See Jacques Brunschwig, "Did Diogenes of Babylon invent the ontological argument?," in *Papers in Hellenistic Philosophy*, trans. Janet Lloyd (Cambridge: Cambridge University Press, 1994), p.181; R. J. Hankinson, *The Sceptics* (London: Routledge, 1995), pp.240–2.

to articulate his understanding of the God of the bible. In this case at least, he may have a point.

A corollary of the proposition that God alone has true being is that he is the source of existence for all other things (remembering that their "existence" is fundamentally different from that enjoyed by God). There is a remarkable statement in *Fug.* 78 (interpreting Dt. 19:5): "And is not life eternal (ζωὴ...αἰώνιος) to take refuge with Him that is (ἡ πρὸς τὸ ὂν καταφυγή), and death to flee away from Him?" It is no coincidence that Philo chooses τὸ ὄν as the designation for God here. In a closely related text, *Spec. Leg.* 1:31, Philo quotes Dt. 4:4 to the effect that "the ones who are devoted to your God who is will live." What is striking is that the LXX reads οἱ προσκείμενοι κυρίῳ τῷ θεῷ ὑμῶν ζῆτε, while Philo has οἱ προσκείμενοι τῷ ὄντι θεῷ ὑμῶν ζῶσι. Given that he quotes the LXX of Dt. 4:4 accurately in *Fug.* 56, the change seems to be tendentious.[162]

What is true of individuals holds true for the creation as a whole. *Mos.* 2: 100 reads:

μόνος γὰρ πρὸς ἀλήθειαν ὤν καὶ ποιητής ἐστιν ἀψευδῶς, ἐπειδὴ τὰ μὴ ὄντα ἤγαγεν εἰς τὸ εἶναι.

For, as He alone really is, He is undoubtedly also the Maker, since He brought into being what was not...

The use of ἤγαγεν to describe the act of creation is taken from *Tim.* 30a5, where Plato describes the demiurge "leading" the universe from chaos to order, but the sentiment is well within the boundaries of Jewish thought.[163] By juxtaposing the divine designation of Ex. 3:14 LXX with the creation account of Genesis, Philo shows that the God Who Is is the source of being for the entire created order.[164] In *Quod Deus* 108, Philo ascribes the creation of the world to "the goodness of the Existent" – ἡ τοῦ ὄντος ἀγαθότης.[165]

Was Philo, then, aware of Jewish traditions which ascribe the creation of the world to the name of God, and specifically to the tetragrammaton? This is a possibility. But it is not necessary to invoke this argument to explain his association of ὁ ὤν and the creation. Plato had laid down the fundamental distinction between τὸ ὄν and ἡ γένεσις. Once God had been equated with ὁ ὤν/τὸ ὄν, it was but a short step to see God as the "ground

---

[162] It is also worth noting that ὄντι functions as the replacement for κυρίῳ of the LXX. This might be adduced as support for the argument that Philo knew of the equivalence YHWH= ὁ ὤν = κύριος.

[163] Runia, *Timaeus*, p.140. Cf. 2 Macc. 7:28, οὐκ ἐξ ὄντων ἐποίησεν αὐτά...

[164] Montes-Peral, pp.47ff. This does not necessarily mean that Philo held to a literal creation *ex nihilo*. See e.g. Runia, *Timaeus*, pp.287ff.; H.F. Weiss, *Untersuchungen zur Kosmologie des hellenistischen und palästinischen Judentums* (Berlin: 1966), pp.59–69.

[165] Goodness is also the motive of the Demiurge in the *Timaeus* (29d ff.).

of Being" for all else. A knowledge of the LXX of Genesis 1 and Ex. 3:14, coupled with a knowledge of the *Timaeus*, is sufficient to explain Philo's language about ὁ ὤν/τὸ ὄν and creation.

We conclude by asking whether Philo took ὁ ὤν/τὸ ὄν to indicate God's everlasting being, or indeed his timeless being. Surely Philo believed that God is eternal (cf. e.g. *Dec.* 67 περὶ τοῦ ζῶντος ἀεὶ θεοῦ). In terms of actual evidence for the association of ὁ ὤν/τὸ ὄν and everlastingness, the best we can do is *Mut.* 12. Shortly after quoting Ex. 3:14, Philo speaks of ὁ πρὸ αἰῶνος, the "life period" of God.[166] This is actually to be linked with Ex. 3:15, however, and the "eternal name" of God, i.e. "the God of Abraham, Isaac, and Jacob."

The direct evidence for "the one who is" as an indication of timelessness is likewise scanty, but what we do have is quite important. On more than one occasion Philo associates ὁ ὤν with *immovability*. *Quod Deus* 4, for instance, speaks of "the unhesitating firmness existing in the God who is" – ...τὴν περὶ τὸ ὄν ἀνενδοίαστον...βεβαιότητα (cf. *Som.* 2: 227–37; *Mut.* 57). We might wish to paraphrase this use of ὁ ὤν as "He who consistently is" or "He who is always the same." But this is not the same thing as timelessness. For this we must turn to *Quod Deus* 32–3. Since this passage also contains a significant use of a *Dreizeitenformel*, we will give an extended discussion.

Philo here is trying to counter the notion that God actually "changed his mind" concerning mankind in Genesis 6. In point of fact, says Philo, nothing is past or future to God: "to God as in pure sunlight all things are manifest."[167] God does not dwell in time, but in eternity, αἰών; and ἐν αἰῶνι δὲ οὔτε παρελήλυθεν οὐδὲν οὔτε μέλλει, ἀλλὰ μόνον ὑφέστηκεν (32). As Whittaker points out, Philo here combines Platonic and Stoic ideas of time. The absence of past and future recalls *Tim.* 37c, while the technical use of ὑφέστηκεν is drawn from Stoicism.[168] Whittaker comments:

> How, then, according to Philo, does God fit into this type of picture? God's life is αἰών (i.e. ἀεὶ ὄν) within which past and future events subsist everlastingly and independently of coming-to-be and passing-away...Thus God's omniscience finds its natural explanation in the fact that His reality is co-extensive with that of past and future events (which Philo would no doubt place within the mind of God). The mind of man embraces the past through memory and the future through expectation[169]...God, how-

---

[166] See Whittaker, *God, Time, Being*, p.35.
[167] Whittaker, *God, Time, Being*, p.37.
[168] Whittaker, *God, Time, Being*, pp.38–9.
[169] See *Leg. All.* 2: 42: ὁ μὲν γὰρ νοῦς τῶν τριῶν ἐφάπτεται χρόνων, καὶ γὰρ τὰ παρόντα νοεῖ καὶ τῶν παρεληλυθότων μέμνηται καὶ τὰ μέλλοντα προσδοκᾷ.

ever, possesses knowledge of past, present, and future through direct acquaintance – the events of all three phases are equally present to Him.[170]

Whittaker is careful to say that this is not necessarily the same thing as Augustine's *totum simul*.[171] But it does indicate some type of "timelessness."[172] The important thing is that Philo follows by saying that he has demonstrated that "the one who is" (τὸ ὄν) does not experience repentance (μετάνοια) (*Quod Deus* 33). The fact that l. 32 echoes *Tim*. 37c, which is speaking precisely about τὸ ὄν and time, makes it likely that the appearance of τὸ ὄν in Philo's summary statement is no accident. It may not be too much to say that the *Timaeus* has helped show Philo the way out of the dilemma posed by the apparent repentance of God in Genesis 6.

Philo, in sum, finds a wealth of meaning hidden in the biblical ὁ ὤν and its counterpart τὸ ὄν. On the negative side, it indicates God's essential namelessness and incomprehensibility, and his imperceptibility by the senses. Positively, it expresses his "real being" in distinction from idols and indeed from all created things; his necessary existence; his role as creator or "ground of being"; (probably) his everlasting being; and (likely) his timeless being. As we have seen, each of these aspects has significant parallels in Greek philosophy, and particularly in Plato. Having said that, there is a strong case for saying that these attributes of God may be reasonably extrapolated from the Hebrew Bible. Whether Philo has Judaised Platonism or Platonised Judaism is impossible to say. What is clear is that Philo finds a convergence of the two in the key terms ὁ ὤν and τὸ ὄν.

Josephus

Josephus offers us little in terms of the meaning of the name YHWH, although he does appear to be familiar with the description of God as ὁ ὤν. In *Ant*. 8:349 he says that at Mt. Carmel Elijah had "convinced the people that the only God was the One who is, whom they had worshipped from the beginning" – πεῖσαι δὲ τὸν λαὸν ὅτι μόνος εἴη θεὸς ὁ ὤν, ὃν ἀπ' ἀρχῆς ἐθρήσκευσαν. Josephus probably has in mind 1 Ki. 18: 39 LXX, where the people cry, Ἀληθῶς κύριός ἐστιν ὁ θεός, αὐτὸς ὁ θεός. At least in this context, Josephus understands ὁ ὤν to mean "the One who *really is* God," in contrast to false gods such as Baal.

---

[170] Whittaker, *God, Time, Being*, p.39.

[171] He does, however, believe Philo has "a somewhat clumsily expressed version of the Neoplatonic doctrine of non-durational eternity" in *Sac*. 76: μηδὲν ἡγεῖσθαι παρ αὐτῷ (sc. God) παλαιὸν ἢ συνόλως παρεληλυθός, ἀλλὰ γινόμενόν τε ἀχρόνως καὶ ὑφεστηκός. See Whittaker, *God, Time, Being*, pp.40-43.

[172] Sorabji (*Time*, pp.121-2) thinks Whittaker does not go far enough, and believes Philo "does touch here on the idea of timeless eternity."

New Testament

Rev. 1:4 represents the clearest "exegesis" of the name YHWH in the New Testament. There are a few other passages, however, that may allude to the traditions surrounding Ex. 3:14.

In Rom. 4:17, Paul says that Abraham believed in God, who ζῳοποιοῦντος τοὺς νεκροὺς καὶ καλοῦντος τὰ μὴ ὄντα ὡς ὄντα. The final clause sounds a familiar theme of early Judaism: God creates the things that are out of things that are not. The phrase shows obvious affinities with Philo, *Mos.* 2: 100, ἐπειδὴ τὰ μὴ ὄντα ἤγαγεν εἰς τὸ εἶναι; and 2 Macc. 7:28, οὐκ ἐξ ὄντων ἐποίησεν αὐτά.[173] If we render ὡς ὄντα, "as if they existed," this might introduce a new element into the tradition. But Cranfield and Dunn make good cases for taking ὡς in the sense of "so that."[174] Seen in this light, Paul is fully in keeping with earlier Jewish teaching and has only made a stylistic alteration to it. Since he is so indebted to the tradition at this point, we cannot say for certain whether he had an opinion about the meaning of the name YHWH. It is at least possible that he would have connected this tradition with the Septuagintal designation of God as ὁ ὤν.

In 1922, Karl Zickendraht made the intriguing suggestion that the divine designation, "the one who was and is and is to come," is hidden in the prologue to John's Gospel.[175] The case has at least a surface plausibility: ἦν appears ten times in John 1:1–18; ἐρχόμενος twice;[176] and ὁ ὤν once.[177] We have seen that the author of Sib. Or. 3: 1–45 appears to have embedded references to the divine name in his text, and thus it would not be out of the question for the author of the prologue to have done the same.[178] References to the name YHWH would be particularly appropriate in a passage which often alludes to the creation narrative, since the tetragrammaton was intimately linked with this event. Seen in light of the gospel as a whole, the

---

[173] For other parallels, see Walter Schmithals, *Der Römerbrief* (Gütersloh: Mohn, 1988), p.144; James Dunn, *Romans 1–9* (Dallas: Word, 1988), p.218; and C.E.B. Cranfield, 2 vols. *The Epistle to the Romans* (Edinburgh: T.&T. Clark, 1975), 1: 245. The use of τὰ ὄντα and τὰ μὴ ὄντα in 1 Cor. 1:28 derives from the traditional motif found in Romans. Most of the Corinthians, in their weakness and lack of learning, were like nothing in the eyes of the world, and yet the creator God was able to make something out of them for his glory.

[174] Cranfield, 1: 244; Dunn, p.218.

[175] Zickendraht, "EGW EIMI," *Theologische Studien und Kritiken* 94 (1922): 162–8.

[176] Once without the article (v.9, ἐρχόμενον εἰς τὸν κόσμον) and once with the article (v.15, ὁ ὀπίσω μου ἐρχόμενος).

[177] In v.18, see discussion below.

[178] This weakens the force of one of Harner's main objection to Zickendraht's thesis, namely that it is "incomprehensible why the Fourth Gospel should conceal its allusion to this expression [the one who is, etc.] in scattered verses of the prologue," given that Revelation uses the title openly. (Harner, p.16.)

"was, is, is coming" motif would serve to foreshadow the "I am" statements which pervade the fourth gospel, some of which are regarded as being expressions of the divine name (see below).

As it turns out, the proposal is ingenious but ultimately unsatisfying. The use of ὁ ὤν in v.18 (ὁ ὤν εἰς τὸν κόλπον τοῦ πατρός) is at best ambiguous. It is perhaps of interest that the sentence as a whole reads θεὸν οὐδεὶς ἑώρακεν πώποτε μονογενὴς θεὸς ὁ ὤν εἰς τὸν κόλπον τοῦ πατρὸς ἐκεῖνος ἐξηγήσατο, such that μονογενὴς θεός immediately precedes ὁ ὤν, the Septuagintal designation for God. But it is more likely that this is simply an ordinary participial use of ὁ ὤν.[179] As for ὁ ἐρχόμενος, the Baptist's words ὁ ὀπίσω μου ἐρχόμενος ἔμπροσθέν μου γέγονεν, ὅτι πρῶτός μου ἦν (v.15) are clearly paralleled in the synoptics (esp. Matt. 3:11: ὁ δὲ ὀπίσω μου ἐρχόμενος ἰσχυρότερός μού ἐστιν ; cf. Mk. 1:7, Lk.3:16). Their appearance in the prologue is thus not surprising, and does not constitute evidence of a hidden *Dreizeitenformel* like that in Rev. 1:4. As for ὁ ἦν, this precise form does not even occur in the prologue.

The primary value of the prologue for our investigation consists rather in its juxtaposition of ἦν and ἐγένετο in vv.1,3: "In the beginning was the Word...all things came to be through him (vv.1,3)." The contrast between εἰμι and γίνομαι is, as we have noted, a Platonic commonplace. Whether the phrase Ἐν ἀρχῇ ἦν ὁ λόγος is to be directly connected with the divine name may be disputed.[180] But surely the author wants to point out the distinction between the eternal word and the created order, and he has done it in a way congenial both to Jewish tradition and Greek philosophy. We will note a similar contrast in John 8:58, where Jesus utters the words πρὶν Ἀβραὰμ γενέσθαι ἐγώ εἰμι. It is to ἐγώ εἰμι that we now turn.

We will see below in our study of the *Memra* that יהוה and אהיה were understood to mean "He is" and "I am" respectively. We have already seen how the LXX rendering of אני הוא as ἐγώ εἰμι virtually ensured that some readers would read ἐγώ εἰμι in the light of Ex. 3:14 and equate it

---

[179] One might compare Rom. 9:5b and 2 Cor. 11:31 in this regard. Rom. 9:5b reads: ὁ ὤν ἐπὶ πάντων θεὸς εὐλογτὸς εἰς τοὺς αἰῶνας, ἀμήν, and 2 Cor. 11:31: καὶ πατὴρ τοῦ κυρίου Ἰησοῦ οἶδεν, ὁ ὤν εὐλογητὸς εἰς τοὺς αἰῶνας, ὅτι οὐ ψεύδομαι. ὁ θεός...ὁ ὤν εὐλογητὸς εἰς τοὺς αἰῶνας is obviously a standardized formula which Paul has adapted for different occasions. Its liturgical sound reminds one of passages like Apostolic Constitutions 8.5.1ff., where ὁ ὤν is used as a divine epithet. This is of course a late text, and the differences in the two are clear, in that Paul's ὁ ὤν functions as a perfectly normal present participle. There is a very slight possibility that Paul consciously used ὁ ὤν as a veiled allusion to God's eternity, in connection with εἰς τοὺς αἰῶνας.

[180] This is emphasized by Hayward in his article "The Holy Name of the God of Moses and the Prologue of St. John's Gospel," *NTS* 25 (1978–9): 28ff. As one might expect, he is particularly concerned with John's possible awareness of the *Memra* in his construction of the prologue. I am not thoroughly convinced that the divine name is in question, but it is a possibility.

with אהיה. The appearance of ἐγώ εἰμι in the Gospels is therefore quite relevant to our study of the divine name in early Judaism. We must reiterate, however, that the literature on this topic is exhaustive and naturally leads into complex questions of the Christology of the early church. Our discussion will be relatively brief. We only aim to demonstrate that "I am" could be taken as a divine designation with close connections to the name YHWH.

For this reason we will focus our attention on the use of ἐγώ εἰμι in the Gospel of John, and in particular John 8:58. The majority of modern commentators (with the notable exception of Rudolf Bultmann[181]) take the "I am" sayings in the fourth gospel to be derived mainly from the Hebrew אני הוא, which we have discussed above.[182] It has been duly noted that this phrase is closely associated with YHWH's uniqueness; his saving activity on behalf of his people; his creative activity; and his eternal being.[183] All of these, we have seen, are related in Jewish tradition to the name YHWH.

This brings us to a consideration of John 8:58, where the connections with Ex. 3:14 seem particularly strong. Harner isolates John 13:19 and 8:58 as the two "absolute" uses of the predicateless ἐγώ εἰμι in the gospel, since in both cases the predicate cannot be supplied from the context.[184] The first verse, "I tell you this in order that when it happens you may believe that I am," may be understood in light of Is. 43:10. There is likely an allusion to the name YHWH here, albeit an indirect one coming via the אני הוא of Is. 43:10.[185] We are thus left with 8:58, "Before Abraham came to be, I am" – πρὶν Ἀβραὰμ γενέσθαι ἐγώ εἰμί.

The saying is the climax of one of Jesus' controversies with "the Jews." Although the precise relationship of the dialogues in chapter 8 is difficult to establish with certainty, it may be of significance that the discourses proceed (following the divisions and titles in the UBS Greek NT) from the "light of the world" (vv.12–20), through "where I am going you cannot

---

[181] Harner (p.58) describes Bultmann as seeing only a "tenuous link" between אני הוא and ἐγώ εἰμι.

[182] Harner, pp.6–7; see also Brown, 1: 536; Dodd, *Interpretation*, pp.93–4; C.K. Barrett, *The Gospel According to St. John*, 2nd ed. (London: SPCK, 1978), p.342; G. R. Beasley-Murray, *The Gospel of John* WBC (Waco, TX: Word, 1987), pp.89–90; Barnabas Lindars, *The Gospel of John* NCB (London: Oliphants, 1972), p.336; Rudolf Schnackenburg, *The Gospel according to John*, trans. Cecily Hastings et al. 3 vols. (London: Burns and Oates, 1968–82), 2: 199–200.

[183] Harner, pp.8–15. Barrett (p.342) alludes to Is.41:4, "I am the first, and with the last" in this regard; cf. Is. 43:13, "Even from eternity. I am he..." MT גם מיום אני הוא; LXX ἔτι ἀπ' ἀρχῆς.

[184] Harner, p.37.

[185] See Ball, pp.198–200.

come" (vv.21–30), "the truth will make you free" (vv.31–38), and "your father the devil" (vv.39–47), to "before Abraham came to be, I am" (vv.48–59). Just as vv.21–30 stress that Jesus is "spatially" on a different plane than the rest of humanity, so v.58 teaches that he is "temporally" unique as well. Lindars sees a progression of meaning in the "I am" statements in the chapter. We move from "I am the light" (v.12) to "I am (he)" (v.24), which signifies, in Lindars' view, "light and all other possible predicates which denote salvation;" and we finish with "I am" (v.58), which denotes "timeless pre-existence."[186]

Of even greater importance, perhaps, is v.51, which precipitates the discussion concerning Jesus' pre-existence and his relationship to Abraham.[187] "Truly, truly, I say to you, if anyone keeps my word, he will not see death forever." Jesus' offer of eternal life draws an incredulous response. Who is he making himself out to be? Does he think he is greater than Abraham and the prophets, who themselves died? The issues of ontology and soteriology are inextricably linked here. If Jesus (as "the Jews" imply) is mortal, then he can hardly claim to be the bestower of eternal life. We will argue below that v. 58 addresses both these issues.

This leads us back to the statement πρὶν 'Αβραὰμ γενέσθαι ἐγώ εἰμί. The commentators agree that there is a temporal, or more properly supratemporal, aspect to Jesus' response here. This dramatic use of the continuous present sends them searching for the appropriate words.[188] We have already noted Lindars' "timeless pre-existence." Schnackenburg speaks of Jesus as "the eternally existent being" who is placed "in God's existence beyond time."[189] Dodd says that he "belongs to a different order of being,"[190] while Hoskyns says the phrase expresses "the contrast between the existence initiated by birth and an absolute existence."[191] Barrett's comment is particularly interesting for our purposes: "The meaning here is: Before Abraham came into being, I eternally was, as now I am, and ever continue to be."[192] However one chooses to phrase the matter, Jesus is clearly speaking of his eternal existence in the verse. Dodd's comment about a "different *order* of being" takes on added weight when we note that in v.58 Jesus employs the classic distinction between that which comes to be (γενέσθαι) and that which is eternally (εἰμί). As we have seen earlier, such a dichotomy is congenial to the Hebrew bible, but the particular con-

---

[186] Lindars, p.336.
[187] Abraham has already been introduced into the narrative in v.33, but there it is a question of his parentage, not his mortality as in vv. 52ff.
[188] See Barrett, p.342.
[189] Schnackenburg, 2: 223.
[190] Dodd, p.261.
[191] Quoted in Beasley-Murray, p.139.
[192] Barrett, p.352.

trast of γενέσθαι and εἰμί would at the very least be immediately comprehensible to a hellenistic audience.[193]

Beasley-Murray, while acknowledging a "real pre-existence," downplays the ontology of the passage: it is a statement "primarily (of) what Jesus means for salvation, rather than of his being."[194] One might question his use of "primarily," but his emphasis on soteriology is a valuable reminder about the context of the passage as a whole; that is, Jesus' offer of eternal life. In fact, the two cannot be separated. "The Jews" have denied Jesus' claim to be God's agent of eternal salvation, since they do not believe he himself possesses the requisite immortality needed for such a task. Jesus responds by saying that, on the contrary, he does share in the everlasting life of the Father. The implication is that he is thereby qualified to share this life with others. As Schnackenburg puts it, "Christology is part of soteriology."[195]

This much seems clear from the text itself. The question remains as to the relevance of Ex. 3:14 to Jesus' words. Bultmann claims that Jesus cannot be using ἐγώ εἰμι as a divine name, since this would cause the phrase to lose its verbal force.[196] Barrett and Lindars feel uncomfortable in affirming Odeberg's claim that this is an "elliptical way of saying "I am the 'I AM'.""[197] Schnackenburg takes a more positive view of the relationship of v.58 to the Exodus text. He agrees that Jesus is not making an absolute identification of himself with YHWH, but he still believes Ex. 3:14 underlies his statement in v.58. He notes the similarity of אהיה to אני הוא, and stresses that the name in Ex. 3:14 represents God's "steadfastness and faithfulness."[198]

The concern over Jesus' apparent identification with YHWH (cf. Odeberg's comments and the responses of Barrett and Lindars) is not the real issue. First, if is problematic that Jesus seems at first glance to equate himself with YHWH here, one must consider statements elsewhere in John

---

[193] Brown, Lindars, Beasley-Murray, and Harner all note the similarity to Ps. 90:2 (LXX 89:2): πρὸ τοῦ ὄρη γενηθῆναι...ἀπὸ τοῦ αἰῶνος ἕως τοῦ αἰῶνος σὺ εἶ. As we noted in our previous discussion of this verse, the MT reads not "you are," but "you are God," אתה אל. ("Come into being" is ילדו in the MT.) Unless the LXX is working with a variant Hebrew tradition, then, it seems likely that they have brought into this text the hellenistic distinction between γίνομαι/εἰμι.

[194] Beasley-Murray, p.139.

[195] Schnackenburg, 2: 223.

[196] See Lindars, p.336.

[197] Lindars, p.336; Barrett, p.352. Barrett says that "Lindars is right in saying there is *no allusion* here to Ex. 3:14" (italics mine), but this may go beyond what Lindars actually intends. He seems only to be criticizing Odeberg's claim that Jesus is specifically adopting the name YHWH as his own. This is different from the possibility of seeing an allusion to Ex. 3:14 in John 8:58.

[198] Schnackenburg, 2: 224.

where similar questions might arise: "I and the Father are one" (10:30) or "And the word was God" (1:1). All these speak of an intimate union with the Father, which does not however preclude the idea of the Father being "greater than" the Son. In terms of v. 58, Jesus can speak of sharing in the absolute existence of God, and thus be *identified with* YHWH, without necessarily making the claim to be *identical to* YHWH. The crowd may not have appreciated this nuance of argument, but their reaction indicates that they did understand him to be taking the divine name to himself. They attempt to stone him in accordance with the law of blasphemy in Leviticus 24.[199]

With this concern set aside, we may see that a reference to Ex. 3:14 might make some sense here. The LXX translation of this verse makes it clear that some Jews took אהיה אשר אהיה as a statement about God's absolute or eternal being. Texts like Ps-Jon.Ex. 3:14 ("I am He who is and who will be has sent me to you;" see below) indicate that this approach to the text was not the exclusive property of Diaspora Judaism. If YHWH means "He who is," it would be appropriate for the one who is God's self-revelation to declare "I am." We will also see that Jewish tradition interpreted Ex. 3:14 as a statement of God's saving activity (cf. Ngl 2 Ex. 3:14, "I am he who was for your support in the captivity of the Egyptians, and I am he who will yet be for your support in all generations"). This, too, fits the context of John. Both ontological and soteriological implications may be reasonably drawn from the Exodus text (the ontological from the use of the verb to be, the soteriological from the context of the Exodus event), and both strands were picked up by Jewish exegetes.

As D. Ball and others have demonstrated, however, John is clearly dependent on Is. 40–55 for many of his "I am" statements.[200] Ball believes Is. 43:10 LXX may be particularly important here because of its contrast between εἰμι and γίνομαι: ...καὶ συνῆτε ὅτι ἐγώ εἰμι ἔμπροσθέν μου οὐκ ἐγένετο ἄλλος θεός...[201] I am not thoroughly convinced by this particular parallel, since the εἰμι/γίνομαι distinction was so common in the ancient world.[202] But the fact remains that Is.40–55 is the immediate source for much of John's "I am" material. Thus, even though the connection with Is. 43:10 may perhaps be forced, it is likely that the theology of Is. 40–55 is of primary importance for interpreting John 8:58.[203]

---

[199] Brown, 1: 367; Harner, p.39.
[200] Ball, pp.176–203. Particularly vivid parallels are Jn. 4:26/Is. 52:6; Jn. 8:18/Is.43:10; Jn. 8:24,8/Is. 43:10; Jn. 13:16–19/Is. 43:10. All are discussed by Ball.
[201] Ball, pp.195–6.
[202] Cf. our note above concerning Ps. 90:2 (LXX 89:2).
[203] Harner (p.40; followed by Ball, pp.196–7) notes that Abraham is introduced "as a model of God's deliverance" in the Targum to Isaiah 41:2, 43:12, 46:11 (cf. the mention of Abraham in MT Is. 41:8, 51:2), and that John may have such verses in mind in his

This hardly makes Ex. 3:14 irrelevant. Is. 40–55 looks back towards Exodus traditions. More importantly, the interpretation of אני הוא/ἐγώ εἰμι as a self-proclamation of God's absolute or eternal existence depends on the equation of these phrases with the אהיה of Ex. 3:14. Ex. 3:14 is the foundational text upon which the other traditions build.

If Jesus' statement πρὶν Ἀβραὰμ γενέσθαι ἐγώ εἰμι is to be connected with the divine name, as is likely, we have further evidence that the name YHWH was understood to mean "He who is" in the New Testament era. This would include not only the idea of eternal being indicated by the continuous present tense, but also the saving activity of God on behalf of his people: "He is there *for us*." Jesus, as the definitive self-disclosure of God, the Logos who is eternally in the bosom of the Father, can thus declare, "Before Abraham came to be, I am."

Rabbinical Literature

The Rabbinical literature, and the Targums in particular, offer some very important parallels to our passage in Revelation. We will note briefly some of the relevant portions of the Talmuds, and then discuss the Targums more extensively.[204] We conclude with a brief look at some later texts which are of relevance to Rev. 1:4.

In our discussion of Philo, we noted that he associated the word κύριος with God's judicial power, and θεός with his merciful power. The Rabbis, on the other hand, tended to do just the reverse: יהוה stood for God's mercy, and אלהים for his judgment. It is difficult to say which one of these formulations was earlier. N. A. Dahl and Alan F. Segal have conducted a thorough investigation of the matter and concluded: "Due to the lack of pre-rabbinic and pre-Philonic evidence, the origin and earliest form of the correlation between divine names and attributes remain unknown."[205] In any case, they believe that the distinction between the names and attributes is of secondary importance: what matters is the *interdependence* of both concepts: "God is just when He shows mercy, and merciful when He judges."[206]

This matter lies on the borderline between the *significance* of the name and its *meaning*. Philo has clearly been influenced by the etymology of κύριος, with its connotations of rulership and power (cf. *Cher.* 27–8), but I do not know anyone who would argue that the rabbis thought that YHWH

---

contrast of Abraham and Jesus. Of course Ex. 3:15 has "the God of Abraham, Isaac, and Jacob," so this alone cannot decide the case.

[204] The Mishnah, as far as I can determine, does not address the etymology of the divine name.

[205] Dahl and Segal, p. 28.

[206] Dahl and Segal, p. 28.

was etymologically linked with words for mercy or kindness. We include the discussion here because the rabbinic teaching does seem to have its roots at least partly in Ex. 3:14.

The identification of YHWH with mercy most likely derives from Ex. 33:12ff., which in turn is a reflection upon the title אהיה אשר אהיה from Ex. 3:14. In Ex. 33:19, God tells Moses that he will proclaim his name, YHWH, before him. This is followed immediately by the statement, "I will have mercy on whom I will have mercy, and I will have compassion on whom I will have compassion" (cf. Ex.34: 6–7). This is an expansion or elucidation of אהיה אשר אהיה, and as such it can be considered an "exegesis" of the divine name.[207] The rabbis appear to have read Ex.3:14 through the lens of Ex. 33:19ff. If this is correct, then in the rabbinical view Ex. 3:14 is not simply an exposition of the fact of, or the nature of, God's existence considered in the abstract. Rather it is an affirmation of his merciful presence with his people.[208]

There is positive evidence in the Talmud to support such a view. B. Ber. 9b interprets Ex. 3:14 as follows:

אני הייתי עמכם בשעבוד זה ואני אהיה עמכם בשעבוד מלכיות
אמר לפניו ובשיע דיה לצרה בשעתה..לך אמר להם אהיה שלחני
אליכם

> I have been with you in this servitude, and I will be with you in the servitude of the kingdoms...He (Moses) said to him, the distress in the present is enough...(God says), Tell them "I am" has sent me to you.

The rabbis often saw significance in words which appeared more than once in a single passage. It is hardly surprising to see them doing so with respect to Ex. 3:14.[209] The first אהיה in b. Ber. 9b stands for God's past and present merciful presence with his people in Egypt, while the second stands for his promise to be with them in their future servitude under the kingdoms (which should be understood to refer to all who subjugate Israel from Assyria and Babylon up through Rome). The third use in Exodus – "I AM has sent me..." – is taken to refer back to the first use. Moses, it seems, has enough things to worry about without troubling himself with the trials of future generations, and so God assures him again that he will be with his people *now*. The motif of past and future sufferings and deliv-

---

[207] Thus Hayward, *Divine Name*, pp.22, 45–6, 123. He introduces the issue as part of his larger argument concerning the theology of the *Memra*, to which we will return later in this section.

[208] See Hayward's chapter in *Divine Name*, "Memra and the Attribute of Mercy," pp.39–56; Pamela Vermes, "Buber's Understanding of the Divine Name Related to Bible, Targum, and Midrash," *JJS* 24 (1973): 150–57.

[209] Hayward, *Divine Name*, pp. 31–2.

erance also calls to mind Is.40–55, as we indicated in our discussion above.

The double use of "I *am*" emphasizes God's active and compassionate presence with his people in their present distress. This serves to make the text applicable for any situation of distress in which God's community might find itself. Pamela Vermes' assertion that in rabbinic tradition God's "being" is a "being with" certainly holds true in the case of b. Ber. 9b.[210]

The Targums, as we have indicated, offer a rich stock of parallels to Rev. 1:4. We are also fortunate that two extensive studies on these texts have already been carried out: Robert Hayward's *Divine Name and Presence: the Memra*; and Martin McNamara's chapter, "The Origin of the Divine Name of the Apocalypse," in his volume *The New Testament and the Palestinian Targum to the Pentateuch*. We will begin with the question of the divine name and the *Memra*, and then move on to the relevant texts.

The word *Memra* appears frequently in the Targums as a part of a designation for God, often in the form "the *Memra* of YHWH." The word has attracted much attention, not only because it is used exclusively in the Targums, but also because of its possible significance for understanding the *logos* doctrine of early Christianity.[211] Scholars have debated whether it is a hypostasis, distinguishable from God (F. Weber, A. Edersheim); a simple translation equivalent for the name of God (Moore); or a theologically significant designation for deity (P. Vermes, Hayward).[212] We cannot hope to solve the problem of the *Memra* here, and so we will concentrate on the thesis advanced by P. Vermes and Hayward that the *Memra* "is God's *'HYH*, His Name for Himself expounded in terms of His past and future presence in Creation and Redemption."[213]

Neither of these scholars is suggesting that every use of *Memra* in the Targums is informed by this theology. At some point the word began to be "a mere replacement for the Tetragram YHWH."[214] But a close inspection of Tg. Neofiti (henceforth N) reveals a significant cluster of texts which connect the *Memra* with the temple, God's glory, God's presence, and God's name. Hayward's thesis may be summarized in the following points:

1. The *Memra* is to be understood as God's אהיה, his name for himself. Central to Hayward's argument here is N's rendering of Ex. 3:12: "And He said, Because I, My *Memra*, will be with you" (ואמר ארום אהווי ממרי עמך). He rejects the suggestion that this should be rendered "I will be with you in (or with) My *Memra*," and believes the text should be read simply as it stands. The אהיה of the original Hebrew has been explained as ממרי. The two are equivalent.

---

[210] P. Vermes, *passim*.
[211] Hayward, *Divine Name*, pp.1–2.
[212] Hayward, *Divine Name*, pp.2–7.
[213] Hayward, *Divine Name*, p.147.
[214] Hayward, *Divine Name*, p.10.

2. The word *Memra* "consists not only of the notion of saying derived from its root *'mr*, but includes as well the idea of *being with*, in that it ultimately means I AM THERE."[215]
3. This *Memra* or אהיה does not signify bare existence, but indicates God's *merciful presence* with his people. Several texts are adduced to emphasize the connection between *Memra* and presence, and *Memra* and mercy.[216]
4. More specifically, this merciful presence can be identified with the covenant of God with Israel, and the oath by which that covenant is ratified.[217]
5. Finally, the *Memra* is often associated with the Jerusalem temple, which Hayward quite rightly argues was the locus *par excellence* of the divine name in early Judaism. This was the meeting place of God with his people, and thus it was appropriate that here he would disclose himself as אהיה, "I am (there)," to which his people might joyfully respond, יהוה, "He is (there)."[218]

Hayward's basic thesis seems essentially sound.[219] If he and P. Vermes are correct, the *Memra* would provide us with evidence that early Judaism not only engaged in serious reflection on the divine name. It also compressed this reflection into a "portable" form such that the theology of the name could be easily introduced into a number of scriptural contexts. Even if one is inclined to dispute the amount of theology that is actually packed into the *Memra*, there is no denying that the texts adduced by Hayward and Vermes point to a sophisticated understanding of the episode of the burning bush in early Judaism, and that they have done a great service by assembling these texts and examining them in detail.

Before we turn to these texts, we must make one minor clarification of Hayward's approach. By consistently translating the verb to be as "to be *with*" or "to be *there*," he highlights the idea of presence as opposed to abstract existence. This might suggest that the rabbis only thought about God's being in terms of his presence with his people. But this view runs into problems in texts like Ngl 1 Ex. 3:14, where God says "I was before the world was created..." This appears to say something about God's being in and of itself, rather than about his relationship with other beings. The emphasis on "being with" is certainly appropriate, but it is not the exclusive meaning of the verb to be in rabbinical theology.[220]

---

[215] Hayward, *Divine Name*, p.24.

[216] Hayward, *Divine Name*, pp.15–56.

[217] Hayward, *Divine Name*, pp.71–98.

[218] Hayward, *Divine Name*, pp.99–113. He regularly adds the word "there" in his translations of the verb to be, in order to emphasize the idea of presence rather than mere existence.

[219] Cf. the approval given by P. S. Alexander in his review of *Divine Name and Presence*, *JJS* 34 (1983): 217–20.

[220] P. Vermes correctly points out that the Targumists were not only concerned with God's presence, but also with his past creative activity, and even with his past existence: "He was always there, he is the Eternal One." P. Vermes, p.152.

We will begin with the Targumic renderings of Ex. 3:14. Not surprisingly, Targum Onqelos gives a conservative rendering of the Hebrew. The principal texts simply reproduce the Hebrew words אהיה אשר אהיה, although some versions emend this slightly to "I will be *concerning* that which I will be" or "I will be *with* whomsoever I will be."[221] The first variant appears to be an attempt to give some grammatical sense to אהיה אשר אהיה, while the second gives us a very concise version of the "theology of presence" which has been noted above.

The other Targums are far more involved. N Ex. 3:14 reads thus:

מן דאמר והיה עלמא מן שרויא ועתיד למימר ליה הווי והווי הוא שלח יתי לוותכון

He who spoke, and the world was from the beginning, and who is to say to it, "Be," and it will be, He has sent me to you. (Hayward, with modifications)

Several comments are in order. The Aramaic phrase מן דאמר והיה עלמא (also used in N Gen. 21:33) is the equivalent of the Hebrew מי שאמר והיה העולם, which appears repeatedly in the *Mekilta de Rabbi Ishmael*.[222] It is uncertain whether this was an independent designation for God which was inserted here by the Meturgeman, or whether it arose directly from the interpretation of Ex. 3:14 itself.[223] In either case, its appearance here makes explicit what is implicit in other texts we have studied: the name YHWH was understood in relation to the command יהי in Gen. 1:3 ff. One might have been inspired by the two-fold use of אהיה in אהיה אשר אהיה to reflect on God's past and future activity. But it can hardly be coincidental that the Meturgeman makes mention of God's words, "Let it be!" in this passage concerning the revelation of the divine name. This is best explained by supposing that the Targum reflects a tradition whereby at least one of the meanings of the name YHWH was "He who causes (the world) to be." We have seen that this is a grammatically possible rendering of the tetragrammaton, and it appears the Meturgemanin availed themselves of it.[224]

Since N simply reproduces the Hebrew phrase אהיה אשר אהיה, Hayward takes "He who said, and the world was, etc." as a gloss upon the single אהיה at the end of the verse. This אהיה is for him equivalent to

---

[221] See *Targum Onqelos to Genesis*, trans. by Bernard Grossfeld, Aramaic Bible (T.&T. Clark: Edinburgh, 1988), at Ex. 3:14.

[222] Marmorstein believes the designation is Tannaitic. See *Old Rabbinic Doctrine*, p.89.

[223] Hayward (*Divine Name*, p.25n) suggests this formula may have "crept into N as a result of its revision by Rabbinic authority."

[224] McNamara (p.108n), in his citation of the text of N Ex. 3:14, notes the opinion of Cross et al. that YHWH means "He who causes to be." He does not, however, offer his own opinion on the matter.

the *Memra*, and so he takes the exposition in N to be an early summary of *Memra* theology.²²⁵ Even if this is technically an expansion of the last אהיה, it seems likely that the two-fold temporal reference has been inspired by אהיה אשר אהיה.²²⁶ If so, the first אהיה is taken to represent God's creative activity at the world's beginning, and the second to represent the creation of the world-to-come. The Meturgeman may have been prompted to include this teaching simply by the fact that the burning bush episode centers on the explanation of the name YHWH. But it is likely that he was also aware of the creation motifs which permeate the Exodus narrative as a whole (e.g. parting of the waters and appearance of dry land at the Red Sea). Israel's deliverance from Egypt is an act of creation by God, and so it is perfectly fitting for the Targum of Ex. 3:14 to hearken back to God's original work of creation, and to look forward to the creation to come. Since God's presence with Moses has already been established in v.12, the Targum works within a framework with striking similarities to the one in Revelation 1:4: God *was* there at the creation of the world; He *is* there with Moses in Egypt; and He *will be* there at the creation of the world-to-come.

The Fragmentary Targum (G)²²⁷ to Ex. 3:14 provides a reading which is very close to N.²²⁸ Perhaps the most significant difference is the positioning of מן שירויא, "from the beginning" directly after דין דאמר לעלמא, "He who spoke to the world..." This appears slightly clearer than the rendering in N and may represent an effort to smooth out an earlier tradition. There is no profound difference in the theology of the two versions.

---

²²⁵ Both he and P. Vermes believe this emphasis on the last אהיה is probably earlier than traditions which devote attention to אהיה אשר אהיה itself. This is possible but difficult to prove. See Hayward, *Divine Name*, pp.18–9; P. Vermes, pp.153–4.

²²⁶ Cf. Hayward's comments on Ngl 2, *Divine Name*, p.19.

²²⁷ Unfortunately the two most thorough works on these Targumic texts, those of Hayward and McNamara, vary in their terminology. The following is a "conversion table":

Hayward	McNamara
FT (G) (the Fragmentary Targum, ed. Ginsburger)	TJII Paris 110
FT (W) (Fragmentary Targum, ed. Walton)	TJII Polyglots
"first Ngl"	Ngl 2 (*sic*!)
"second Ngl"	Ngl 1 (*sic*!)
Ps-Jon.	TJI

I have adopted Hayward's designations, since they are the more recent. For the sake of convenience, however, I label his "first Ngl" as Ngl 1, and "second Ngl" Ngl 2:

²²⁸ Cf. the similar readings in FT (W) Ex. 3:14 and Ngl 1 Ex. 3:14. See Hayward, *Divine Name*, pp.18–9. All these texts omit "from the beginning."

The second gloss of N, (Ngl 2), on the other hand, represents a different tradition indeed:

אנא הוויתי עד לא איתברא עלמא ואנא הוויתי מן דאיתבריה עלמא
אנא הוא דהוויתי בסעדכון בגלותא דמצראי ואנא הוא דעתיד למחווי
בסעדכון בכל דר ודר...אהיה שלח יתי לוותכון

I was before the world was created, and I was after the world was created. I am He who was for you support in the captivity of the Egyptians, and I am He who is to be for your support in every generation...I am has sent me to you. (Hayward, with modifications)

The verbs of speaking are absent from this version, although one still finds the creation of the world used as a frame of reference for describing the eternity of God. Ngl 2 stays closer to the text of Exodus by retaining the first person, "I was before the world was created..." rather than the "He who spoke..." of the previous two readings. The repeated phrase אנא הוא, meanwhile, appears to be the equivalent of אני הוא in texts like Is.48:12. The expression in the first explanation offered, אנא הוויתי, looks to be derived from a similar source.

Ngl 2 is not simply meditating on God's activity in the past, present, and future. Instead, in Ngl 2, God reveals himself to be the eternally existent one, who was before the world was created.[229] But this fact is not presented in a vacuum. Ngl 2 immediately ties this to God's present care for Israel in Egypt, and his care for Israel in future generations. The idea of God's eternity is introduced to provide confirmation of his ability to watch over his people at all times. The final clause of Ex. 3:14 is given in something quite close to its Hebrew form.[230] Presumably we are to take אהיה here as inclusive of all the characteristics previously mentioned.

The person responsible for Ngl 2 may have stitched together two traditional interpretations of Ex. 3:14, the first one emphasizing God's eternity (cf. Ex. R. 3:6), and the other emphasizing God's presence with his people in their distress (cf. b.Ber 9b).[231] Alternatively, he may have made an independent contribution by reading Ex. 3:14 in the light of Is. 40–55, whose theology he appears to see encapsulated in the phrase אני הוא (see esp. Is. 41:4;43:10–13;44:6;46:4;48:12). In any event, his expansion of the text seems entirely appropriate. The Exodus text does speak of God's being in very allusive terms, and the repetition of אהיה invites reflection on the question of God and his relationship to time. The context, however, demands that attention also be paid to God's merciful presence with his servants in their captivity. The composer of Ngl 2 has adopted the simple, but effective, method of placing these two ideas side by side, so that the reader

---

[229] Cf. P. Vermes, p.152.
[230] McNamara, p.107.
[231] Cf. McNamara, p.107.

The Meaning of the Name

may infer that God's eternity undergirds his promise to be there for his people not only now, but for all time to come as well.

Ps-Jon. also shows some significant variations:

דין דאמר והוה עלמא אמר והוה כולא...אנא הוא דהוינא ועתיד
למיהוי שדרני לוותכון

> He who spoke and the world was; who spoke and all things were...I am He who is and who will be has sent me to you. (McNamara)

The Meturgeman may have taken the two instances of אהיה in אהיה אשר אהיה as being in a kind of poetic parallelism. The two forms are the same, and hence so are their meanings: "He who spoke and the world was; who spoke and all things were." In any event, the final אהיה receives more attention than it has in the other Targums. While the past creation event has been accounted for in the rendering of אהיה אשר אהיה, the presence (or at least the existence) of God in the present and the future is associated with the אהיה שלחני of the MT. Interestingly, however, Ps-Jon. has not employed שלח itself, as do the other versions, but rather introduces שדרני. Perhaps the difference is inconsequential, but it at least suggests a certain independence on the part of Ps-Jon. Such independence is also evidenced in its unique conflation of apparently traditional elements. The speaking/past creation motif is preserved, albeit in modified form. But unlike N and FT (G), it is not conjoined with the idea of a future creation. Nor is there an emphasis on God's presence with his people. It may implicit in the latter portion of the verse, but all that is stated is the rather vague, "I am he who is and who will be..." Finally, the key phrase אנא הוא דהוינא ועתיד למיהוי seems dependent upon the "first and last" texts of Isaiah 40ff., particularly 48:12.

We conclude this section with a text *not* taken from Ex. 3:14, but which nonetheless shows the closest parallels to our expression in Revelation: Ps-Jon. Dt. 32:39. The Targum is interpreting the phrase, "See now that I, even I, am He...(ראו עתה כי אני אני הוא). It reads as follows:

חמון כדון ארום אנא הוא דהוי והוית ואנא הוא דעתיד למהוי ולית
אלהא הורן בר מיני

> See now that I am he who is and who was and I am he who will be, and there is no other God beside me. (McNamara)

The parallels with, e.g., Is.48:12, are striking. The appearance of אני הוא in both Dt. 32:39 and Is. 48:12 would make a conflation of the texts quite natural. At the same time, apart from the addition of הוית, this formula is quite close to the one used in Ps-Jon. Ex. 3:14. The Meturgeman may have connected the two appearances of אני in Deuteronomy with the two appearances of אהיה in Exodus, and thus used the exegetical traditions of Ex. 3:14 and Is. 40–55 to illuminate Dt. 32:39.

As for the relevance of Ps-Jon. Dt. 32:39 to our text in Revelation, we begin with McNamara's conclusions on the matter:

> Here we encounter the same divine Name we have already met in TJI [= our Ps-Jon.] Ex 3,14, but now in its tripartite form. This text of TJI Dt 32,39 is a perfect parallel to the divine Name in the Apocalypse. דהוי is the relative particle ד + הוי the participle, in the meaning of the present. It is then the exact equivalent of ὁ ὤν. הוית is again the perfect qal, with the relative particle ד presupposed and is the exact equivalent of ὁ ἦν. עתיד למהוי would correspond to ἐσόμενος rather than to ἐρχόμενος. We have seen, however, that ἐρχόμενος is probably either a Christian addition or a Christian adaptation of some other term or terms...It appears that ὁ ὤν καὶ ὁ ἦν καὶ ὁ ἐρχόμενος of the Apocalypse is a servile rendering of the Aramaic דהוי (sic)א (ו)הוית ו(ד)עתיד למיתא) and is perfectly paralleled in TJI Dt 32,39...[232]

McNamara's basic point is valid, even if it is stated in somewhat extreme terms. The verbal parallels are quite remarkable, and we will return to them when we examine the grammatical peculiarities of the texts in Revelation in the final chapter of the thesis. Although dating passages in the Targums is always a problem, McNamara produces evidence that suggests that Ps-Jon. Dt 32–33 contains some very early material. In our specific instance, it would seem more probable that a Christian writer would borrow this type of Jewish formulation rather than vice versa.[233]

Some questions do remain, however. Calling John's phrase a "servile" rendering of the Aramaic is hardly fair, given that he radically alters it by the replacement of the final verb to be with ἐρχόμενος. (This in addition to the perhaps minor point that והוית is not a *perfect* equivalent of ὁ ἦν, since the ד is only understood in Ps-Jon. and is not actually present there.) The appearance of the participle דהוי also requires some explanation. It is true that Aramaic has a certain preference for the participle.[234] But is it a coincidence that this form, as McNamara himself points out, may be the exact equivalent of ὁ ὤν? We have seen that the introduction of ὁ ὤν into the interpretation of Ex. 3:14 was due to the exigencies of Greek grammar. While the introduction of דהוי may have been an independent contribution, it is at least possible that the Targum depends on the Septuagint translation of Ex. 3:14.[235]

---

[232] McNamara, p.112.
[233] Cf. Hayward, *Divine Name*, p.34. Aune (*Revelation 1–5*, pp.32-3) is not convinced by McNamara's dating of the Targum, and prefers to speak of a common liturgical tradition behind Ps-Jon. and Revelation. It is certainly safer to speak of such a "tradition" rather than to insist that John knows Ps-Jon. itself.
[234] As James Davila has reminded me. His comments on this section have been of great help.
[235] One might argue that Ps-Jon. Dt. 32:39 is dependent on אנא הוא דהוינא in Ps-Jon. Ex. 3:14. But this only pushes the problem back a step. Why is there a participle in Ps-Jon.Ex. 3:14?

We must also reckon with the possibility of Greek influence on the three-fold structure itself.[236] The reading in Ps-Jon. Dt. 32:39 could have developed from earlier Jewish bi-partite formulations, so that the resemblance with Greek descriptions of deity is purely coincidental. But the work of Hengel and others has established that early Judaism did not develop in a vacuum. We hasten to add that "influence" need not, and in fact should not, imply a passive reception of ideas from the "superior" Greek culture. I believe the traditions surrounding Ex. 3:14 and related texts indicate an awareness of the Greek descriptions of deity we have studied in our first chapter. I also believe that the *Dreizeitenformel* in Tg. Dt. 32:39 may constitute a polemical retort to the claims of Zeus or Isis or Aion. They are false claimants to the eternity that belongs only to the God of Israel. This idea is certainly not foreign to the Hebrew bible, and may be found within Deuteronomy 32 itself (see 32:40, חי אנכי לעלם).

The Targums, then, express a number of different perspectives on the significance of Ex. 3:14, which may be summarized as follows:

1. God has been with his people in their captivity in Egypt, and will continue to be with them in the future (b. Ber. 9b; Ngl 2)
2. God spoke the present world into existence (Ps-Jon.), and will speak the future world into existence (N; FT (G); FT (W))
3. God existed before the world was created; still exists after the creation of the world (Ngl 2); and will exist in the future (Ps-Jon. Dt. 32:39).

God's name, then, is understood to indicate something about God's *presence*, his *creative activity*, and/or his *being*. Whatever hesitations one might have about Targumic exegesis in general, it must be admitted that all of these explanations are plausible readings of the Exodus text, particularly as it is read through the lens of Is.40–55. The idea of presence is signalled both by the general context of the deliverance from evil, and from the specific mention of God's *being with* Moses in 3:12. The connection of the Exodus event and the creation narrative has been noted above. As for the question of God's *being*, the Targums are hardly alone in believing that Ex. 3:14 has something to say about God's eternity or his existence independent of the creation. Nor must we necessarily posit a conflict amongst varying schools of interpretation. The Meturgemanin may well have differed on what was the "proper" understanding of the passage, but it is equally possible that the obscurity of God's response to Moses was taken as an opportunity to read the texts in a number of different but harmonious

---

[236] See Heinrich Kraft, *Die Offenbarung des Johannes*, HNT 16a (Tübingen: J.C.B. Mohr (Paul Siebeck), 1974), p.31; Friedrich Büchsel, "εἰμι," *TDNT* 2: 399. Note that Aune devotes most of his attention to Greek sources in his comments on Rev. 1:4; the information on the Targumim appears in a small print excursus (*Revelation 1–5*, pp.30–33).

ways (cf. especially Ngl 2). It can be argued that the treatment of Ex. 3:14 represents one of the high points of Targumic exegesis.

We close our discussion with some later Rabbinical texts which deal with the divine name. We are not arguing that the traditions they contain pre-date the writing of Revelation – although this is possible – but they do show the continuity of tradition concerning the reading of Ex. 3:14. The list is not meant to be exhaustive, but is merely intended to show some of the ways the discussion proceeded in later centuries.

The first text is Mekilta de R. Ishmael. Shir. 3.25:[237]

היה לי ויהיה לי היה לי לשעבר ויהיה לי לעתיד לבא

He was (there) for me and He will be (there) for me; He was (there) for me for the past, and He will be (there) for me for the future. (Trans. Hayward, with modifications, p.30; text, Lauterbach)

The first thing which catches one's eye is the appearance of לבא for "future." While this is not used of God *per se*, it raises the possibility that at least the word for "come" may have formed some part of the interpretative heritage of Ex. 3:14 and related passages. The present text is actually a gloss upon Ex. 15:2, ויהי לי לישׁוּעה, hence the incorporation of לי in the reading of the Mekilta. But the two-fold temporal reference indicates that this may hearken back to traditional readings of Ex. 3:14. The association of the two verses may simply be due to similar content, namely the Exodus deliverance of God's people. But one wonders if the presence of יהי in Ex. 15:2 formed the crucial link in mind of the author of the Mekilta. If so, this would provide us with more evidence for a connection between the name YHWH and יהי, the word which is so central to the creation account. It also bears repeating that the Mekilta frequently employs the designation מי שׁאמר והיה העולם, "Who spoke and the world was," as a designation for God. Finally, this passage demonstrates again the close connection between God's *being* and his *being with* his people. God not only "is"; he "is-for-me."

Exodus Rabba 3:6, meanwhile, reads:

אני שהייתי ואני הוא עכשו ואני הוא לעתיד לבוא

I am He who was, and I am now, and I am for the future (Hayward, with modifications)

Exodus Rabba may date in its present form to as late as 1000 CE.[238] Nevertheless, the tripartite scheme is of interest. Note the phrases אני שהייתי,

---

[237] The *Mekilta* is traditionally dated to the time of the Mishnah; cf. the introduction in vol. I of Lauterbach's *Mekilta de Rabbi Ishmael* (Philadelphia: Jewish Publication Society of America, 1949). Hayward (*Divine Name*, pp.29–30) notes the recent critiques of its antiquity by Wacholder, but says these critiques must be seen as "not proven." An early date would not fundamentally alter our discussion.

which bears a close resemblance to ὁ ἦν of Revelation; and לעתיד לבוא (see above on the Mekilta).

Finally, there is Alphabet of R. Akiba on Ex. 3:14:

אני שהייתי ואני הוא עכשו ואני הוא לע״ל לכן כתיב אהיה ג׳ פעמים

I am he who was and I am he (who is) now, and I am he (who will be) forever." Wherefore is it said thrice, "I am." (Text and Translation in McNamara, p.x5)

This work is also fairly late,[239] and its similarity to Ex. R. 3:6 may indicate a common, and late, reading of Ex. 3:14. It is included because it makes explicit what is elsewhere implicit in the rabbinic approach to the text: "*Wherefore* it is said three times..." (One could easily substitute "two times" to reflect the mentality of those interpreters who interpret אהיה אשר אהיה alone.) The three-fold appearance of אהיה calls for an explanation, which is supplied by "Akiba."

The *Dreizeitenformel* in Jewish Literature

The "three times formula" is not used in the Old Testament. This is not to say that the idea of God's everlasting existence is unknown in the Hebrew Scriptures (see e.g. Is. 48:12).[240] It is this precise way of speaking about God's everlasting existence which is absent, perhaps because of the structure of the Hebrew verbal system. Variations of the formula do occur, however, in later Jewish literature. We will survey those occurences here, and then briefly look at some Christian, Greek, and Gnostic sources which post-date Revelation.

Jewish Literature

We are especially interested in formulae which describe God as existing in the past, present, and future. The most important examples are those from the Targums (e.g. Tg. Ps-Jon. Ex. 3:14; Tg. Ps-Jon. Dt. 32:39; cf. Ex. R. 3:6). We have also made reference to the similar description of God in Sib. Or. 3:16:

ἀλλ' αὐτὸς ἀνέδειξεν αἰώνιος αὐτὸς ἑαυτόν/ὄντα τε καὶ πρὶν ἐόντα, ἀτὰρ πάλι καὶ μετέπειτα.

---

[238] C. Evans, *Non-Canonical Writings and New Testament Interpretation* (Peabody, MA: Hendrickson, 1992), p.133.

[239] McNamara, p.105.

[240] Nor, of course, is it unknown in later Jewish literature where the *Dreizeitenformel* is not present. A good example is LAB 21:4, "...you who are before all ages and after all ages still live..." (trans. Harrington, *OTP* 2: 330).

But he himself, eternal, revealed himself as existing now, and formerly, and again in the future.[241]

We noted that the context may suggest an allusion to Ex. 3:14. At the same time, the content of the description recalls the "Zeus was, Zeus is, Zeus will be" of the Dodona oracle, and its form has certain affinities with *Il.* 1.70 (cf. ὄντα τε καὶ πρὶν ἐόντα and τά τ' ἐόντα τά τ' ἐσσόμενα πρό τ' ἐόντα). Such a combination of Jewish and hellenistic motifs is not at all surprising in a text like Sib. Or. 3:1–45, which appears to be a typical hellenistic Jewish apologetic piece.[242]

A related formula appears in the Jewish Orphic works and in Josephus *Ap.* 2:190: "God is (or holds) the beginning, middle, and end of all things."[243] As we have seen, the phrase goes back before the writing of Plato's *Laws*. Plato begins the address to the new colonists of Magnesia with a reference to ὁ...θεός...ἀρχήν τε καὶ τελευτὴν καὶ μέσα τῶν ὄντων ἁπάντων ἔχων (*Laws* 715 e ff.). According to Plato, this is a παλαιὸς λόγος. Variations of the formula were popular throughout antiquity.[244] But we should not jump to the conclusion that the phrase is of immediate relevance to Rev. 1:4. First of all, the quotation from Plato does not say God *is* the beginning, middle, and end of all things, but rather that he *holds* the beginning, middle, and end of all things. This is how the formula appears in the Jewish Orphic fragment preserved in Eusebius.[245] Secondly, it may at times have a *cosmological* rather than a temporal connotation. How is the universe held together? God holds the beginning, middle, and end.[246] Finally, even if one takes these references to be temporal, one cannot assume that "the beginning, middle, and end of all things" has any kind of eschatological meaning. It is more likely that in some, if not most, instances (e.g. *Laws* 715e, Orphic fragment; ps-aristotelian *De Mundo* 401b

---

[241] Trans. Collins, OTP 1: 362.

[242] Collins (*OTP* 1: 360) notes the affinities with the Jewish Orphic fragments and with Philo. The most overtly hellenistic element is the mention of "strong mother Tethys" in l. 22.

[243] On this see van Unnik, *Het Godspredikat, passim*; and Carl R. Holladay, *Fragments from Hellenistic Jewish Authors, Volume IV: Orphica* (Atlanta: Scholars Press, 1996), pp.190–92.

[244] Again see van Unnik, C. Holladay.

[245] Pr. Ev. 13:12.5.4 (= Orphic poem "E," l.39 in *OTP*, 2: 800): ἀρχὴν αὐτὸς ἔχων καὶ μέσσην ἠδὲ τελευτήν (text in Karl Mras, ed., *Eusebius Werke*, vol. VIII, pt. 1; Berlin: Akademie-Verlag, 1954); see the discussion of variants in C. Holladay, pp.189–90). M. LaFargue (*OTP*, 2: 800) translates this: "Being 'the beginning, middle, and end'," making it apply directly to God (or to Moses, if one adopts LaFargue's suggestion that ll.32–9 refer to him). "Being" is a possible interpretation of ἔχων, but "having" or "holding" seems more natural. I much prefer Holladay's rendering (p.188), "since he controls their beginning, as well as their middle and end."

[246] See van Unnik, *Het Godpredikat*, pp.62–3.

25²⁴⁷), the phrase means that God is in control of the various cycles that occur in the world: the birth and death of human beings; the rise and fall of cities; the beginnings and endings of the seasons; and so on.²⁴⁸

Josephus' use of "the beginning, middle, and end" in *Ap.* 2:190 is still of some interest. It occupies a prominent place in his argument, coming at the beginning of his discourse on the ten commandments ("What, then, are the precepts and prohibitions of our Law?"). He cleverly adapts Plato's formula to suit his own needs. The word ἔχω is retained, but is shifted to the initial phrase "God holds (ἔχει) the universe...." This leaves Josephus with a verbless ἀρχη, μέσα, τέλος, which he puts in the nominative so that it applies to God himself. God does hold everything, as in Plato; Josephus adds that God in fact *is* the beginning, middle, and end of all things. The distinction in meaning between Josephus and Plato may not amount to much, but the fact that Josephus uses it as a title for God rather than as a description of his activity makes his formulation that much closer to Rev. 1:4. The appearance of the phrase at the beginning of his discourse about God is another important parallel with our text in Revelation. It is not a question of literary dependence, nor even of a common source. The overt differences between the texts may disabuse us of that notion. Rather, Josephus and John exhibit a similar mind-set. If you want to speak about God and his control of the world, it is good to begin with a dramatic three-part formula that expresses something of his power and his control over history.

The Homeric description of prophecy as the knowledge of τά τ' ἐόντα τά τ' ἐσσόμενα πρό τ' ἐόντα exercised its influence not only on later Greek writers but also on Jewish ones. It is not surprising to find a variant of this *Dreizeitenformel* in the first Sibylline Oracle (1:4), which has marked hellenistic influence.²⁴⁹ The Sibyl will speak concerning ὁππόσα πρὶν γέγονεν, πόσα δ' ἐστίν, ὁπόσσα δὲ μέλλει/ἔσσεται κόσμῳ διὰ δυσσεβίας ἀνθρώπων.²⁵⁰ This provides us with an important conceptual bridge between Homer and Revelation. The "things that were before" commence with a particularly Jewish account of creation and follow with a summary of biblical history (Sib. Or. 1:5 ff.). The things that "will come upon the world" include the eschatological rule of the Hebrews (Sib.Or.2: 174 ff.). The Greek *Dreizeitenformel* serves as the overture for a Jewish account of history.

---

²⁴⁷ Note that the author of the *De Mundo* mentions the three-fold division of time with regards to the Fates (401b 15 ff.) immediately before the quotation.

²⁴⁸ The *De Mundo*, for instance, gives no evidence of eschatology in the Jewish or Christian sense. On the contrary, at 397a 9 ff. the author declares that the celestial bodies move in orderly arrangement from infinity to infinity.

²⁴⁹ See Collins' introduction, in *OTP* 1: 334.

²⁵⁰ Text in Geffcken.

An even earlier example of the prophetic three-times formula may be found in the Exagoge of Ezekiel.[251] The influence of Greek culture on the poem, especially on its form, is obvious. In ll.68–82, Moses has a dream which is then interpreted by his father-in-law. Our concern is the interpretation of Moses' words, "I gazed upon the whole earth round about/things under it, and high above the skies (ll.77–8)." His father-in-law tells him: "As for beholding all the peopled earth/and things below and things above God's realm:/things present, past, and future you shall see (ὄψει τά τ' ὄντα τά τε προτοῦ τά θ' ὕστερον; ll.87–9)."[252] Like most writers who employ a *Dreizeitenformel*, Ezekiel adds a few personal touches, but the idea derives ultimately from *Il.* 1.70. Moses, as the prophet *par excellence*, can hardly be bereft of the credentials enjoyed by even an "ordinary" seer such as Calchas. This is not to suggest that Ezekiel is creating a prophetic Moses *ex nihilo*. Given a traditional understanding of the Pentateuch, it is quite appropriate to see Moses as the great revealer of the past (the Genesis narratives, particularly the creation account); the present (the revelation of the Law); and the future (e.g. the predictions in the book of Deuteronomy). What Ezekiel does is to take this traditional material and give it a familiar Greek label.[253]

We conclude this section with Wis. 7:17–8, where Solomon declares that he knows "the beginning and end and middle of times."[254] The words are close to *Laws* 715e *et al.*, though the temporal dimension is clearly marked. What differs is that Solomon *knows* the beginning, end, and middle of times. As it happens, Solomon's knowledge is more "scientific" than prophetic. His understanding of what exists (τῶν ὄντων) includes "the structure of the world and the activity of the elements; the beginning and end and middle of times, the alternations of the solstices and the changes of the seasons; the cycles of the year and the changes of the seasons" etc.

---

[251] Second century BCE, according to R.G. Robertson in *OTP* 2: 804. The translations quoted are from this edition.

[252] Greek text in Eusebius, Pr. Ev. 9.29.6.5, ed. Mras. Note that the division of time into past, present, future is represented *in the vision* by a division of space into heaven, earth, below the earth. The parallel does not hold strictly for John, since he is willing to present a four-fold division of creation in e.g. 5:13, "every creature in heaven and on the earth and under the earth and on the sea..."

[253] We may compare the words of Enoch in 2 En. 39:5 (J): "I have been sent today to you from the lips of the Lord, to speak to you whatever has been and whatever is now and whatever will be until the day of judgment." Trans. F.I. Andersen, in *OTP*, 1: 162. The uncertainty of the date and provenance of the work make further discussion difficult. It is of interest, however, that Enoch here receives the type of insight ascribed to Moses in the Exagoge.

[254] Gk. εἰδέναι...ἀρχὴν καὶ τέλος καὶ μεσότητα χρόνων.

(7:17-19 RSV). "The beginning, end, and middle of times" refers to the cycles of the natural world rather than to eschatology.[255]

The underlying assumption of these texts is that God knows the past, present, and future, hence he can bestow such understanding upon prophets and wise men. Judith prays, "For thou hast done these things and those that went before and those that followed; thou hast designed the things that are now, and those that are to come (Jud. 9:5, RSV)."[256] God not only knows the past, present, and future. He knows them because he causes all things to happen according to his will. God's overview of human history is bound up in Jewish thinking with his control of that history. We have already noted Philo's use of a *Dreizeitenformel* in a related way in *Quod Deus* 32.

Early Jewish literature, then, does show acquaintance with the *Dreizeitenformel*. It could be used to describe prophecy, recalling the Homeric model in *Il*. 1.70. It could also on occasion be used to describe God himself. Many, if not most, of the instances we have cited are found within works which exhibit a strong hellenistic influence (e.g. Wisdom, Philo's works; Ezekiel Trag.; Sibylline Oracles). It seems most plausible to me that the formula entered Judaism from the Greek world, and was adapted by Jewish writers to describe their faith in a way that made sense within that world. This did not necessarily involve a change in the content of the Hebrew scriptures. God's eternity is presupposed in many writings, while the ability of the prophet to speak of the past, present, and future was evident in the activity of Moses in the Pentateuch. What had changed was the idiom.

Later Materials

Van Unnik's survey of *Dreizeitenformeln* in the ancient world[257] includes a considerable sampling of material which post-dates the composition of Revelation, and his work need not be duplicated here. We will only underscore the fact that the three-times formula remained a popular way of describing God or prophecy within both Christian and pagan circles. It appears in the Epistle of Barnabas (1:7; 5:3); the *Apology* of Theophilus (1:14; 2:9); Irenaeus *Adv. Haer.* 4:33.1; Hippolytus *De Antichristo* 2; and

---

[255] Not that these are gifts are not from God: In 1 Ki. 4:33 Solomon's God-given wisdom includes knowledge of the natural world.

[256] Gk. σὺ γὰρ ἐποίησας τὰ πρότερα ἐκείνων καὶ ἐκεῖνα καὶ τὰ μετέπειτα καὶ τὰ νῦν καὶ τὰ ἐπερχόμενα διενοήθης. Cf. Sir. 42:19: "He (= God) declares what has been and what is to be...(RSV)"; 2 Bar. 21:5: "You...have seen the things which are to come as well as those which have passed" (trans. A.F.J. Klijn, in *OTP* 1: 628); 1 En. 39:11: "...he knows what is forever and what will be from generation to generation..." (trans. E. Isaac in *OTP* 1: 31).

[257] van Unnik, "Formula," pp.86–94.

Ps-Clementine Homilies, Hom. 2:6.1.[258] Examples can also be found in the Apocryphon of John ; a magical papyrus; Orphic Hymn 25:4–5; the Tübingen Theosophy; and the Hermetic treatise Asclepius 14,29,34.[259] None of the formulae are especially close to what we have in Revelation. They are closer to the versions found in Homer or the Presocratic philosophers. This gives us further evidence that: a) John's use of the *Dreizeitenformel* was not unique, but was rather part of a widespread pattern in the ancient world; and b) His particular *formulation* of the *Dreizeitenformel*, while close to that of the Targums, is nonetheless unique, and shows considerable theological reflection.

Summary: The Name's Encounter with Hellenism

It is evident that there was Greek influence on at least some Jewish interpretations of the name YHWH. This is most evident (not surprisingly) in works written in Greek, and reaches its climax in the writings of Philo. It is also present in some rabbinic writings. But speaking about "influence" without further ado is somewhat pointless. What is important is *how* Greek thinking influenced Jewish reflection on the name; or, better, how Jewish thinkers faced the challenges posed by Hellenism.

For heuristic purposes we may distinguish between the *form* and *content* of Jewish interpretations of the name. We start with form. One should not forget that any writer working in Greek was thereby "influenced" by Greek culture. If nothing else, they were acknowledging that the Greek language was a suitable medium for telling Israel's story. The effect on the name might seem slight in some instances; for example, when the name Iao was transliterated into Greek characters. At other times, the introduction of a Greek term – most notably ὁ ὤν – would open up a new range of associations in philosophy or religion. It is possible that a "philosophical" etymology like ὁ ὤν was introduced in part out of a desire to match corresponding hellenistic formulae such as "Zeus is the one through whom all things have life." We have also argued that the *Dreizeitenformel* was originally a Greek form. While a tri-partite description of time seems quite natural to us, it is not attested in Jewish literature before the hellenistic era.

The interpretations of YHWH show varying levels of engagement with Greek culture in their content, as well. The rabbinic exegesis of Ex. 3:14 focused on the name's meaning for Israel, and the content was drawn largely from the Hebrew bible (most notably Is. 40–66). God's name could

---

[258] All these citations, with Greek or Latin text, may be found in van Unnik, "Formula," pp.88–9.
[259] Texts in van Unnik, "Formula," pp.90–3.

refer to his role as creator of the world (Tgs. N, Ps-Jon. Ex. 3:14); as deliverer at the Exodus (b. Ber. 9b; Tg. Ngl 2); as present help in Israel's troubles (b. Ber. 9b); or as the future hope for his people in the world to come (Tgs. N, FT (G,W) Ex. 3:14). The Greeks and Romans factor in only as those who are currently oppressing Israel. They are slotted into the role of Pharaoh and are thus completely submerged into Israel's traditional story.

Even when we depart from the rabbinic writings, we find that the understanding of YHWH stands largely in continuity with the biblical tradition. This is true even for the quintessentially "hellenistic" designation ὁ ὤν. The original use of this term in Ex. 3:14 LXX is embedded in the biblical text, and must receive its primary interpretation from the surrounding context. Later uses of ὁ ὤν develop it in various ways, but they seldom depart from themes found in the Hebrew Bible. For Josephus, Philo (at times), and the authors of the Wisdom of Solomon and the third Sibylline Oracle, ὁ ὤν expressed the true Being of God versus the Not-Being of idols. The third Sibylline Oracle also appears to take ὁ ὤν as a short-hand designation for God's eternity, which can be expanded into the formula "...he himself, eternal, revealed himself as existing now, and formerly, and again in the future." God's eternity is likewise in view in AC 8.5.1ff. 4 Ezra 8:7 affirms that only God has independent existence, a view which could easily be extrapolated from the biblical teaching of God as creator.

At times, of course, the connection with the biblical tradition could be more tenuous. We have suggested that echoes of Platonism may be heard in the unlikely environs of Qumran, where the idea of τὸ ὄν as the "blueprint" for the universe appears to have found its way into 1QS and 1QH. The effect of Greek philosophy on Philo is more readily apparent. Basing himself, at least in part, on Ex. 3:14 LXX, Philo develops the ideas of God's necessary existence and timelessness in ways that go somewhat beyond what one finds in the actual biblical text. At times the tension between the traditional religion and Greek philosophy becomes more keen. When Philo, probably quoting a Greek source, states in *Mut.* 27 that τὸ γὰρ ὄν, ᾗ ὄν ἐστιν, οὐχὶ τῶν πρός τι, the sensitive reader might well cringe. How can the God who speaks in the Pentateuch be described as *not* of the πρός τι?

What may we conclude from all this? Hellenization was a reality, and its impact was felt in the Jewish interpretation of the name YHWH. But we must also remember that Hellenism did not spring fully born into the world, like Athena from Zeus' head. It was a part of the ancient world, and even its greatest philosophers regularly drew upon ideas and images from the broader ancient Mediterranean milieu. The Greeks, to take the most apposite example, did not invent the verb to be. Moreover, Hellenism was itself shaped by the cultures it had conquered. This was not simply in its adoption of "foreign" gods – hellenistic philosophy was profoundly influenced by thinkers from outside the Greek mainland.

When we take all this into account, the Jewish interpretation of YHWH must be seen as a positive response to the challenge of Hellenism. The Jewish thinkers we have examined effectively maintained their traditional beliefs, and at the same time they addressed the legitimate questions posed by Greek philosophy. For some people, any gesture towards the West might have been interpreted as a "Platonizing" of the ancient faith. But to ignore the philosophical conversation would be to admit that the Jewish faith was an irrelevant middle eastern cult which was uninterested in, or incapable of dealing with, the profound issues that perplexed the Greeks. This would hardly be in keeping with a faith which proclaimed that its God was the creator of the world and the sovereign Lord of the universe.

God's declaration of his name, "I am who I am," served as a natural bridge between Jewish and Greek thinking. The rabbis were willing to explain this in a Greek fashion at times, that God was and is and will be in the future. This is admittedly a minor borrowing, but a borrowing nonetheless. What is remarkable is that even when Jewish writers made a more significant gesture towards Hellenism, as in the use of ὁ ὤν, they usually remained firmly rooted in Israel's story. If anything, philosophical discourse was drawn into the Jewish tradition, and the "Greek" concepts were eclipsed by the biblical narrative. Rather than speaking of the "hellenization" of YHWH, it might be better to speak of the "judaization" of τὸ ὄν. The disparate notions of "Being" in Greek thought have been captured and redefined in the light of the God of Israel, "the One who is."

As with any encounter with a foreign culture, there was a risk involved. In the case of the name, this risk may be seen most clearly in the writings of Philo, who at times seems to blur (or obliterate) the distinctions between hellenistic philosophy and the biblical tradition. But Philo is, after all, still commenting on the Pentateuch, and he remains a faithful member of the visible Jewish community. And even his most radical statements connected with the name (such as τὸ ὄν ᾗ ὄν not being of the πρός τι) might be seen as extreme statements of legitimate biblical principles concerning God's distinction from the creation.

The Jewish encounter with Greek thinking did not cease with the fall of Jerusalem. It continues in one form or another to this day, and not the least of its concerns is the name and Being of God. But that story must be told some other time. We must now turn to the final chapter of our story, the interpretation of the name by the author of the Apocalypse. In what form does YHWH come to Patmos?

Chapter 4

Revelation

As we turn at last to Rev. 1:4 itself, we will organize our discussion around three basic questions. What was the source(s) for John's formula ὁ ὢν καὶ ὁ ἦν καὶ ὁ ἐρχόμενος? Why did John choose to include this formula in his book? How does John use the formula in 1:4 and elsewhere in the book?

Sources

The Old Testament nowhere describes God as one who "was, is, and is to come/will be." If any Christian used the expression before John, we have no record of it. We have noted some of the problems of positing a Persian background to the phrase in our discussion of the oracle from Dodona. Even if one could demonstrate that the description of Ahura Mazda in *Bund.*1:3 is the earliest example of the *Dreizeitenformel* being applied to deity, it is exceedingly unlikely that John would have known about it first hand. The probability is that John adapted his formula either from the pagan hellenistic world or from early Judaism.

We will first consider the possibility that John drew directly upon Greek sources. This option has not appealed to most commentators, and as we will see there are admittedly serious difficulties with it. But even raising the question may yield some insights into John's situation. While the following considerations are put forth merely as suggestions, they build upon premises which most scholars would accept, namely: 1) John wrote Greek; 2) John considered himself to be in some sense to be a prophetic figure; and 3) John had a certain authority within the churches of the province of Asia.

Whether John employed an amanuensis is uncertain, but if he did, the amanuensis did nothing to smooth over John's language.[1] It would seem that John is responsible for the text as we have it. If he wrote Greek, then he presumably could read and speak Greek as well. He would thus have

---

[1] For examples of John's aberrant Greek see e.g. H. B. Swete, *The Apocalypse of Saint John* (London: Macmillan, 1906), pp.cxxiv ff.

had ample opportunity to be exposed to hellenistic culture. David Aune has unearthed a significant amount of hellenistic imagery within Revelation.[2] John, he writes, "used pagan imagery and practices as part of a broad apologetic assault on Graeco-Roman culture itself."[3] Part of John's apologetic program consists in the re-interpretation of traditional mythology from a Christian perspective, the most notable instance of which is the apparent use of the Typhon myth (among others) in Revelation 12.[4]

If such allusions indicate a broader interest in Greco-Roman religion and mythology, John might have had occasion to read the works of Homer or Hesiod, which would have been widely available. This must not be dismissed out of hand, since Homer and Hesiod clearly influenced the Jewish portions of the first and second Sibylline Oracles, which appear to have been written in Asia Minor a generation before John.[5] As we have pointed out, the *Dreizeitenformeln* occupy a prominent position in the early parts of the *Iliad* and the *Theogony*, and they are both concerned with prophetic utterance. Is it unthinkable that John, a prophet himself, could have been interested in his hellenistic "competition" in the sphere of prophecy? It will be argued below that Rev. 1:19, "Write therefore what you have seen, what they are and what is going to happen after them," is (in part) a statement of John's prophetic vocation, which is deliberately modeled on the three-fold description of God in 1:4. The comparable Homeric formula, ἤδη τά τ' ἐόντα τά τ' ἐσσόμενα πρό τ' ἐόντα, had currency (at least in literary circles) down to the imperial age and beyond. The appearance of the formula at the beginning of John's work, meanwhile, recalls the use of *Dreizeitenformeln* in the proem to Hesiod's *Theogony*.

Let us turn to the matter of John's authority within the churches of Asia. Not everyone has been convinced by the attempts of Ramsay and Hemer to identify precise local references throughout the messages to the twelve churches.[6] At the same time, it seems improbable that John's insights into the situation of each congregation were gained purely at second-hand (see

---

[2] See his commentary, *passim*.

[3] David E. Aune, "The Apocalypse of John and Graeco-Roman Revelatory Magic," *NTS* 33 (1987): 481.

[4] See George R. Beasley-Murray, *The Book of Revelation* (London: Oliphants, 1974.), pp.191–7; Elisabeth Schüssler Fiorenza, *Revelation: Vision of a Just World* (Edinburgh: T.&T. Clark, 1993), pp.26–31.

[5] See Collins, in *OTP* 1: 330–4; Alfons Kurfess, "Homer und Hesiod im 1. Buch der Oracula Sibyllina," *Philologus* 100 (1956): 147–53; Trebilco, pp.95–6.

[6] W. M. Ramsay, *The Letters to the Seven Churches of Asia* (London: Hodder and Stoughton, 1904); Colin J. Hemer, *The Letters to the Seven Churches of Asia in their Local Setting* (Sheffield: JSOT, 1986). See also John M. Court, *Myth and History in the Book of Revelation* (London: SPCK, 1979), pp.20–42. For a recent critique of the first two works, see Steven J. Friesen, "Revelation, Realia, and Religion: Archaeology in the Interpretation of the Apocalypse," *HTR* 88 (1995): 291–314.

e.g. 2:21). If one grants that John was in Patmos because of conspicuous Christian activity, we have further evidence that he was a notable leader of the church in this region (even if that authority may not have been universally acknowledged).[7] Assuming John was such a leader, we might expect him to be engaged in defending the Christian faith against pagan as well as Jewish critiques. John's opposition to the synagogue – at least insofar as particular synagogues set themselves against the Christian church – is clear enough from Revelation. We cannot exclude the possibility that John also had to respond to philosophical queries from interested (or hostile) Gentiles within the Asian cities. Whether some would-be philosopher, clutching his handbook of philosophical opinions, ever questioned John about what "was, is, and will be" is impossible to say, but it cannot be excluded *prima facie*.

John's knowledge of Homer, Hesiod, or the Greek philosophers may well be questioned. The above examples are put forward merely as possibilities. There is, however, good reason for viewing John against the backdrop of hellenistic "cosmic religion." The attempts to read John in this way have unfortunately tended to excess, and have ignored or underestimated more traditional approaches.[8] This should not prevent us from seeing that John's work does have a significant connection with, for instance, the ps-aristotelian *De Mundo* or Cleanthes' *Hymn to Zeus*. Like them, John is concerned to speak about the whole of reality, and particularly the nature of the God who rules the cosmos. It is also worth remembering that the characters in the works of both Parmenides and Plato (in the Phaedrus) learn about "that which (really) is" by piercing through the heavenly dome. This is precisely how John encounters "the One who is." This does not of course prove that John was directly familiar with either Parmenides or Plato, but it does suggest a common way of looking at the world.[9]

We have proposed that the *Dreizeitenformel* used with respect to deity was a part of the religious *koine* of this "cosmic religion," and as such may

---

[7] Bauckham (*Theology*, p.4) suggests that John may not have been exiled to Patmos, but rather went there in order to receive the revelation. Leonard Thompson argues in a similar vein that John may have gone to Patmos to preach (pp.172–3). For arguments in favor of the traditional argument that John was banished to Patmos, see A.Y. Collins, *Crisis and Catharsis: The Power of the Apocalypse* (Philadelphia: Westminster, 1984), pp.102–4; Beasley-Murray, pp.12–4.

[8] Notably F. Boll, *Aus der Offenbarung Johannis* (Amsterdam: Hakkert, 1967; repr. Leipzig: Teubner, 1914), and more recently Bruce Malina, *On the Genre and Message of Revelation* (Peabody, MA: Hendrickson, 1995), see esp. pp. 1–10, 12–8. Malina's work does contain much helpful comparative material, although in my opinion he presses it too hard to prove that Revelation is "astral prophecy."

[9] Recall, too, that the "wisdom" possessed by the writers of 1QS 10–11 and 1QH 20 consists in part of the knowledge of the *heavenly bodies* as they relate to the proper seasons for worship.

have been known to John. Variations of the formula may be found at two major religious centers in Greece, Dodona and Eleusis; in Egypt (the inscription at Saïs); and in Asia Minor (Rev. 1:4). There is a wide geographical spread. (The inscription at Eleusis is the work of Romans, which indicates the phrase may also have had currency in Italy.) If John were aware of such formulations, we may suppose that he would have reacted negatively to them. "Zeus was, Zeus is, Zeus will be, O mighty Zeus!" for instance, would hardly be a rallying cry for John. While some Jews, like the author of the Letter of Aristeas, seemed willing to concede that "Zeus" might be an appropriate epithet for God, at least for pagans, it is hard to imagine John being among their number.[10] It is equally hard to imagine John writing as effusively about Isis as does Plutarch. The inscription at Saïs implicitly identifies Isis/Athena/Neïth as the goddess of revelation, as is indicated by the use of ἀπεκάλυψεν, and Plutarch goes on to say that she reveals τὸ ὄν, "that which is." Surely John would perceive the devotees of Isis as his religious rivals.

The Aion inscription is especially instructive. If one interprets it as an expression of the deity of the eternal cosmos itself, this would constitute a blasphemous blurring of boundaries between the creation and the One who "created all things" (Rev.4:11). John's cosmos, moreover, in no way "remains exactly the same" (lines b.1-2 of the Eleusis inscription). The heavenly bodies themselves, which are the epitome of stability in the cosmic religion of the hellenistic age, are subject to disruption at the command of God (see especially Rev. 6:12-14). Even if one puts the best face on it (from a Christian perspective) and envisions Aion as simply the force which created and continues to order the universe, it seems unlikely that John would wish to substitute the quasi-personal name "Aion" for other more traditional titles of God. He is perfectly willing to describe God as "the one who lives forever and ever" (4:9: ...τῷ ζῶντι εἰς τοὺς αἰῶνας τῶν αἰώνων), but this stops well short of making Aion itself a divine name. John may in fact be making a subtle distinction between God and Aion in chapter 1 by reference to the divine name Ἰαώ, which may be an answer to the claims of *ΑΙΩΝ*.[11]

---

[10] Some of John's names for God, such as "the Beginning and the End," may have parallels in pagan religions (cf. van Unnik's *Het Godspredikat*), but he does not describe God with personal divine names drawn from the hellenistic milieu. The one possible reference to a pagan divine name – Ἀπολλύων (Rev.9:11), which may be a pun on Apollo – is hardly positive.

[11] The similarity of Iao and Aion has been noted by many scholars, including F. Dornseiff, cited by Traugott Holtz, *Die Christologie der Apokalypse des Johannes*, 2nd. ed. (Berlin: Akademie-Verlag, 1971, p.149n); and Austin Farrer, *A Rebirth of Images* (Westminster: Dacre Press, 1949), p.264. I argue below for the influence of Iao on v. 8. I

Aion also suffered from "guilt by association." The inscription from Eleusis explicitly invokes Aion to prop up the Roman state, not to mention the Eleusinian mysteries themselves, which were no doubt equally abhorrent to John.[12] The relief plates from Aphrodisias present Aion in the same role, although here, as far as we can tell, the point is made with images rather than words. While the continuance of Rome may have conjured up images of enduring peace and prosperity to some people, John's reaction would have been more in keeping with George Orwell's vision of the future: "Imagine a boot stamping on a face – forever." From John's perspective, "Eternal Rome" could only translate as "Eternal Oppression."[13] One could easily envision the *Dreizeitenformel* serving as a slogan for Aion devotees not only at Eleusis but in Asia Minor as well. If this is so, John's description of God as "the One who is and was and is coming" could serve as a direct attack on the (false) god who was believed to be the guarantor of Roman rule.[14]

I believe the connection with Aion is the most promising option of all the ones surveyed above. Before we conclude, however, that John's immediate source was Aion veneration – or more particularly, Aion veneration as a means of maintaining Roman rule – we must examine the Jewish evidence. The parallels in the Targums given by McNamara are hard to dismiss, and commentators are almost universally agreed that Rev. 1:4 heark-

---

am not necessarily convinced that John was deliberately contrasting Iao and Aion in this text, but it is a distinct possibility.

[12] It is worth remembering that Josephus treats the name of God as a great mystery, and indeed uses language reminiscent of the Eleusinian mysteries when discussing the name.

[13] See e.g. J. Nelson Kraybill, *Imperial Culture and Commerce in John's Apocalypse* (Sheffield: JSOT, 1996), esp. pp.57–101. On p.57 he cites a graffito in Ephesus, "Rome, queen over all, your power will never end." Cf. Rev. 18:7, "I sit as a queen and I am not a widow, and I will never see mourning..." The destruction of Babylon/Rome "in a single day" (18:8) may be an ironic retort to Rome's claim to eternity. See also John Sweet, *Revelation* (London: SCM Press, 1990; Philadelphia: Westminster Press, 1990), p.61, who contrasts John's vision of the future with the *aeternitas* on Roman coinage.

[14] We may compare with this the designation "Our Lord and God" (ὁ κύριος καὶ θεὸς ἡμῶν), which bears a striking resemblance to Domitian's (alleged) self-description as *dominus et deus noster*. (See, e.g. Holtz, *Christologie*, p.12; Thompson, pp.15 ff.; Kraybill, pp. 62ff. Whether Domitian actually called himself that is immaterial; it is clear the phrase was associated with him.) The application of the title to God is a polemical transformation of the imperial title. In a similar way, van Unnik believes John appropriates the designation "the Beginning and the End" from hellenistic culture (at least in part) and says in effect, "Our God fulfills this." (van Unnik, *Het Godspredikat*, p.76). Cf. Aune, "Magic," p.489. For OT backgrounds see G.K. Beale, "The Old Testament Background of Rev. 3:14," *NTS* 42 (1996): 133–52. As is the case 1:4, both the Greek and the OT backgrounds must be taken with full seriousness. There may also be an ironic reference to Rome as the "eternal city" in 18:7.

ens back to Ex. 3:14 directly or indirectly.[15] The fact that the traditions adduced by McNamara derive from Exodus traditions solidifies his case.[16] John makes frequent use of Exodus motifs throughout the Apocalypse (e.g. in the plague sequences of the visions).[17] Chapter 1 itself makes use of the kingdom/priests motif (v.6, cf. Ex.19:6,23:22); the Sinai theophany (v.10, cf. Ex.19:16);[18] and the golden lampstands (vv.12-13, cf. Ex.25). A reference to the episode of the burning bush would not be out of place.

In fact, it would admirably suit John's purposes. John's book may be fairly described as a "New Exodus," as God delivers his people from their oppressors. (This is not to deny, of course, that many other OT motifs, notably the role of Babylon, are essential to Revelation.) It would be most fitting to introduce such a work with a reference to YHWH, the personal name of the God of the Exodus, the name which was revealed to Moses at the beginning of the Exodus deliverance. It is noteworthy that in Rev. 1:4-8, the nature of God is primarily articulated through the *names* or titles of God, particularly the names related to YHWH.[19] The connection of "the One who is and who was and who is to come" (1:4) with the name YHWH should be evident by this point. We will argue below that the designations in 1:8 are likewise derived from three variations of the name YHWH; namely, Ἰαώ ("the Alpha and the Omega"); YHWH Elohim ("the Lord God"); and YHWH Sabaoth ("...who is and who was and who is to come, the Almighty"). Apparently John felt that an interpretation of these divine

---

[15] See e.g. Beasley-Murray, p.54; J. Massyngbe Ford *Revelation* (Garden City, NY: Doubleday, 1975), pp.376-7; R.H. Charles. *A Critical and Exegetical Commentary on the Revelation of St. John.* 2 vols. (Edinburgh: T.&T. Clark, 1920), 1: 10; Isbon T. Beckwith, *The Apocalypse of John* (London: Macmillan, 1919), p.424; Swete, p.5.

[16] This is true even of Tg. Ps-Jon. Dt. 32:39. As we have argued above, this appears to be a conflation of traditions surrounding Ex. 3:14 and Isaiah 40 ff.

[17] For more references see, e.g., McNamara, pp.97-8.

[18] The unusual expression "I turned to *see* the voice that was speaking to me" (Rev. 1:12: καὶ ἐπέστρεψα βλέπειν τὴν φωνὴν ἥτις ἐλάλει μετ' ἐμοῦ) may well derive from Ex. 20:18: וכל העם ראים את הקולת ..."And all the people perceiving (or *seeing*) the thunders/noises..." The LXX reads καὶ πᾶς ὁ λαὸς ἑώρα τὴν φωνήν. For discussion see Aune, *Revelation 1-5*, pp.87-8.

[19] Apart from the divine names I mention, all that is said of God in Chapter 1 is that He gives the revelation (v.1) and that He is the Father of Jesus Christ (v.6). There are also two occurrences of the "word of God" (vv.2,9). We are of course speaking in very precise terms here. Since Jesus himself ultimately reveals God, what is said of Jesus may from a certain perspective apply equally to the Father (note, e.g., the parallels between vv.12-16 and the visions of God in Daniel and Ezekiel). The point is that the explicit references to God the Father focus on divine titles. (I also concur with Bauckham, *Theology*, p.24, that John deliberately alters traditional titles such as "God our Father" for his own purposes. I have nonetheless retained them here for convenience, since John also is deliberately "Trinitarian" in his presentation of God (again see Bauckham, *Theology*, p.24).)

names would provide the best introduction to the God whose majesty will become evident in the following visions.

The use of traditions drawn from Ex. 3:14 would not only aid John in his presentation of God. It would also implicitly bolster his self-presentation as a prophet of God. The burning bush episode is a revelation both of the authority of God, and the derivative authority of his spokesman Moses. This is not to say that John portrays himself as a "second Moses" or downgrades Moses to exalt himself. Moses was viewed as the prototype of Israel's prophets (Dt. 18:15), and the prophets' call narratives often echo that of their forebear (see e.g. Jeremiah 1:4–19). Indeed, the narrative of divine revelation was a common motif of the ancient world, as the example of Hesiod shows. If you were going to speak about things normally hidden from humanity, you had to have a good explanation for your authority for doing so.[20] What makes John's use of Exodus interesting, as we have noted, is the fact that he combines the divine designation ("the One who is and who was and who is to come") with a similar formula concerning his prophetic vocation ("Write what you have seen and what they are and what is going to happen after them," 1:19).

That John does in fact avail himself of the traditions surrounding Ex. 3:14 becomes clear when we compare Rev. 1:4 with texts such as Tg. Ps-Jon. Dt. 32:39, which itself depends on the ancient exegesis of Ex. 3:14[21]:

חמון כדון ארום אנא הוא דהוי והוית ואנא הוא דעתיד למהוי ולית
אלהא הורן בר מיני

See now that I am he who is and who was and I am he who will be, and there is no other God beside me. (McNamara)

It is almost certain that the Jewish tradition does not depend on Revelation, but rather that John is dependent on a Jewish tradition like that represented above.[22] John has of course adapted it for his own purposes. While the aberrant Greek of Rev.1:4 may well have been influenced by the Targumic tradition, it still represents a deliberate choice on John's part. He could have translated the tradition into better Greek (e.g. by inserting ἀπὸ τοῦ... before ὁ ὤν),[23] but he did not. He may have wished to stress the "indecli-

---

[20] See Aune's comment (*Revelation 1–5*, p.31): "Just as Moses was told by God to accredit his message by telling the people that ὁ ὤν had sent him, so John appears to be authenticating his prophetic book by claiming that its actual source is none other than ὁ ὤν..."

[21] For John's use of the Targums in general, see (in addition to the commentaries) McNamara, pp.117–25; and Mark Bredin, "The Influence of the Aqedah on Revelation 5:6–9," *Irish Biblical Studies* 18 (1996): 26–43.

[22] Hayward, p.34.

[23] See, e.g., Ernst Lohmeyer, *Die Offenbarung des Johannes* 2nd ed. (Tübingen: J.C.B. Mohr (Paul Siebeck), 1953), p.10. Note, too, that John includes the article (which

nability" of God's name.[24] The grammatical solecism would also draw attention to the fact that he is alluding to the OT, in keeping with his practice elsewhere in Revelation.[25] Most importantly, of course, he deviates from the tradition by employing ὁ ἐρχόμενος as his final element.

The proximate source for John's formula, then, appears to have been something like the tradition preserved in Ps.-Jon. Dt. 32:39. But we have already noted that there was likely some Greek influence on this tradition itself. Moreover, Sibylline Oracles 1 and 3 give evidence that ὁ ὤν and the *Dreizeitenformel* were used elsewhere as a part of an apologetic program for Judaism. Thus while John is obviously indebted to his Jewish heritage for this designation of God, we cannot exclude the possibility that he employed the tradition in a polemical fashion. If the veneration of Aion in Asia Minor included the use of the phrase, "was and is and will be," John would have been able to draw upon the Jewish traditions to counter a clear and present danger to the faith of his audience – the veneration of a false god who was invoked to prop up the despised Roman empire. If John were not aware of the association of the *Dreizeitenformel* with Aion, "the One who is and who was and who is to come" would still provide a dramatic opening for a work committed to exalting the one God above any rivals.

Use of the *Dreizeitenformel*

The preceding paragraph gives a brief answer to *why* John used the *Dreizeitenformel* in his work. Before this question can be fully answered, however, it is necessary to look in depth at *how* John uses the formula in 1:4 and in the rest of Revelation. We will first look at the context of Rev. 1:4; we will follow this with a section on the significance of *names* in Revelation; and then we will examine the components of the formula one by one.

This last point may require some justification. It is evident that the elements "the One who is," "the One who was," and "the One who is to

---

is strictly speaking not present in וְהֹוֶית) in ὁ ἦν, probably to maintain a symmetry with ὁ ὤν and ὁ ἐρχόμενος.

[24] See e.g. Beckwith, p.424; Lohmeyer, p.10: "Gott ist indeklinabel, daher der Nom." (The word "God," of course, is declined throughout Revelation (e.g. 1:2).). G. B. Caird writes, "God is, so to speak, always in the nominative, always the subject..." (*A Commentary on the Revelation of St. John the Divine*; London: A.&C. Black, 1966), p.16. But Sweet (p.65) aptly remarks that this "cannot be pressed, or it must apply to the devil, too (20:2)!"

[25] G.K. Beale has noted that John's grammatical "errors" frequently serve to highlight Old Testament allusions in the text of Revelation. See his forthcoming commentary on Revelation (Grand Rapids, MI: Eerdmans/Exeter: Paternoster).

come" cannot be completely divorced from the formulae in which they occur. They are not *necessarily* each independent divine epithets. At the same time, the widespread use of ὁ ὤν as a divine title, coupled with the unusual grammatical form of the phrase, makes one suspect that John could have seen each term as meaningful in and of itself, as well as making a contribution to the whole.[26]

Context

John adapts traditional *Dreizeitenformeln* for his own purposes in Revelation. In a similar way, John adapts the traditional greeting formula of Christian letters in order to express his unique theological perspective. In place of the expected, "Grace and peace to you from God our Father and the Lord Jesus Christ,"[27] we have, "Grace to you and peace from the one who is and who was and who is to come, and from the seven spirits which are before his throne and from Jesus Christ, the faithful witness, the firstborn of the dead and the ruler of the kings of the earth."[28] If nothing else, this dramatic expansion of the usual form would have roused the attention of listeners for whom the greeting had become a meaningless prelude to the "real" content of the letter.

Since our phrase recurs a number of times in Revelation in various guises, its appearance in the greeting formula cannot be the sole guide to its meaning. Nonetheless, its presence here indicates the importance John attached to the designation "the One who is and who was and is to come." He wants his readers and hearers to know that the God in whose name John offers "grace and peace" is not simply a treasured part of their religious heritage, nor one option in the marketplace of hellenistic religion. He is the God who created the cosmos, who rules over it, and who is coming to renew that cosmos and deliver his people. His involvement with humanity is so intimate that he achieves his kingdom through the sacrifice of his own Son.

What is in a Name?

There are sound exegetical reasons for seeing "the One who is and who was and who is to come" as an interpretation of the name YHWH. The

---

[26] See Aune, *Revelation 1-5*, pp.30-1.

[27] Rom. 1:7; 1 Cor. 1:3; 2 Cor. 1:2, etc.; cf. 1 Pet. 1:2-3; 2 Jn. 3; Jude 1-2.

[28] This is noted by most commentators; see e.g. Beasley-Murray, pp.53-4; Kraft, p.31; Sweet, p.61. O. Hofius points out that the three-fold description of Christ (faithful witness/firstborn/ruler) matches the three-fold description of God in the previous verse. See Hofius, "Das Zeugnis der Johannesoffenbarung von der Gottheit Jesu Christi," in *Geschichte - Tradition - Reflexion: Festschrift für Martin Hengel zum 70. Geburtstag; Vol. III: Frühes Christentum*, ed. Hermann Lichtenberger (J.C.B. Mohr (Paul Siebeck), 1996: 511-28), p.512.

power of names in antiquity is well documented, and the use of divine etymologies had a long history in both Jewish and Greek thought. We have taken a special interest in the widespread use of the formula "Zeus is the one through whom all things have life." While there is no evidence that John was aware of this etymology, his own use of the name YHWH is comparable. In place of a traditional divine name, John offers his readers a sophisticated "unpacking" of the name which reveals its universal significance. The tetragrammaton was well-positioned for such etymological uses. By the time John was writing, it had acquired a certain air of mystery, particularly with regards to its pronunciation. Yet it was not so obscure as to be completely beyond the knowledge of at least some of John's audience. Furthermore, there was a history of interpretation of the name YHWH, beginning with the writing of Ex. 3:14 itself, upon which John could draw. It is hardly surprising that John, with his keen interest in signs and their interpretation, should have been drawn to the tetragrammaton.

For the sake of completeness we should mention the general significance of names in Revelation. Names are quite important to John, as a scan of his use of τὸ ὄνομα reveals. Jesus possesses a name which no one knows but himself (19:12), although the name by which he is called is "the Word of God" (19:13). The faithful hold to the name of Jesus (2:13; 3:8) and suffer for it (2:3). In return they receive "the name of my God, and the name of the city of my God...and my own new name" (3:12;cf. 2:17, 14:1, 22:4). Their names are in the book of life (3:5). The beast, by contrast, has a blasphemous name on his heads (13:1; cf. the harlot in 17:3,5), and his followers are marked with his name on their right hand or forehead (13:16-7). Their names are not in the book of life (13:8,17:8).

Names in Revelation primarily serve to designate ownership or allegiance.[29] This is an interesting topic in and of itself, but for reasons of space we will restrict ourselves to the question of whether the name of God referred to in 3:12; 14:1; and 22:4 is in fact the tetragrammaton.[30] John could have in mind the YHWH inscription on the headdress of the high priest. According to the Targums Neofiti and Ps-Jon (Ex. 32:25), the wilderness generation as a whole shared in this privilege, wearing golden crowns inscribed with "the great and glorious name" (though they were removed after the incident of the golden calf). Since John's people are likewise a kingdom of priests (1:6; cf. Ex. 19:6), he could have availed

---

[29] Cf. Charles, 1: 92.

[30] Charles believes the "seal" in 7:3 is in fact the divine name. Others suggest that the seal may refer to the sign given to the believer at baptism – the *tau* (cf. Ezek. 9:4) which according to J. Daniélou, represents the divine name (see Daniélou, *Primitive Christian Symbols*; trans. Donald Attwater; Baltimore: Helicon Press, 1964, pp.140–1; cf. Sweet, p.105). Daniélou provides no evidence for this association of *tau* and YHWH, so I cannot endorse his opinion. Beasley-Murray (p.143) does not believe 7:3 refers to baptism.

himself of a similar image. We must also remember that the name was "put on Israel" in the benediction from Num. 6:22 ff., a practice that continued down to the New Testament era.[31] The name in the Numbers text is undoubtedly YHWH, which is repeated three times in the blessing. All of this indicates that John probably had the tetragrammaton in mind when he spoke of the name being "on" people in Revelation.

What remains uncertain, however, is whether the phrase in 3:12 "*my* (=Jesus') new name" likewise refers to the tetragrammon. As we have seen, early Christianity knew of traditions in which Jesus "received" or "bore" the divine name. Whether John knew of them is another question. The problem is that Jesus' "new name" in v.12 is distinguished from the "name of my God" earlier in the verse. It would appear that the overcomer receives the name of God (presumably YHWH); the name of the new Jerusalem (signifying citizenship[32]); and the new name of Jesus (which is left a secret). It is possible that John did have the tetragrammaton in mind in both the first and last cases, in which case we would have a further instance of John's high christology. But I find this unlikely. If one were to see Jesus' new name as the tetragrammaton, this might shed more light on John's description of God as the One who *is to come*: because Jesus shares God's name, it is appropriate to interpret that name in light of God's coming-in-Christ. The uncertainly surrounding 3:12, however, keeps this in the realm of speculation.

ὁ ὤν

McNamara writes that John was not "in any way influenced by this LXX usage..." in his use of ὁ ὤν.[33] While we cannot prove that John read Ex. 3:14 LXX, it is surely not impossible that he did so. In any case, the Septuagint translation is crucial as the foundation for all subsequent uses of ὁ ὤν. We have shown that ὁ ὤν, while by no means omnipresent, was nonetheless a significant feature of early Judaism and early Christianity alike. This may be traced back to Ex. 3:14 LXX. It is quite possible that Ps-Jon. Dt.32:39 itself is heavily indebted to the work of the Septuagint translators. This is not a matter of simple temporal priority. The translators of the LXX had taken a bold step with their rendering, one that put the etymology of YHWH in direct engagement with Greek religious and philosophical thought. A later author might conceivably either strengthen the philosophi-

---

[31] Beasley-Murray, p.333.

[32] Thus Aune, *Revelation 1–5*, p.243.

[33] McNamara, p.103. Most other commentators at least refer to the LXX; see e.g. Beasley-Murray, p.54; Swete, p.5; Caird, p.16; Sweet, p.65. Aune devotes the most attention to Ex. 3:14 LXX and the ensuing history of ὁ ὤν (*Revelation 1–5*, pp.30–1). I am obviously quite sympathetic to his point of view.

cal sense of ὁ ὤν (e.g. Philo) or diminish it (John?), but the philosophical overtones could not be wholly stripped away.

The most obvious meaning of ὁ ὤν in the context of Rev. 1:4 is, "the One who *now* is." If nothing else, John wants to assure his readers that God always exists. While one could indicate this with a two-fold formula (e.g. "the First and the Last"), the inclusion of the third element may give the expression a greater weight or a more pronounced poetic effect. It may also emphasize God's presence with his people *now*, despite appearances to the contrary (see below). As we have noted in our discussion of the Septuagint translation of Ex. 3:14, however, "The One who is" is an open-ended description that fairly begs for further explanation. This forces us to reckon with a number of different possibilities of interpretation, which may not be mutually exclusive. John may have wished to keep several nuances in play. Even if he had a definite meaning in mind, his readers may have understood it in a different way. We thus offer some of the major interpretative options in addition to the overt meaning of "the One who now is."

We may first consider the "veridical aspect" of the verb to be: "what is" is equivalent to "what is true or real." In the case of God, "the One who is" could therefore mean "the One who is true, the One who *really is* God." Wis. 13:1 and Sib. Or. 3:33 use ὁ ὤν in this way, contrasting the true God with idols, which are not God (cf. LXX Esther 4:17q). J. Ramsey Michaels has argued convincingly that John frequently exploits the veridical aspect of the verb to be in the book of Revelation. Although Michaels is particularly concerned with Rev. 1:19, he adduces numerous examples throughout the book in which "is" or "are" indicate not the present tense, but rather the *reality* of a thing or situation.[34] Although John does not explicitly refer to idols as "non-existent" (cf. LXX Esther), he comes close to this in Rev. 9:20: "The rest of mankind, who were not killed by these plagues, did not repent of the works of their hands nor give up worshipping demons and idols of gold and silver and bronze and stone and wood, which cannot either see or hear or walk..." There is a more pointed contrast between the God who *is* and would-be gods who *are not* in 17:8, where the beast is described with the words "...was, and *is not*, and is to ascend from the abyss and go to destruction." God fundamentally *is*; the Beast fundamentally *is not*.[35]

God is not simply distinct from false gods, of course. He is distinct from all other things as well. God is thus not only existent, he is *independently*

---

[34] Michaels, "Rev. 1.19 and the Narrative Voices of the Apocalypse," *NTS* 37 (1991): 604–20. Some of the clearest examples come from the messages to the churches, where people claim to be Jews or apostles, but are *not really* so (οὐκ εἰσιν; 2:2,9; 3:9).

[35] We will discuss this passage in detail below.

or *necessarily* existent. This is one of the pillars of Philo's theology of ὁ ὤν (*Mos.* 1: 74–6; *Det.* 160), and it also informs the statement *Solus enim es* in 4 Ez. 8:7. Since John does not use explicitly philosophical terms like "independently" or "necessarily" existent, we cannot demonstrate that he had this in mind when he used ὁ ὤν. But we might infer that John believes God is necessarily existent from the fact that God is the creator of all other entities.[36]

A third possibility is that ὁ ὤν is intended to emphasize God's presence with his people – "I am (or will be) *with you.*" Assuming that a writer has some familiarity with the context of Ex. 3:14 (especially 3:12), this idea could be borne by the Greek phrase ὁ ὤν.[37] As for Revelation, the messages to the seven churches depict Christ's intimate knowledge of his followers, and include promises of succor and discipline for them. The "seven Spirits" are likewise "the presence and power of God on earth."[38] God's continual existence undergirds his promise to be with his people. This would connect our text with the only other *Dreizeitenformel* in the NT, "Jesus Christ is the same yesterday, today, and forever" (Heb. 13:8). While one would not want to deny that God is in some sense present with his people, even in the midst of their tribulation, ὁ ὤν cannot be used unconditionally of "God's presence with his people." Revelation also recognizes a hope for God's people which is yet to be realized, and so ὁ ὤν must be read along with ὁ ἐρχόμενος.

Finally, we come to the temporal aspect of ὁ ὤν. We have seen that it may mean "God *now* is." We must also reckon with the possibility that it means God is the one who *always* is. Outside of Revelation, this interpretation is evidenced in Apostolic Constitutions 8:12 and in the inscription on the altar at Pergamum. In both cases ἀεί is added to ὁ ὤν to make the meaning clear. John does not do this, but he does use formulae like "the One (or God) who lives forever" (4:9,10; 10:6; 15:7) to express the eternity of God.[39] This may explain the priority of ὁ ὤν in 1:4. "God is the one who is – *that is*, he was and (implicitly) is and is to come."[40] Ὁ ὤν, in

---

[36] Cf. Bauckham, *Theology*, pp.50–1.

[37] See, e.g., T. Holtz in his essay "Gott in der Apokalypse" (in *L'Apocalypse johannique et l'Apocalyptique dans le Nouveau Testament*, ed. J. Lambrecht; Gembloux: Duculot/Louvain: University Press, 1980, p.250): "So ist Gott, gerade weil er der Schöpfer ist, immer auch der gegenwärtige Gott...Schon die Vorordnung von ὁ ὤν vor ὁ ἦν, die der gewöhnlichen Reihenfolge der Glieder widerspricht, hebt das Gegenwärtig-sein Gottes hervor..."

[38] Bauckham, *Theology*, p.113.

[39] Cf. Christ's words in 1:18, "...and behold I am living (ζῶν εἰμι) forever and ever."

[40] Farrer, p.267; cf. Anton Vögtle, "Der Gott der Apokalypse," in *La notion biblique de Dieu*, ed. J. Coppens; Gembloux: Duculot/Louvain: University Press, 1976, p.380. This would not keep John from using it as a "normal" present tense in, e.g. 4:8.

other words, is an abbreviated way of talking about the everlasting existence of God.

Does this mean, then, that John uses ὁ ὤν in anything like a Platonic sense, to express God's "timeless eternity"? The phrase in and of itself does not demand such an interpretation, but it could be taken that way by Christians, as Eusebius' favorable citation of Plutarch's *De E ap. Delphos* indicates. We can collect *testimonia* from modern scholars on both sides of the issue. Oscar Cullmann, for one, vehemently denies that the biblical God, in Revelation or elsewhere, is depicted as "timeless":

> Primitive Christianity knows nothing of a timeless God. The "eternal" God is he who was in the beginning, is now, and will be in all the future, "who is, who was, and who will be (sic)" (Rev. 1:4). Accordingly, his eternity can and must be expressed in this "naïve" way, in terms of endless time.[41]

G. B. Caird, by contrast, is willing to speak of God's "eternal present," a view which is endorsed by Minear,[42] and E. Lohmeyer makes the distinction between time and eternity (or timelessness) one of the keys to understanding the entire book of Revelation.[43]

The first step in attacking this problem is to isolate two senses in which people speak about "timelessness." The first, which we may call the "hard line," takes timelessness to be *non-durational eternity*. This might imply a certain "frozenness" in God, and some may prefer to speak of the *totum simul* of Augustine: God comprehends all of time in a single moment. The second, or "soft line," takes timelessness to mean that God surveys the whole of time, without speculating on whether he experiences things all at once. God is thus not subject to time, although he may freely intervene within the space-time continuum. Cullmann expresses this as God's "lordship over time." God alone "can conceive, survey, and control this endless line [of time], since in its unlimited form it is only his own line. Only to him does eternity belong..."; and "...God is superior to time. He rules over time..."[44]

---

[41] Cullmann, *Christ and Time*, Rev. Ed., trans. Floyd V. Filson (London: SCM, 1962), p.63. See also Mathias Rissi, *Time and History*, trans. Gordon C. Winsor (Richmond, VA: John Knox Press, 1966), pp.22–54, esp. p.32: "To be absolutely avoided, however, is the conception which Sasse works into the New Testament, the 'eternity which transcends time'." Note, however, that he is willing to speak of the eschaton in different terms (p.47) : "God's coming will then have become an eternal present."

[42] Caird, (p.16, cf. p.291) writes, "Yet at all times past and future are embraced in his eternal present." Cf. Paul Minear, *I Saw a New Earth: An Introduction to the Visions of the Apocalypse* (Washington/Cleveland: Corpus, 1968), p. 18. Vögtle (pp.378–9) uses the term *Überzeitlichkeit* in a similar fashion. Sweet writes (p.115): "...John has moved into heaven, where past, present, and future exist as one whole."

[43] Lohmeyer, pp.189.

[44] Cullmann, pp.69–70.

With regards to the "hard" line, it is certain that John is no strict Platonist according to the standard of the *Timaeus*. To begin with, it is difficult to convey the idea of non-durational eternity even when one uses sophisticated philosophical vocabulary – how much more so in the absence of such vocabulary. We have suggested that one might be able to extrapolate the idea of "necessary existence" from the data in Revelation. But non-durational eternity, it seems, lies at a far deeper level of abstraction. As it happens, the material we do have in Revelation is difficult to square with the "hard line." The Septuagintal shift from τὸ ὄν to ὁ ὤν creates the first problem. One can imagine a number or a concept being "timeless" (e.g. two times two *is* four, irrespective of time). It is more difficult (though not perhaps impossible) to imagine a personality, a living being, as timeless in this sense.[45] If this were not enough, John goes on to employ a past tense ("who was") and a type of future tense ("who is coming") in his introductory formula. As we have indicated numerous times, this would run counter to Plato's statement in the *Tim.* 37e ff., "We say that it was and is and shall be; but 'is' alone really belongs to it and describes it truly; 'was' and 'shall be' are properly used of becoming which proceeds in time, for they are motions."

We must go further than this. The appearance of ὁ ἐρχόμενος in his formula would be particularly jarring to philosophically minded Greeks, since it describes not only God's future existence, but his coming to consummate human history. Commentators have rightly stated that such an idea would be offensive, or even patently absurd, to many educated Greeks.[46] Even more perplexing is the intrusion of the human history of Jesus into the heavenly realm itself. Jacques Ellul observes: "The terrestrial event [i.e. Jesus' incarnation, death, and resurrection] provokes the celestial event...What happens in the divine world is defined, determined, provoked by the venture of Jesus upon the earth."[47] The Lamb is worthy to open the scroll because he *was* slain (ἐσφάγης, 5:9). Even if one reads 13:8 as "the book of life of the Lamb who was slain from the foundation of

---

[45] See Paul Helm, *Eternal God* (Oxford: Oxford University Press, 1988), pp.56–72. While Helm argues that a personal being can be timeless, he also provides a survey of arguments to the contrary. Another contemporary philosopher who defends God's timelessness is Brian Leftow, in his book *Time and Eternity* (Ithaca: Cornell University Press, 1991); see especially pp.267–82. (Note that he is not entirely convinced by Helm's arguments and finds it necessary to offer an alternative approach to the problem.)

[46] See Beasley-Murray, p.54; cf. Sweet, p.65.

[47] Ellul, *Apocalypse*, trans. George W. Schreiner (NY: Seabury, 1977), pp.47–8. See also Farrer, p.276.

the world," one cannot discount the importance of the actual death of Christ in time and space for John's theology (cf. 1:18, 2:8).[48]

The "hard line" on timelessness does not offer much help for understanding John's view of God. The "soft line" – God is not subject to time – looks more promising. If it is difficult to conceive of the God of Revelation as being "non-durational," it is equally difficult to conceive of him as existing within the same temporal framework as that of the creation. We have seen that in the ancient world, time was viewed as a function of the motion of the heavenly bodies (cf. *Tim.* 37e ff.; *De Caelo* 279a17–28; Gen. 1:14). It is no coincidence that in the *Phaedrus* Plato "locates" the Forms beyond the outermost sphere of the heavens, since this would place them (literally) beyond time. John works within the same basic cosmological system, as is evidenced by his ascent into heaven through the "door" of Rev. 4:1. It is perfectly reasonable to suppose that he would also have believed that the God who thus transcends the space of the creation would also transcend the time of the creation.

John himself enjoys an unusual relationship to time by virtue of his journey to heaven. As Leonard Thompson writes:

> Time takes a curious turn in the Book of Revelation, for past, present, and future are not separated by fixed, absolute boundaries. The seer, rising above time as in an airplane, takes a transcendent view and traces the past, present, and the future on his temporal map. Boundaries in the future are as visible to him as boundaries of the past, and those future boundaries share characteristics and homologies with present and past.[49]

Surely John's ability to see into the past and future is dependent upon the vision given by "the One who is and who was and who is to come." God does not merely control history from within, as an emperor might. He is the one who, in the words of Is. 46:10, "declares the end from the beginning."

Time is disrupted further by the frequent use of mythic imagery in the book.[50] Rome is not simply Rome, it is Babylon, the "Anti-city." The four beasts of Daniel, mythical representations themselves, combine to form

---

[48] This question will probably never receive a definitive answer, but I am inclined to think 13:8 should be read "...the Lamb who was slain from the foundation of the world." (Those in favor of such a reading include Caird, p.168; Sweet, pp.211–2; Beasley-Murray, pp.213–4; among those who disagree are Swete, p.167, and Beckwith, p.638.) John may be playing with two early Christian traditions concerning ἀπὸ (or πρὸ) καταβολῆς κόσμου. In one, Christians are chosen before the foundation of the world (e.g. Eph. 1:4). In the other, Christ is predestined for sacrifice before the foundation of the world (1 Pet. 1:20; cf. Acts 2:23). John refers to the first in 17:8 and the second in 13:8.

[49] Thompson, p.84.

[50] See especially Court, *passim*; and Minear, "Ontology and Ecclesiology in the Apocalypse," *NTS* 12 (1966): 89–105.

beasts of Daniel, mythical representations themselves, combine to form one super-Beast. Examples could be multiplied. One would not want to label these evil forces as eternal, since they are created and will be destroyed. But they do persist in a way that is different from individual human beings or empires.

Finally, we have a certain transcendence of time in the heavenly worship. While we have noted that there is "action" in heaven (e.g. the presentation of the Lamb), it is significant that the four living creatures are not subject to the alterations of times and seasons which govern earthly worship. They *never cease*, day or night, praising God (4:8).[51] Farrer aptly remarks: "The divine eternity is here seen reflected in the endless worship of the creatures: to them God's worshipfullness was and is, and stretches into a future without end."[52] God is not subject to the ravages of time, and so it is fitting that he is worshipped continually in heaven.[53]

ὁ ἦν

For the purist, John's grammar goes from bad to worse as we move to the second element of our formula. Not only does he retain the nominative definite article, he employs it with a finite verb. In the absence of a past participle for εἰμι, John would be left with the option of employing ὁ γεγονώς (cf. Derveni theogony, 15:6; Plato, *Tim.* 37b–c; Plutarch, *De Is.* 354c). Commentators have suggested that he avoids this lest he imply that God is subject to "becoming."[54] This seems quite reasonable, and all the more so in light of the fact that γίνομαι could imply birth itself, as well as "becoming."[55] This sort of distinction between God's being and creation's becoming is evidenced elsewhere in the New Testament, of course, e.g. in John 1:1–3 and 8:58. A cursory knowledge of the Septuagint would associate γίνομαι with the creation (e.g. the very title of the book of ΓΕΝΕΣΙΣ).

---

[51] This point is not present in Isaiah 6, although it may be implied in 1 En. 39:12.

[52] Farrer, p.276.

[53] This idea comes into play at the human level in 2 Bar. 51:9. In the eschaton, "time will no longer make them [= the righteous] grow older." (trans. Klijn, *OTP* 1: 638). Kraft (p.101) suggests that this picture of worship in Revelation 4–5 reflects "Greek" thinking, in that a timeless God is worshipped by time-bound creatures (*Zeithaftigkeit*). I would question whether the heavenly worship scene is distinctively "Greek," but his comment merits reflection. God *sits on the throne* while the creation worships him. There is some sense in which God's stability contrasts with the movement of his creatures. At the same time, God is also the one who "is to come" to the creation, so that we must not suppose his sitting on the throne implies inactivity or lack of concern.

[54] See Kraft, p.31. We may recall the statement attributed to Chrysippus that the sun, moon, etc. γενητοί εἰσιν ὁ δὲ Ζεὺς ἀΐδιος ἐστιν (*SVF* 2: 309, #1049).

[55] See Bauer's lexicon, s.v. γίνομαι. We may also say that the use of the *perfect* ὁ γεγονώς would also imply that God has *come into* being, which would be even more inappropriate for Jewish and Christian theology.

Having said this, it does not at all follow that John has a "static" conception of God. He simply wishes to maintain a dividing line between the Creator and the creation. We might add that, for all its grammatical oddity, ὁ ἦν does have a certain euphony within the phrase. This may not be insignificant given the almost liturgical sound of this designation.

As for its meaning, "the one who was" clearly implies "the one who has always been." It may also imply that God is the creator – he existed (or *already* existed) at the beginning of the world. We have seen that the LXX description of God as ὁ ὤν came in part as a response to the idea that Zeus was the one "through whom all things have life." Later Jewish interpretations of Ex. 3:14 make a connection between the name YHWH and the creation of the world (Tg. Neof. Ex. 3:14; FT (G,W) Ex. 3:14; Ps-Jon. Ex. 3:14). There is some evidence within Revelation that John may be aware of this tradition associating the name YHWH with the creation. In 4:8, the formula from 1:4 is repeated, but in a different order. The four living creatures sing, "Holy, holy, holy, Lord God Almighty, *who was and who is and who is to come.*" As McNamara indicates, the appearance of ὁ ἦν in the first position should be read in the context of 4:8–11, where God is praised as the Creator of all things.[56] We might wish to compare Ps-Jon. Ex. 3:14: "He who spoke and the world was; who spoke and all things were...I am He who is and who will be has sent me to you" (McNamara). Since the first two items in this interpretation are synonymous, we have the same pattern here as in Rev. 4:8: *was* (with reference to the creation); *is*; *will be/is to come.*

We may add a few comments here on the unusual phrase in 4:11:

---

[56] McNamara, p.100. Pierre Prigent notes that Jewish liturgical tradition based on Is. 6:3 likewise celebrated God as Creator (Prigent, *L'Apocalypse de Saint Jean*; Geneva: Labor et Fides, 1988, pp.87–8). Cf. Sweet, p.120. A similar understanding of God is found in other early Jewish writings. Charles understands 1 En. 39:11, "There is no ceasing before him...," to mean, "Past, present, and future are before Him." (Charles, *The Book of Enoch*, Oxford: Oxford University Press, 1893, p.117.) While this phrase could simply indicate that worship never ceases from before God (cf. 39:12, "those who slumber not..."), Charles' theory is supported by the remainder of the verse, "...before the world was created, he knows what is forever and what will be from generation to generation." (Trans. Isaac, *OTP* 1: 31; S. Uhlig gives an almost identical rendering in his German version in *JSHRZ*. This assumes the validity of the reading "what is forever..." The variant in Aeth. 2 (noted by Uhlig), "what it (= the World) is..." may indicate an ambiguity in a putative original עולם, which could be either "world" or "eternity.") 2 Bar. 21:5 reads, "You who gave commandments to the air with your sign and have seen the things which are to come as well as those which have passed." (*OTP* 1: 628; cf. v.8, "You alone know the end of times before it has arrived"; and vv. 9–10, where God is described as "the Living One.") The idea that God planned future events before the creation is also notable in, e.g., Ap.Abr. 22:1–5; 4 Ezra 6 and 1QS 3. The concept is present in the OT (e.g. Isaiah 40 ff.) but seems to be intensified in later Judaism.

ὅτι σὺ ἔκτισας τὰ πάντα καὶ διὰ τὸ θέλημά σου ἦσαν καὶ ἐκτίσθησαν

....because you created all things, and through your will they were and they were created.

Assuming the text in Nestle-Aland is correct (and there is no strong reason not to),[57] we are left with the problem of why John uses both ἦσαν and ἐκτίσθησαν for God's creative activity. It may simply be a poetic device. Rather than repeating himself ("you created...they were created"), he varies the formula ("they were and were created") for heightened effect.[58] The repetition of the -ησαν would add to the effect. Another possibility is that John is consciously reflecting on the יהי, "let it be," of Genesis 1. The meaning then would be: "They came to be and *thus* they were created." The ἦσαν of v.11 would serve as a literary counterpart to the ἦν of the divine title in v.8, and the ἐκτίσθησαν would reiterate that the "was" of the created order does not extend into eternity past, as does the "was" of the creator. The problem with this interpretation is that we would expect a form of γίνομαι to appear rather than a form of εἰμι.[59]

Some commentators have suggested that ἦσαν καὶ ἐκτίσθησαν refers to the fact that all things first exist in the "eternal will of God," and then become "actual" through God's creative activity.[60] This interpretation might appear tendentiously Platonic at first glance. But there was of course a widespread view within early Judaism and Christianity that God had future events in mind before the creation of the world (cf. especially 1 En. 39:11, which comes in a context of heavenly worship quite close to that of Rev. 4:11; and Ap.Abr. 22:1–5).[61] John himself mentions (certainly) names being written in the book of life before the foundation of the world (17:8) and (perhaps) the Lamb being slain before the foundation of the world (13:8). Two points must be made, however. First, if John was intending to speak about God's planning and God's actual creating, he has done it in such an oblique fashion that one can never be sure of it. Second, even if

---

[57] A few MSS (e.g. 046) hopefully add οὐκ before ἦσαν. This eliminates our problem so well it is excluded by *lectio difficilior*. 2329 attempts to remove the ambiguity of ἦσαν (has the universe existed forever, like God?) by substituting ἐγένοντο, while others do the same thing by placing ἦσαν in the present tense (1854, 2050, etc.). One could try and argue that ἦσαν was introduced by homoioteleuton (ἐκτίσθ*ησαν*), but there is no textual support for this.

[58] Beckwith (p.504) suggests that the καὶ functions epexegetically.

[59] See previous footnote, on ms. 2329.

[60] See, e.g. Robert H. Mounce, *The Book of Revelation* (Grand Rapids, MI: Eerdmans, 1977), p. 140; Vögtle, pp.378–9; Kraft, p.101; Swete, p.75. Prigent, pp.91–2, suggests this as an option, although he also says it may mean "les choses arrivent à l'être par la création." Beckwith, by contrast, argues that there is "no idea...of a *potential* existence...(p.504)."

[61] For the NT, see especially Eph. 1:3 ff.

one accepts this interpretation, one should be wary of equating John's "they were" with the τὸ ὄν of Plato (particularly with respect to the Eternal Living Creature, the "blueprint" of creation in the *Timaeus*). Since those who support the view outlined above tend to speak in terms reminiscent of Platonic reality, I am hesitant to endorse their position. I believe it is best to rest content with our first proposal, that the ἦσαν καὶ ἐκτίσθησαν is a poetic device which serves to re-iterate the glory of God in creation. Ontological speculations should not be pressed.

ὁ ἐρχόμενος

The individual elements of the *Dreizeitenformel* in Greek were subject to wide variation. One finds participles and finite verbs, forms of εἰμι and forms of γίνομαι, in a variety of combinations. But John's unprecedented use of ὁ ἐρχόμενος is one of the most radical adaptations of the formula we possess. While one could use ἔρχομαι simply as a way of indicating the future tense (as in the English, "I *am going to* do something), John clearly has more in mind: "...the one who is to come" indicates not merely God's future existence, but his coming to the world to consummate his kingdom.

The idea of a god "coming" to the aid of his or her people was not foreign to Greek thinking.[62] The Homeric gods frequently came to earth on behalf of their beloved heroes (e.g. Athena and Odysseus). We recall too the injunctions of the magicians for the gods to "Come! Come! Quick! Quick!" What is unusual is John's fusion of a transcendent, almost philosophical conception of God ("the One who is and was and [will be]") with a highly personal and decidedly interventionist one ("...is to come"). This combination is one of John's supreme theological achievements.

We begin with the question of whether there is any significance to the precise form ὁ ἐρχόμενος. We have argued that ὁ ὤν had a well-recognized independent status as a designation of God from the time of the Septuagint translation onward. This is less apparent in the case of ὁ ἐρχόμενος. I have been unable to find any examples in the OT, early Judaism, or the NT (outside of Rev. 1:4,8) where God is referred to by this title. Nor was it used in early Judaism as a designation of the Messiah.[63] The Gospels do describe Christ as the one "coming after" John the Bap-

---

[62] See J. Schneider, ἔρχομαι, in *TDNT* 2: 666–7.
[63] See C. F. Evans, *Saint Luke* (London: SCM/Philadelphia: Trinity Press International, 1990), p. 351; and R. H. Gundry, *Matthew* (Grand Rapids: Eerdmans, 1982), p.205. Schneider (p. 670) says that ὁ ἐρχόμενος did describe the Messiah in Judaism, but this may simply be his way of saying the Messiah was expected to come, which no one would dispute. He offers no evidence for actual occurrences of ὁ ἐρχόμενος or the equivalent in any Jewish literature.

tist,⁶⁴ or as the one "coming in the name of the Lord" (quoting Ps.118:26).⁶⁵ The only places where it may function as an independent title are Matthew 11:3 (= Lk. 7:20) and Heb. 10:37. In Matthew, John the Baptist asks via his disciples, "Are you the coming one (ὁ ἐρχόμενος) or should we expect another one?" Explanations differ as to who exactly this "coming one" is (cf. John 6:14 ὁ προφήτης ὁ ἐρχόμενος εἰς τὸν κόσμον), but it seems to be some sort of messianic reference.⁶⁶ Heb. 10:37, meanwhile, reads ὁ ἐρχόμενος ἥξει. This is a citation of Hab. 2:3, לא יאחר כי בא יבא (LXX: ὅτι ἐρχόμενος ἥξει). The apparently tendentious addition of the article indicates that the author of Hebrews has given a messianic application to the text of Habbakuk, such that "the Coming One" likely refers to Jesus (cf. Heb. 9:28).⁶⁷

The "coming" of Christ is of obvious interest for the interpretation of Rev. 1:4.⁶⁸ It is possible that earlier Christian use of ὁ ἐρχόμενος for Christ influenced John's composition of Rev. 1:4. But the absence of references outside Revelation to *God* as ὁ ἐρχόμενος make it equally likely that John uses this particular form primarily as way of keeping the symmetrical structure initiated by ὁ ὤν. (This would appear to be the case with ὁ ἦν as well.) If one does not find the exact words ὁ ἐρχόμενος used of God outside Revelation, however, one does find the idea of God's coming throughout the OT and early Judaism.⁶⁹ Judges 5:4 ff. puts this in quite personal terms: "YHWH, in your going out from Seir...the earth shook..." (cf. the Song of Moses, Exodus 15; Is. 29:5–6). In the prophets, the "coming" of the Day of the Lord meant judgment and vindication for the people of God in the OT (see especially Joel 2:1, בא יום יהוה; cf. 3:4). We may also cite Is. 40:10, "Behold, my Lord YHWH comes with strength, and his arm rules for him..." and Zech. 14:5, "And YHWH my God will come, and all the holy ones with him."

---

⁶⁴ Matt. 3:11, ὁ δὲ ὀπίσω μου ἐρχόμενος ἰσχυρότερός μού ἐστιν. Mark and Luke, by contrast, have respectively ἔρχεται ὁ ἰσχυρότερός μου ὀπίσω μου and ἔρχεται δὲ ὁ ἰσχυρότερός μου. Cf. John 1:15, ὁ ὀπίσω μου ἐρχόμενος.

⁶⁵ Matt. 21:9: εὐλογημένος ὁ ἐρχόμενος ἐν ὀνόματι κυρίου. This portion of the Matthean citation matches the LXX, although Matt. has ὡσαννὰ for LXX σῶσον δή (118:25). Cf. Mk. 11:9; Lk.19:38, Jn. 12:13; Lk. 13:35.

⁶⁶ For a list of options see W.D. Davies and Dale C. Allison, *The Gospel according to Saint Matthew* 2 vols. (Edinburgh: T.&T. Clark, 1988), 1: 312–14. They conclude that it probably refers to Elijah or to the Messiah, and more likely to the latter.

⁶⁷ See G. W. Buchanan, *To the Hebrews* (Garden City, NY: Doubleday, 1972), p.175; R. McL. Wilson, *Hebrews* (Grand Rapids: Eerdmans/Basingstoke: Marshall, Morgan, & Scott, 1987), p.199; F. F. Bruce, *The Epistle to the Hebrews* (London/Edinburgh: Marshall, Morgan, & Scott, 1964), pp.271–4.

⁶⁸ See Hofius, "Das Zeugnis", p.513.

⁶⁹ For examples of God's coming in early Judaism, see Fitzmyer, *The Gospel According to Luke I–IX* (Garden City, NY: Doubleday, 1981), p.666.

These last two examples are particularly relevant because they were applied by the early Christians to the parousia of Christ (see e.g. Matt.16:27, 25:31; 1 Thess. 4:16–7). In their view, YHWH's coming *is* Christ's coming. John fits well in this tradition.[70] Shortly after describing God as ὁ ὢν καὶ ὁ ἦν καὶ ὁ ἐρχόμενος, he offers a conflation of Dan. 7:13 and Zech. 12:10:

> Ἰδοὺ ἔρχεται μετὰ τῶν νεφελῶν, καὶ ὄψεται αὐτὸν πᾶς ὀφθαλμὸς καὶ οἵτινες αὐτὸν ἐξεκέτησαν, καὶ κόψονται ἐπ' αὐτὸν πᾶσαι αἱ φυλαὶ τῆς γῆς (Rev. 1:7; cf. Matt. 24:30[71]).

The one "coming with the clouds" is clearly Christ. We may compare this with the declarations at the close of the book, "I am coming soon" (22:7,12,20). The words which follow v. 20, "Amen. Come, Lord Jesus" identify this coming one as Christ. The rider on the white horse in chapter 19 is likewise the returning Christ, though the word "come" is not explicitly used there. As Roloff points out, the fact that only the coming of Christ is spoken of elsewhere in Revelation does not contradict the formula found in 1:4; "rather, it interprets the coming of Jesus as the event in which God's power over history is visibly achieved."[72]

As for the temporal significance of ὁ ἐρχόμενος, it is God's eschatological coming in Christ which predominates in the book. While we do find references to Christ "coming" to the church within history (e.g. 2:5; perhaps 2:16, 3:11), most of the uses of ἔρχομαι refer to God's coming to consummate history. The most natural reading of the invocations to "Come!" in chapter 22 is that they refer to the parousia of Christ which will usher in the new heavens and new earth. We may also note that in 11:17 and 16:5, the formula from 1:4 appears, but this time without ὁ ἐρχόμενος. The reason for its absence is that in these passages God's final judgement on the world has begun – he *has* come (see discussion below).

In summary, John's alteration of the expected "will be" into "the one who is to come" is a move with profound theological significance. God defines his own future not as an infinite extension of existence, but as the deliverance of his people. As Bauckham writes, "This is the biblical God, who chooses as his own future, his coming to his creation, and whose creation will find its future in him (cf. 21:3)."[73] We may also say that for John, the definition of who God is cannot be separated from Jesus Christ.

---

[70] See, e.g., Caird, p.19; Minear, *New Earth*, pp.17–8; Jürgen Roloff, *The Revelation of John*, trans. John E. Alsup (Minneapolis: Fortress Press, 1993), p.24. Hofius (p.513) writes: "Für Johannes ereignet sich in der Parusie des Sohnes Gottes das eschatologische „Kommen" Gottes selbst."

[71] Beckwith, p.431.

[72] Roloff, p.24.

[73] Bauckham, *Theology*, p.30.

God is defined as "the one who is to come;" but this coming is in the person of Christ. Finally, we should not overlook the fact that John does not simply talk about God's coming as an incidental attribute. It is rather a part of his name, his identity. The coming of God to his creation is not simply a future possibility for John, it is the inevitable consequence of God's being who he is. As J. Comblin writes:

> Dieu est ainsi...celui qui est l'existence absolue. Mais l'existence absolue, vue dans son rapport aux hommes, se présente comme une venue future absolument immanquable. Aussi vrai que Dieu existe, il viendra.[74]

Variations on the Formula of 1:4

We have already touched upon many of the variations of the formula in 1:4 which occur throughout the book of Revelation. The following section gives more exegetical detail on those passages which warrant further comment.

Rev. 1:8

Rev. 1:8 concludes the greeting *cum* doxology section 1:4–8, forming an inclusio with the description of God in v.4. The saying is of great importance in and of itself, since it constitutes one of the two occasions in Revelation where God himself speaks (the other is 21:5–6, where "the Alpha and the Omega" also appears). The formula in v.4 is expanded to read:

> Ἐγώ εἰμι τὸ ἄλφα καὶ τὸ ὦ, λέγει κύριος ὁ θεός, ὁ ὢν καὶ ὁ ἦν καὶ ὁ ἐρχόμενος, ὁ παντοκράτωρ.
>
> I am the Alpha and the Omega, says the Lord God, who is and who was and who is to come, the Almighty.

It may be that John is adapting a hellenistic Jewish liturgical formula for his own purposes. We have previously noted the text Apostolic Constitutions 8.5.1ff., which appears to derive from Jer. 1:6 LXX and which contains the phrase ὁ ὤν, δέσποτα κύριε ὁ θεὸς ὁ παντοκράτωρ, ὁ μόνος ἀγέννητος καὶ ἀβασίλευσας, ὁ ἀεὶ ὢν καὶ πρὸ τῶν αἰώνων ὑπάρχων. John may have availed himself of such a tradition, with "the Alpha and the Omega" being perhaps his own contribution.

I will argue here that John is doing more than adapting a pre-existing formula. Rather, John ends his greeting the same way he began, with an interpretation of the name YHWH. In v.8, however, he employs *three dif-*

---

[74] J. Comblin, *Le Christ dans L'Apocalypse* (Paris: Descleé, 1965), p.52. Cf. Beasley-Murray, p.54: "It is of his nature that he 'comes' from the future and works his gracious and powerful will."

ferent versions[75] of the name YHWH: Iao, YHWH Elohim, and YHWH Sabaoth.[76] John has already used a three-fold formula for the divine name in 1:4. We might suppose that 1:8 is constructed in an analogous way, as a compound of three versions of the name YHWH, rather than as a string of four or more names (taking Elohim, Sabaoth, etc. as independent names).

The phrase "the Alpha and the Omega" is generally agreed to mean something like "the one who controls the beginning and end of history."[77] As such it has obvious affinities with "the First and the Last" of Is.44:6. The precise source of the title is more disputed. Many have suggested a connection with the first and last letters of the Hebrew alphabet, *aleph* and *tau*. Apart from understanding these as a general way of speaking about totality, people have regarded *aleph* and *tau* as representing the first letters of Elohim and Sabaoth (*sic*!);[78] or the Urim and Thummim;[79] or as a shortened version of the word אמת, "truth."[80] Others have noted parallel uses of the first and last letters of the alphabet in Greco-Roman texts.[81] Since the phrase itself is not our primary concern, we will not assess each of these options. The most plausible view would be one which takes "Alpha" and "Omega" as symbols for the beginning and end. This could have come from a Jewish or a Greek source, and it may well have appeared in both traditions.

Whatever the source might have been, I would argue that John employs it here because of its affinities with the Iao form of the divine name. The connection between "the Alpha and the Omega" and 'Ιαώ has been suggested before.[82] I believe this theory may receive support from a tradition found in the Gnostic text Pistis Sophia. In P.S. 4:136, Jesus says 'Ιαώ three times. We then read, "...this is its interpretation: iota, because the All came forth; alpha, because it will return again; omega, because the completion of

---

[75] This is assuming that 'Εγώ εἰμι is simply an introductory speech formula, rather than a play on the word אהיה.

[76] E.-B. Allo does not recognize the influence of Iao on the first element, but he does note the presence of YHWH Elohim and YHWH Sabaoth in the text. See Allo, *Saint Jean: L'Apocalypse* (Paris: Lecoffre, 1933), p.8.

[77] E.g. Beasley-Murray, p.59. Cf. Holtz, *Christologie*, pp.148ff.

[78] Cf. Kraft, pp.36–7.

[79] Ford, p.379.

[80] Kraft, pp.36–7.

[81] Charles, 1: 20. Beasley-Murray, p.59.

[82] By, e.g. Bauckham, *Theology*, pp.27–8; Aune, "Magic", pp.489–90. The most extended discussion is given by Farrer, pp. 261ff. While his comments are at times illuminating, I believe he goes too far in arguing that Iao (and also Ia) shapes both the form and content of many of the divine epithets in Revelation. I am particularly concerned that he does not give evidence as to why the *iota* in these names should refer to the "is" of God's present activity, as opposed to the *alpha* (=past) and *omega* (=future). This supposition informs much of his discussion.

all completions will happen."[83] There are obviously problems with bringing this text into the discussion, not the least of which is its late date. The Pistis Sophia, for instance, mentions *iota*, where none is discernible in the Revelation text.[84] We might also have hoped to see "alpha" representing the creation, or at least some event in the past, but this may be attributable to the vagaries of Gnostic doctrine. Nonetheless, it is significant that the letters of the Iao name could be disassembled to yield a formula which included alpha and omega as some sort of boundary markers of history. Since the Pistis Sophia is obviously not dependent on the Revelation text, it appears likely that John was not creating his "Alpha and Omega" designation *de novo*, but rather was working with an existing tradition of interpreting the Iao name.

The second element in the formula in 1:8, YHWH Elohim, is easily gleaned from κύριος ὁ θεός.[85] The latter is familiar from the LXX (e.g. Gen.2:8 ff.) and needs no further comment. YHWH Sabaoth appears in a more convoluted form. If it is granted, however, that ὁ ὢν καὶ ὁ ἦν καὶ ὁ ἐρχόμενος stands for YHWH, we need only demonstrate that ὁ παντοκράτωρ may serve as a translation of Sabaoth. This can be done by comparing, for example, the MT of Am. 3:13 יהוה אלהי הצבאות with its counterpart in the LXX, κύριος ὁ θεὸς ὁ παντοκράτωρ.[86]

The three-fold occurrence of titles with the name YHWH may be nothing more than a sophisticated stylistic device to expand and enhance the title given in 1:4. It is possible that something more may be involved. David Aune has argued that "the Alpha and the Omega" should be read against the background of Greco-Roman revelatory magical practices.[87]

---

[83] Trans. in *Pistis Sophia*, text ed. Carl Schmidt, trans. Violet MacDermot (Leiden: Brill, 1978).

[84] Contra Farrer. One might take *iota* as *yod*, and understand *yod* as an abbreviation of the name YHWH, yielding "YHWH is Alpha and Omega," of which John uses only the latter portion. This is possible but not demonstrable. See also Aune, *Revelation 1–5*, p.57.

[85] Bauckham (*Theology*, p.30) argues that Rev. 1:8 splits the expected form κύριος ὁ θεὸς ὁ παντοκράτωρ and inserts ὁ ὢν καὶ ὁ ἦν καὶ ὁ ἐρχόμενος in the middle of it. He cites 4:8 (ἅγιος ἅγιος ἅγιος κύριος ὁ θεὸς ὁ παντοκράτωρ, ὁ ἦν καὶ ὁ ὢν καὶ ὁ ἐρχόμενος) in support of this. This may well be correct. But we are still left with the problem of *why* John inserts ὁ ὢν κτλ. where he does. It could be for the sake of variety. We suggest that it is to preserve the play on the name YHWH.

[86] As indicated in the Nestle-Aland margin to Rev. 1:8. The presence of נאם אדני before this phrase in the MT (missing in the LXX) is interesting, but it does not materially effect our point. Charles (1: 20) notes that παντοκράτωρ appears elsewhere in the NT only in an OT quotation (2 Sa. 7:8) in 2 Cor. 6:18

[87] Aune, "Magic", *passim*. See also his commentary, pp.57–8. The Egyptian provenance of the magical texts we possess by no means excludes the possibility that similar invocations were used in Asia Minor. Magic was an international phenomenon, and no doubt popular texts would have circulated throughout the Mediterranean world like any

Vocalic cries and divine names were both manipulated as a means of calling upon divine power for the service of the magician. John's use of "the Alpha and the Omega," according to Aune, is a polemical response to this practice.

I would like to take this same thought in a slightly different direction. One of the most common motifs in magical texts is the piling up of divine epithets in hopes of securing the favor of a god or gods. Jewish names for God were not excluded in such lists; indeed, they seem to be used with particular frequency. They may be employed along with magical formulae, as in *PGM* XXXVI: 35f.: "IAO SABAOTH ADONAI ELOAI ABRASAX ABLANATHANALBA..." They also appear in hymnic praise like Ladder of Jacob 2:17–18: "Holy, Holy, Holy, Yao, Yaova, Yaoil, Yao, Kados, Chavod, Savaoth..." The most pertinent text for us is *PGM* LXXI:3–4, which contains the formula ὁ ὤν θεὸς ὁ Ἰαώ, κύριος παντοκράτωρ.

Is John deliberately copying such invocations of deity? We have argued that underlying Rev. 1:8 is the tri-fold description of God: Iao, YHWH Elohim, YHWH Sabaoth. Such a list would not be at all out of place in the magical papyri. Of course John's use of the phrase is very different from that of the magical papyri. It is framed not as an invocation of the deity, but as a self-disclosure of the deity. Moreover, in the Greek sentence in which our posited formula actually appears in Revelation, it is a very meaningful and profound self-disclosure. By transforming the at times meaningless repetition of divine names into an exposition of the grandeur of God's being, John reclaims these names for the Christian community.

Whatever one makes of this connection with magical practice, we hope to have demonstrated that in v.8, John is again expressing central points of his theology through the interpretation of the name YHWH.

Rev. 1:17–8

A Christological variation of the *Dreizeitenformel* may be found in Rev. 1:17–8:

ἐγώ εἰμι ὁ πρῶτος καὶ ὁ ἔσχατος καὶ ὁ ζῶν καὶ ἐγενόμην νεκρὸς καὶ ἰδοὺ ζῶν εἰμι εἰς τοὺς αἰῶνας τῶν αἰώνων

...*I am the First and the Last and the Living One, and I became dead and behold I am living for ever and ever...*

The punctuation in Nestle-Aland 26 rightly maintains the unity of the first three elements ὁ πρῶτος...ὁ ἔσχατος...ὁ ζῶν, which is implied by the

---

other valued commodity. To take but one example, Acts 19:19 reports of numerous magical scrolls being burnt by converts in Ephesus.

repetition of the definite article.[88] The expression "the First and the Last" is drawn from the divine title of Is. 44:6, although it would have resonance in the hellenistic milieu as well.[89] The "Living One" is likewise a common title for God in Jewish and Christian tradition, e.g. Sir. 18:1 ὁ ζῶν εἰς τὸν αἰῶνα ἔκτισεν τὰ πάντα κοινῇ.[90] Farrer makes the cogent remark: "'He that lives', ὁ ζῶν, is as near a sound to 'he that is', ὁ ὤν, as the Greek tongue can pronounce."[91] In form, content, and even sound, this self-designation of Christ echoes the self-designation of God in 1:4,8. It is difficult to imagine a clearer statement of John's high Christology.[92] Beasley-Murray goes so far as to say that this verse combines Is. 44:6 and Ex. 3:14 such that "Christ is above the limitations of time."[93]

The differences between the formulae in 1:4 and 1:17–8 should not be overlooked. Whatever one makes of New Testament Christology, it should be agreed that the New Testament writers, including John, wish to preserve a distinction between God the Father and Jesus Christ. Lohmeyer is perhaps correct to say that the best commentary on "the Living One" is John 5:26: Jesus, like the Father, and as the Father's gift, has life "in himself."[94] At the same time, "the Living One" used with respect to Christ must also be connected with his experience of death and resurrection. This is done in the latter half of v. 18. For the committed Platonist, the use of ἐγενόμην for a divine figure would be bad enough; ἐγενόμην νεκρός would be the *reductio ad absurdum*. It would be no less offensive to a Jewish audience.

John is willing to let the paradox stand. Indeed, he seems almost to revel in it. On the one hand, he freely uses divine attributes – we may say *incommunicable* divine attributes – for Jesus: he is the First and the Last and the Living One. The tri-partite formula recalls the explication of the name YHWH given in 1:4,8. But the life Christ has, and the power he exercises over past and future events, must be viewed through the prism of his death and resurrection. Bauckham sums up the matter in these words:

---

[88] See also Holtz, *Christologie*, p.82; Kraft, p.48; Beasley-Murray, p.67; Hofius, "Das Zeugnis," p.515; and Lohmeyer, pp.18–19. Charles (1: 31) denies that the phrase is tripartite, arguing that "the First and the Last" is complete in itself. Cf. Swete, p.19; Beckwith, p.441.

[89] For which see van Unnik, *Het Godspredikat, passim*.

[90] Lohmeyer, p.19. Cf. (with Nestle-Aland mg.) Dt. 32:40, καὶ ἐρῶ Ζῶ ἐγὼ εἰς τὸν αἰῶνα...; Ps. 41:3 LXX (Heb. 42:3): ...πρὸς τὸν θεὸν τὸν ζῶντα." For other references see Charles, 1: 32; Swete, pp.19–20.

[91] Farrer, p.275. Recall also the juxtaposition of ὤν and ζῶν in the amulet from Caernarvon discussed in chapter 2.

[92] See Hofius, "Das Zeugnis," pp.515–6. Cf. Holtz' understanding of the formula (*Christologie*, p.82) : "Er ist der Ewige, der Anfang und Ende der Zeit in sich begreift."

[93] Beasley-Murray, p.67.

[94] Lohmeyer, p.19.

The declaration [of vv.17–8] begins by asserting Christ's participation in the eternal being of God, the origin and goal of all things...and then continues by asserting the particular – indeed, extraordinary – way in which he, as 'the living one'...shares God's eternal livingness. Whereas of God it is said that he is 'the One who is and who was and who is to come'...or that he is 'the One who lives forever and ever'...Christ says: 'I was dead, and behold, I am alive forever and ever'...His eternal livingness was interrupted by the experience of a human death, and he shares the divine life of God through triumph over death.[95]

Rev. 1:19

Rev. 1:19 has attracted much comment, most of it concerning the implications of the verse for the outline of the book of Revelation. Our present concern is not so far reaching, and we will bypass the myriad interpretative options that have been put forward.[96] We are primarily interested in pointing out that this "prophetic commissioning" reflects the description of God in 1:4, such that John's inspired utterance about the past, present, and future is connected with the God who controls history.

The verse reads:

γράψον οὖν ἃ εἶδες καὶ ἃ εἰσὶν καὶ ἃ μέλλει γενέσθαι μετὰ ταῦτα.

Write therefore the things which you have seen, and the things which are, and the things which shall take place after these things (NASB).

This description of John's prophetic office accords well with the classical models of Homer and Hesiod. It would also fit with some of the formulations we mentioned in our section on the *Dreizeitenformel* in Jewish literature, e.g. T.Job 47:9: "And the Lord spoke to me in power, showing me things present and things to come."[97] The fact that it appears in close proximity to the description of God as "the One who is and who was and

---

[95] Bauckham, *Theology*, p.56. Cf. Beasley-Murray, p.67; Charles, 1:31; Minear, *New Earth*, p.32.

[96] The options are conveniently summarized in G. K. Beale, "The Interpretative Problem of Rev. 1:19," *NovT* 34 (1992): 360–87. See also Michaels, pp.604–20. I will adopt the view that "the things which you have seen" represents the inaugural vision; "the things which are" represent the present, particularly the present state of the congregations in Asia Minor (which I see at least partially reflected in the visions of chs.4–22 as well as in the messages to the congregations in chs. 2–3); and "the things which shall take place after these things" represent the future. Whether this is the distant future or the immediate future is immaterial to our argument. I am also willing to concede that ἃ εἰσιν may have a secondary nuance, "what they (that is, the visions) *mean*," exploiting the veridical nuance of εἰμι, as argued by Michaels. He finds this sense of the verb to be in e.g. Rev. 1:20; 4:5;5 :6,8; 7:14; 11:4,12;14:4–5;16:13–4;17:7–18. All are discussed in Michaels, pp.608ff.

[97] Trans. R.P. Spittler, *OTP* 1: 865. See also Sib.Or. 4:19–20: "He it is who drove a whip through my heart within/to narrate accurately to men what now is,/and what will yet be (ὅσα νῦν τε καὶ ὁππόσα ἔσσεται)..." (trans. Collins, *OTP* 1: 384; text in Geffcken).

proximity to the description of God as "the One who is and who was and who is to come" indicates that John wishes us to read the former in light of the latter. John is qualified to speak about the present and the future because he is called to do so by a God who holds all time and history in his hands.[98] It is true that the formula only mentions the present and the future, but this is probably attributable to the fact that there is little reflection upon the past in the book.[99] Note, too, that we at least have a past *tense*, namely εἶδες, so that there is a three-fold structure of some sort in the verse.

Rev. 4:8

In 4:8, we meet with our original *Dreizeitenformel* in slightly modified form:

ἅγιος ἅγιος ἅγιος κύριος ὁ θεὸς ὁ παντοκράτωρ, ὁ ἦν καὶ ὁ ὢν καὶ ὁ ἐρχόμενος.

Holy, holy, holy, is the Lord God Almighty, who was and who is and who is to come.

The use of Is. 6:3 is apparent. Pierre Prigent describes Rev. 4:8 as a "liturgical adaptation" of the Isaianic text.[100] John first expands the divine title in Isaiah, departing from the יהוה צבאות of the MT (LXX κύριος σαβαωθ) and employing κύριος ὁ θεὸς ὁ παντοκράτωρ (= Heb. יהוה אלהי הצבאות; cf. Hos. 12:6; Amos 3:13; 4:13).[101] The expansion is probably a stylistic device to maintain the pattern of "threes," which will of course culminate in the designation "who was and is and is to come."[102]

The more drastic alteration of Is. 6:3 is the replacement of "the whole earth is full of his glory" with "who was and is and is to come." Is this change simply a stylistic one? John creatively re-works the Old Testament tradition throughout Revelation, so we need not posit a one-to-one correspondence between every element in Is.6:3 and Rev. 4:8. On the other hand, we have evidence that other commentators altered Is. 6:3 in an effort

---

[98] Thompson (p.84) makes this association: "John sees both 'what is and what is to take place hereafter' (1:19), and John's God is 'the one who is and was and is to come.'"

[99] Sweet (p.73); Beasley-Murray (p.68); and Caird (p.26) argue that past, present, and future are all mixed together in the visions. This may be true to some extent (e.g. the ascension of Christ in ch.12 is a past event), but the past is far less evident in the book than the present and the future. This is not to deny that motifs from the past, notably the Exodus, are fundamental to the understanding of Revelation. The deliverance of God in the present and future is in continuity with his past acts of deliverance.

[100] Prigent, pp.87–8. Aune (*Revelation 1–5*, pp.302–307) has a very thorough discussion. See also Thompson, pp.57–8; Charles, 1: 119 ff.

[101] Bauckham, *Theology*, p.30.

[102] Farrer, p.267.

to articulate the meaning of the text.[103] The Isaiah Targum, for instance, reads "Holy *in the heavens of the height, his sanctuary;* holy *upon the earth, the work of his might;* holy *in eternity* is the Lord of Hosts; the whole earth is filled with *the brilliance of* his glory."[104] 1 En. 39:12, we have seen, gives "Those who sleep not bless thee; they stand before thy glory, saying: Holy, holy, holy, is the Lord of spirits: he fills the earth with spirits."[105]

The Targum, in typical fashion, attempts to give a reason for the threefold occurence of "holy" in the text.[106] "Brilliance" is added either to explain what God's glory is like (i.e. brilliant light) or, more likely, to suggest that what one finds on earth is a reflection or a diffusion of God's glory rather than the glory itself. Also, the Meturgamin appears to situate the passage in heaven, rather than in the earthly temple (as one might read the original of Isaiah 6) and therefore stresses that God's glory is not restricted to earth. As for 1 Enoch, the author appears to believe that God's glory is manifest on the earth through the spirits he creates to inhabit it (or perhaps "visit it," if angelic messengers are in mind).

John's alteration of Isaiah ("the one who was and is and is to come" for "the earth is filled with his glory") may derive in part from similar traditions. We have noted that the name YHWH is often associated with the creation. The glory of God as creator lies at the heart of the adoration in Revelation 4 (cf. v.11).[107] If one accepts the proposal that 1 Enoch's "he fills the earth with spirits" is an interpretation of the *divine name* יהוה צבאות, then John may be working with a traditional theme by including

---

[103] For discussion of the use of the Trishagion in later Judaism, see David Flusser, "Sanktus und Gloria," in *Abraham unser Vater*, eds. O. Betz, M. Hengel, P. Schmidt (Leiden/Köln: Brill, 1963): 129–52; and Eric Werner, "The Doxology in Synagogue and Church," *HUCA* 19 (1945–6): 275–351. Clement of Rome (1 Cor. 34:6) cites the LXX of Is. 6:3 almost verbatim, but substitutes κτίσις for LXX γῆ. In later formulations (e.g. Exod.Rab. 30.6,44a; Questions of Ezra A29; Ladder of Jacob 2:12) Isaiah's words were expanded to include "heaven and earth are full of your glory." See Werner, pp.292ff.

[104] Trans. in B. D. Chilton, *The Isaiah Targum* (Edinburgh: T.&T. Clark, 1987).

[105] Trans. in Black. Note that "those who sleep not" has no parallel in Isaiah 6, but it does remind one of Rev. 4:8, where it is said that the living creatures never stop praising God day or night.

[106] Cf. Aune, *Revelation 1–5*, pp.306–7.

[107] Although 3 Enoch is admittedly a late text, it does contain an interesting link between the Trishagion, the Name, and Creation. After the recitation of the Trishagion, "then all the explicit names that are graven with a flaming style on the Throne of Glory fly off like eagles with sixteen wings..." (39:1; trans. Odeberg). P. Alexander (in *OTP* 1: 290) notes that these names are either multiple occurrences of YHWH or different permutations containing the name YHWH. At the conclusion of the Trishagion account, Metatron proceeds to tell Ishmael "the letters by which heaven and earth were created..." (41:1). As Alexander (p.292) notes, these are probably the 22 letters of the alphabet, but the connection is still of interest.

an interpretation of the name YHWH ("the one who was and is and is to come") in the Trishagion. 1 Enoch likewise puts an emphasis on the *eternal* praise of God (see 39:6–7,10–11,14), as is common in doxologies.[108] John's formulation fits in well with this pattern.[109]

But John also departs significantly from his predecessors when it comes to the question of God's glory on earth. Both the MT and LXX of Is. 6:3 lack the auxiliary verb, such that the phrase is literally "...the whole earth full of his glory." The Targum and 1 Enoch, like modern translations, take this as a reference to the present time: the earth *is* full of his glory (or "filled with spirits" in Enoch's interpretation). But this seemingly innocuous insertion leads to an immense theological problem: If the whole earth *is* full of God's glory, why does injustice seem so often to reign? This may help explain why John interprets the statement in Isaiah the way he does.[110] The problem is not (as it is for the Targum and 1 Enoch) *how* God fills the earth with his glory, but rather *whether* God's glory in fact fills the earth at the present time.

John surely recognizes God's wonderful creative activity, and he emphasizes this by placing "was" in the first position. But the presence of "is to come" points towards a *future* realization of God's kingdom on earth. John, it appears, reads Is. 6:3 in the light of other OT passages which speak of the hope that God's glory *will* fill the earth. The most pertinent text is Psalm 72, particularly the concluding verses[111]:

ברוך יהוה אלהים אלהי ישראל עשה נפלאות לבדו וברוך שם כבודו
לעולם וימלא כבודו את כל הארץ אמן ואמן

Blessed be the Lord God, God of Israel, who alone does wonders; and blessed be the name of his glory forever, and may his glory fill all the earth, Amen and Amen (Ps. 72:18–19).

While one might conceivably take וימלא as a converted imperfect with a present tense meaning, the translation "*may* his glory fill all the earth..."[112] makes much better sense of the psalm as a whole, which looks forward to the *future* rule of the king of Israel over all the nations.[113] The parallels to

---

[108] See Werner, p.277: he asserts that "doxology" may be defined as the "proclamation of God's praise *coupled with an affirmation of his infinity in time*" (italics his). He supports this with evidence from both the Bible and later Jewish liturgy. Cf. Flusser, pp.131–39.

[109] Aune cites a very interesting parallel from the hekalot literature. Several lines after the Trishagion we read "And the earth says, 'The Lord was king, the Lord is king, the Lord will be king for ever and ever.'" See Aune, *Revelation 1–5*, p.307.

[110] See Bauckham, *Theology*, pp.46–7.

[111] My attention was drawn to these verses by Werner, p.279.

[112] Cf. LXX καὶ πληρωθήσεται τῆς δόξης αὐτοῦ πᾶσα ἡ γῆ.

[113] The messianic overtones would help explain why John makes use of the psalm in his interpretation of Is. 6:3.

Is. 6:3 are obvious. We would only emphasize the fact that it is God's *name* which is to be blessed forever.

John's description of God as "the One who was and who is and who is to come," then, may well be his way of handling the ambiguity inherent in Is. 6:3. God has created the world, and so is worthy to receive praise, both now and forever. This much would already be a part of the tradition of the depiction of heavenly worship. But John realizes that God's glory is not fully revealed on earth at present. For this to happen, there must be a redemption of humanity and a renovation of the cosmos. This new creation is inaugurated by the death and resurrection of Christ, and will find its completion in his coming to earth. By using the phrase "the one who was and is and is to come," John offers us an interpretation of Is. 6:3 in which Theology and Christology are not easily distinguished. God comes, but he comes in Christ. The revelation of God's glory on earth stems from the redemptive work of the Lamb, and they share in the praise of the redeemed creation (5:13, 21:23).

Rev. 11:17, 16:5

In both these verses we meet with a shortened version of the *Dreizeitenformel* from 1:4. Rev. 11:17 reads:

...εὐχαριστοῦμέν σοι, κύριε ὁ παντοκράτωρ, ὁ ὢν καὶ ὁ ἦν, ὅτι εἴληφας τὴν δύναμίν σου τὴν μεγάλην καὶ ἐβασίλευσας...

16:5 reads:

...δίκαιος εἶ, ὁ ὢν καὶ ὁ ἦν, ὁ ὅσιος, ὅτι ταῦτα ἔκρινας...

John uses two-part formulae for God elsewhere ("the Alpha and the Omega," "the First and the Last"), but the adjustments to the *Dreizeitenformel* in 11:17 and 16:5 are obviously not merely stylistic. The absence of ὁ ἐρχόμενος is deliberate. In chapter 11, God is invoked as ὁ ὢν καὶ ὁ ἦν just before the description of his judgment in v.19. This would appear to be the final judgment, since it concludes the cycle begun in chapter 8. In chapter 16, God is likewise in the midst of executing his judgments upon the earth ("the seven plagues, which are the *last*...," 15:1) when he receives this title. As Bauckham writes, "The shorter versions (11:17; 16:8) occur at points in the vision which anticipate the end, when God will have 'come' in his eschatological kingdom. The expectation of his coming is now fulfilled."[114]

---

[114] Bauckham, *The Climax of Prophecy* (Edinburgh: T.&T. Clark, 1993), p.32. Cf. McNamara, p.101.

The beast which you saw was and is not and is going to ascend from the abyss and goes to destruction (Τὸ θηρίον ὃ εἶδες ἦν καὶ οὐκ ἔστιν καὶ μέλλει ἀναβαίνειν ἐκ τῆς ἀβύσσου καὶ εἰς ἀπώλειαν ὑπάγει), and the inhabitants of the earth, those whose names are not written in the book of life from the foundation of the world, will marvel, seeing the beast, that it was and is not and will be present...and the beast which was and is not, he is himself an eighth and is one of the seven, and goes to destruction (17:8,11)

The words used here of the beast are an obvious parody of the divine titles in 1:4 and parallels.[115] As such they enhance John's presentation of the dragon's kingdom as a blasphemous imitation of the kingdom of God. But this formal similarity to the divine title is overshadowed by some crucial differences. The description of the beasts uses neither definite articles nor participles, as is the case with the divine name. It is only a description, not a title. John will only go so far in asserting parallels between the beast and God. Even more obvious is the alteration of "...is to come" to "...is going to ascend from the abyss and goes to destruction." While the second occurrence of the description says that the beast "will be present" (v. 8b), John is still careful to avoid an exact equivalence of God and the beast by using παρέσται rather than a form of ἔρχομαι or even the simple εἰμι.[116] The keynote remains "goes to destruction." God, through Christ, comes in triumph. The beast goes to a shameful defeat.

Finally, there is the transformation of ὁ ὤν into οὐκ ἔστιν. At one level, this may indicate something about the deceptively peaceful political situation in John's time. The beastly character of the Empire may *seem* to have disappeared ("is not") but it will emerge again.[117] Others may wish to see here a reflection of the Nero legend. Nero, the beast *par excellence*, is not present at the moment, but he will return. In any case, there is an obvious contrast with the description of God as ὁ ὤν, and Christ as ὁ ζῶν (1:18). The former is obvious and will be taken up in the next paragraph. As for the latter, Bauckham has argued convincingly that the parody in ch. 17 is as much a parody of Christ as it is of God the Father. The beast's ascent from the abyss is a counterpart to the return of Christ.[118] Thus we may contrast the three-fold formula for the beast with Christ's words in 1:17-18, "I am the First and the Last and the Living One, and I became dead and behold I am living forever and ever..." The beast parodies Christ's death, resurrection, and return, but he cannot say, "I died and now live forever."

---

[115] This is noted by most commentators. See, e.g., Bauckham, *Climax of Prophecy*, pp.431–41; Caird, p.215; Beasley-Murray, p.254; Kraft, p.217.

[116] As Bauckham (*Climax of Prophecy*, p. 436) notes, the connection between παρέσται and παρουσία is not as significant as it may appear, since John does not use παρουσία for the return of Christ.

[117] See Sweet on 17:8; Caird, p.216.

[118] Bauckham, *Climax of Prophecy*, pp.434–5.

Where Christ's *Dreizeitenformel* has ὁ ζῶν as its present tense element, and God's has ὁ ὤν, the beast's has οὐκ ἔστιν.

The ontological implications of this contrast have not been lost on commentators. Minear writes, "Does the contrast between a perfect and an imperfect formula [i.e. ὁ ὤν vs. οὐκ ἔστιν] constitute the prophet's way of denying ultimate 'Being' to the demonic powers which are set against God? I believe it does."[119] Farrer is even more emphatic:

> In relation to God's world, he [= the beast] is nothingness incarnate, he is already annihilated...As the epitome of not-being, as the type of the working lie, he is the perfect object of idolatrous worship for the idols, we know, are nothing in the world..."[120]

Does the "is not" in fact refer in some way to the "Being" of the beast – or more properly, its Not-Being? There is evidence that it does. We have argued that ὁ ὤν may have had some ontological resonance, and so we might expect something similar in its counterpart οὐκ ἔστιν. One should also note the opening statement of v. 8: Τὸ θηρίον ὃ εἶδες ἦν καὶ οὐκ ἔστιν καὶ μέλλει ἀναβαίνειν κτλ. The formula "which you saw...it is" is a recurring motif in the book of Revelation. As Michaels points out, the "is" represents the truth about a person or situation, comparable to Kahn's "veridical aspect" of the verb to be.[121] Might John be playing with this idea here in order to indicate that the "truth" about the beast is precisely his *Not*-Being?[122] This supposition finds support in the final element of the formula, "...and goes to destruction." The beast's ultimate destiny is annihilation, nothingness. Just as God's "coming" is predicated upon his eternal being (cf. the quote of Comblin above), so the beast's "going to destruction" is the inevitable outworking of his Not-Being.

Another indication that John may be making an ontological statement about the beast comes through John's use of Is. 47:7,8 in his account of the fall of Babylon (18:7). Compare the MT, the LXX, and Revelation:

---

[119] Minear, "Ontology and Ecclesiology," p.100 n.
[120] Farrer, p.291; cf. Vögtle, p.382.
[121] Michaels, *passim*.
[122] Cf. Michaels, p.614, who suggests the οὐκ ἔστιν may connote falsity, as in 2:2,9; 3:9.

Is. 47:7,8 MT
ותאמרי לעולם אהיה גברת עד...האמרה בלבבה אני ואפסי עוד לא
אשב אלמנה ולא אדע שכול

Is.47:7,8 LXX
καὶ εἶπας Εἰς τὸν αἰῶνα ἔσομαι ἄρχουσα...ἡ λέγουσα ἐν τῇ καρδίᾳ αὐτῆς Ἐγώ
εἰμι, καὶ οὐκ ἔστιν ἑτέρα οὐ καθιῶ χήρα οὐδὲ γνώσομαι ὀρφανείαν

Rev. 18:7
ὅτι ἐν τῇ καρδίᾳ αὐτῆς λέγει ὅτι κάθημαι βασίλισσα καὶ χήρα οὐκ εἰμὶ καὶ
πένθος οὐ μὴ ἴδω

The claim of Babylon אני ואפסי עוד is obviously a blasphemous arrogation of the divine prerogatives expressed in the אני הוא of Is.40 ff.. In point of fact, the nations are *as nothing* (כאין) before God (Is.40:17).[123] What is interesting is how John deliberately eliminates Babylon's pretensions to possess independent "Being." He switches the verbs to be (אהיה!) and to sit, so that "I will be a queen forever...I will not sit as a widow" becomes "I sit as a queen...I am not a widow." The claim "I am and there is no other" is by-passed altogether.[124]

I would concur with Minear and Farrer that the three-fold description of the beast in chapter 17 does refer to the "ontological status" of the beast vis-à-vis God. God fundamentally is, the beast fundamentally is not. Idols may exist, in some sense. The political power of the beast may equally have some claim to reality. But insofar as the beast opposes the God who is, it forfeits whatever right it may have had to true existence, and ensures only its own destruction.

Comparison with Other Formulae in Revelation

Now that we have examined the use of the formula "the One who is and was and is to come" in Revelation, we must ask what relationship it bears to other, similar formulae in the book. Why does John feel compelled to include this *Dreizeitenformel* alongside such designations as "the First and

---

[123] Cf. Wis. 14:13, which says regarding idols: οὔτε γὰρ ἦν ἀπ' ἀρχῆς οὔτε εἰς τὸν αἰῶνα ἔσται.

[124] We may compare with this Sib. Or. 5: 173–4: ἀλλ' ἔλεγες »μόνη εἰμὶ καὶ οὐδείς μ' ἐξαλαπάξει«; νῦν δὲ σὲ καὶ σοὺς πάντας ὀλεῖ θεὸς αἰὲν ὑπάρχων, speaking now of Rome rather than Babylon. Collins (in *OTP* 1: 397) notes the connections between this line and Ex. 3:14 and Is. 47:8, 41:4. Cf. Sib. Or. 3:310, where it is said of Babylon καὶ τότ' ἔσῃ, ὡς ἦσθα πρὸ τοῦ, ὡς μὴ γεγονυῖα. According to Sib. Or. 5:34, the returning Nero will declare himself equal to God, "but will prove that he is not" – ἐλέγξει δ' οὐ μιν ἐόντα. While this may allude to his "Not-Being," it more likely means only "will prove that he is not God."

the Last," "the Alpha and the Omega," and "the Beginning and the End" – all of which seem to be saying approximately the same thing?

We cannot discount *aesthetic considerations*. This is no minor concern in a liturgical or quasi-liturgical work like Revelation, where symmetry and image are a crucial part of the communication of the message.[125] At a very basic level, John is seldom content to use one description when several are available. Divine titles appear to be particularly ripe for such multiplication, since the piling up of epithets and attributes was already a part of Jewish worship.[126] John is also very aware of numbers, and given the traditional significance of the number three,[127] it is not surprising that he would choose to employ a tri-partite formula in his description of God. A three-fold formula would be all the more attractive because of its parallels with the Trishagion of Isaiah 6, and with incipient trinitarian formulae such as Rev. 1:4 (God, "seven spirits," Jesus Christ).

John also had the weight of *tradition* with which to reckon. *Dreizeitenformeln* like the one used by John had already been employed at the beginning of other works in antiquity, most notably Hesiod's *Theogony*, the (presumptive) hymn to the gods from Dodona, and the Sibylline Oracles Books 3 and 5. John's use of a similar phrase in 1:19 announces his intention to speak about events from the privileged perspective of the prophet. Depending on what one makes of our suggestion that John may have been aware of pagan descriptions of the gods like those at Dodona and Eleusis, one might also see a *polemical* intent in John's use of the *Dreizeitenformel*. If false gods are going to claim that they "were, are, and will be," John will answer them in kind.

Did John use ὁ ὢν καὶ ὁ ἦν καὶ ὁ ἐρχόμενος only for the above reasons, or did this phrase communicate something more than "the Beginning and the End," "the First and the Last," and "the Alpha and the Omega"? I would say that it did. To begin with, the use of "the One who is and was and is to come" brings the alert reader back to the Exodus (whether via the LXX or traditions preserved in the Targums). We have already noted how such an allusion serves both to confirm John's prophetic calling and to connect the book of Revelation with God's previous acts of deliverance. The description of God as ὁ ὢν is especially useful. Not only does it provide an explicit avowal of ὢν's present existence, which is only implicit

---

[125] It is possible, of course, that the formula was already a part of Christian liturgy and thus available for John's use. Liturgies, however, must emerge somewhere, and we will work under the assumption that John himself is responsible for the formula as we have it.

[126] See, e.g. 1 En. 27:3; Ap. Abr. 17:8ff.; Ladder of Jacob 2:17–18.

[127] E.g. Aristotle (*De Caelo* 268a10, quoted from Guthrie 1: 193), who says the Pythagoreans believed "the whole world and all things in it are summed up in the number three; for end, middle and beginning give the number of the whole, and their number is the triad."

in phrases like "the Beginning and the End." Far more importantly, it evokes various aspects of God's divine glory, from his supra-temporality to his genuineness to his presence with his people.

Finally, John's transformation of the expected "will be" into "is to come" creates a dynamic image which sets it apart from both the two-part formulae in Revelation and the *Dreizeitenformeln* in extra-biblical literature. "The Beginning and the End," for instance, evokes an image of God embracing all of history. He defines its limits, ordering its origins and its consummation. As such, it fits fairly congenially with similar phrases in Greek literature, such as *Laws* 715e ff. The idea that God *is to come* to consummate history sets up a different image, of God intruding into history. As we have remarked numerous times, this would be most disconcerting to a Greek philosopher. "Zeus was, Zeus is, Zeus will be" might be likened to the sun, maintaining its (perceived) course above the earth in a reliable, endless cycle. With "the one who is and was and is to come," it is as though this sun comes down to earth.

Conclusion

We have attempted in this study to shed some light on an obscure period in the history of the name YHWH. One is tempted to speak of the "silent years" of the tetragrammaton. There is of course some justification for this. As we have shown, there was a widespread custom of not pronouncing YHWH "according to its letters" in the second temple period. The custom probably began with the restriction of the name in oaths and curses and was then extended to a general prohibition. The sectaries at Qumran were particularly attentive to the question of the divine name, and treated even the written tetragrammaton with extreme delicacy.

But this is only a part of the story. For all the efforts to draw a veil over the name, it keeps peeking out behind the shrouds. The High Priest almost certainly pronounced the name on the day of atonement, and it is likely that the name was also pronounced during the daily blessing of the priests. We must reckon, then, with a substantial proportion of the population who knew the "proper" pronunciation of the divine name, even if we only consider those Jews who were actually present during these ceremonies. It seems more likely than not that many of these people would have shared this knowledge at least with their family and Jewish friends. It is not then surprising to hear the rabbis tell of ordinary Jews using the name to curse their fellows.

If these were the "silent years", then, we must say that it was a very loud silence – and not only because many people probably knew the name, and some apparently used it. The silence itself spoke. When someone like Josephus informed his readers that he was "not permitted" to share the name of his god with outsiders, he was making a very clear statement about the boundaries of his community and the uniqueness of the Jewish faith. If the name had simply been forgotten, there would be no more for us to say. As it stands, the deliberate restriction of the name to Jews was a proclamation of their unwillingness to melt into the wider hellenistic culture.

We have also seen that the interpretation of the name gave expression to central themes in Jewish theology. The voice from the burning bush was still echoing in early Judaism. The name could underscore the glory of the God in whom they trusted: the God who *was always there* and who created the world, *would always be there* and would create the world to come. More pointedly, the name could serve to affirm Israel's unique identity over against the peoples. The God who *was* there for Israel in Egypt *would be* there for them in their captivity to Rome. Here again, the question of the meaning of the name cannot be separated from the issue of Jewish identity in the hellenistic world.

But the interpretation of the name was not simply a way of affirming the old stories in a familiar way. Jewish thinkers also used the name to address the legitimate questions posed by Greek philosophy, and in so doing broadened the understanding of what YHWH might mean for the world. Yet they did it in such as way as to maintain a substantial continuity with the tradition. We have argued that the capstone of this endeavor is the Septuagint translation of Ex. 3:14, which manages to do a capable job of handling a difficult Hebrew text, while simultaneously addressing – and radically redefining – the question of Being as posed by Parmenides, Plato, and their successors. This in turn supported the deep engagement with Greek thought found in Philo and the early Greek Fathers.

It is against such a background that we must view John's description of God in Rev. 1:4. John may have had his vision of YHWH on an island, but he was hardly isolated from the religious and political currents of his day. It seems reasonably certain that he was drawing on a Jewish tradition which described God as the one who "is and was and will be." But this Jewish description was itself a response to pagan claims that Zeus or the world "was, is, and will be." We have seen evidence to suggest that John may have been aware of some of these pagan claims, and that his use of the *Dreizeitenformel* had a polemical thrust to it. In this respect he was following in the footsteps of his Jewish forbears. He proclaimed the name of God in a way that was comprehensible to the wider world, while at the same time he asserted that this God was the only true claimant to the title, "the One who is and was and is to come." The Greeks may receive due credit for the euphony of the phrase, but it is at heart a Jewish message.

It is, however, a very distinctive Jewish message. John seems to have been the first to substitute "is to come" for the expected "will be." But even this could still sit comfortably within a first century Jewish context. What sets John's description apart is the fact that this "coming" of God is inextricably linked with the coming of Christ. It is surely no coincidence that in between the *Dreizeitenformeln* in 1:4,8, John gives his conflated quotation of Dan. 7:13 and Zech. 12:10: "Behold he is coming with the clouds, and every eye will see him..." (Rev. 1:7). John cannot utter the name of God without at the same time invoking the person of Christ.

Bibliography

Albrektson, Bertil. "On the Syntax of אהיה אשר אהיה in Exodus 3:14." In *Words and Meanings*. Edited by Peter R. Ackroyd and Barnabas Lindars. Cambridge: Cambridge University Press, 1968: 15-28.
Albright, W. F. "Contributions to Biblical Archaeology and Philology: The Name Yahweh." *JBL* 43 (1924): 370-78.
Alexander, P. S. Review of *Divine Name and Presence*, by Robert Hayward. *JJS* 34 (1983): 217-20.
Alföldi, A. *Aion in Mérida und Aphrodisias*. Madrider Beiträge 6. Mainz am Rhein: Zabern, 1979.
―――. "From the *Aion Plutonios* of the Ptolemies to the *Saeculum Frugiferum* of the Roman Emperors." In *Greece and the Eastern Mediterranean in Ancient History and Prehistory*. Edited by K. H. Kinzl. Berlin/New York: Walter de Gruyter, 1977: 1-30.
―――. "Redeunt Saturnia Regna." *Chiron* 3 (1973): 131-42.
Allen, R. E. *Plato's 'Parmenides'*. Oxford: Blackwell, 1983.
Allen, Thomas W., ed. *Homeri Ilias*. Oxford: Oxford University Press, 1931.
Allo, E. B. *Saint Jean: L'Apocalypse*. Paris: Lecoffre, 1933.
Alon, Gedalyahu. *Jews, Judaism, and the Classical World*. Translated by Israel Abrahams. Jerusalem: Magnes Press, 1977.
Andersen, Francis I. and Freedman, David N. *Amos*. AB. New York: Doubleday, 1989.
Aristotle. *On the Cosmos*. Translated by D. J. Furley. LCL. London: Wm. Heinemann/Cambridge: Harvard University Press, 1955.
―――. *On the Heavens*. Translated by W. K. C. Guthrie. LCL. London: Wm. Heinemann/Cambridge: Harvard University Press, 1939.
―――. *The Metaphysics*. Translated by Hugh Tredennick. 2 vols. LCL. London: Wm. Heinemann/Cambridge: Harvard University Press, 1933-5.
―――. *Metaphysics*. Translated by by Christopher Kirwan. 2nd Edited by Oxford: Oxford University Press, 1993.
―――. *Physica*. Translated by R. P. Hardie and R. K. Gaye. Oxford: Oxford University Press, 1930.
―――. *The Physics*. Translated by Philip H. Wicksteed and F. M. Cornford. 2 vols. LCL. London: Wm. Heinemann/Cambridge: Harvard University Press, 1934.
Arnold, W. R. "The Divine Name in Ex. 3:14." *JBL* 24 (1905): 107-65.
Athanassakis, Apostolos N. *The Orphic Hymns*. Missoula, MT: Scholars Press, 1977.
Aune, David E. "The Apocalypse of John and Graeco-Roman Revelatory Magic." *NTS* 33 (1987): 481-501.
―――. *Revelation 1-5*. Word Biblical Commentary. Dallas: Word, 1997.
Ball, David M. *'I Am' in John's Gospel*. JSNTSS 124. Sheffield: JSOT, 1996.
Bamberger, Bernard J. "The Dating of Aggadic Material." *JBL* 68 (1949): 115-123.
Baneth, Eduard, ed. *Mishnajot: Teil II, Ordnung Mo'ed*. Basel: Victor Goldschmidt, 1968.

Barker, Margaret. *The Great Angel*. London: SPCK, 1992.
Barnes, Jonathan. *The Pre-Socratic Philosophers*. 2 vols. London: Routledge and Kegan Paul, 1979.
————. ed. *The Cambridge Companion to Aristotle*. Cambridge: Cambridge University Press, 1995.
Barr, James. *The Semantics of Biblical Language*. Oxford: Oxford University Press, 1961.
Barrett, C. K. *The Gospel According to St. John*. 2nd ed. London: SPCK, 1978.
Bates, W. H. "The Composition of the Anaphora of Apostolic Constitutions VIII." *Studia Patristica* 13/II (1975): 343–355.
Bauckham, Richard. *The Climax of Prophecy*. Edinburgh: T.&T. Clark, 1993.
————. *Jude and the Relatives of Jesus in the Early Church*. Edinburgh: T.&T. Clark, 1990.
————. *The Theology of the Book of Revelation*. Cambridge: Cambridge University Press, 1993.
Baudissin, Wolf W. G. *Kyrios als Gottesname*. 4 vols. Giessen: Alfred Topelmann, 1929.
Baumgarten, Joseph M. " את הו הכול - אונ הו הכול: A Reply to M. Kister." *JQR* 84 (1994): 485–87.
————. "A New Qumran Substitute for the Divine Name and Mishnah Sukkah 4.5." *JQR* 83 (1992): 1–5.
Beale, G. K. *Revelation*. NIGTC. Grand Rapids, MI: Eerdmans/Exeter: Paternoster, forthcoming.
————. "The Interpretative Problem of Rev. 1:19." *NovT* 34 (1992): 360–87.
————. "The Old Testament Background of Rev. 3:14." *NTS* 42 (1996): 133–52.
Beasley-Murray, George R. *The Book of Revelation*. NCB. London: Oliphants, 1974.
————. *The Gospel of John*. WBC. Waco, TX: Word, 1987.
Beattie, D. R. G., and McNamara, M. J., eds. *The Aramaic Bible: Targums in their Historical Context*. Sheffield: JSOT, 1994.
Beckwith, Isbon T. *The Apocalypse of John*. London: Macmillan, 1919.
Belardi, Walter. "Omero, A 70." *Maia* 3 (1950): 54–6.
Belayche, N. "Aïôn: vers une sublimation du temps." In *Le temps chrétien de la fin de l'antiquité au moyen âge, IIIe–XIIIe siècles*. Edited by Jean-Marie LeRoux. Paris: Éditions du Centre National de la Recherche Scientifique, 1984: 11–29.
Bertrand, Daniel A. *La vie grecque d'Adam et Ève*. Paris: Adrien Maisonneuve, 1987.
Betz, H. D., ed. *The Greek Magical Papyri in Translation*. 2 vols Chicago: University of Chicago Press, 1986.
Beyer, Klaus. *Die aramäischen Texte vom Toten Meer*. Göttigen: Vandenhoeck and Ruprecht, 1984.
Bickel, Ernst. "Senecas Briefe 58 und 65." *Rheinisches Museum für Philologie* n. f. 103 (1960): 1–20.
Black, Matthew. *The Book of Enoch or 1 Enoch*. Studia in Veteris Testamenti Pseudepigrapha 7. Leiden: Brill, 1985.
Boll, F. *Aus der Offenbarung Johannis*. Amsterdam: Hakkert, 1967; repr. Leipzig: Teubner, 1914.
Bonner, Campbell. *Studies in Magical Amulets: Chiefly Graeco-Egyptian*. Ann Arbor: University of Michigan Press, 1950.
Bousset, Wilhelm. *Kyrios Christos*. Translated by John E. Steely. Nashville: Abingdon, 1970.
Bredin, Mark. "The Influence of the Aqedah on Revelation 5:6–9." *Irish Biblical Studies* 18 (1996): 26–43.

Brenk, Frederick. "An Imperial Heritage: The Religious Spirit of Plutarch of Chaironeia." *ANRW* II.36.1: 248-349.
Brown, Raymond. *The Gospel according to John.* 2 vols. AB Garden City, NY: Doubleday, 1966-70.
Bruce, F. F. *The Epistle to the Hebrews.* New London Commentaries on the New Testament. London/Edinburgh: Marshall, Morgan, & Scott, 1965.
Brunschwig, Jacques. "Did Diogenes of Babylon invent the ontological argument?." In Brunschwig, *Papers in Hellenistic Philosophy.* Translated by Janet Lloyd. Cambridge: Cambridge University Press, 1994: 170-89.
———. "The Stoic theory of the supreme genus and Platonic ontology." In *Papers in Hellenistic Philosophy*: 92-157.
Buchanan, G. W. *To the Hebrews.* AB. Garden City, NY: Doubleday, 1972.
Büchsel, Friedrich. "εἰμι." *TDNT* 2: 398-400.
Burkett, Delbert. *The Son of Man in the Gospel of John.* JSNTSS 56. Sheffield: JSOT, 1991.
Byington, Steven T. "יהוה and אדני." *JBL* 76 (1957): 58-9.
Caird, G. B. *A Commentary on the Revelation of St. John the Divine.* BNTC. London: A.&C. Black, 1966.
Caquot, A., and Geoltrain, P. "Notes sur le texte éthiopien des 'Paraboles' d'Henoch." *Semitica* 13 (1963): 39-54.
Caster, Marcel, ed. *Clement: Les Stromates* I. SC 30. Paris: Cerf, 1951.
Cazelles, Henri. *Autour de L'Exode.* Sources bibliques. Paris: LeCoffre, 1987.
Cerbelaud, Dominique. "Le nom d'Adam et les points cardinaux: récherche sur un thème patristique." *Vigiliae Christianae* 38 (1984): 285-301.
Charles, R. H. *The Book of Enoch.* Oxford: Oxford University Press, 1893.
———. *A Critical and Exegetical Commentary on the Revelation of St. John.* 2 vols. ICC. Edinburgh: T.&T. Clark, 1920.
Charlesworth, James H. "A Prolegomenon to the New Study of the Jewish Background of the Hymns and Prayers in the New Testament." *JJS* 33 (1982): 264-85.
———. ed. *The Old Testament Pseudepigrapha.* 2 vols. NY: Doubleday, 1983.
Childs, Brevard. *Exodus.* Old Testament Library. London: SCM Press, 1974.
Chilton, B. D., trans. *The Isaiah Targum.* Aramaic Bible. Edinburgh: T.&T. Clark, 1987.
Clay, Jenny Strauss. "What the Muses Sang." *Greek, Roman, and Byzantine Studies* 29 (1988): 323-33.
Cohon, Samuel S. "The Name of God: A Study in Rabbinic Theology." *HUCA* 23, Part 1 (1950-51): 579-604.
Collins, A. Y. *Crisis and Catharsis: The Power of the Apocalypse.* Philadelphia: Westminster, 1984.
Colpe, C. "Geister (Dämonen)." In *Reallexikon für Antike und Christentum* 9 (Stuttgart: Anton Hiersemann, 1976): 618-19.
Comblin, J. *Le Christ dans L'Apocalypse.* Paris: Descleé, 1965.
Cook, A. B. *Zeus.* 3 vols. Cambridge: Cambridge University Press, 1914-40.
Cornford, F. M. *Plato and Parmenides.* London: Kegan Paul, Trench, Tubner, 1939.
———. *Plato's Cosmology.* London: Kegan Paul, Trench, Tubner/New York: Harcourt, Brace, 1937.
Court, John M. *Myth and History in the Book of Revelation.* London: SPCK, 1979.
Cowley, A. *Aramaic Papyri of the Fifth Century.* Oxford: Oxford University Press, 1923.
Cranfield, C. E. B. *The Epistle to the Romans.* 2 vols. ICC. Edinburgh: T.&T. Clark, 1979.

Cross, F. M. *Canaanite Myth and Hebrew Epic*. Cambridge: Harvard University Press, 1973.
Cullmann, Oscar. *Christ and Time*. Rev. ed. Translated by Floyd V. Filson. London: SCM Press, 1962.
Cumont, Franz. *Les religions orientales dans le paganisme romain*. 4th ed. Paris: Librairie Orientaliste Paul Geuthier, 1929.
Dahl, N. A. and Segal, Alan F. "Philo and the Rabbis on the Names of God." *JSJ* 9 (1978): 1–28.
Danby, Hebert, trans. *The Mishnah*. Oxford: Oxford University Press, 1933.
Daniélou, Jean. *Primitive Christian Symbols*. Translated by Donald Attwater. Baltimore: Helicon Press, 1964.
Davies, W. D. and Allison, Dale C. *The Gospel according to Saint Matthew*. 2 vols. ICC. Edinburgh: T.&T. Clark, 1988.
Davila, James R. "The Name of God at Moriah: An Unpublished Fragment from 4QGenExod[a]." *JBL* 110 (1991): 577–82.
de Vaux, Roland. "The Revelation of the Divine Name YHWH." In *Proclamation and Presence: OT Essays in Honor of G. H. Davies*. Edited by John I. Durham and J. R. Porter. London: SCM Press, 1970: 48–75.
de Vries, G. J. *A Commentary on the Phaedrus of Plato*. Amsterdam: Hakkert, 1969.
Delcor, Matthias. "La signification de l'E delphique et Exode 3,14–15." In *De la Tôrah au Messie*. Edited by M. Carrez, J. Doré, and P. Grelot. Paris: Desclée, 1981: 361–8.
———. *Les hymnes de Qumran: Hodayot*. Autour de la Bible. Paris: Letouzey et Ané, 1962.
Delling, Gerhard. "Die Altarinschrift eines Gottesfürchtigen in Pergamon." *NovT* 7 (1964-5): 73–80.
"Der Orphische Papyrus von Derveni." *Zeitschrift für Papyrologie und Epigraphik* 47 (1982): after p.300.
des Places, Édouard. "La langue philosophique de Platon: Le vocabulaire de l'être." *CRAI* (1961): 88–94.
Diels, Hermann, and Kranz, Walther, eds. *Die Fragmente der Vorsokratiker*. Eleventh ed. 3 vols. Zürich/Berlin: Weidmannsche, 1964.
Dillon, John. *The Middle Platonists*. London: Duckworth, 1977.
Discoveries in the Judaean Desert I. Edited by D. Barthélemy and J. T. Milik. Oxford: Oxford University Press, 1955.
Discoveries in the Judaean Desert of Jordan IV. Edited by James Sanders. Oxford: Oxford University Press, 1965.
Discoveries in the Judaean Desert VII. Edited by Maurice Baillet. Oxford: Oxford University Press, 1982.
Discoveries in the Judaean Desert IX. Edited by Patrick W. Skehan, Eugene Ulrich, and Judith E. Sanderson. Oxford: Oxford University Press, 1992.
Discoveries in the Judaean Desert XIII. Edited by Harold Attridge, et al. Oxford: Oxford University Press, 1994.
Dittenberger, Wm., ed. *Sylloge Inscriptionum Graecorum*. 3rd ed. Leipzig: Hirzel, 1920.
Dodd, C. H. *The Bible and the Greeks*. London: Hodder and Stoughton, 1935.
———. *The Interpretation of the Fourth Gospel*. Cambridge: Cambridge University Press, 1953.
Dunn, James. *Romans 1–9*. WBC. Dallas: Word, 1988.
Dupont-Sommer, André. "Le syncrétisme religieux des Juifs d'Éléphantine d'après un ostracon araméen inédit." *Revue de l'histoire des religions* 130 (1945): 17–28.

———. "'Yaho' et 'Yaho Seba'ot' sur des ostraca araméens inédits d'Éléphantine." *CRAI* (1947): 175-191.
Eerdmans, B. D. "The Name Jahu." *Oudtestamentische Studiën* 5 (1948): 1-29.
Ellul, Jacques. *Apocalypse*. Translated by George W. Schreiner. NY: Seabury, 1977.
Epictetus. *Works*. 2 vols. Translated by W. A. Oldfather. LCL. London: Wm. Heinemann/NY: Geo. Putnam's Sons, 1925-8.
Euripedes. *Works*, vol. I. Translated by by A. S. Way. LCL. London: Wm. Heinemann/NY: Macmillan, 1912.
Evans, Craig A. "Mishna and Messiah 'in Context': Some Comments on Jacob Neusner's Proposals." *JBL* 112 (1993): 267-89.
———. *Non-Canonical Writings and New Testament Interpretation*. Peabody, MA: Hendrickson, 1992.
Evans, C. F. *Saint Luke*. London: SCM/Philadelphia: Trinity Press International, 1990.
Farrer, Austin. *A Rebirth of Images*. Westminster: Dacre Press, 1949.
Fauth, W. "Aion." In *Der Kleine Pauly: Lexikon der Antike*. Vol. 1. Edited by Konrat Ziegler and Walther Sontheimer. Stuttgart: Druckenmüller, 1964: 185-8.
Feeney, D. C. *The Gods in Epic*. Oxford: Oxford University Press, 1991.
Feldman, Louis H. *Jew and Gentile in the Ancient World*. Princeton: Princeton University Press, 1993.
———. "Introduction." In *Josephus, Judaism, and Christianity*. Edited by Louis H. Feldman and Gohei Hata. Detroit: Wayne St. University Press, 1987.
———. "Josephus' Portrayal of the Hasmoneans." In *Josephus and the History of the Greco-Roman Period*. Edited by Fausto Parente and Joseph Sievers. Leiden: Brill, 1994: 41-68.
Festugière, A. J. "À propos des arétalogies d'Isis." *HTR* 42 (1949): 209-34.
———. *La Révélation d'Hermès Trismégiste*, 4 vols.; vol. 2: *Le dieu cosmique*. Paris: Libairie LeCoffre, 1944-54.
———. *La Révélation d'Hermès Trismégiste*; vol. 4, *Le dieu inconnu*.
Fiensy, David. "The Hellenistic Synagogal Prayers: One Hundred Years of Discussion." *JSOP* 5 (1989): 17-27.
———. "Redaction History and the Apostolic Constitutions." *JQR* 72 (1982): 293-302.
Fitzmyer, Joseph. *The Gospel According to Luke*. AB. Garden City, NY: Doubleday, 1981.
———. "New Testament Kyrios and Maranatha and their Aramaic Background." In *To Advance the Gospel: New Testament Studies*. NY: Crossroad, 1981: 218-35.
———. "The Semitic Background of the New Testament *Kyrios*-Title." In *A Wandering Aramean: Collected Aramaic Essays*. SBL Monograph Series 25. Missoula, MT: Scholars Press, 1979: 115-42.
Flusser, David. "Sanktus und Gloria." In *Abraham unser Vater*. Edited by O. Betz, M. Hengel, and P. Schmidt. Leiden/Köln: Brill, 1963: 129-52.
Foerster, Werner. "κυριος." *TDNT*, 3:1039-98.
Ford, J. Massyngbe. *Revelation*. AB. Garden City, NY: Doubleday, 1975.
Fossum, Jarl E. *The Name of God and the Angel of the Lord*. WUNT 36. Tübingen: J. C. B. Mohr (Paul Siebeck), 1985.
Fränkel, Hermann. *Early Greek Poetry and Philosophy*. Translated by Moses Hadas and James Willis. Oxford: Blackwell, 1975.
Freedman, David N. "The Name of the God of Moses." *JBL* 79 (1960): 151-56.
Freedman, David N., and O'Connor, M. P. "YHWH." *TDOT* 5: 500-21.
Freeman, Kathleen. *Ancilla to the Pre-Socratic Philosophers*. Oxford: Blackwell, 1956.

Freudenthal, J. "Septuagint: Are there Traces of Greek Philosophy in the Septuagint?" *JQR* 2 (1890): 205–222.
Friesen, Steven J. "Revelation, Realia, and Religion: Archaeology in the Interpretation of the Apocalypse." *HTR* 88 (1995): 291–314.
Furth, Montgomery. "Elements of Eleatic Ontology." In *The Presocratics*. Edited by Alexander Mourelatos. Garden City, NY: Doubleday, 1974: 241–70.
Gabel, J. B., and Wheeler, C. B. "The Redactor's Hand in the Blasphemy Pericope of Leviticus XXIV." *VT* 30 (1980): 227–9.
Ganschinietz. "Iao." *PW* 7: 698–722.
Ganschinietz. "Israel." *PW* 9: 2233–4.
García Martínez, Florentino, trans. *The Dead Sea Scrolls Translated*. Second Edition. Translated by Wilfred G. E. Watson. Leiden: Brill/Grand Rapids, MI: Eerdmans, 1996.
Geffcken, J. *Die Oracula Sibyllina*. GCS 8. Leipzig: J. C. Hinrichs'sche, 1902.
Gersh, Stephen. *Middle Platonism and Neoplatonism: The Latin Tradition*. 2 vols. Notre Dame: U. of Notre Dame Press, 1986.
Gifford, Edwin H., trans. and ed. *Eusebius: Preparation for the Gospel*. Oxford: Oxford University Press, 1903.
Gigon, Olof. "Die Theologie der Vorsokratiker." In Gigon, *Studien zur antiken Philosophie*. Edited by Andreas Graeser. Berlin/New York: Walter de Gruyter, 1972: 41–68.
Ginzberg, L. *Legends of the Jews* 7 vols. Philadelphia: Jewish Publication Society of America, 1946.
Gladigow, Burkhard. "Götternamen und Name Gottes." In *Der Name Gottes*. Edited by H. von Stietencron. Düsseldorf: Patmos, 1975: 13–32.
Goldenberg, David M. "Antiquities IV: 277 and 288 Compared with Early Rabbinic Law." In *Josephus, Judaism, and Christianity*: 198–211.
Goodenough, E. R. *Jewish Symbols in the Greco-Roman Period*. 13 vols. NY: Pantheon, 1953–68.
Griffiths, J. Gwyn. *Plutarch's De Iside et Osiride*. Swansea: U. of Wales Press, 1970.
Groarke, Leo. "Parmenides' Timeless Universe." *Dialogue* 24 (1985): 535–41.
Gundry, R. H. *Matthew: A Commentary on his Literary and Theological Art*. Grand Rapids, MI: Eerdmans, 1982.
Guthrie, W. K. C. *A History of Greek Philosophy*. 6 vols. Cambridge: Cambridge University Press, 1962–78.
———. *Orpheus and Greek Religion* 2nd ed. London: Methuen, 1952.
Hallo, William. "Scurrilous Etymologies." In *Pomegranates and Golden Bells*. Festschrift for Jacob Milgrom. Edited by David P. Wright, David Noel Freedman, and Avi Hurvitz. Winona Lake, IN: Eisenbrauns, 1995: 767–76.
Hankinson, R. J. *The Sceptics*. London: Routledge, 1995.
Harl, Marguerite; Dorival, Gilles; and Munnich, Olivier. *La Bible greque des Septante*. Paris: Cerf, 1988.
Harner, Philip B. *The 'I Am' of the Fourth Gospel*. Facet Books, Biblical Series. Philadelphia: Fortress, 1970.
Harrington, D. J. "The *Raz Nihyeh* in a Qumran Wisdom text." *RQ* 65–8 (1996): 549–53.
Hata, Gohei. "The Story of Moses Interpreted within the Context of anti-Semitism." In *Josephus, Judaism, and Christianity*, eds. Feldman and Hata: 180–197.
Hawthorne, Gerald. *Philippians*. WBC. Dallas: Word, 1983.
Hayward, Robert. *Divine Name and Presence: The Memra*. Totowa, NJ: Allanhead, Osmun, and Co., 1981.

———. "The Holy Name of the God of Moses and the Prologue of St. John's Gospel." *NTS* 25 (1978-9): 16-32.
Heitsch, Ernst, ed. *Hesiod*. Darmstadt: Wissenschaftliche Buchgesellschaft, 1966.
Held, Klaus. *Heraklit, Parmenides, und der Anfang von Philosophie und Wissenschaft*. Berlin/New York: Walter de Gruyter, 1980.
Helm, Paul. *Eternal God*. Oxford: Oxford University Press, 1988.
Hemer, Colin J. *The Letters to the Seven Churches of Asia in their Local Setting*. JSNTSS 11. Sheffield: JSOT, 1986.
Hengel, Martin. *Jews, Greeks, and Barbarians*. Translated by John Bowden London: SCM Press, 1980.
———. *Judaism and Hellenism*. 2 vols. Translated by John Bowden. London: SCM Press, 1974.
Hofius, Otfried. *Der Christushymnus Philipper 2:6-11*. WUNT 14. Tübingen: J. C. B. Mohr (Paul Siebeck), 1976.
———. "Das Zeugnis der Johannesoffenbarung von der Gottheit Jesu Christi." In *Geschichte - Tradition - Reflexion: Festschrift für Martin Hengel zum 70. Geburtstag; Vol. III: Frühes Christentum*, ed. Hermann Lichtenberger. J. C. B. Mohr (Paul Siebeck), 1996: 511-28.
Holladay, Carl R. *Fragments from Hellenistic Jewish Authors, Volume IV: Orphica*. Atlanta: Scholars Press, 1996.
Holladay, William. *A Concise Hebrew and Aramaic Lexicon of the Old Testament*. Grand Rapids, MI: Eerdmans, 1971.
Holm-Nielsen, Svend. *Hodayot: Psalms from Qumran*. Aarhus: Universitetsforlaget, 1960.
Holtz, Traugott. *Die Christologie der Apokalypse des Johannes*. 2nd. ed. Berlin: Akademie-Verlag, 1971.
———. "Gott in der Apokalypse." In *L'Apocalypse johannique et l'Apocalyptique dans le Nouveau Testament*. Edited by J. Lambrecht. BETL 53. Gembloux: Duculot/Louvain: University Press, 1980: 247-65.
Howard, George. "The Tetragram and the New Testament." *JBL* 96 (1977): 63-83.
Hurtado, Larry W. *One Lord, One God: Early Christian Devotion and Ancient Jewish Monotheism*. Philadelphia: Fortress Press, 1988.
Hyatt, J. Philip. *Exodus*. NBC. London: Marshall, Morgan, and Scott, 1971.
Jaeger, Werner. *The Theology of the Early Greek Philosophers*. London: Oxford University Press, 1947.
Jervell, Jacob. "Imagines und Imago Dei: Aus der Genesis-Exegese des Josephus." In *Josephus-Studien*. Edited by Otto Betz, Klaus Haacker, and Martin Hengel. Göttingen: Vandenhoeck and Ruprecht, 1974: 197-204.
Josephus. *Works*. 9 vols. Translated by H. St. J. Thackeray, Ralph Marcus, Allen Wickgren, and L. H. Feldman. LCL. London: Wm. Heinemann/NY: Geo. Putnam's Sons/Cambridge: Harvard University Press, 1926-65.
Kahn, Charles H. "Some Philosophical Uses of "to be" in Plato." *Phronesis* 26 (1981): 105-34.
———. *The Verb "Be" in Ancient Greek*. The Verb 'Be' and Its Synonyms: Philosophical and Grammatical Studies, Part 6. Series ed. John W. M. Verhaar. Dordrecht: Reidel, 1973.
Kern, Otto, ed. *Orphicorum Fragmenta*. Berlin: Weidmann, 1922.
Ketchum, Richard. "Plato on Real Being." *American Philosophical Quarterly* 17 (1980): 213-20.

Kirk, G. S.; Raven, J. E.; and Schofield, M. *The Pre-Socratic Philosophers*. 2nd ed. Cambridge: Cambridge University Press, 1983.
Kneale, W. "Time and Eternity in Theology." *Proceedings of the Aristotelian Society* 61 (1960–1): 87–108.
Kotansky, Roy. *Greek Magical Amulets: Part I*. Opladen: Westdeutscher Verlag, 1994.
Kraft, Heinrich. *Die Offenbarung des Johannes*. HNT 16a. Tübingen: J. C. B. Mohr (Paul Siebeck), 1974.
Kraub, Samuel. *Die Mishna: Sanhedrin, Makkot*. Giessen: A. Töpelmann, 1933.
Kraut, Richard. "Introduction to the Study of Plato." In *The Cambridge Companion to Plato*. Edited by Richard Kraut. Cambridge: Cambridge University Press, 1992.
Kraybill, J. Nelson. *Imperial Culture and Commerce in John's Apocalypse*. JSNTSS 132. Sheffield: JSOT, 1996.
Kurfess, Alfons. "Homer und Hesiod im 1. Buch der Oracula Sibyllina." *Philologus* 100 (1956): 147–53.
L.-Duhaime, Jean. "L'Instruction sur les deux esprits et les interpolations dualistes à Qumrân 1QS III, 13–IV, 26." *Revue biblique* 84 (1977): 566–594.
Lacocque, André. *Le devenir de Dieu*. Encyclopédie Universitaire. Paris: Éditions Universitaires, 1967.
Lane, Eugene N. "Sabazius and the Jews in Valerius Maximus: A Re-examination." *Journal of Roman Studies* 69 (1979): 35–38.
Lange, Armin. *Weisheit und Prädestination: Weisheitliche Urordnung und Prädestination in den Textfunden von Qumran*. STDJ 18. Leiden: Brill, 1995.
Lanne, Emmanuel. "Les ordinations dans le rite copte." *L'Orient syrien* 5 (1960): 81–106.
Lattimore, Richard, trans. *The Iliad of Homer*. Chicago: University of Chicago Press, 1951.
Lauterbach, Jacob, trans. *Mekilta de Rabbi Ishmael*. 3 vols. Philadelphia: Jewish Publication Society of America, 1949.
Le Boulluec, Alain, and Sandevoir, Pierre. *La Bible d'Alexandrie: L'Exode*. Paris: Cerf, 1989.
Le Déaut, R. *Introduction à la Littérature Targumique*. Part I. Rome: Pontifical Biblical Institute, 1966.
―――. *The Message of the New Testament and the Aramaic Bible*. Subsidia Biblica 5. Rome: Pontifical Biblical Institute, 1982.
―――, trans. *Targum du Pentateuque*. SC. Paris: Cerf, 1978–80.
Leftow, Brian. *Time and Eternity*. Ithaca: Cornell University Press, 1991.
Le Glay, Marcel. "Abrasax." In *Lexicon Iconographicum Mythologiae Classicae*, I/1 (Zurich and Munich: Artemis, 1981): 2–7.
Levine, Etan. "The Biography of the Aramaic Bible." *Zeitschrift für die Altestamentliche Wissenschaft* 94 (1992): 353–379.
Lexicon Iconographicum Mythologiae Classicae, I/2 (Zurich and Munich: Artemis, 1981).
Lindars, Barnabas. *The Gospel of John*. NCB. London: Oliphants, 1972.
Lindblom, J. "Noch einmal die Deutung des Jahwe-Namens." *Annual of the Swedish Theological Institute* 3 (1964): 4–15.
Lohmeyer, Ernst. *Die Offenbarung des Johannes*. 2nd ed. HNT 16. Tübingen: J. C. B. Mohr (Paul Siebeck), 1953.
Lohse, Eduard, ed. *Die Texte aus Qumran*. 3rd ed. Darmstadt: Wissenschaftliche Buchgesellschaft, 1981.
Long, A. A. *Hellenistic Philosophy*. London: Duckworth, 1974.

Long, A. A., and Sedley, D. N. *The Hellenistic Philosphers*. 2 vols. Cambridge: Cambridge University Press, 1987.
MacKinnon, D. M. "Aristotle's Conception of Substance." In *New Essays in Plato and Aristotle*. Edited by Renford Bambrough. London: Routledge and Kegan Paul, 1965: 97–119.
Maehler, Herwig. *Die Auffassung des Dichterberufs im frühen Griechentum bis zur Zeit Pindars*. Göttingen: Vandenhoeck & Ruprecht, 1963.
Malcolm, John. "Plato's Analysis of τὸ ὄν and τὸ μὴ ὄν in the *Sophist*." *Phronesis* 12 (1967): 130–46.
Malina, Bruce. *On the Genre and Message of Revelation*. Peabody, MA: Hendrickson, 1995.
Marmorstein, A. *The Old Rabbinic Doctrine of God*. London: Oxford, 1927.
———. "Philo and the Names of God." *JQR* 22 (1931): 295–306.
Martin, J. P. "La Primera Exegesis Ontologica de 'Yo soy El que es' Exodo 3,14–LXX." *Stromata* 5: 93–115.
Martin, Ralph P. *Carmen Christi: Philippians 2:5–11 in Recent Interpretation and in the Setting of Early Christian Worship*. Rev. ed. SNTSMS 4. Grand Rapids: Eerdmans, 1983.
Masson, Olivier. "Le 'roi' carthaginois Iômilkos dans des inscriptions de Délos." *Semitica* 29 (1979): 53–57.
Mazon, Paul, ed. *Hésiode*. Paris: Société d'Édition, 1967.
McGregor, Leslie John. *The Greek Text of Ezekiel: An Examination of its Homogeneity*. Septuagint and Cognate Studies 18. Atlanta: Scholars Press, 1985.
McKnight, Scot. *A Light among the Gentiles: Jewish Missionary Activity in the Second Temple Period*. Minneapolis: Fortress Press, 1991.
McNamara, Martin. *The New Testament and the Palestinian Targum*. Analecta Biblica 27. Rome: Pontifical Biblical Institute, 1966.
Meinhold, Johannes. *Die Mischna: Joma*. Giessen: A. Töpelmann, 1913.
Merlan, Philip. "ὄν ᾗ ὄν und πρώτη οὐσία: Postskript einer Besprechung." *Philosophische Rundschau* 7 (1959): 148–53.
Mettinger, Tryggve. *In Search of God: The Meaning and Message of the Divine Names*. Translated by Frederick H. Cryer. Philadelphia: Fortress Press, 1988.
Metzger, Marcel, trans. *Les Constitutions Apostoliques*. 3 vols. SC 300,329,336. Paris: Cerf, 1985–87.
Meyer, Eduard. "Hesiods Erga und das Gedicht von den fünf Menschengeschlechtern." In *Hesiod*. Edited by Ernst Heitsch. Darmstadt: Wissenschaftliche Buchgesellschaft, 1966: 471–522.
Michaels, J. Ramsey. "Rev. 1.19 and the Narrative Voices of the Apocalypse." *NTS* 37 (1991): 604–20.
Minear, Paul S. *I Saw a New Earth: An Introduction to the Visions of the Apocalypse*. Washington/Cleveland: Corpus, 1968.
———. "Ontology and Ecclesiology in the Apocalypse." *NTS* 12 (1966): 89–105.
Mohr, Richard D. "Plato on Time and Eternity." *Ancient Philosophy* 6 (1986): 39–46.
Montes-Peral, Luis Angel. *Akataleptos Theos: Der unfassbare Gott*. ALGHJ 16. Leiden: Brill, 1987.
Moore, George Foot. *Judaism in the First Centuries of the Christian Era*. Cambridge: Harvard University Press, 1927.
Mounce, Robert H. *The Book of Revelation*. NICNT. Grand Rapids, MI: Eerdmans, 1977.
Mourelatos, Alexander, ed. *The Presocratics*. Garden City, NY: Doubleday, 1974.
Mras, Karl, ed. *Eusebius Werke*. Vol. 8, pt. 1. Berlin: Akademie-Verlag, 1954.

Muraoka, T. *Emphatic Words and Structures in Biblical Hebrew.* Jerusalem: Magnes Press/Leiden: Brill, 1985.
Mylonas, George E. *Eleusis and the Eleusinian Mysteries.* Princeton: Princeton University Press/London: Routledge and Kegan Paul, 1961.
Nagata, Takeshi. *Philippians 2:5-11: A Case Study in the Contextual Shaping of Early Christology.* Diss. Princeton, 1981.
Nebe, G. Wilhelm. "Der Buchstabenname Yod als Ersatz des Tetragramms in 4Q511, Frag.10, Zeile 12?" *Revue de Qumran* 12 (1986): 283-4.
Neitzel, Heinz. "Hesiod und die lügenden Musen." *Hermes* 108 (1980): 387-401.
Neusner, Jacob. *The Mishnah: A New Translation.* New Haven/London: Yale University Press, 1988.
―――. "The Mishna in Philosophical Context and out of Canonical Bounds." *Journal of Biblical Literature* 112 (1993): 291-304.
―――. *The Tosefta: Nashim.* New York: KTAV, 1979.
―――. "The Use of the Mishnah for the History of Judaism Prior to the Time of the Mishnah." *JSJ* 11 (1980): 177-85.
Newsom, Carol. *Songs of the Sabbath Sacrifice.* Harvard Semitic Studies 27. Atlanta: Scholars Press, 1985.
Nikiprowetzky, V. *Le commentaire de l'Écriture chez Philon Alexandrie.* ALGHJ 11. Leiden: Brill, 1977.
Nilsson, Martin P. "À propos du tombeau de Vincentius." *Revue archéologique.* 31-2 (1949): 764-9.
―――. "The Anguipede of the Magical Amulets." *Harvard Theological Review* 44 (1951): 61-64.
―――. *Geschichte der griechischen Religion.* 2nd ed. 2 vols. Munich: C. H. Beck'sche, 1961.
―――. "Zwei Altäre aus Pergamon." *Eranos* 54 (1956): 167-173.
Nitzan, Bilha. "Hymns from Qumran — 4Q510-4Q511." In *The Dead Sea Scrolls: Forty Years of Research.* STDJ 10. Edited by Devorah Dimant and Uriel Rappaport. Leiden: Brill, 1992: 53-63.
Nock, A. D. "A Vision of Mandulis Aion." *HTR* 27 (1934): 53-104.
―――. "Oracles théologiques." *Revue des études anciennes* 30 (1928): 280-90.
―――. Review of Harder's *Karpocrates von Chalkis. Gnomon* 21 (1949): 221-28.
Norden, Eduard. *Agnostos Theos.* Leipzig: B. G. Teubner, 1913.
Norin, Stig. "Die Wiedergabe JHWH-haltiger Personnamen in der Septuaginta." *SJOT* 1 (1988): 76-95.
O'Brien, Peter. *The Epistle to the Philippians.* NIGTC. Grand Rapids: Eerdmans, 1991.
Ó'Fearghail, Fearghas. "Sir. 50, 5-21: Yom Kippur or The Daily Whole Offering?" *Biblica* 59 (1978): 301-316.
Owen, G. E. L. "Eleatic Questions." *CQ* n. s. 10 (1960): 84-102.
―――. "Plato and Parmenides on the Timeless Present." in Mourelatos, ed. *The Presocratics*: 271-92.
Oxford Annotated Apocrypha. Edited by Bruce Metzger NY: Oxford University Press, 1965.
Parke, H. W. "Mighty Zeus." *Hermathena* 111 (1971): 24-33.
―――. *The Oracles of Zeus.* Oxford: Blackwell, 1967.
Parke-Taylor, G. H. *Yahweh: The Divine Name in the Bible.* Waterloo, Ont.: Wilfrid Laurier University Press, 1975.
Patterson, Richard. "On the Eternality of Platonic Forms." *Archiv für Geschichte der Philosophie* 67 (1985): 27-46.

Patzig, G. "Theology and Ontology in Aristotle's *Metaphysics*." In *Articles in Aristotle: 3: Metaphysics*. Edited by Jonathan Barnes, Malcolm Schofield, and Richard Sorabji. London: Duckworth, 1979: 33–49.
Petuchowski, Jakob. "Judaism as 'Mystery' — The Hidden Agenda?" *HUCA* 52 (1981): 141-152.
Philo, *Works*. 10 vols and 2 suppl. Translated by F. H. Colson, G. H. Whitaker, J. W. Earp, and Ralph Marcus. LCL. London: Wm. Heinemann/NY: Geo. Putnam's Sons/Cambridge: Harvard University Press, 1929–62.
Philonenko, Marc. "L'Anguipède alectorocéphale et le dieu Iao." *CRAI* (1979): 297–304.
———. "Une intaille magique au nom de Iao." *Semitica* 30 (1980):57–60.
Philonenko, Marc, and Philonenko-Sayar, Belkis. *Die Apokalypse Abrahams*. JSHRZ 5.5. Gütersloh: Mohn, 1982.
Pietersma, Albert. "Kyrios or Tetragram: A Renewed Quest for the Original Septuagint." In *De Septuaginta*. Edited by Albert Pietersma and Claude Cox. Mississauga, Ontario: Benben Publications, 1984: 85–101.
Pistis Sophia. Text edited by Carl Schmidt. Translated by and notes by Violet MacDermot. Nag Hammadi Studies 9. Leiden: Brill, 1978.
Plato, *Cratylus*. Translated by H. N. Fowler. LCL. London: Wm. Heinemann/Cambridge: Harvard University Press, 1926.
———. *Oeuvres Complètes* Vol. 5, part 2, Edited by Louis Méridier Paris: Société d'Édition "Les belles lettres." 1931
———. *Phaedrus*. Translated by C. J. Rowe. Warminster: Aris And Phillips, 1986.
———. *Republic 5*. Translated by S. Halliwell. Warminster: Aris and Phillips, 1993.
———. *The Republic of Plato*. Edited by James Adam, 2nd ed. by D. A. Rees. Cambridge: Cambridge University Press, 1963.
———. *Republic* Translated by R. Waterfield. Oxford: Oxford University Press, 1993.
———. *The Sophist and The Statesman*. Translated by A. E. Taylor. London: Thomas Nelson, 1961.
———. *Theaetetus*. Translated by R. Waterfield. Harmondsworth: Penguin, 1987.
———. *Timaeus and Critias*. Translated by A. E. Taylor: London: Methuen, 1929.
———. *Timaeus...* Translated by R. G. Bury. LCL. London: Wm. Heinemann/Cambridge: Harvard University Press, 1952.
Plutarch, *Moralia*. vol. 5 Translated by Frank Cole Babbitt. LCL. London: Wm. Heinemann/Cambridge: Harvard University Press, 1936.
———. *Sur l'E de Delphes*, Edited by and Translated by Robert Flacelière. Annales de l'Université de Lyon Paris: Société d'Édition *Les Belles Lettres*, 1941.
Pohlenz, Max. *Stoa und Stoiker*. Zürich: Artemis, 1959.
Porten, Bezalel. "Elephanine Papyri." In *The Anchor Bible Dictionary*. Vol. 2. Edited by David N. Freedman. (Garden City, NY: Doubleday): 445–55.
Preuß, H. D. *Theologie des Alten Testaments*. Band 1. Stuttgart: Kohlhammer, 1991.
Prigent, Pierre. *L'Apocalypse de Saint Jean*. CNT 2nd series. Geneva: Labor et Fides, 1988.
Proclus. *Commentaire sur le Timée*. Translated by and notes by A. J. Festugière. Paris: Librairie Philosophique J. Vrin, 1966.
Procopé-Walter A. "Iao und Set." *ARW* 30 (1933): 34–69.
Pucci, Pietro. *Hesiod and the Language of Poetry*. Baltimore: Johns Hopkins University Press, 1977.
Puech, Émile. "Une apocalypse messianique 4Q521." *Revue de Qumran* 60 (1992): 475–519.

Ramsay, W. M. *The Letters to the Seven Churches of Asia*. London: Hodder and Stoughton, 1904.
Rengstorf, Karl H. *A Complete Concordance to Flavius Josephus*. Leiden: Brill, 1975.
Reynolds, Joyce. *Aphrodisias and Rome*. London: Society for the Promotion of Roman Studies, 1982.
Richter, Will. "Kritisches und Exegetisches zu Senecas Prosaschriften." *Hermes* 84 (1956): 182–98.
Rissi, Mathias. *Time and History*. Translated by Gordon C. Winsor. Richmond, VA: John Knox Press, 1966.
Rist, J. M. "Seneca and Stoic Orthodoxy." *ANRW* II, 36.3: 1993–2012.
Roloff, Jürgen. *The Revelation of John*. Translated by John E. Alsup. Continental Commentaries. Minneapolis: Fortress Press, 1993.
Rose, Martin. *Jahwe*. Theologische Studien 122. Zürich: Theologischer Verlag, 1978.
Rowland, Christopher. *The Open Heaven*. London: SPCK, 1982.
Runia, David. "Naming and Knowing: Themes in Philonic Theology." In *Knowledge of God in the Graeco-Roman World*. Edited by R. van den Broek, T. Baarda, and J. Mansfeld. Leiden: Brill, 1988: 69–91.
―――――. *Philo of Alexandria and the Timaeus of Plato*. Philosophia antiqua 44. Leiden: Brill, 1986.
Russell, D. A. *Plutarch*. London: Duckworth, 1973.
Safrai, Samuel, ed. *The Literature of the Sages, Part 1*. Compendia Rerum Iudaicarum ad Novum Testamentum. Assen/Maastricht: Van Gorcum/Philadelphia: Fortress Press, 1987.
Sandbach, F. H. *The Stoics*. Ancient Culture and Society. London: Chatto and Windus, 1975.
Sanders, E. P. *Jewish Law from Jesus to the Mishnah*. London: SCM, 1990.
―――――. *Judaism: Practice and Belief 63 BCE–66 CE*. London: SCM/Philadelphia: Trinity Press International, 1992.
Sarna, Nahum M. *Exodus*. JPS Torah Commentary. Philadelphia: Jewish Publication Society, 1991.
Schiffman, Lawrence. *Sectarian Law in the Dead Sea Scrolls*. Brown Judaic Studies 33. Chico, CA: Scholars Press, 1983.
Schild, E. "On Exodus 3:14 – I am that I am." *VT* 4 (1954): 296–302.
Schlatter, Adolf. "Das Verhältnis Israels zu den Völkern." In *Zur Josephus-Forschung*. Edited by Abraham Schalat. Darmstadt: Wissenschaftliche Buchgesellschaft, 1973: 157–203.
Schlesier, Renate. "Les Muses dans le prologue de la 'Theogonie' d'Hésiode." *Revue de l'histoire des religions* 199 (1982): 131–67.
Schmidt, Werner. "Der Jahwename und Ex 3,14." In *Textgemäss: Aufsätze und Beiträge dur Hermeneutik des alten Testaments*. Göttingen: Vandenhoeck and Ruprecht, 1979: 123–38.
Schmithals, Walter. *Der Römerbrief*. Gütersloh: Mohn, 1988.
Schnackenburg, Rudolf. *The Gospel according to John*. 3 vols. Translated by Cecily Hastings et al. Herders Theological Commentaries on the New Testament. London: Burns and Oates, 1968–82.
Schneider, Johannes. "ἔρχομαι." *TDNT* 2: 666–84.
Schofield, Malcolm. "Did Parmenides Discover Eternity?" *Archiv für Geschichte der Philosophie* 52 (1970): 113–35.
Scholem, Gershom G. *Jewish Gnosticism, Merkabah Mysticism, and Talmudic Tradition*. NY: Jewish Theological Seminary, 1960.

Schürer, Emil. *The History of the Jewish People in the Age of Jesus Christ (175 B. C.–A. D. 135)*. Revised and edited by G. Vermes, F. Millar, and M. Black. 3 vols. Edinburgh: T.&T. Clark, 1973–87.

Schüssler Fiorenza, Elisabeth. *Revelation: Vision of a Just World*. Rev. ed. Edinburgh: T.&T. Clark, 1993.

Schwartz, E. "Diodorus." *PW* 5: 663–704.

Segal, M. H. "The Promulgation of the Authoritative Text of the Hebrew Bible." *JBL* 72 (1953): 35–47.

Seligman, Paul. *Being and Not-Being: An Introduction to Plato's Sophist*. The Hague: Martinus Nijhoff, 1974.

Seneca. *Ad Lucilium Epistulae Morales 1*. Translated by Richard M. Gummere. LCL. London: Wm. Heinemann/NY: Geo. Putnam's Sons, 1917.

Sextus Empiricus. *Outlines of Pyrrhonism*. 3 vols. Translated by R. G. Bury. LCL. London: Wm. Heinemann/Cambridge: Harvard University Press, 1933–6.

Siegel, Jonathan P. "The Employment of Paleo-Hebrew Characters for the Divine Names at Qumran in the Light of Tannaitic Sources." *HUCA* 42 (1971): 159–72.

Siegmann, Ernst. "Zu Hesiods Theogonieproömium." In *Hesiod*, ed. Heitsch: 316–23.

Sigal, Phillip. "Early Christian and Rabbinic Liturgical Acculturation." *NTS* 30 (1984): 63–90.

Skehan, Patrick W. "The Divine Name at Qumran, In the Masada Scroll, and in the Septuagint." *Bulletin of the International Organization for Septuagint and Cognate Studies* 13 (1980): 14–44.

Skehan, Patrick W., and DiLella, Alexander A. *The Wisdom of Ben Sira*. AB. New York: Doubleday, 1987.

Smith, Morton. "The Image of God: Notes on the Hellenization of Judaism." *Bulletin of the John Rylands Library* 40 (1957–8): 473–512.

―――. "The Jewish Elements in the Magical Papyri." *SBL Seminar Papers* 25 (Atlanta: Scholars Press, 1986): 455–62.

Sorabji, Richard. *Matter, Space, Motion*. London: Duckworth, 1988.

―――. *Time, Creation, and the Continuum*. London: Duckworth, 1983.

Starobinski-Safran, Esther. "Ex. 3,14 dans l'oeuvre de Philon d'Alexandrie." In *Dieu et l'Être: Exégèses d'Exode 3,14 et de Coran 20,11–24*. Edited by A. Caquot et al. Centre d'Études des Religions du Livre. Paris: Études Augustiniennes, 1978: 47–55.

Stegemann, Hartmut. "Religionsgeschichtliche Erwägungen zu den Gottesbezeichnungen in den Qumrantexten." In *Qumran: Sa piété, sa théologie et son milieu*. Edited by M. Delcor. BETL 46. Paris: Duculot/Leuven: University Press, 1978.

―――. "Zu Textbestand und Grundgedanken von 1QS III, 13 – IV,26." *Revue de Qumran* 13 (1988): 95–131.

Stern, Menahem, ed. *Greek and Latin Authors on Jews and Judaism*. 3 vols. Jerusalem: Israel Academy of Sciences and Humanities, 1974.

Steudel, Annette. "4Q408: A Liturgy on Morning and Evening Prayer — Preliminary Edition." *Revue de Qumran* 63 (1994): 313–334.

Stevenson, J. G. "Being qua Being." *Apeiron* 9 (1975): 42–50.

Strabo. *Strabonis Geographica: Band 4 Strabon von Amaseia*. Translated by Wolfgang Aly. Bonn: Rudolf Habelt, 1957.

Strack, Hermann L. and Stemberger, Günter. *Einleitung in Talmud und Midrasch*, 7th ed. Munich: Beck'sche, 1982.

Stroh, Wilfried. "Hesiods lügende Musen." In *Studien zum antiken Epos*. Edited by Herwig Görgemanns and Ernst A. Schmidt. Beiträge zur klassischen Philologie 72. Meisenheim am Glen: Anton Hain, 1976: 85–112.

Stuhlmacher, Peter. *Paul's Letter to the Romans*. Translated by Scott Hafemann. Louisville: Westminster/John Knox, 1994.
Sweet, John. *Revelation*. New Testament Commentaries. London: SCM Press/Philadelphia: Westminster Press, 1990.
Swete, H. B. *The Apocalypse of Saint John*. London: Macmillan, 1906.
Targum Onqelos to Genesis. Translated by Bernard Grossfeld. Aramaic Bible. T.&T. Clark: Edinburgh, 1988.
Targum Pseudo-Jonathan of the Pentateuch: Text and Concordance. Edited by E. G. Clarke. Hoboken, NJ: KTAV, 1984.
Thackeray, H. St. J. *The Septuagint and Jewish Origins*. British Academy Schweich Lectures 1920. Oxford: Oxford University Press, 1921.
Thalmann, William G. *Conventions of Form and Thought in Early Greek Epic Poetry*. Baltimore: Johns Hopkins University Press, 1984.
The Scrolls from Qumran Cave 1. Photographs by John C. Trever. Jerusalem: Albright Institute and Shrine of the Book, 1972.
Theiler, Willy. *Poseidonios: Die Fragmente*. 2 vols Berlin: De Gruyter, 1982.
―――――. *Die Vorbereitung des Neuplatonismus*. Berlin/Zürich: Weidmannsche, 1964; repr. of 1934 ed.
Thierry, G. J. "The Pronunciation of the Tetragrammaton." *Oudtestamentische Studiën*, Deel V (1948): 30–42.
Thompson, Leonard. *The Book of Revelation*. NY/Oxford: Oxford University Press, 1990.
Tov, Emanuel. "The Literary History of the Book of Jeremiah." In *Empirical Models for Biblical Criticism*. Edited by Jeffrey H. Tigay. Philadelphia: University of Pennsylvania Press, 1985: 211–37.
―――――. *The Septuagint Translation of Jeremiah and Baruch*. Harvard Semitic Monographs 8. Missoula, MT: Scholars Press, 1976.
Trebilco, Paul. *Jewish Communities in Asia Minor*. SNTSMS 69. Cambridge: Cambridge University Press, 1991.
Uhlig, Siegbert. *Das äthiopische Henochbuch*. JSHRZ 5.6. Gütersloh: Mohn, 1984.
Urbach, E. E. *The Sages*. 2 vols. Translated by Israel Abrahams. Jerusalem: Magnes Press, 1975.
van den Broek, R.; Baarda T.; and Mansfeld, J., eds. *Knowledge of God in the Graeco-Roman World*. Leiden: Brill, 1988.
van der Horst, P. W. "The Unknown God." In *The Knowledge of God in the Graeco-Roman World*, eds. van den Broek et al.: 19–42.
van Unnik, W. C. "A Formula Describing Prophecy." *NTS* 9 (1962): 86–94.
―――――. *Het Godspredikat "Het Begin en Het Einde" bij Flavius Josephus en in de Openbaring van Johannes* Amsterdam: Noord-Hollandsche Uitgevers Maatschappij, 1976.
VanderKam, James C. "Simon the Just: Simon I or Simon II" in *Pomegranates and Golden Bells*, eds. Wright et al.: 303–18.
Verdenius, W. J. "Notes on the Proem of Hesiod's *Theogony*." *Mnemosyne* 25 (1972): 225–60.
Vermes, Geza, trans. *The Dead Sea Scrolls in English*. 3rd ed. Sheffield: JSOT, 1987.
Vermes, Pamela. "Buber's Understanding of the Divine Name Related to Bible, Targum, and Midrash." *JJS* 24 (1973): 147–66.
Vlastos, Gregory. "Theology and Philosophy in Early Greek Thought." In *Studies in Pre-Socratic Philosophy*. Vol. 1. Edited by David J. Furley and R. E. Allen. London: Routledge and Kegan Paul/New York: Humanities Press, 1970: 92–129.

Vögtle, Anton. "Der Gott der Apokalypse." In *La notion biblique de Dieu*. Edited by J. Coppens. BETL 41. Gembloux: Duculot/Leuven: University Press, 1976: 377–98.
von Arnim, J., ed. *Stoicorum Veterum Fragmenta*. Leipzig: Teubner, 1903.
von Leyden, W. "Time, Number, and Eternity in Plato and Aristotle." *Philosophical Quarterly* 14 (1964): 35–52.
von Rad, Gerhard. *Old Testament Theology*. Vol. 1. Translated by D. M. G. Stalker. Edinburgh: Oliver and Boyd, 1962.
Waddell, W. G. "The Tetragrammaton in the LXX." *JTS* 45 (1944): 158–61.
Waltke, B., and O'Connor, M. *An Introduction to Biblical Hebrew Syntax*. Winona Lake, IN: Eisenbrauns, 1990.
Weingreen, J. "The Case of the Blasphemer." *VT* 22 (1972): 118–123.
Weinreich, Otto. "Aion in Eleusis." *ARW* 19 (1919): 174–90.
Weiss, H. F. *Untersuchungen zur Kosmologie des hellenistischen und palästinischen Judentums*. TU 97. Berlin: Akademie Verlag, 1966.
Wernberg-Møller, P. *The Manual of Discipline*. STDJ 1. Leiden: Brill, 1957.
Werner, Eric. "The Doxology in Synagogue and Church." *HUCA* 19 (1945–6): 275–351.
Wernicke, "Aion." *PW* 1: 1042–3.
West, M. L. *Hesiod: Theogony; Works and Days*. The World's Classics. Oxford: Oxford University Press, 1988.
———. *The Orphic Poems*. Oxford: Oxford University Press, 1983.
West, E. W. *Pahlavi Texts Part 1: The Bundahis; Bahman Yast, and Shâyast Lâ-Shâyast*. Sacred Books of the East, Vol. 5. Oxford: Oxford University Press, 1880.
Wevers, William. *LXX: Notes on the Greek Text of Exodus*. Septuagint and Cognate Studies 30. Atlanta: Scholars Press, 1990.
Whittaker, John. "Ammonius on the Delphic E." *CQ* n. s. 19 (1969): 185–92.
———. "The 'Eternity' of the Platonic Forms." *Phronesis* 13 (1968): 131–44.
———. *God, Time, Being*. Symbolae Osloenses Fasc. Supp. 23. Oslo: Universitetsforlaget, 1971.
———. "Moses Atticizing." *Phoenix* 21 (1967): 196–201.
———. "Seneca, Ep. 58.17." *Symbolae Osloenses* 50 (1975): 143–48.
———. "Plutarch, Platonism, and Christianity." In *Neoplatonism and Early Christian Thought*. Edited by H. J. Blumenthal and R. A. Markus. London: Variorum, 1981: 50–63.
Whittaker, Molly. *Jews and Christians: Graeco-Roman Views*. CCWJCW 6. Cambridge: Cambridge University Press, 1984.
Williams, A. Lukyn. "Yaho." *JTS* 28 (1927): 276–83.
Williams, C. J. F. "Being." In *A Companion to Philosophy of Religion*. Blackwell Companions to Philosophy. Eds. Philip L. Quinn and Charles Taliaferro. Oxford: Blackwell, 1997: 223–28.
Williams, Ronald. *Jews in the Hellenistic World: Philo*. CCWJCW v.1, pt. 2. Cambridge: Cambridge University Press, 1989.
Wilson, R. McL. *Hebrews*. NCB. Grand Rapids, MI: Eerdmans/Basingstoke: Marshall, Morgan, & Scott, 1987.
Winston, David. *The Wisdom of Solomon*. AB. Garden City, NY: Doubleday, 1979.
Wolfson, Harry A. *Philo*. 2nd printing revised. 2 vols. Cambridge: Harvard University Press, 1948.
Wright, David P.; Freedman, David Noel; and Hurvitz, Ari, eds. *Pomegranates and Golden Bells*. Festschrift for Jacob Milgrom. Winona Lake, IN: Eisenbrauns, 1995.
Yadin, Yigael. *The Temple Scroll: The Hidden Law of the Dead Sea Sect*. London: Weidenfeld and Nicolson, 1985.

York, Anthony D. "The Dating of Targumic Literature." *JSJ* 5 (1974): 49–62.
Zaehner, R. C. *Zurvan: A Zoroastrian Dilemma*. Oxford: Oxford University Press, 1955.
Zahn, Theodor. *Forschungen zur Geschichte des neutestamentlichen Kanons und der altkirchlichen Literatur*. Vol. 3. Erlangen: Deichert, 1884.
Zepf, Max. "Der Gott Αἰών in der hellenistischen Theologie." *ARW* 25 (1927): 225–44.
Zickendraht, Karl. "EGW EIMI." *Theologische Studien und Kritiken* 94 (1922): 162–8.
Zuntz, Günther. *Aion: Gott des Römerreichs*. Abhandlungen der Heidelberger Akademie der Wissenschaften, Philosophisch-historische Klasse 1989/2. Heidelberg: Carl Winter Universitätsverlag, 1989.
―――――. *ΑΙΩΝ in der Literatur der Kaiserzeit*. Wien: Österreichische Akademie der Wissenschaften, 1992.
―――――. *ΑΙΩΝ im Römerreich: Die archäologischen Zeugnisse*. Abhandlungen der Heidelberger Akademie der Wissenschaften, Philosophisch-historische Klasse 1991/3. Heidelberg: Carl Winter Universitätsverlag, 1991.

Index of Sources

Old Testament

Genesis
1	130, 168, 213
1:3 ff.	180
1:14	210
2:8 ff.	219
6	168-9
15	215
15:2	61 n, 186
15:7	133 n
19:6	200, 204
19:16	200

Exodus
3	42
3:12	136, 178, 181, 185, 207
3:14	1-5, 7, 12-3, 26, 31, 33, 37, 58, 81, 83, 117-8, 123, 131-41, 152, 155-9, 161-5, 167-8, 170-7, 180-8, 192-4, 200-1, 204-7, 212, 221, 229 n, 233
3:15	81, 108 n, 159, 168, 176 n
4:13	133 n
11:6	143 n
15:11	70
17:15	130 n
20:2	133 n
20:7	63 n, 110
20:18	200 n
22:27	83 n, 86 n
23:21	124-6
23:22	200
23:13	64, 147 n
25	200
28:36	82
32:25 ff.	124
33	125
33:6	124
33:12 ff.	177
33:19	177
34:14	130 n, 147 n
39:30	82

Leviticus
11:45	133 n
16:21	110
16:30	100
19:12	71 n
19:36	133
20:24	133 n
24:10-6	58, 62-3, 73, 78 n, 86, 108-10, 112, 175
24:11	62-3
24:12	100 n
24:14	63
24:15-6	62, 83
24:16	62-5

Numbers
5:11 ff.	84, 110
5:23	85
6:24-7	79, 110, 205
15:34	100 n
16:22	153 n
16:26	65 n
27:16	153 n
27:20	106 n
30:2	68 n

Index of Sources

Deuteronomy
4:4	167
5:11	63 n
12:5	114, 124
12:11	114, 124
12:26	68 n
18:15	201
19:5	167
23:2-4	69
28:10	124
28:58	73
32	215
32:39	140, 183
32:40	185, 221 n

Joshua
23:7	64, 65 n

Judges
4:18	161
5:4 ff.	215

Ruth
2:4	104, 106
4:1	161

1 Samuel
4:18	64 n
21:20	147 n
23:13	133 n

2 Samuel
7:8	219 n
7:22	147 n

1 Kings
8	126
8:16-9	114, 124
8:20	126
8:27	126
8:30	126
8:34	126
8:36	126
9:3	114, 124
17:1	153 n
18:39	169

2 Kings
8:1	133 n

1 Chronicles
17:20	147 n
21:17	132-4

Ezra
4:18	100 n

Psalms
19:10	69 n
42:3 (LXX 41:3)	221 n
45:12	153 n
72:18-9	225
90:2 (LXX 89:2)	155, 174 n 175 n
118:25	69, 104-5
118:26	215
129:4	70
130:1	70
138:1	67
145:1	67

Proverbs
3:19-20	149-50, 152
3:21	150
8	150, 152
8:14	150
8:23	150
11:26	62 n
30:1	75 n

Isaiah
6:3	153, 212 n, 223-6, 230
11:1-5	70
28:16	61
29:5-6	215
40-55	131, 138-41, 148, 175, 178, 182-3, 185, 200 n, 212 n, 229
40-66	192
40:10	215
40:17	229
40:28	138
41:4	138, 140, 172 n, 182, 229 n
41:8	175 n
41:12	147
41:22-3	138
41:22	144
42:6	68
42:8	68, 140 n, 147
42:9	138
43:10	138-9, 141, 172, 175
43:10-3	182
43:11	140 n

43:12-3	138 n, 139	39:16-7	137
43:13	138, 172 n	*Ezekiel*	
43:18-9	138	1:28	106
43:25	138, 140-1	7:19	160
44:6	138, 140, 182, 218, 221	9:4	204 n
44:7	138	21:28	64 n
45	127	24	63 n
45:3	140 n, 147, 148 n	29:16	64 n
45:3 ff.	147-8	40-48	99
45:4	148		
45:5	140 n	*Daniel*	
45:6	146	2:19	76 n
45:14	147	7:13	216, 233
45:17	138		
45:23	127	*Hosea*	
46:3	138	1:9	118
46:4	138-9, 141, 182	12:5	223
46:9-10	138	13:4	147 n
46:10	210	LXX	
47:7-8	228-9	12:6	223
47:8	155, 229 n	*Joel*	
48:1	64 n, 72 n	2:1	215
48:11	147	2:2	143 n
48:3 ff.	138	3:4	215
48:12	138-40, 182-3, 187	3:5	61
49:1	64 n		
51:2	175 n	*Amos*	
51:6	138	3:13	219, 223
51:12	138, 140	4:13	223
51:13	138	6:10	58, 62-5, 72 n
52:6	138, 175 n		
62:2	62 n	*Nahum*	
66:3	64 n	1:2	68
		Habbakuk	
Jeremiah		2:3	215
MT			
1:4-19	201	*Zephaniah*	
16	63 n	1:18	160
20:9	64		
32:16-7	137	*Zechariah*	
LXX		4:5	216
1:6	137, 158, 217	12:10	216, 233
14:13	137	14	115
23:36	64 n		

Apocrypha

1 Esdras
1:48   76 n

Tobit
1:3   76
1:4   76
1:13   76
4:11   76

Judith
5:6   90 n, 92
9:5   191
9:7   76 n

Esther (LXX Additions)
4:17a-17z   76
4:17o   154, 206
4:17q   154, 206

Wisdom of Solomon
2:2   153 n
7:17   145 n, 190-1
7:17-9   190-1
12:23 ff.   154
12:8   154
13:1   154, 165, 206
13:6   154
13:10   154
14:13   154, 229 n
14:21   78 n

Sirach
4:10   76
7:9   76
7:15   76
17:28   153 n
18:1   221
23:9-10   78
23:12   78 n
24:23   76
36:12   77 n, 124 n
42:19   143 n, 191 n
43:27   69
45:15   76 n, 79
47:18   73
50:1-6   102
50:20   79, 102

Baruch
1:1-3:8   76 n
1:10 ff.   76
2:15   77 n, 124 n
3:1   76
3:9-5:9   76 n

Bel and the Dragon
25   76

Prayer of Manesseh
1   76
3   128

1 Maccabees
2:61   76
4:24   76

2 Maccabees
6:7   88, 89 n
7:28   18, 153, 167 n, 170
8:15   77 n, 124 n

Psalms of Solomon
9:9   77 n, 124 n

Pseudepigrapha

Apocalypse of Abraham
10:3   75, 125
10:4   75 n, 77, 115
10:8   75, 125
10:9   75 n
17:8 ff.   230 n
17:13   75, 125

22:1-5	144 n, 151-2, 212 n, 213	39:14	225
25:4	151	69:6 ff.	129 n
		69:13-26	129
		69:14	77 n

Apocalypse of Elijah
1:9   77 n, 124 n

2 Enoch
39:5 (J)   190 n

Apocalypse of Moses
29:4   75, 125
33:5   75, 125

3 Enoch
12:5   124
39:1   224 n

Apocalypse of Zephaniah (A)
     76 n, 77-8, 115

Exagoge of Ezekiel
68-89   190

Apostolic Constitutions (Hellenistic Synagogal Prayers)
7.33-8   158
7.33.7   158
8.5.1 ff.   137-8, 158, 171 n, 193, 217
8.12.6 ff.   158, 207

4 Ezra
1:15   76
4:25   77 n, 124 n
6   212 n
8:4-5   155
8:7   155, 193, 207
9:18   155 n

Letter of Aristeas
15-17   10, 136

Joseph and Aseneth
11:17   65 n

Ascension of Isaiah
1:7   77 n
7:37   77 n

Jubilees
36:7   78 n, 129

2 Baruch
6:6   76 n
17:2   76 n
21:8-10   212 n
21:5   191 n, 212 n
21:5-8   144 n
21:17   144 n
48:2 ff.   144 n
48:23   77 n, 124 n
51:9   211 n

Ladder of Jabob
2:12   224 n
2:17-8   75, 125, 220, 230 n

Liber Antiquorum Biblicorum (LAB)
21:4   187 n
26:12   75 n
19   76 n
98   76

Life of Adam and Eve (Vita)
14:2   75

4 Baruch
6:13   78 n

Lives of the Prophets
2:16   77

1 Enoch
8:1 ff.   129 n
9:4   70-1
10:9   70-1
27:3   230 n
39:6-7   225
39:10-11   225
39:11   144 n, 191 n, 212 n, 213
39:12   153, 211 n, 212 n, 222

Odes of Solomon
8:19   77 n, 124 n
22:6   77 n, 124 n

Prayer of Jacob
     74

Questions of Ezra
A29   224 n

Sibylline Oracles

fr.1:35	155
1:4 ff.	189
1:137-46	156, 202 n
2:174 ff.	189
3:8	157
3:11	77 n
3:11 ff.	156
3:17-26	157
3:16	187
3:18-9	77-8
3:33	156-7, 206
3:310	154 n, 229 n
3:1-45	156-7, 170, 188, 202 n
3:192-4	90 n
3:608-25	90 n
4:19-20	223
5:34	154 n, 229 n
5:173-4	155, 229 n
10:22	77 n, 124 n

Testament of Daniel

6:7	77 n, 124 n

Testament of Job

47:9	222-3

Testament of Solomon

18:15-6	75

Testament of the Twelve Patriarchs

	77 n, 124 n

New Testament

Matthew

1:22	97 n
3:3	97 n
3:11	171
11:3	215
16:27	216
21:9	215 n
25:31	216
24:30	216

Mark

1:7	171
11:9	215 n
12:29	97 n

Luke

3:16	171
4:19	97 n
7:20	215
13:35	215 n
19:38	215 n

John

1:1	171, 175
1:1-3	211
1:3	171
1:1-18	170-1
1:9	170 n, 215 n
1:15	170 n, 171
1:18	170 n, 171
4:26	175 n
5:26	221
8:12	173
8:12-20	172
8:18	175 n
8:21-30	173
8:24	173
8:31-8	173
8:33	173 n
8:39-47	173
8:48-59	173
8:51	173
8:58	171-6, 211
10:30	175
12:13	215 n
13:19	172
13:16-9	175 n
17:6 ff.	126 n
17:11	126 n

Acts

2:21	97 n
2:23	210 n
19:13	65 n
19:19	220 n

Romans

1:7	1 n, 203 n

4:8	97 n	*Revelation*	
4:17	18, 170	1	42
9:5	171 n	1:1	56, 200 n
10:9	61	1:2	200 n, 202 n
10:11	61	1:4	1, 2, 4, 6, 11, 16, 47, 57, 62, 123, 138, 144, 146, 160-1, 170-1, 176, 178, 181, 184, 185 n, 188-9, 195-217, 219, 221, 229-33
10:12	61		
10:13	61		
1 Corinthians			
1:3	1 n, 203 n		
1:28	170 n		
16:22	98	1:4-5	1, 203
		1:4-8	200
2 Corinthians		1:6	200, 204
1:2	1 n, 203 n	1:7	216, 233
6:18	219 n	1:8	158 n, 198 n, 200, 214, 217-20, 221
11:31	171 n		
		1:9	200 n
Ephesians		1:10	200
1:3 ff.	213 n	1:12-3	200
1:4	210 n	1:17-8	220-3, 228
1:21	126	1:18	161, 207 n, 227
		1:19	196, 201, 206, 222, 223 n
Phillipians			
2:5-11	126-8	1:20	222 n
2:9	126-8	2:2	206 n, 228 n
2:10-1	126-8	2:3	204
		2:5	216
1 Thessalonians		2:8	210
4:16-7	216	2:9	206 n, 228 n
		2:13	204
2 Timothy		2:16	216
2:19	65 n	2:17	204
		2:21	197
Hebrews		3.5	85 n, 204
1:4	126	3:8	204
9:28	215	3:9	206 n, 228 n
10:27	215	3:11	216
13:8	207	3:12	204-5
		4	224
1 Peter		4-5	127, 128 n, 211 n
1:2-3	1 n, 203 n	4:1	210
1:20	210 n	4:5	222 n
		4:8	207 n, 211-2, 219 n, 223-7
2 Peter			
2:4	41 n	4:8-11	212
		4:9	198, 207
2 John		4:10	207
3	1 n, 203 n	4:11	198, 212-3, 224
		5:5-6	128 n
Jude		5:6-8	222 n
1-2	1 n, 203 n		
6	41 n		

5:9	209	16:13-4	222 n
5:13	226	17:3	204
6:12-4	198	17:5	204
7:3	204 n	17:7-18	222 n
7:14	222 n	17:8	204, 206, 210 n, 213, 227-9
9:11	41, 198 n		
9:20	206	17:8-10	50
10:6	207	17:11	227-9
11:4	222 n	18:7	199 n, 228-9
11:12	222 n	18:8	199 n
11:17	216, 226-7	19	216
12	41 n, 196, 223 n	19:12	204
13:1	204	19:13	204
13:8	204, 209, 210 n, 213	21:3	217
13:16-7	204	21:5-6	217
14:1	204	21:23	226
14:4-5	222 n	22:4	204
15:1	226	22:7	216
15:7	207	22:12	216
16:5	216, 226	22:20	216

Dead Sea Scrolls

		11:15	69
Covenant of Damascus (CD)		11:11	142 n, 143, 148
2:9-10	142 n	11:18	142 n
9:5	68	11:17-8	148
15:1	71 n	11:19	148-9
1QH		*Temple Scroll*	
7:28	70	17:13	66
10:8	153 n	63:8	141
18:2	142 n	63:4	141
20:4	144		
20:5-8	144, 197 n	*1QSa*	
20:9-11	144-8, 150-3, 193	2:4	69
20:11 ff.	144	*1QSb*	
1QIs^a	68, 70	5:25	69-70
1QM	70	*1Q14*	16
17:5	142	*1Q15*	16
1QS		*1Q19*	71 n
3:15-4:26	142		
6:27-7:2	71-4, 101 n, 108 n, 112	*1Q26*	143 n
8:13	68	*1Q27*	143 n
8:14	68 n		
11:3 ff.	144, 148-53, 193		
10:7-8	148		

4Qpap4QLXXLev^b			
fr.20:4	58-9, 65, 70, 92, 119	4Q270	73 n
4QEn^b	70-1, 98	4Q402	142 n
4QGenExod^a	70 n	4Q408	69-70
4QpHab	66	4Q409	69
4QIs^c	66-7	4Q416	143 n
4QpPs^a	66	4Q417	143 n
4QSam^c	68	4Q418	142, 143 n
4Q134	70	4Q511	69, 142 n
4Q162	66 n	4Q521	68 n
4Q163	66 n	11QPs^a	66-7, 70
4Q166-70	66 n	16:7	67
		21:2	67
4Q171	66	28:7	69
4Q175-6	68	8HevXIIgr	59-60
4Q180	142	11Q11	
4Q216	74 n	1:2-4	74 n
4Q266	69, 104-5		

Rabbinical Literature

Mishnah		Tamid	
		3:8	101 n
Berakoth		7:2	101, 102 n
9:5	104, 107	Yoma	
Megillah		3:8	100
4:10	110	4:2	100
		6:2	100
Sanhedrin			
7:5	102-3, 108, 112	Talmud, Babylonian	
10:1	103-4, 112		
		'Abodah Zarah	
Sotah		18a	103 n, 108 n
1:4	98		
7:6	101	Berakoth	
		9b	67, 177-8, 182, 185, 193
Sukkah			
4:5	69, 104-7		

Hagigah
16a	106
49b	108

Makkoth
11a	129 n
16a	109, 112

Nedarim
7b	108

Pesaqim
50a	108 n, 115

Qiddushin
71a	106-8

Rosh Hashanah
18b	108 n

Sanhedrin
60a	108
102b	99

Shabbath
61b	99 n
104b	99
120b	99 n

Shebu'oth
21a	109, 112
35b	109 n

Sotah
7a,b	84, 98
37a-38b	79, 101 n

Sukkah
53b	129 n

Temurah
3a	109, 112

Yoma
8a	99
69b	101 n

Talmud, Jerusalem

Megillah
1:9 (71d)	67

Nedarim
9:1	59 n

Sanhedrin
29a,b	129 n

Shebu'oth
3:10	109, 112

Sukkah
54c	105 n

Tamid
3:8	108 n

Yoma
3:7 (40d)	106-7, 109, 113 n

Tosefta

Berakoth
7:23	69 n, 104, 106, 113 n

Sotah
8:6	102
10:1	102
13:8	101
15:3-4	102

Targums

Fragmentary Targum G
Exodus
3:14	181, 183, 185, 193, 212

Fragmentary Targum W
Exodus
3:14	181 n, 185, 193, 212

Neofiti
Genesis
21:33	180

Exodus
3:12	178
3:14	180-1, 183, 185, 193, 212
32:25 ff.	113 n, 124, 204
33:6	113 n, 124

Leviticus
24:11 ff.	109-10, 112
24:16	110

Numbers
6:24-6	110

Deuteronomy
32:3	110 n

Ngl1
Exodus
3:14	179, 181 n, 185

Ngl2
Exodus
3:14	175, 182-3, 185-6, 193

Onqelos
Exodus
3:14	180
20:7	110, 112

Numbers
6:24-6	110

Ps-Jonathan
Exodus
2:21	128
3:14	175, 183, 184 n, 185, 187, 193, 212
4:20	128
21:17	110
28:30	129 n
32:25 ff.	113 n, 124, 204
33:6	113 n, 124

Leviticus
16:21	110
24:11 ff.	109-10, 112

Numbers
5:19	110
6:24-6	110-11
20:8	128
31:8	128

Deuteronomy
5:11	110
9:19	128
28:10	124
32:3	110 n
32:39	183-5, 187, 200 n, 201-2, 205

Tg. Isaiah
6:3	224
41:2	175 n
43:12	175 n
46:11	175 n

Tg. Jeremiah
4:2	110
12:10	110

Tg. Zephaniah
1:5	110

Tg. Zechariah
5:3	110 n

Other Works

Aboth de R. Nathan
103 n

Alphabet of R. Akiba
Ex.3:14	187

Ecclesiastes Rabbah
3:11	109

Exodus Rabbah
1:29	101 n, 108 n
3:6	182, 186-7
30:6 (44a)	224 n

Mekilta de R. Ishmael
Shir. 3:25	186
16	109 n

Pesiqta de R. Kahana
148a	103 n

Ruth Rabbah
4:5	104 n

Sifre on Numbers
6:23	101 n
6:27	101 n
14	109 n

Sifre Zuta on Numbers
6:27	106

Ancient Authors

Alexander of Aphrodisias

Commentary on Aristotle
Topica IV, p.15   33

Anaxagoras

fr.1	19
fr.12	20, 45, 46 n
fr.14	12, 20
fr.17	19

Aristotle

De Caelo

268a10	230 n
279a28	52
279a11-18	32
279a17-28	11, 31-2, 210
279a22-279b1	29-30

Categories (Cat.)

2a11 ff.	27 n

Metaphysics (Met.)

985b4 (A4)	20 n
10003a21 (Γ1)	27, 28, 166
E1	27-9
Z1	13
Z	29
H	29
Θ	29
Λ	28
Λ9	41 n
1071b3 ff. (Λ)	28-9
1072b13-5 (Λ)	28, 30
1072b29 ff. (Λ)	32
1073a23 ff. (Λ)	29
1074a35 ff. (Λ)	29 n

Physics (Phys.)

187a1	20 n
187a34	18
221a26 ff.	31-2
259a4-5	30

Epistle of Barnabas

1:7	191
5:3	191

Bundahisn

1:3	49-50, 195

Cicero

De Natura Deorum

1:31	80 n, 88 n

Oratio post reditum ad Quirites

7	48 n, 57

Clement of Alexandria

Stromata (Strom.)

1.1.11	118 n
5.6.34	95 n, 118, 120 n
5.14.121, 1-3	77

Clement of Rome

1 Cor. 34:6	224 n

Contest of Homer and Hesiod

97-8	48 n

Cornelius Labeo see Macrobius, Saturnalia

Demosthenes

De Corona

260	89

Diodorus Siculus

Bibliotheca Historica

1, 94:2	91-3
1, 44:1	93 n
9, 3.2	48 n
40, 3	76 n

Index of Sources

Diodorus of Tarsus
fr.64   118

Diogenes Laertes
7.135-6   36 n
7.147   10
7.148   33 n

Empedocles
fr.12   19
fr.17   19
fr.30   129-30
fr.71   19

Epictetus
3, 13.4 ff.   51
fr.8   48 n

Euripedes

Helen
13-4   42 n

Eusebius

Praeparatio Evangelica (Pr. Ev.)
9.29.6.5   190 n
13.12.5.4   188
15.14.2   48 n
527b ff.   12 n, 39 n

Gorgias
fr.1   20

Heraclitus
fr.1   46 n
fr.30   46, 51
fr.90   46 n

Hermetica

Asclepius
14, 29, 34   192

Herodotus

History
5:50.2   14

Hesiod

Theogony (Th.)
1-115   42, 196
30-9   43
32-4   43-5, 230
34   14
36 ff.   45 n
43-4   45 n
44   44
66 ff.   44
77 ff.   8
80 ff.   44 n
105   44
195 ff.   8
207 ff.   8
569 ff.   44 n

Hippolytus

De Antichristo
2   191

Philosoph.
21, 1   33

Refutatio omnium Haeresium (Ref.)
1.7.1   46

Homer

Iliad (Il.)
1.1 ff.   41-2
1.70   42-4, 48 n, 188-91, 196
1.71   42

Horace

Satirae
1:9.67-72   89 n

Irenaeus

Adversus haereses (Adv. haer.)
4:33:1   191

Jerome

Ep.25 ad Marcellam
   59

Liber Interp. Heb. Nom.
118 n

Prologue galeatus
28:594-5   60 n

Josephus

Antiquitates Judaicae (Ant.)
1:9-10	86 n
2:331-2	84
2:275	85-6
3:90	85
3:91	84-5, 112
3:187	84 n
3:270	84
4:202	86, 112
4:207	83 n, 86
8:349	169
12:22	10, 136
13:68	86
14:72	85
20:90	86

Contra Aponiem (Ap.)
2:82	86 n
2:79-80	97 n
2:94	86 n
2:106	86 n
2:112-4	97 n
2:190	47, 188-9
2:237	83 n, 86

Bellum Judaicum (Bell.)
1:541	85
5:235	82 n, 84

Vita (Vit.)
275   85

Julius Africanus

Kestos
18   95 n

Juvenal

Saturae
14:97	76 n
14:102	92

Lactantius

De vera sap.
9   33 n

Livy

History
Book 102   87-8, 92

Lucan

Pharsalia
2:593   87 n

J. Lydus

De Mensibus
4:53   87-8, 91-2

Macrobius

Saturnalia
1:18:18-21   88, 92 n

Melissus

fr.1	19 n
fr.2	18-9

Metrodorus

fr.1	20
fr.2	20

Numenius

fr. 22   135

Origen

Contra Celsum
4.14	33 n
5.6	76 n

Orphic Hymns

25.4-5   46 n, 192

Ovid

Art of Love
1.75-6, 413-6   89 n

Metamorphoses (Met.)
517-8   48 n

Papyri Graecae Magicae (PGM)

1:14-8	96
1:216	96 n
2:15	95 n
3:75	95 n
3:145	95
3:572	95 n
4:605 f.	94 n
4:1167-1206	54 n
4:1217-26	93, 94 n
4:1376	96 n
4:1815	95
4:1460-95	94 n
4:3007-86	93
4:3034	95
5:102	95
5:115	94 n
12:5	95
12:237-8	94 n
13:424 f.	94 n
22b:1-26	95 n
23:31	95
36:35 f.	95, 220
36:259	96
71:3-4	220

Parmenides

fr.2	15
fr.8:1-38	15-8

Pausanias

10.12.10	49-50, 188, 230-1

Philo

De Abrahamo (Abr.)
124   80-1

De Cherubim (Cher.)
27-8	81, 176
49	163 n
56	80 n
83	61 n

De Decalogo (Decal.)
8   165

67	168
82 ff.	83 n, 112

De Fuga et Inventione (Fug.)
56	167
78	167
141	80 n
165	163

De Gigantibus (Gig.)
45	61 n
54	83 n

De Legatione ad Gaium (Leg.)
353   83 n

Legum Allegoriarum (Leg. All.)
1:82	164 n
1:95	60
2:1-2	166
2:42	168 n
3:42-3	47 n
3:207	81 n

De Migratione Abrahami (Mig.)
103	82
168-9	61 n
182-3	164 n

De Mutatione Nominum (Mut.)
7 ff.	162-3, 165
11	80 n, 162-3, 165-6
11-5	80 n
12	168
12 f.	80
13	80 n
14	80 n
15	80
27	162 n, 166, 193
57	168

De Opificio Mundi (Op.)
15 ff.	164
125	61 n

De Plantatione (Plant.)
21-2	164
85 f.	61 n

De Posteritate Caini (Post.)
15	162 n, 165 n
15 ff.	80 n, 164
20	164

166-7	165 n
167	162 n, 164 n, 165
168-9	164 n

De Praemiis et Poenis (Praem.)
37-8	164 n
39	163-4
39-40	80 n

De Sacrificiis Abelis et Caini (Sac.)
76	169 n
87	61 n

De Sobrietate (Sob.)
55	61 n

De Somniis (Som.)
1:66	165 n
1:67	80 n, 164 n
1:230	80 n, 163-4
1:231	164 n
1:232	80
2:227-37	168

De Specialibus Legibus (Spec. Leg.)
1:31	167
1:32 ff.	164 n
1:37 ff.	164 n
1:41	80 n
1:46 ff.	164
1:46-9	163 n

Quod Deterius Potiori Insidiari soleat (Det.)
160	165, 207

Quod Deus Sit Immutabilis (Deus)
4	168
32-3	168-9, 191
62	80 n
110	61 n

Quis rerum divinarum heres sit (Quis. Her.)
22 ff.	61
166	61 n
170	80, 83, 164 n

De Virtutibus (Virt.)
215	164

De Vita Mosis (Mos.)
1:74-6	81, 207
1:75	80 n, 165
2:100	165, 167, 170
2:114	82-3
2:132	82
2:192 ff.	83, 112
2:203-4	83
2:208	83

Philodemus

περι ευσεβειας
12	10

Pistis Sophia
4:136	219

Plato

Charmides
173c-174b	47

Cratylus
396a-b	9-10, 50, 136

Laws
715e ff.	47, 50, 53, 188-9, 190, 231

Parmenides
140e ff.	25 n

Phaedo
78d	21 n

Phaedrus
	136
246 ff.	23-4, 164
247c	24, 151
247d	24, 151, 164
247e	24
248a ff.	24
249c	24, 151, 164-5

Republic (Rep.)
477a	22, 165 n
477b ff.	21 n, 165 n
478d	22, 165 n
478e ff.	23
485a-b	22, 165
490a	22, 165 n, 166
509b	23, 26 n, 33
518c	22
521d	21 n

522c ff.	23	373a	38, 39 n
523a	21 n	375c	38 n
527b	23, 165		
617c	47		

Quaestiones Convivales (Quaest. Conviv.)

4, 6:1-2	89-90

Theaetetus

	21 n
185c	21 n

Proclus

Commentary on the Timaeus

27d6 ff.	36-7

Timaeus (Tim.)

	150-1
27d	36-7, 39, 152
27d-28a	24, 36, 164 n, 165
28c	80 n
29d ff.	167 n
34a	14 n, 53 n
37c	168-9
37d	25, 52
37e ff.	24-6, 39, 209-10
38b-c	47, 211
41b	14 n

Protagoras

fr.1	20
fr.4	20

Ps-Aristotle

De mundo

	197
379a9 ff.	189 n
401a	10-11
401b	11, 188-9

Sophist (Soph.)

	21 n, 22 n
248e	22 n
262c	21 n

Ps-Clementine Homilies

2:6:1	192

Plutarch

Scholia in Lucanum

2:593	87

De animae procreatione in Timaeo (De proc. an. in Tim.)

1013b	35 n
1019e	35 n
1020c	35 n

Scriptores Historiae Augustae

Divus Claudius

2:4	88 n

De defectu oraculorum (De def. orac.)

433d-e	40 n

Seneca

De E apud Delphos (De E)

387a-b	48 n
388f.	8 n
392a	38
392b-c	38
392e	38-9
393a	14 n, 39
393b	8, 40

De Brevitate Vitae (De brev. vit.)

10.2	47 n

Epistulae Morales

24:19-20	39 n
58	34-7, 135, 165
58:7-15	34
58:16-22	34
58:17	36
58:22 ff.	36
58:27	37
58:22-8	38 n
65	34, 41

De Iside et Osiride (De Is.)

352a	8, 38
354b	37-8
354c	55-7, 198, 211
354c-d	56

Sextus Empiricus

Adversus Mathematicos. (Adv. math.)
9   48
9:134 ff.   166

Outlines of Pyrrhonism
3:142 ff.   47 n

Tacitus

Historiae
4.11-18   89 n
5.5:5   88

Tertullian

Apologeticus (Apol.)
21   33 n

Theodoret

Haeret. fab.
5, 3   118

Quaest. in Exod. Interr.
15   118

Theophilus

Apology
1:14   191
2:9   191

Virgil

Georgics
4.392-3   46 n, 48 n

Index of Modern Authors

Adam, J. 22, 75, 157
Albrektson, B. 3, 134
Albright, W. F. 72, 130, 153
Alexander, P. S. 16, 30, 33, 79, 84, 92, 179, 224
Alföldi, A. 54
Allen, R. E. 15, 23, 25, 42, 84
Allison, D. C. 215
Allo, E. B. 218
Alon, G. 100, 102, 104
Aly, W. 93
Andersen, F. I. 63, 64, 190
Arnold, W. R. 132
Athanassakis, A. N. 8
Attridge, H. 74
Aune, D. E. 2, 159, 160, 184, 185, 196, 199, 200, 201, 203, 205, 218, 219, 223, 224, 225
Babbitt, F. C. 39
Baillet, M. 69, 149
Ball, D. M. 138, 139, 172, 175
Bamberger, B. J. 109
Baneth, E. 107
Barker, M. 125
Barnes, J. 14, 19, 28, 29
Barr, J. 134, 135
Barrett, C. K. 172, 173, 174
Barthélemy, D. 71
Bates, W. H. 158
Bauckham, R. 1, 98, 197, 200, 207, 216, 218, 219, 221, 222, 223, 225, 226, 227
Baudissin, W. W. G. 3, 59, 60, 63, 75, 76, 81, 84, 86, 92, 93, 95, 96, 116, 118, 121, 125
Baumgarten, J. M. 68, 69, 73, 104, 105, 106
Beale, G. K. 2, 199, 202, 222

Beasley-Murray, G. R. 172, 173, 174, 196, 197, 200, 203, 204, 205, 209, 217, 218, 221, 222, 223, 227
Beattie, D. R. G. 109
Beckwith, I. T. 2, 200, 202, 210, 213, 216, 221
Belardi, W. 42
Belayche, N. 54
Bertrand, D. A. 75, 125
Betz, H. D. 85, 93, 94, 95, 223
Beyer, K. 70, 71
Bickel, E. 34, 35, 36
Black, M. 71, 101, 129, 153, 202, 224
Boll, F. 197
Bonner, C. 96, 159, 160
Bousset, W. 68
Bredin, M. 201
Brenk, F. 38
Brown, R. 138, 172, 174, 175
Bruce, F. F. 74, 197, 215
Brunschwig, J. 33, 34, 166
Buchanan, G. W. 215
Büchsel, F. 185
Burkett, D. T. 138, 139, 140, 141
Bury, R. G. 24
Byington, S. T. 70
Caird, G. B. 202, 205, 208, 210, 216, 223, 227
Caquot, A. 129, 164
Caster, M. 118
Cazelles, H. 133
Cerbelaud, D. 157
Charles, R. H. 2, 13, 21, 200, 204, 212, 218, 219, 221, 222, 223
Charlesworth, J. H. 74, 75, 95, 157, 158
Childs, B. 3, 5, 135
Chilton, B. D. 224
Clarke, E. G. 110
Clay, J. S. 42, 43, 44, 45

Cohon, S. S. 62, 100, 104, 108
Collins, A. Y. 90, 156, 188, 189, 196, 197, 222, 229
Colpe, C. 97
Colson, F. H. 80
Comblin, J. 217, 228
Cook, A. B. 10
Cornford, F. M. 21, 23, 24, 25, 30
Court, J. M. 196, 210
Cowley, A. 93
Cranfield, C. E. B. 61, 170
Cross, F. M. 130, 153, 180
Cullmann, O. 208
Cumont, F. 89, 90, 91
Dahl, N. A. 61, 81, 176
Danby, H. 99, 100
Daniélou, J. 204
Davies, W. D. 215
Davila, J. R. 70, 184
de Vaux, R. 3, 133
Delcor, M. 60, 135, 145, 146
Delling, G. 159
des Places, É. 21
Diels, H. 15
DiLella, A. A. 79
Dillon, J. 33, 35, 37, 41, 53
Dittenberger, Wm. 51
Dodd, C. H. 78, 105, 138, 140, 141, 172, 173
Dorival, G. 134
Dunn, J. 170
Dupont-Sommer, A. 116
Eerdmans, B. 118, 119
Ellul, J. 209
Evans, C. A. 99, 187
Evans, C. F. 214
Farrer, A. 198, 207, 209, 211, 218, 219, 221, 223, 228, 229
Fauth, W. 51, 52
Feeney, D. C. 10
Feldman, L. H. 84, 86, 87, 89, 134
Festugière, A. J. 22, 51, 52, 53, 54, 55, 56
Fiensy, D. 157, 158
Fitzmyer, J. 65, 71, 98, 128, 215
Flacelière, R. 8, 38, 39
Flusser, D. 223, 225
Foerster, W. 75, 76, 86
Ford, J. 200, 218

Fossum, J. E. 3, 4, 75, 123, 124, 125, 128, 129, 130
Fowler, H. N. 10
Fränkel, H. 15, 16, 17, 18, 46
Freedman, D. N. 2, 8, 63, 64, 79, 116, 117, 130, 153
Freeman, K. 20
Freudenthal, J. 134
Friesen, S. J. 196
Furley, D. J. 10, 11, 15
Furth, M. 16
Gabel, J. B. 62
Ganschinietz 125, 94, 95, 96, 97, 118
García Martínez, F. 72, 73, 74, 143, 144, 145, 146, 148, 149
Gaye, R. K. 30
Geffcken, J. 155, 189, 222
Geoltrain, P. 129
Gersh, S. 35, 36, 37
Gifford, E. H. 39
Gigon, O. 15, 20
Ginzberg, L. 75, 128
Gladigow, B. 94
Goldenberg, D. M. 84
Goodenough, E. R. 94, 95, 96, 97, 159
Griffiths, J. G. 38, 55, 56
Groarke, L. 17
Grossfeld, B. 180
Gummere, R. M. 36
Gundry, R. H. 214
Guthrie, W. K. C. 8, 9, 11, 13, 15, 16, 17, 18, 19, 20, 27, 29, 30, 31, 41, 45, 46, 230
Halliwell, S. 21
Hallo, W. 7, 8
Hankinson, R. J. 166
Hardie, R. P. 30
Harl, M. 134
Harner, P. B. 105, 138, 140, 170, 172, 174, 175
Harrington, D. J. 75, 143, 187
Hata, G. 84, 86, 87
Hawthorne, G. 127
Hayward, R. 3, 4, 113, 124, 134, 171, 177, 178, 179, 180, 181, 182, 184, 186, 201
Heitsch, E. 43, 45
Held, K. 25, 46
Helm, P. 209
Hemer, C. J. 196

Hengel, M. 10, 76, 78, 85, 87, 88, 89, 91, 94, 115, 132, 134, 142, 143, 185, 203, 223
Hofius, O. 126, 203, 215, 216, 221
Holladay, C. R. 188
Holladay, W. 62, 72
Holm-Nielsen, S. 144, 145, 146, 147
Holtz, T. 198, 199, 207, 218, 221
Howard, G. 59, 60, 68, 97
Hurtado, L. W. 125, 127
Hyatt, J. P. 136
Jaeger, W. 8, 9, 15, 19, 20, 29, 46
Jervell, J. 85
Kahn. C. H. 13, 14, 16, 21, 42, 228
Kern, O. 9
Ketchum, R. 21, 22, 23
Kirk, G. S. 8, 9, 15, 16, 17, 18, 19, 20, 45, 46, 130
Kirwan, C. 27, 28
Kneale, W. 32
Kotansky, R. 94, 160, 161
Kraft, H. 185, 203, 211, 213, 218, 221, 227
Kranz, W. 15
Kraub, S. 103
Kraut, R. 22
Kraybill, J. N. 199
Kurfess, A. 196
L.-Duhaime, J. 142, 144
Lacocque, A. 131, 135
Lane, E. N. 89, 90, 91
Lange, A. 142, 143, 145
Lanne, E. 158
Lattimore, R. 42
Lauterbach, J. 186
Le Boulluec, A. 5, 118, 132, 134
Le Déaut, R. 109, 110
Le Glay, M. 97
Leftow, B. 209
Levine, E. 109
Lindars, B. 3, 172, 173, 174
Lindblom, J. 133
Lohmeyer, E. 201, 202, 208, 221
Lohse, E. 72
Long, A. A. 33, 34, 48
MacDermot, V. 219
MacKinnon, D. M. 27, 28
Maehler, H. 43
Malcolm, J. 21
Malina, B. 197

Marcus, R. 84
Marmorstein, A. 3, 62, 78, 81, 99, 102, 103, 107, 180
Martin, J. P. 162, 166
Martin, R. P. 126, 127, 128
Mazon, P. 43
McGregor, L. J. 59, 60
McKnight, S. 90
McNamara, M. 4, 109, 178, 180, 181, 182, 183, 184, 187, 199, 200, 201, 205, 212, 226
Meinhold, J. 100, 107
Méridier, L. 10
Merlan, P. 27, 28, 29, 30, 166
Mettinger, T. 2, 117, 133
Metzger, M. 74, 155, 157, 158
Meyer, E. 43, 44
Michaels, J. R. 206, 222, 228
Milik, J. T. 71
Millar, F. 101, 145
Minear, P. S. 208, 210, 216, 222, 228, 229
Mohr, R. D. 25, 26
Montes-Peral, L. A. 162, 163, 164, 165, 167
Moore, G. F. 63, 108, 178
Mounce, R. H. 213
Mourelatos, A. 16, 17
Mras, K. 188, 190
Munnich, O. 134
Muraoka, T. 140
Mylonas, G. E. 86
Nagata, T. 126, 127
Nebe, G. W. 69
Neitzel, H. 44, 45
Neusner, J. 99, 101, 107
Newsom, C. 145
Nikiprowetzky, V. 80, 81, 82, 83
Nilsson, M. P. 8, 49, 51, 52, 54, 89, 91, 92, 97, 159
Nitzan, B. 94
Nock, A. D. 54, 55, 92
Norden, E. 87, 92
Norin, S. 116
Owen, G. E. L. 15, 17, 18, 19, 23, 25
Parke, H. W. 49, 50, 51, 52
Parke-Taylor, G. H. 3, 116, 130
Patterson, R. 25, 27, 28, 29, 30
Patzig, G. 166
Petuchowski, J. 101, 128

Philonenko, M. 94, 97, 125
Philonenko-Sayar, B. 125
Pietersma, A. 59, 60, 61
Pohlenz, M. 33, 34
Porten, B. 116, 119
Preuß, H. D. 5, 131
Prigent, P. 212, 213, 223
Pucci, P. 43, 44
Puech, É. 68, 69
Ramsay, W. M. 196
Raven, J. E. 8, 9, 15, 16, 17, 18, 19, 20, 45, 46, 130
Rengstorf, K. H. 85
Reynolds, J. 54
Richter, W. 35, 36
Rissi, M. 208
Rist, J. M. 34, 35
Roloff, J. 216
Rose, M. 2, 3, 116, 117
Rowe, C. J. 24
Rowland, C. 125
Runia, D. 80, 81, 164, 166, 167
Russell, D. A. 37, 38
Safrai, S. 99
Sandbach, F. H. 34
Sanders, E. P. 98, 99
Sanders, J. 67
Sanderson, J. E. 59
Sandevoir, P. 5, 118, 132, 134
Sarna, N. M. 133
Schiffman, L. 71, 72, 73, 78, 102, 104, 108, 109
Schild, E. 3, 132, 133, 134
Schlatter, A. 86
Schlesier, R. 44
Schmidt, W. 117
Schmithals, W. 170
Schnackenburg, R. 172, 173, 174
Schneider, J. 214
Schofield, M. 8, 9, 15, 16, 17, 18, 19, 20, 28, 45, 46, 130
Scholem, G. G. 96
Schürer, E. 101
Schüssler Fiorenza, E. 196
Schwartz, E. 93
Sedley, D. N. 33, 48
Segal, A. F. 61, 81, 176
Segal, M. H. 67
Seligman, P. 21, 22
Siegel, J. P. 66, 67, 68, 70, 98

Siegmann, E. 45
Sigal, P. 158
Skehan, P. W. 59, 60, 66, 67, 68, 69, 70, 72, 73, 74, 79
Smith, M. 93, 94, 95, 96, 132
Sorabji, R. 15, 17, 18, 25, 28, 31, 32, 39, 40, 41, 169
Starobinski-Safran, E. 164, 166
Stegemann, H. 60, 65, 66, 67, 68, 71, 142
Stemberger, G. 103
Stern, M. 76, 87, 88, 89, 90, 91, 92, 93, 97
Steudel, A. 70
Stevenson, J. G. 28, 29
Strack, H. L. 103
Stroh, W. 43
Stuhlmacher, P. 61
Sweet, J. 199, 202, 203, 204, 205, 208, 209, 210, 212, 223, 227
Swete, H. B. 2, 195, 200, 205, 210, 213, 221
Taylor A. E. 21, 24
Thackeray, H. St. J. 84, 85, 86, 137
Thalmann, W. G. 42, 43, 44, 45
Theiler, W. 34, 35, 93
Thierry, G. J. 117, 118, 119, 120
Thompson, L. 159, 197, 199, 210, 223
Tov, E. 137
Trebilco, P. 90, 91, 159, 196
Tredennick, H. 29, 32
Trever, J. C. 72
Uhlig, S. 129, 212
Ulrich, E. 59
Urbach, E. E. 3, 98, 102, 103, 104, 105, 106, 107
van der Horst, P. W. 87, 88
van Unnik, W. C. 4, 8, 41, 46, 48, 49, 56, 57, 188, 191, 192, 198, 199, 221
VanderKam, J. C. 79, 102
Verdenius, W. J. 20, 43, 44, 45
Vermes, G. 71, 72, 73, 101, 145, 146, 149
Vermes, P. 4, 177, 178, 179, 181, 182
Vlastos, G. 15
Vögtle, A. 207, 208, 213, 228
von Arnim, J. 33
von Leyden, W. 30, 32
von Rad, G. 5, 131
Waddell, W. G. 59

Waltke, B. 140
Waterfield, R. 21, 23
Weingreen, J. 62, 63
Weinreich, O. 2, 4, 41, 51, 52, 55
Weiss, H. F. 167
Wernberg-Møller, P. 72, 149
Werner, E. 8, 117, 224, 225
West, E. W. 49, 50
West, M. L. 9, 43, 44, 46
Wevers, W. 5, 132, 134
Wheeler, C. B. 62
Whittaker, J. 5, 8, 12, 16, 17, 18, 25, 26, 31, 32, 35, 36, 37, 38, 39, 40, 80, 135, 164, 168, 169
Whittaker, M. 89, 90

Wicksteed, P. H. 30
Williams, A. L. 119
Williams, C. J. F. 13
Williams, R. 79
Wilson, R. McL. 215
Winston, D. 154
Wolfson, H. A. 79, 80, 82, 164
Yadin, Y. 66, 67, 68
York, A. D. 109
Zaehner, R. C. 49, 50
Zahn, T. 118
Zepf, M. 52, 53
Zickendraht, K. 170
Zuntz, G. 51, 52, 53, 54

Index of Subjects

Adam 75, 157
Ahura Mazda 49-50
Aion
– at Aphrodisias 54-5
– definition of as "always being" 31-2
– as divinity 11, 30, 32, 51-3, 185, 198-9, 202
– at Eleusis 51-3, 198-9
Aisa (=Destiny) 11
All, the 69
Alpha and Omega 200, 217-20, 226, 230
Altar, at Pergamum 159
Ammonius, views on Being 38-40
Amulets, containing divine name 93, 97, 160-1
Anaximenes, on air 46-7
Anguipede 97
Apollo
– equated with Being 38-40
– as god of revelation 40
– name meaning " not many" 8
Babylon 229
Beast 227-9
Beginning, God as b., middle, end 47, 188-9
Being
– of Beast 228-9
– vs. Becoming 21-7, 36, 135, 142-3, 165, 167-8, 171-5, 211, 213
– as corporeal 33-4
– "dynamic" vs. "static" 134-5, 211-12
– equated with God 12-5, 34-41, 137, 162-9
– in Greek thought 5, 13-41
– in Parmenides 15-8
– terms for in Plato 21 n
– "that which is" vs. "things that are" 16, 19
– 3 levels of in Plato 23

– qua Being 27-31, 166
– six modes of 34-7
– as Spirit 34
– symbolized by Osiris 38
– "veridical aspect" 13-4, 21, 42 n, 206
Calendar 144-5, 148
Christology, in Revelation 221-2, 226
Copula 140 n
Creation
– ex nihilo 30
– by name of God 4, 128-31, 142 n, 152, 157, 167-8, 170-6, 180-1, 183-5, 212-3, 224 n
– by wisdom of God 150-3
Decree, of God 145-52, 212 n
Demiurge 14 n, 36, 53, 167
Derveni Theogony 9 n, 46, 211
Dieu cosmique (="cosmic religion") 53, 197
Diogenes of Babylon, and ontological argument 47 n
Dionysus, identified with Jewish God 88-9
Dodona, oracle at 49-51
Domitian 199 n
Dreizeitenformel
– of Aion 51-3
– of God/gods 44-5, 49-56, 139-40, 156-7, 170-1, 183-9, 191-2, 195, 230
– inappropriate for true Being 16-8, 24-6, 39-40, 47, 209
– of prophecy 42-5, 48, 189-92
– summary of 56-7
– as synonym for "all things" 43 n, 45-6, 48
Duration, as process 18 n, 25-6
E (=Epsilon), at Delphi 38-40
Eternal
– vs. everlasting 17-8, 48, 168-9
– "eternal present" 17 n, 168-9, 208-11

Eternal Living Creature 24, 53
Eternity (see also Aion)
– as timeless 16-8, 25-6, 29-32, 39-40, 168-9, 208-11
Etymology
– of Greek gods 8-11
– of Marduk 7-8
Eudorus 35-6
Existence, of God
– contrasted with essence 163-4
– contrasted with idols 153-6, 165, 169, 193
– as independent 31 (of Aion), 156, 166, 193, 206-7, 229
– as necessary 166-7, 206-7
Exodus, motifs used in Revelation 200-1, 223 n, 230
Fire
– in Heraclitus 46-7, 50-1
– in Stoics 34, 48 n, 51
First and Last 138, 140, 183, 220-1, 226, 229-30
Forms
– as having true Being 22-7, 35-7, 40
– and God 37, 41, 136, 150-3, 163-5
God/gods (see also under YHWH)
– coming of 205, 209, 214-7, 225-8, 21, 233
– compared with Lord in Philo and rabbis 81, 176-7
– eternity of 136-41, 152, 156-8, 168-9, 172-6, 179, 182, 185-8, 193, 207-8, 222
– glory of 223-7, 231
– Greek ideas of 12-4, 20, 32, 40-1, 44, 48, 214
– identical with intellect in Aristotle 41
– identification of Jewish God with Greek gods 88-91, 92 n
– as nameless 77-81, 87-8, 94, 115, 163
Good, the 23
Greeting formula 203
Iael (see Iaoel)
Iao
– and Aion 53, 198
– in Greco-Roman texts 89, 91-3
– in Greek letters 59
– in Jewish texts 75, 105, 116-22, 125, 192
– in magical texts, amulets 92-7, 160-1, 219-20
– and Revelation 198, 218-9
Iaoel 75, 125
Idols 153-6, 165, 169, 193
Isis
– as revealer of Being 38
– as world ruler 55-6, 185
Jesus
– coming of 214-7, 233
– and name 61, 65 n, 98, 126-8, 171-76, 204-5, 215-7, 221
John (author of Revelation)
– and Greek language 195-6, 201-2
– and Greek culture 195-9
– as prophet 196, 200, 222-3
Kyrios
– compared with God in Philo 81
– in Josephus 86
– in LXX 60-2, 75-7
– meaning of in Philo 61
– in NT 61, 97-8, 126-8
Living One, the 220-2
Logos 33-4
Lord of Spirits 153
Lord (see *kyrios*)
Love, and Strife 19, 46, 129-30
LXX (see Septuagint)
Memra 4, 110, 171 n, 178-81
Metatron 125
Mind, in Anaxagoras 12, 20
Muses 42-3, 45 n
"Mystery of existence" 143-4, 149
Name of God (see YHWH)
Names, in Revelation 204-5
Negative theology 163-5
Not-being 18, 21, 153-4, 228-9
One, the, as superior to Being 33
Ontology, equated with theology in Aristotle 27-8
Orphic Theogony 9, 46
Pherecydes 8-9
Prime Mover 28-31
Proteus 8 n
Pypy (divine name) 59
Revelation (divine), at Qumran 144-5, 148-9
Rome 155-6, 199, 227-9
Sabazius 90-1
Sabbath 89-91

Index of Subjects

Saïs 55-6, 198
Septuagint (see also Scripture Index, esp. Ex.3:14)
– attitudes of translators 132, 134-5
– and Greek philosophy 134-7, 151-3, 194-5, 205-6, 233
Simon, the Righteous 101-2
Speucippus, on Being 33
Tetragrammaton (see YHWH)
Three-times formula (see *Dreizeitenformel*)
Time (see also Eternity)
– as having parts 24-5
– in Aristotle 31-2
– God and 39-40, 168-9, 207-11
– as tripartite 47-8
Totum simul (see eternity, timeless)
Trishagion 223-7
Valerius 90-1
Varro, on Jewish God 88, 91-2, 94
Void 20
Wisdom, of God 149-52
YHWH
– angel bearing name of 124-5
– in Aramaic script 70-1
– associated with "Let it be" 130-1, 142 n, 180
– blasphemy of 62-3, 83, 86, 102-3, 108-10, 112, 175
– in blessings 70, 73-4, 79, 100-2, 106
– connected with salvation 174-6
– correcting of 66-7
– cursing with 62-3, 72-4, 85, 109-10, 112
– "disguising" of 69, 101, 104-7
– engraved on high priest's mitre 82, 84
– erasing of 99
– exorcisms with 74 n
– as "expressed name" 100
– as four-lettered 65, 67-8, 82, 108, 120, 157, 160-1
– in Greek 58-9, 70-1
– in greetings 63 n, 104
– as ineffable 77-8, 115, 156-7
– Jesus and 126-8
– letters of identical to "He is" 141-2
– linked with mercy 176-7
– magical use of 93-7, 103-4, 109, 112
– meaning of 6, 131-94
– "naming the name" of 62-5, 83, 86
– oaths with 71 n, 72-4, 78, 85, 108-9, 112, 129
– omission of 68
– origin of 116-7
– in paleo-Hebrew 59-60, 66-8
– power of 128-31
– in prayer 63 n
– prefixes, suffixes with 67
– and presence 125-6, 177, 179, 182, 185-6, 206-7
– profaning of 73 n
– prohibition against speaking 62-5, 69-74, 77-8, 82-6, 101-9, 111-6, 232
– as "proper" name 80-1
– proper pronunciation of 95 n, 105-6, 116-22
– as riddle 156
– in Scripture reading 73-4
– significance of 123-31
– spoken on day of atonement 100-1, 110-1
– spoken in temple 62 n, 79, 100-2, 120-1
– substitutions for 68-70, 76-7, 101, 104, 111, 114-5, 120
– and temple 113-4, 124, 126, 179
– and test of adulterous woman 84-5, 98, 110
– upon Israel 77 n, 124, 205
– writing of 58-9, 65-71, 232
YHWH Elohim 125, 218-20
YHWH Sabaoth 130-1, 153, 218-20
Zeus
– Cleanthes' hymn to 13, 197
– equated with God/intelligence/fate 33 n
– equated with Jewish God 88
– equated with Moira/air/breath 46
– equated with world-fire 51
– and Isis 56
– meaning of name 8-11, 136, 192
– "was, is, will be" 49-51, 185, 188

www.ingramcontent.com/pod-product-compliance
Lightning Source LLC
Chambersburg PA
CBHW070338230426
43663CB00011B/2368